Communication History in Canada

Edited by Daniel J. Robinson

OXFORD
UNIVERSITY PRESS

1904 ❧ 2004

100 YEARS OF
CANADIAN PUBLISHING

OXFORD

UNIVERSITY PRESS

70 Wynford Drive, Don Mills, Ontario M3C 1J9
www.oup.com/ca

Oxford University Press is a department of the University of Oxford.
It furthers the University's objective of excellence in research, scholarship,
and education by publishing worldwide in

Oxford New York

Auckland Bangkok Buenos Aires Cape Town Chennai
Dar es Salaam Delhi Hong Kong Istanbul Karachi Kolkata
Kuala Lumpur Madrid Melbourne Mexico City Mumbai Nairobi
São Paulo Shanghai Taipei Tokyo Toronto

Oxford is a trade mark of Oxford University Press
in the UK and in certain other countries

Published in Canada
by Oxford University Press

National Library of Canada Cataloguing in Publication

Communication history in Canada / edited by Daniel J. Robinson.

Includes bibliographical references and index.

ISBN 0-19-541929-4

1. Mass media—Canada—History. I. Robinson, Daniel J.

P92.C3C564 2003   302.23'0971   C2003-905528-0

Cover and text design: Brett Miller

1 2 3 4 - 07 06 05 04
This book is printed on permanent (acid-free) paper ♾
Printed in Canada

Contents

For my mother, Patricia Robinson.

Preface

The idea for this essay collection arose from my experience as a trained historian teaching media studies. Where possible, I tried to provide my students with historical context for the contemporary subjects under discussion, if only to demonstrate that 'New Media' was in fact an old concept, and that the advent of newspapers and radio were at least as socially transformative as the arrival of the Internet. What I found, however, was that the available communication history texts and readers presented a problem: while fine in many respects, they offered little in the way of Canadian content, focusing almost entirely on American and European experiences. Students reading these texts would learn nothing about William Lyon Mackenzie, the Canadian Broadcasting Corporation, or *Chatelaine* magazine. Communication systems and the mass media evolved differently in Canada than in either the United States or Europe, owing to the country's distinctive blend of history, geography, government, economics, and biculturalism. Without a Canadian perspective, students could not acquire the proper historical foundation for understanding present-day media and communications in Canada.

The group of essays contained in this volume attempts to redress this historical omission. As seen below, there is a well-established tradition of historical writing on Canadian communications, perhaps not surprisingly given the country's special interest in broadcasting and telecommunications. The works contained here range in scope from nineteenth-century newspapers to music television in the 1980s. The authors represent a wide cross-section of disciplines, among them history, communication studies, sociology, journalism, political science, and film studies. Analytical approaches range from neo-Marxism

to postmodern theories of reader response. Not included are works dealing specifically with French-speaking Canada, in large part because many of the key works in this area are in French only.

The readings are grouped into five sections. The first section explores theoretical issues concerning the relationship between media, society, and human thought, focusing on concepts like time, space, technology, and nationality. Section 2 discusses postal systems and telecommunications centring on the telegraph, the telephone, and computers. The third section describes the origins and diffusion of newspapers and magazines, with a particular emphasis on the commercializing roles of advertising and market research. Section 4 charts the rise of radio broadcasting during the inter-war years and of television broadcasting from the 1950s until the 1980s. The final section examines film and sound recording in Canada. In most cases, the readings address media or communication systems in their initial phases, highlighting the social, economic, and political consequences of their establishment in this country.

While these articles are grouped mainly by media type, other thematic threads are noteworthy. The theme of commercialization recurs, mostly in terms of accelerating marketing and advertising that have reconfigured media industries and media content. Second, the theme of political economy is important because of Ottawa's extensive role in the development of media and communication systems. From state patronage of newspapers in the 1800s to the CRTC's pervasive influence on broadcast content and competition, the state has been a core stakeholder throughout much of this history. Finally, the issue of Canadian nationalism—and related themes like Canadian identity and cultural sovereignty—figures prominently. The threat posed by a growing American presence, whether cultural, economic, or political, has been a persistent concern for federal policy makers and media interests alike. Defending and promoting English-Canadian culture, however ill-defined, has been an animating aspect of media policy in Canada.

For their assistance and encouragement, I would like to thank Bob Babe, Mike Gasher, Suzanne Geba, Jack Granatstein, Russell Johnston, Keir Keightley, Alex Markus, Anna Maurutto, Paula Maurutto, Jessica McEwan, David Spencer, Paul Rutherford, Eric Sinkins, and Jon van der Veen. A special note of thanks is owed to Megan Mueller, my editor at Oxford University Press, whose early support for this project—and later patience with its progress—made this book possible.

Time, Space, Technology, and Nation

How do communication systems shape our understandings of society and human history? How is cultural expression—our patterns of symbolic interaction—informed by society's primary media technologies? To what extent is a society's world view indicative of the dominant mode of communication that articulates it, whether oral, print, celluloid, electronic, or digital? Do some media promote democracy and egalitarianism while others engender totalitarian rule and imperial conquest? For decades, communication scholars and historians have dealt with these questions in order to learn how media have configured human experience at different times and in different parts of the world. Their inquiries reflect social-scientific and philosophical orientations. Psychologists have conducted numerous studies on the behavioural effects of mass media, while anthropologists and philosophers, among others, have explored how concepts like myth, spiritualism, symbolic expression, reason, and justice are intertwined with communication systems and media technologies.

Historian Gerald Friesen has studied the way Canadian Aboriginal societies draw on oral traditions for cultural sustenance. In his essay here, he shows how the tradition of passing stories down through generations made speechmaking and storytelling highly valued activities, while forging a deep-seated connection with the past, both quotidian and spiritual. Historical and mythical pasts were interwoven, as seen with the Dream Map of Aggan Wolf, which was both diagram of animal and human trails and 'sketch of the path to eternity'. First Nations people understood time in ecological and generational terms, not calendrical ones, and used temporal units rather than spatial ones to measure such things as canoe routes. But beginning in the sixteenth century, European traditions of literacy and typography challenged the Aboriginal world view. Printed messages, when read later in different places, were seen by Aboriginal people as 'foretelling the future'. Jesuit missionaries presented biblical scripture as superior to Native spiritualism because it did not 'vary like the oral word of man', which was 'almost by nature false'. That First Nations people have managed to preserve a cultural heritage in spite of such challenges to the legitimacy of oral history is a testament to their unshaken 'belief in an unbroken chain between past and present'.

Concepts of time and space were central to Harold Innis, a distinguished Canadian historian and political economist. His transnational research, spanning centuries, examined links between a society's dominant form of communication and its social, cultural, and political attributes. Societies with durable communication media like stone tablets and parchment reflected a time-biased orientation. Those centred on impermanent media like papyrus and paper were space-biased in nature. Time-biased societies were rooted in oral traditions, valuing activities like poetry or storytelling. Space-biased societies promoted centralization and instrumentalism, and often tended towards imperialism, as seen with Roman rule in the Mediterranean basin or the British reign in Asia. 'The sword and the pen worked together,' Innis writes, stressing the interdependence of military and administrative capabilities.

If communication technologies are thought to shape cognitive structures and patterns of human social relations, then the computer, George Grant argues, is an exemplar of the technocratic ethos. A Canadian conservative philosopher, Grant challenged the dominance of liberal instrumentalism in Western society, notably the conflation of truth, goodness, and beauty with the technological imperative. In his essay, Grant takes issue with the view that computers are value-neutral, inert devices, whose subsequent purposes and applications are determined by the freestanding choices of human beings. Computers do not appear spontaneously but are the end product of an *a priori* 'paradigm of knowledge' encompassing metallurgy, chemistry, mathematics, corporate organization, and educational priorities. Computers are bound up with our 'civilizational destiny', as much in morality as in the material. Without this precondition, computers could not exist. Suggestive of Innis, Grant views the computer as an instrument of imperialism and control because of its ability to classify and homogenize disparate social identities and groupings.

Like Innis, Marshall McLuhan was interested in the relationship between media technologies and human society. The University of Toronto professor, who became an academic and media sensation during the 1960s, is best known for the aphorism, 'the medium is the message'. Here he discusses, controversially, the cognitive and affective features of radio and its status as a 'hot' medium, unlike the 'cool' medium of television. Group listening promoted 'depth involvement' with radio programming, fusing psyche and society 'into a single echo chamber'. Radio thus functioned as an extension of the collective nervous system, which in the case of Adolph Hitler's Third Reich tapped into and ignited the 'tribal mode' of the German nation. While literacy and visual modes of reasoning promoted liberal individualism and human reason, radio countered this trend through an ominous ability to 're-tribalize mankind'.

The relationship between a medium of communication and national identity is also addressed by Maurice Charland. In his excerpt, he examines how the Canadian state discursively employed the railroad and broadcasting as elements of 'technological nationalism'. A nation's technology, not its people or polis, serves as the central metaphor for national identity and collective purpose. The very idea of Canada, its historical and mythical origins, is bound up in the sagas of the Canadian Pacific Railway and the Canadian Broadcasting Corporation. Here, too, there are echoes of Innis, as Charland argues that the CPR in the 1880s forged a 'network of domination', extending the power of the Canadian state to the Western frontier and its Native inhabitants. The technological nationalism produced by the creation of the CBC in the 1930s was defensive in nature, meant to safeguard Canada's 'ether and consciousness' from American radio. But the technological triumph of coast-to-coast radio and television transmission could not prevent, ironically, the influx of American programming on those very airwaves.

Questions for Critical Reading

1. How was the world view of Aboriginal peoples framed by understandings of time and space?
2. What challenges did literacy and print pose to the oral culture of Canada's First Nations?
3. How do print-based and oral-based cultures differently interpret the past? How do their senses of history differ?
4. According to Innis, what are the main differences between time-biased and space-biased media? How do they influence social organization and political governance? From a communications perspective, what similarities existed between Jesuit missionaries and Roman administrators?
5. What does Grant mean by the 'civilizational destiny' of the computer?
6. Outline Grant's overall view of the role of technology in Western society.
7. What does McLuhan mean when he refers to radio as a 'hot' medium and to television as a 'cool' one?
8. How did radio function to 're-tribalize mankind'?
9. Discuss the similarities and differences between McLuhan's views on oral societies and those presented in the Innis and Friesen articles.
10. How did the railroad and broadcasting differ as agents of technological nationalism?
11. How was Canada historically and mythically constituted by technology and not its people? What are the chief drawbacks to this type of nationalism?

Further Readings

Acland, Charles and William J. Buxton, eds. *Harold Innis in the New Century: Reflections and Refractions.* Montreal: McGill–Queen's University Press, 1999.
   • This is a collection of revisionist essays on Innis by an interdisciplinary group of scholars bringing Innis's ideas to bear on recent issues involving cultural policy, communtion studies, gender, and postmodernism.
Babe, Robert E. *Canadian Communication Thought: Ten Foundational Writers.* Toronto: University of Toronto Press, 2000.
   • This book features chapters on each of Innis, McLuhan, and Grant, covering biographical information and outlining their respective theories.
Christian, William and Sheila Grant, eds. *The George Grant Reader.* Toronto: University of Toronto Press, 1998.
   • This reader offers a selection of Grant's philosophical writings on a range of subjects, including technology, continentalism, the Vietnam War, and Friedrich Nietzsche.
McLuhan, Eric and Frank Zingrone, eds. *Essential McLuhan.* Toronto: Anansi, 1995.
   • This collection offers wide-ranging selections from many of Marshall McLuhan's most important works.
Otter, A.A. Den. *The Philosophy of Railways: The Transcontinental Railway Idea in British North America.* Toronto: University of Toronto Press, 1997.
   • Den Otter uses the concept of 'technological nationalism' to illustrate the discursive dimension of nineteenth-century railway expansion.

Interpreting Aboriginal Cultures

Gerald Friesen

If Aboriginal views do not underlie Canada's economic institutions, and if Aboriginal genealogies do not convince today's Canadians of their country's indebtedness to Aboriginal precursors, how, as Harold Innis suggests, are Aboriginal people 'fundamental to the growth of Canadian institutions'? The answer lies in two related realms—in their cultures and in their politics. First Nations people once experienced the basic dimensions of life, the dimensions of time and space, in terms of their relations with the natural world. They did so in specific, identifiable places in northern North America. The dominant mode of communication in their communities was speech. What is more, their political commitment, evident in hundreds of episodes of community solidarity and resistance, has ensured that their knowledge of their group's distinctiveness—their connection to place—lies at the heart of today's Canada.

I

Summer of the Loucheux illustrates this Aboriginal sense of continuity. The climax of the film occurs when the Andre family travels across the river to visit the fishing camp where Alestine's grandmother, 93 years old, is living. Alestine says that she had always known that her grandmother was a very special person and that 'we had to prepare a place for her. That's one of the important things that I learned from my grandma—that you always look after your old people.' The very old woman was uncertain about whether to participate in the film project. However, she decided to do so and prepared carefully for the arrival of family and film crew, to the extent that she clothed herself in a striking rabbitskin coat that she had woven years earlier. When all was ready for the filming, she lit her pipe, leaned forward, and began to speak in Dene dialect. In voice-over, a narrator reads Hyacinthe's translation of her speech:

I was born at the mouth of Travier River. I grew up in the country with Sandy River to the east and Tree River to the west, so I was born in the middle. That's why I think of all this country as my own. It's just mine.

Now I am going to tell a story about up the Arctic Red River [Tsiigehtchic]. Nobody stayed in towns then. By this time in the summer, the people had left for the bush already. From the mouth of the Arctic Red River, you can paddle less than a mile. From there, you have to tie a rope to your canoe. Then you walk along and pull the canoe. That's the way we travelled, all the way up the river, for a long way.

Now we leave the canoe, we are heading for the mountains. Lots of mosquitoes. We take no white man's food. Sometimes we've got nothing to eat.

Now we come to a fish lake. We set nets on that lake and get a few fish. When we get to the mountains, we see mountain sheep—way on the top of the mountain. The sheep are coming down—right to the foot of the mountain. They look just like rabbits. We hunt the mountain sheep there until early fall. And when we finish we soon begin to see lots of caribou in the high meadows. We are living on good food then. Why would we stay in town?

When we've got enough dry meat, we go

Excerpts from chapter 2 from *Citizens and Nation: An Essay on History, Communication, and Canada*, by Gerald Friesen (Toronto: University of Toronto Press, 2000), 31–47. Reprinted by permission of the publisher.

back to the forest to trap for the winter. Now there's lots of snow. We've got caribou skins to live in. We build a big lodge. We get fur and we go to the fish lake. And the women stay there.

The men go to Fort MacPherson for some supplies. When the men come back, we start to move again, to the mountains. The men go first. They go on snowshoes just with an axe and a gun. The women load up the sled, follow the men, and look for the axe. When you find your husband's axe, that's where you set up your camp.

The children are crying. They're so cold. You pack the children next to you. I don't know how many times I pack your father like that. That much I looked after him. And today my own boy, he looks after me like a baby.

I like to tell old stories about all those good people and what they're doing. I talk about it, but, right away, I just feel full of tears in my heart.[1]

Grandmother's story is effective as drama. It is also an invaluable historical document. Students watching the film respond to the old woman and listen carefully to her tale. They readily recognize that she illustrates the place of history and narrative in a community. And this is an important insight. To grasp the significance of the old woman and her story is to grasp the implications of Harold Innis's statement about the Aboriginal place in Canadian life. But how to articulate and communicate this lesson?

The film's achievement is that it captures the feeling of continuity—the sense of historical connectedness—embedded in these individuals. This structure of feeling is, I suspect, what attracted filmmaker McCrea to Alestine's story. And it is undoubtedly what prompted him to place grandmother's narrative at the climax of his work. Although her story seems to lack drama or action, it is powerful because it conveys authority. It constitutes the assertion of an Aboriginal sense of self and sense of place. It also communicates a message of hope: Grandma is telling her son, granddaughter, and great-granddaughter that their people survived in the past, through good times and bad; that there have always been times just like the moment they are enjoying as she speaks, when their people feel at ease in the land, telling stories as the sun sets and the fire burns low on a warm summer's evening; and, just as these times have been rekindled today, so shall they occur again. Alestine comments when speaking of her grandmother: 'By the stories that are being told . . . it gives you a sense of pride that there were times back in the old days not only up in this area but other parts of Canada where Indian people were very independent.'

Let us examine grandmother's reflections on her life, using time and space as entry points to the structures of feeling contained therein.

II

Time and space are complicated notions. In today's world, we divide time into minutes, days, years, and centuries, and we often experience it as an insistent, linear, and even monetized unit of life's dimensions. In the past century or so, developments in scientific analysis have extended the range of human comprehension of time as far back as an event billions of years ago, the 'Big Bang', from which moment the evolution of the universe is said to have begun. Such intellectual breakthroughs may not be a regular part of daily conversation, but they have established for all of us an extraordinary vista of measured moments from 'the beginning of time' to the present. Is it any wonder that, in the modern age, time seems to be a fixed measuring rod of not quite infinite proportions?

Space is, in contrast, increasingly vague. We all know that it can be measured in kilometres and cubic centimetres, described in terms of shapes, sold by volume and area, mapped by distance and nationality, and that, in each of these contexts, it is a concrete and seemingly objective thing. But we also know that, in the last several centuries, space has been made to seem a less definitive, and even less important, dimension of life. After all, from the steam-engine and telegraph to television, satellites, and e-mail, the world's inventors have enabled the rest of us to transcend the limitations of space. All of which is to say that, despite their seemingly determinate characteristics in our own age, time and space vary a great deal depending on the society and epoch in which they are experienced.

It is true that our everyday calculations of time seem to build on natural occurrences. As Anthony Aveni, a student of anthropology and astronomy, has written: 'Rare is the element in any of the calendars . . . that does not grow out of the repeatable phenomena of nature's cycles, both physical and biological.'[2] Many traditional societies, for example, organized their economic activities around an _ecological time_ that coincides with the solar and lunar cycles and the seasons. They also employed a second measure, _structural time_, that marks the passing of the generations and explains the interaction of groups within them. Aveni explains: 'These people do not believe in history the way we do, though they do have a sense of history. As in the events and relationships that comprise tribal life, there is a kind of immediacy to both cyclic ecological time and linear structural time among these tribal societies. [. . .]'[3] These societies placed great store on continuity and duration. The Mayas, whose leaders were guided by sophisticated astronomical observers in their struggle to maintain dynastic power, 'did not segregate past from future as we do. For them, the past could and, indeed, did repeat itself. If you paid close enough attention to time, you could see that the past already contained the future.'[4]

This may seem to be a paradox. How can the past contain the future? . . . A Canadian illustration will clarify the point. In the winter of 1994–5, an Aboriginal man residing on a reserve in northwestern Ontario saved a life in remarkable circumstances. The Ojibwa man had been restless the previous night, bothered by a dream

in which a hand had appeared out of a lake or out of an ice-bound landscape. In the morning, he made plans to drive on the new winter road, a route ploughed across the lake, from Pikangikum to the laundromat in Red Lake. He was impatient, urging his companion to hurry up, and finally they departed. Their truck was travelling fairly rapidly across the great broad sweep of newly scraped road when he spotted a hand sticking out of the ice. He immediately called on his friend to stop; they skidded some distance and turned around, raced back, and were in time to pull a grader operator to safety. The machine had been maintaining the winter road when it plunged through the ice to the bottom of the lake. Its operator had managed to escape from the cab but was near exhaustion, immersed in shattered ice and freezing water, when he was dragged to safety. The Aboriginal rescuer, having foreseen the crisis in his dream, had been able to respond in a timely fashion. And he now had a story to tell.

How should we understand these events? The man's dream foretold the event. The fact of the foretelling, along with the drama of the rescue itself, made the story worth repeating. That is, what became history—worthy of telling as a story—had been experienced twice, in dream and in reality, or in future and in past. History in this sense was what had been foretold, a fact that both emphasized the importance of the event and made its telling worthy of contemplation by others. In this storytelling process, one's sense of time is subject to revision. Time is less fixed, less rigid and unbending, to the Aboriginal storyteller and to those who lend an ear to his or her narrative than it might seem to observers unaccustomed to this perspective or unsympathetic to such notions.[5]

Traditional approaches to time have often been recorded in the history of northern North America. Like other communities that have relied on nature's rhythms, Aboriginal people have used natural changes—days and seasons—to measure ecological time. A northern hunting band's annual calendar might include two major seasons, winter and summer, with four additional subdivisions for early and late spring and fall; the biggest distinction lay between the time of cold and the time of warmth because of the differences in diet, transport, social organization, and band location in those two periods. The Huron names for the time units that were the equivalents of months, for example, distinguished 'days growing longer after winter, water beginning to flow in spring, . . . fish running, berries flowering and becoming fruit, crops maturing, birds returning, deer yarding, and bears giving birth.'[6]

The Blackfoot 'winter count'—a kind of community chronicle—built on the longer rhythms of the annual cycle of winter and summer to record a structural time representing a chronology that extended over several generations, each 'year' associated with a memorable event.[7] Indeed, as Aveni observed in the case of a Dakota Sioux equivalent, 'Absolute time was marked not by the date or the number in a cycle, but rather by the most significant event occurring between consecutive winters. They painted each event in the form of a sequence of picture writings on buffalo hide: the inundation, the war, the great snowfall, the disastrous hunt, the construction of a new town by the whites, and so on. These major events constituted the Sioux's winter count—a year calendar not unlike our month calendar. In the Dakota Sioux's calendar, time and history appear to be the same.'[8]

Although these versions of ecological and structural time will seem entirely familiar, it is none the less the case that Huron and Blackfoot versions of time are not like the dimensions in which Canadians live today. Rather, they constitute a quite different notion of time itself. And it is not easy to perceive why or how the divergence in perspective occurs. Claude Lévi-Strauss, the French anthropologist, once argued that traditional peoples inhabited a 'timelessness';[9] Calvin Martin, the American historian, wrote of Aboriginal peoples' 'astounding ability

to annul time, their remarkable capacity to repudiate systematically time and history.'[10] Such metaphors require some thought.

Perhaps the best way to appreciate the divergence is to see it in action. Robin Ridington, an anthropologist, has illustrated such abstractions by referring to stories that he was told by members of a Beaver (Dunne-za) Indian community in northeastern British Columbia, with whom he lived in the 1960s. One of his contacts there, a man named Johnny, was willing to translate the last stories of his father, Japasa, for Ridington: 'My dad said that when he was a boy, about nine years old, he went into the bush alone. He was lost from his people. In the night it rained. He was cold and wet from the rain, but in the morning he found himself warm and dry. A pair of silver foxes had come and protected him. After that, the foxes kept him and looked after him. He stayed with them and they protected him. Those foxes had three pups. The male and female foxes brought food for the pups. They brought food for my dad too. They looked after him as if they were all the same. Those foxes wore clothes like people. My dad said he could understand their language. He said they taught him a song.'

Noting that when he visited this community Japasa was near death, Ridington explained that he recorded the subsequent events with care:

Japasa began to sing. The song seemed to be part of his story. It must have been the song the foxes gave him. It must have been one of his medicine songs. I believe he sang the song to give it away. He did not want to become 'too strong'. He was prepared to follow his dreams toward Yagatunne, the Trail to Heaven. I did not know, then, that a person could sing his medicine song only when death was near to him or to the listener. I did not know that the song had power to restore life or to take it away. I did not know he was giving up power the foxes gave to him in a time out of time, alone in the bush in the 1890s. The song fell away and Japasa resumed his narrative. Johnny continued to whisper a translation:

> My dad said he stayed out in the bush for twenty days. Ever since that time, foxes have been his friends. Anytime he wanted to, he could set a trap and get foxes.[11]

. . .

What is central about this approach to time is its creation of links between the reality of the everyday and the spiritual reality that we might prefer to describe as mythic; the links are the product of a person's power or knowledge. As Riel and Tanner suggested in their discussions of foreknowledge in hunting, so in this approach to the dimensions of time and history the individual is enabled to live simultaneously in what we perceive as two dimensions, whether labelled 'past and present' or 'this world and the next'. According to Calvin Martin: 'The key here is one's cultural conception of time. Archaic societies maintain their strikingly vivid relationship with Nature because of their *a priori* commitment to living in mythic, rather than in historic, time.'[12] This prior commitment distinguishes traditional from contemporary Canadian experience. It can be described as knowledge or understanding of these other dimensions. Indeed, Ridington concludes: 'For northern hunting people, knowledge and power are one. To be in possession of knowledge is more important than to be in possession of an artefact.'[13] And time thus could be bent to fit the shapes established by spiritual understanding.

The perception of space, particularly as nature and land, is as important as the perception of time in distinguishing between the traditional Aboriginal universe and today's cultural assumptions. The evidence begins in Aboriginal myths because, as is evident in the setting for the story told by Alestine's grandmother, telling stories and making speeches are among the most highly valued arts in traditional cultures. The land provides many of the characters: river and mountain, caribou and mountain goat, summer sun and winter snow offer context and actors for these tales. Whitefish and grouse and rabbits are the faithful supports of human existence. Other creatures take on the characteristics of humans. Thus for certain Aboriginal groups Bear is the warrior, Wolf the isolated spirit, Wolverine the outcast. In offering models of leadership, Crane is wise and Loon is ambitious. For Aboriginal storytellers, music might be evoked by the song of a bird, the winds of the forest, and the waves on a lake—sounds that are actually providing a backdrop as they speak. The rhythm of life is reflected in the succession of the seasons: in an Ojibwa story, harsh Winter wages war against gentle Summer, but neither secures permanent victory. These are not only the expressions of widely observed human experiences, although they do have that status, but they carry too the messages of specific locations on the earth's surface. James Bay and Hudson Bay and Lake Superior and Lake Winnipeg—their names today—figure in these stories; the Rocky Mountains and the Atlantic Ocean are boundaries of experience; and the distinctive combinations of nature's family in this part of the globe—mosquito and seal and magpie and muskrat—are unmistakable signposts of place.[14]

The rituals of hunting bands are drawn from hunting itself and are associated with special moments or stages in life, forecasts of game, and control of the weather. A typical rite of passage is the Mistassini Cree 'walking out' ceremony, which occurs soon after children learn to walk. It formally marks the moment when a child can begin to be active outside the dwelling. Young children are led straight out of the doorway of the household and along a path to a small decorated tree, where they perform a symbolic act such as shooting an animal or gathering fuel. They then circle the tree and return to the dwelling and family for a special meal. Each element in this ritual, including the walk itself, the tree (a vehicle of communication between human and animal), the meal, and the symbolic task, carries a spiritual message translated into the language of the land.

Cree dwellings often face a body of water and the rising sun, partly for physical reasons (prevailing winds, for example) and partly to permit communication with certain spirits of the natural world. The consumption and disposal of animals after a successful hunt also involve rules and rituals that convey the band's expectation of comparable harvests in the future, expressed in the languages of the hunt and the land. They imply a sense of belonging to the universe that is predictable and reassuring, but, in their use of the identifiably local characteristics of the boreal forest of northern North America, they denote also a specific sense of place.

Aboriginal maps or abstract depictions of the environment have rarely survived the passage of centuries. However, the few pieces of evidence that have been passed on reveal clues about the way in which different cultures shape the environment according to different principles. The canoe routes through northern Canada's intricate networks of rivers and lakes that Aboriginal people mapped at the request of fur traders were customarily measured in time rather than in spatial units, so that an easy downstream paddle of fifty miles and a difficult portage of eight miles might occupy the same space on a diagram because they required equal time to traverse. Such diagrams frequently ignored the distinction between river, portage, and trail, presumably because they were 'parts of a single communication network'. Moreover, and for similar reasons, small strategic creeks might be represented as equal to major water courses.[15]

It was a short step from depictions of canoe routes to depictions of hunting resources and, most essential of all, to depictions of the link between earthly spaces and the supernatural. The experience of Hugh Brody in northern British Columbia offers just such an insight into the hunters' spatial imagination. Brody was investigating Indian land use. He learned that members of the band might fish a particular pool or pick berries in a certain patch only once in five or ten years, but they remembered the location of the resource clearly and regarded it as theirs; the maps that they drew of their patterns of land use indicated clear boundaries between the customary hunting areas of one community and those of another.

The relation between these secular drawings of patterns of resource use and the spiritual depiction of the land was even more striking. The people with whom Brody lived, like the Indians in fur trade journals, described how the most skilled and perceptive hunters could dream the hunting trails, find the quarry and dream-kill it, then awake and collect the animal just as had been foretold. These men and women knew where the animals came from, where the berries grew, where the trails converged, and even where they originated; the best men and women—the strong dreamers—could map the animal trails and the berry patches and follow the trails to the points of convergence and from there, 'where the trails to animals all meet', draw the route to heaven.

At a public hearing concerning plans for an oil pipeline in this area, after the speeches and the testimony were over and a community supper had begun, Brody witnessed an Aboriginal map reading that demonstrated the interconnection between the present world and another one:

Jimmy Wolf's brother Aggan and Aggan's wife Annie brought a moosehide bundle into the hall. Neither Aggan nor Annie had spoken earlier in the day, but they went directly to the table at which the elders had sat. There they untied the bundle's thongs and began very carefully to pull back the cover.

At first sight the contents seemed to be a thick layer of hide, pressed tightly together. With great care, Aggan took this hide from its cover and began to open the layers. It was a magnificent dream map.

The dream map was as large as the table top, and had been folded tightly for many years. It was covered with thousands of short, firm, and variously coloured markings . . . Abe Fellow and Aggan Wolf explained. Up here is heaven; this is the trail that must be followed; here is a wrong direction; this is where it would be worst of all to go; and over there are all the animals. They explained that all of this had been discovered in dreams.

Aggan also said that it was wrong to unpack a dream map except for very special reasons. But the Indians' needs had to be recognized; the hearing was important. Everyone must look at the map now . . . They should realize, however, that intricate routes and meanings of a dream map are not easy to follow. There was not time to explain them all . . .

A corner of the map was missing and one of the officials asked how it had come to be damaged. Aggan answered: someone had died who would not easily find his way to heaven, so the owner of the map had cut a piece of it and buried it with the body. With the aid of even a fragment, said Aggan, the dead man would probably find the correct trail, and when the owner of the map died, it would all be buried with him. His dreams of the trail to heaven would then serve him well.

This moosehide dream map was an extraordinary document and artifact; it was at once a diagram of the region, a representation of animal trails and other resources, and a sketch of the path to eternity.[16]

What were the salient characteristics of the Aboriginal cultural order? The culture, first, was constructed on a particular sense or dimension of time. Second, it postulated a unity of experience among humans, the animal world, and the rest of the natural universe—that is, it recognized an accessible, direct link between this world and a dream trail. Third, it relied on the land. These three points, which emphasize the role of the land in traditional culture and the unity of experience between this world and another, constitute fundamental characteristics of a perception of time and space that differ from the conventional perceptions today. Fourth,

human interactions within these distinctive time–space dimensions occurred in known locations—*this* river, *that* chain of mountains, *those* hunting sites—in a specific part of the world. The unmistakable link between people and place dating from time immemorial, when combined with their cultural distinctiveness, substantiates Harold Innis's sweeping judgment about the Aboriginal foundation of Canadian institutions: the very community sites, the places where people now live, have been occupied from time immemorial—that is, from the earliest versions of time and space—by the ancestors of individuals who live in these locations today.

III

Robert Bear, then in his eighties and an elder on the Little Pine Reserve, offered a succinct summary of world cultural history for the museum in Prince Albert, Saskatchewan, when a new exhibit was being prepared in the 1980s: 'The Indian was the first here and this is where he was created; the white man was created overseas and came here afterwards. The Bible we were given was nature itself; the white man was given a book.'[17] In other words, as the mythic narratives and the dream map reveal, many of the crucial elements in hunting band life in the Americas were conveyed from one generation to the next by oral tradition. Dreams and diagrams were not recorded for posterity in the pages of a book but rather depended on the insights of new dreamers to revitalize band beliefs and on the words of wise elders to aid in the interpretation of complex visions. Aboriginal communication before European contact relied on the spoken word, and to a considerable degree the oral message has remained the vehicle of religious perspectives.

Can one seriously contend that the culture sustained by oral traditions has survived in our literate age? Can it actually constitute a foundation for Canadian institutions? Knowledge in a society that relies exclusively on oral transmission of its culture is extremely fragile, writes James Axtell, 'because its very existence depends on the memories of mortal people, often specialists who are entrusted with major portions of the corporate wisdom. Abnormally high death rates in one or more generations sever the links of knowledge that bind the culture together.'[18] Moreover, for four centuries, Aboriginal spiritual or cultural beliefs have been the targets of European criticism and indeed of direct assaults by European missionaries and teachers. If the Aboriginal cultures drew their strength from the land, they were also undermined by the very characteristics—the orality and the land-based metaphors—that sustained them.

The Aboriginal peoples' reception of print in the seventeenth century shows what a devastating impact the Europeans' literacy had on their society. One story must suffice. The Récollet priest Gabriel Sagard reported that, when he was on a trip to Quebec with some Hurons and discovered that one of the canoes was leaking, he sent a note to a priest colleague back in the village whence they had come to ask for another canoe: 'When our canoe arrived,' Sagard wrote, 'I cannot express the admiration displayed by the natives for the little note I had sent to Father Nicolas. They said that the little paper had spoken to my brother and had told him all the words I had uttered to them here, and that we were greater than all mankind. They told the story to all, and all were filled with astonishment and admiration at this mystery.'

To the Aboriginal observer, as James Axtell says, print 'duplicated a spiritual feat that only the greatest shamans could perform, namely, that of reading the mind of a person at a distance and thereby, in an oral context, foretelling the future'. This was a feat identical in form, in the Aboriginal cultural perspective, to that of the greatest hunters who could foretell the kill of an animal or map the trails to Heaven.[19] It was identical too to the story about the 1995 rescue of the roadgrader operator.

The First Nations were introduced to the powers of print by missionaries, particularly by the Bible, the missionaries' means of reference to their deity. The existence of such a holy work redoubled the Europeans' authority, in the view of some Aboriginal people, because it seemed to promise that the priests had continuous contact with their God. These Aboriginal 'radicals', as they might be labelled to distinguish them from 'conservatives' who wished to retain inherited or traditional perspectives, argued that the priests possessed tangible proof of their doctrines: 'Christian doctrine was immutable', they could claim, 'and therefore superior to Native religious traditions, because it was preserved in a printed book as it had been delivered by God.' Axtell suggests also that print was a crucial weapon in the missions of New France: 'Wherever they went, the Jesuits hammered home the point that "the Scripture does not vary like the oral word of man, who is almost by nature false." Huron converts had been so persuaded by their resident Black Robes that they would interrupt the traditional history recitations performed at council elections to make the same argument . . . When Father Joseph Le Mercier reported to his superiors in 1638, he drew up a list of what inclined the Hurons to Christianity. At the top of the list was "the art of inscribing upon paper matters that are beyond sight".'[20]

Literacy and Christianity constituted a powerful challenge to Aboriginal cultures and were wielded like weapons within them. Still, it would be wrong to think that the cultural link between past and present in Aboriginal society has been broken by the twin forces of literacy and Christianity. A convincing display of resistance is the Andre family itself: grandmother, the story she tells, and the listeners who absorb her message exemplify cultural continuity.

It is obvious that orality, as a dominant mode of communication, has been vanquished by literacy and print. One cannot recover a world without clocks, books, lists, and codified laws and regulations. But Aboriginal culture has not been obliterated. Aboriginal people are not simply like other Canadians. Why not? Their belief in an unbroken chain between past and present remains unshaken, as is evidenced by a thousand stories about Aboriginal cultural resurgence in contemporary Canada.

Notes

1   Graydon McCrea, *Summer of the Loucheux* (1983).

2   Anthony F. Aveni, *Empires of Time: Calendars, Clocks, and Cultures* (New York: Kodansha International, 1995), 81.

3   Ibid., 183.

4   Ibid., 209.

5   CBC Information Radio, Noon Edition, transcript of interview script for discussion conducted by Jim Rae, 'Smith Keeper Saves Man', 6 Jan. 1995, Winnipeg CBW.

6   John L. Steckley, 'Why I Study an Extinct Canadian Language', *Language and Society* 37 (Jan. 1992), 11–12.

7   Hugh A. Dempsey, *Crowfoot: Chief of the Blackfeet* (Edmonton: Hurtig, 1972), 14, and *A Blackfoot Winter Count* Occasional Paper No. 1 (Calgary: Glenbow-Alberta Institute, 1965).

8   Aveni, *Empires of Time*, 122.

9   Claude Lévi-Strauss, *The Savage Mind* (Chicago: University of Chicago Press, 1966), 262–3; the object of such traditional peoples, he wrote, was 'to grasp the world as both a synchronic and a diachronic totality'.

10 Calvin Martin, ed., *The American Indian and the Problem of History* (New York: Oxford University Press, 1987), 16.

11 Robin Ridington, *Trail to Heaven: Knowledge and Narrative in a Northern Native Community* (Vancouver: Douglas and McIntyre, 1988), 57–8.

12 Martin, 'Epilogue: Time and the American Indian', in *American Indian*, 207–8.

13 Ridington, Fox and Chickadee,' in Martin, *American Indian*, 134.

14 Catherine McLellan et al., *Part of the Land, Part of the Water: A History of the Yukon Indians* (Vancouver: Douglas & McIntyre, 1987), offers insights into the stories and cultures of the Dene.

15 G. Malcolm Lewis, 'Indian Maps: Their Place in the History of Plains Cartography', *Great Plains Quarterly* 4, no. 2 (Spring, 1984), 104.

16 Hugh Brody, *Maps and Dreams: Indians and the British Columbia Frontier* (Harmondsworth: Penguin Books, 1981), 266–7.

17 This statement by Robert Bear appears in the exhibit on Aboriginal elders that was on display in the Prince Albert Museum in 1996.

18 James Axtell, *The Invasion Within: The Contest of Cultures in Colonial North America* (New York: Oxford University Press, 1985), 14–15; also 'The Power of Print in the Eastern Woodlands', *William and Mary Quarterly* 3rd Series 44 (April 1987), 300–9; note the work of Walter Ong, *Orality and Literacy: The Technologizing of the Word* (London: Routledge, 1982), and of Jack Goody, *The Logic of Writing and the Organization of Society* (Cambridge: Cambridge University Press, 1986) and *The Interface between the Written and the Oral* (Cambridge: Cambridge University Press, 1987).

19 Axtell, 'The Power of Print', 304–5, and *The Invasion Within*, 102–3.

20 Axtell, 'The Power of Print', 306–7.

From *Empire and Communications*

Harold A. Innis

. . .

It has seemed to me that the subject of communication offers possibilities in that it occupies a crucial position in the organization and administration of government and in turn of empires and of Western civilization. But I must confess at this point a bias which has led me to give particular attention to this subject. In studies of Canadian economic history or of the economic history of the French, British, and American empires, I have been influenced by a phenomenon strikingly evident in Canada, which for that reason I have perhaps over-emphasized. Briefly, North America is deeply penetrated by three vast inlets from the Atlantic—the Mississippi, the St Lawrence, and Hudson Bay, and the rivers of its drainage basin. In the northern part of the continent or in Canada extensive waterways and the dominant Precambrian formation have facilitated concentration on bulk products the character of which has been determined by the culture of the aborigines and by the effectiveness of navigation by lake, river, and ocean to Europe. Along the north Atlantic coast the cod fisheries were exploited over an extensive coastline; decentralization was inevitable; and political interests of Europe were widely represented. The highly valuable small-bulk furs were exploited along the St Lawrence by the French and in Hudson Bay by the English. Continental development implied centralization. Competition between the two inlets gave the advantage in the fur trade to Hudson Bay, and after 1821 the St Lawrence region shifted to dependence on the square timber trade. Monopoly of the fur trade held by the Hudson's Bay Company checked expansion northwestward from the St Lawrence until Confederation was achieved and political organization became sufficiently strong to support construction of a transcontinental railway, the Canadian Pacific, completed in 1885. On the Pacific coast the discovery of placer gold was followed by rapid increase in settlement, exhaustion of the mines, and the development of new staples adapted to the demands of Pacific Ocean navigation such as timber. The railway and the steamship facilitated concentration on agricultural products, notably wheat in western Canada and, later on, products of the Precambrian formation such as precious and base metals and pulp and paper. Concentration on the production of staples for export to more highly industrialized areas in Europe and later in the United States had broad implications for the Canadian economic, political, and social structure. Each staple in its turn left its stamp, and the shift to new staples invariably produced periods of crises in which adjustments in the old structure were painfully made and a new pattern created in relation to a new staple. As the costs of navigation declined, less valuable commodities emerged as staples—precious metals, dried fish exported to Spain to secure precious metals, timber to support defence, in the words of Adam Smith 'perhaps more important than opulence', and finally wheat to meet the demands of an industrialized England. An attempt has been made to trace the early developments elsewhere but little has been done to indicate clearly the effects of the development of the pulp and paper industry. The difficulty of studying this industry arises partly

Excerpts from the introduction to *Empire and Communications*, by Harold A. Innis, revised by Mary Q. Innis (Toronto: University of Toronto Press, 1972). Reprinted by permission of the publisher.

from its late development and partly from the complexity of the problem of analyzing the demand for the finished product. Concentration on staple products incidental to the geographic background has involved problems not only in the supply area but also in the demand area, to mention only the effects of specie from Central America on European prices, the effects of the fur trade on France, of wheat production on English agriculture, the impact on Russia of the revolution, and of pulp and paper production on public opinion in Anglo-Saxon countries. The effects of the organization and production on a large scale of staple raw materials were shown in the attempts by France to check the increase in production of furs, in the resistance of English purchasers to the high price of timber ending in the abolition of the Navigation Acts, in the opposition of European agriculture to low-cost wheat, and in the attempt to restrain the sensationalism of the new journalism, which followed cheap newsprint.

In this reference to the problem of attack it will be clear that we have been concerned with the use of certain tools that have proved effective in the interpretation of the economic history of Canada and the British Empire. It may seem irreverent to use these tools in a study of public opinion and to suggest that the changing character of the British Empire during the present century has been in part a result of the pulp and paper industry and its influence on public opinion, but I have felt it wise to proceed with instruments with which I am familiar and which have proved useful. The viewpoint is suggested in a comment of Constable to Murray: 'If you wish to become a great author your chance will be bye and bye when paper gets cheaper.'[1] In any case I have tried to present my bias in order that you may be on your guard.

I shall attempt to outline the significance of communication in a small number of empires as a means of understanding its role in a general sense and as a background to an appreciation of its significance to the British Empire. Bryce has stated that

from the time of Menes down to that of Attila the tendency is generally towards aggregation: and the history of the ancient nations shows us, not only an enormous number of petty monarchies and republics swallowed up in the Empire of Rome, but that empire itself far more highly centralized than any preceding one had been. When the Roman dominion began to break up the process was reversed and for seven hundred years or more the centrifugal forces had it their own way . . . From the thirteenth century onwards the tide begins to set the other way . . . neither Democracy nor the principle of Nationalities has, on the balance of cases, operated to check the general movement towards aggregation which marks the last six centuries.[2]

In attempting to understand the basis of these diverse tendencies, we become concerned with the problem of empire, and in particular with factors responsible for the successful operation of 'centrifugal and centripetal forces'. In the organization of large areas, communication occupies a vital place, and it is significant that Bryce's periods correspond roughly first to that dominated by clay and papyrus, second to that dominated by parchment, and third to that dominated by paper. The effective government of large areas depends to a very important extent on the efficiency of communication.

The concepts of time and space reflect the significance of media to civilization. Media that emphasize time are those that are durable in character, such as parchment, clay, and stone. The heavy materials are suited to the development of architecture and sculpture. Media that emphasize space are apt to be less durable and light in character, such as papyrus and paper. The latter are suited to wide areas in administration and trade. The conquest of Egypt by Rome gave access to supplies of papyrus, which became the basis of a large administrative empire. Materials that emphasize time favour decentralization and hierarchical types of institutions, while those that emphasize space favour centralization and systems of government less hierarchical in character. Large-scale political organizations such as empires must be considered from the standpoint of two dimensions, those of space and time, and persist by overcoming the bias of media which over-emphasize either dimension. They have tended to flourish under conditions in which civilization reflects the influence of more than one medium and in which the bias of one medium toward decentralization is offset by the bias of another medium towards centralization.[3]

We can conveniently divide the history of the West into the writing and the printing periods. In the writing period we can note the importance of various media such as the clay tablet of Mesopotamia, the papyrus roll in the Egyptian and in the Greco-Roman world, parchment codex in the late Greco-Roman world and the early Middle Ages, and paper after its introduction in the Western world from China. In the printing period we are able to concentrate on paper as a medium, but we can note the introduction of machinery in the manufacture of paper and in printing at the beginning of the nineteenth century and the introduction of the use of wood as a raw material in the second half of that century.

It would be presumptuous to suggest that the written or the printed word has determined the course of civilizations, and we should note well the warning of Mark Pattison that 'writers with a professional tendency to magnify their office have always been given to exaggerate the effect of printed words.' We are apt to overlook the significance of the spoken word and to forget that it has left little tangible remains. We can sense its importance[4] even in contemporary civilization and we can see its influence in the great literature of the heroic age[5] of the Teutonic peoples and of Greece and in the effects[6] of its discovery in the sagas of Europe in the late eighteenth century on the literature of the north. Prior to the introduction of writing, music played its role in

emphasizing rhythm and metre, which eased the task of memory. Poetry is significant as a tribute to the oral tradition. Sapir has noted that 'many primitive languages have a formal richness; a latent luxuriance of expression that eclipses anything known to languages of modern civilization.' The written tradition has had a limited influence on them.

It is scarcely possible for generations disciplined in the written and the printed tradition to appreciate the oral tradition. Students of linguistics have suggested that the spoken word was in its origins a halfway house between singing and speech, an outlet for intense feelings rather than intelligible expression.[7] Used by an individual, it was in contrast with language described as the sum of word-pictures stored in the mind of all individuals with the same values. In the words of Cassirer[8] language transformed the indeterminate into the determinate idea and held it within the sphere of finite determinations. The spoken word set its seal on and gave definite form to what the mind created and culled away from the total sphere of consciousness. But the speech of the individual continued in a constant struggle with language and brought about constant adjustment. 'The history of language when looked at from the purely grammatical point of view is little other than the history of corruptions' (Lounsbury).[9] Herbert Spencer wrote that 'language must be regarded as a hindrance to thought, though the necessary instrument of it, we shall clearly perceive on remembering the comparative force with which simple ideas are communicated by signs.'[10] Perhaps it is a tribute to the overwhelming power of printed words that Maeterlinck could write: 'It is idle to think that, by means of words, any real communication can ever pass from one man to another . . . from the moment that we have something to say to each other we are compelled to hold our peace.'[11]. . .

The significance of a basic medium to its civilization is difficult to appraise since the means of appraisal are influenced by the media, and indeed the fact of appraisal[12] appears to be peculiar to certain types of media. A change in the type of medium implies a change in the type of appraisal and hence makes it difficult for one civilization to understand another. The difficulty is enhanced by the character of the material, particularly its relative permanence. Pirenne has commented on the irony of history in which as a result of the character of the material much is preserved when little is written and little is preserved when much is written. Papyrus has practically disappeared, whereas clay and stone have remained largely intact, but clay and stone as permanent material are used for limited purposes, and studies of the periods in which they predominate will be influenced by that fact. The difficulties of appraisal will be evident, particularly in the consideration of time. With the dominance of arithmetic and the decimal system, dependent apparently on the number of fingers or toes, modern students have accepted the linear measure of time. The dangers of applying this procrustean device in the appraisal of civilizations in which it did not exist illustrate one of numerous problems. . . .

I have attempted to meet these problems by using the concept of empire as an indication of the efficiency of communication. It will reflect to an important extent the efficiency of particular media of communication and its possibilities in creating conditions favourable to creative thought. . . .

Much has been written on the developments leading to writing and on its significance to the history of civilization, but in the main studies have been restricted to narrow fields or to broad generalizations. Becker[13] has stated that the art of writing provided man with a transpersonal memory. Men were given an artificially extended and verifiable memory of objects and events not present to sight or recollection. Individuals applied their minds to symbols rather than things and went beyond the world of concrete experience into the world of conceptual relations created within an enlarged time and space universe. The time world was extended beyond the range of remembered things and the space world beyond the range of known places. Writing enormously enhanced a capacity for abstract thinking which had been evident in the growth of language in the oral tradition. Names in themselves were abstractions. Man's activities and powers were roughly extended in proportion to the increased use and perfection of written records. The old magic was transformed into a new and more potent record of the written word. Priests and scribes interpreted a slowly changing tradition and provided a justification for established authority. An extended social structure strengthened the position of an individual leader with military power who gave orders to agents who received and executed them. The sword and pen worked together. Power was increased by concentration in a few hands, specialization of function was enforced, and scribes with leisure to keep and study records contributed to the advancement of knowledge and thought. The written record signed, sealed, and swiftly transmitted was essential to military power and the extension of government. Small communities were written into large states and states were consolidated into empire. The monarchies of Egypt and Persia, the Roman Empire, and the city-states were essentially products of writing.[14] Extension of activities in more densely populated regions created the need for written records which in turn supported further extension of activities. Instability of political structures and conflict followed concentration and extension of power. A common ideal image of words spoken beyond the range of personal experience was imposed on dispersed communities and accepted by them. It has been claimed that an extended social structure was not only held together by increasing numbers of written records but also equipped with an increased capacity to change ways of living. Following the invention of writing, the special form of heightened language, characteristic of the oral tradition and a collective society, gave way to private writing. Records and messages displaced the collective memory.

Poetry was written and detached from the collective festival.[15] Writing made the mythical and historical past, the familiar and the alien creation available for appraisal. The idea of things became differentiated from things and the dualism demanded thought and reconciliation. Life was contrasted with the eternal universe and attempts were made to reconcile the individual with the universal spirit. The generalizations which we have just noted must be modified in relation to particular empires. Graham Wallas has reminded us that writing as compared with speaking involves an impression at the second remove and reading an impression at the third remove. The voice of a second-rate person is more impressive than the published opinion of superior ability.

Such generalizations as to the significance of writing tend to hamper more precise study and to obscure the differences between civilizations insofar as they are dependent on various media of communication. We shall attempt to suggest the roles of different media with reference to civilizations and to contrast the civilizations.

Notes

1 Thomas Constable, *Archibald Constable and His Literary Correspondents* (London, 1873), 270.

2 James Bryce, *Studies in History and Jurisprudence* (London, 1901), 254–5.

3 For a discussion of the background of political organization see F.J. Teggart, *The Processes of History* (New Haven, 1918).

4 This does not refer to the mechanical spoken word which apparently Hitler had in mind in *Mein Kampf*. 'I know that one is able to win people far more by the spoken than the written word. The greatest changes in the world have never been brought about by the goose quill. The power which set sliding the great avalanches of a political and religious nature was from the beginning of time, the magic force of the spoken word.'

5 See H.M. Chadwick, *The Heroic Age* (Cambridge, 1926).

6 See Emery Neff, *A Revolution in European Poetry 1660–1900* (New York, 1940), ch. 2.

7 See Otto Jesperson, *Mankind, Nation and Individual from a Linguistic Point of View* (Oslo, 1925), 5–13.

8 Ernst Cassirer, *Language and Myth* (New York, 1946), 38.

9 Cited in Jesperson, *Mankind, Nation and Individual* (Oslo, 1925), 139.

10 Herbert Spencer, *Philosophy of Style: An Essay* (New York, 1881), 11.

11 Cited in Graham Wallas, *The Great Society* (London, 1914), 263.

12 For a discussion of conditions favourable to historical writing see F.J. Teggart, *Theory of History* (New Haven, 1925).

13 See C.L. Becker, *Progress and Power* (Stanford University, 1936); see also A.C. Moorhouse, *Writing and the Alphabet* (London, 1946).

14 Edwyn Bevan, *Hellenism and Christianity* (London, 1921), 25.

15 See Christopher Caudwell, *Illusion and Reality: A Study of the Sources of Poetry* (London, 1937), 51.

Thinking about Technology

George Grant

. . .

A computer scientist recently made the following statement about the machines he helps to invent: 'The computer does not impose on us the ways it should be used.' Obviously the statement is made by someone who is aware that computers can be used for purposes of which he does not approve—for example, the tyrannous control of human beings. This is given in the word 'should'. He makes a statement in terms of his intimate knowledge of computers which transcends that intimacy, in that it is more than a description of any given computer or of what is technically common to all such machines. Because he wishes to state something about the possible good or evil purposes for which computers can be used, he expresses, albeit in negative form, what computers are, in a way which is more than their technical description. They are instruments, made by human skill for the purpose of achieving certain human goals. They are neutral instruments in the sense that the morality of the goals for which they are used is determined outside them.

Many people who have never seen a computer, and only slightly understand the capacity of computers, have the sense from their daily life that they are being managed by them, and have perhaps an undifferentiated fear about the potential extent of this management. This man, who knows about the invention and use of these machines, states what they are in order to put our sense of anxiety into a perspective freed from the terrors of such fantasies as the myth of Doctor Frankenstein. His perspective assumes that the machines are instruments, because their capacities have been built into them by human beings, and it is human beings who operate those machines for purposes they have determined. All instruments can obviously be used for bad purposes, and the more complex the capacities of the instrument, the more complex can be its possible bad uses. But if we apprehend these machines for what they are, neutral instruments which we in our freedom are called upon to control, we are better able to come to terms rationally with their potential dangers. The first step in coping with these dangers is to see that they are related to the potential decisions of human beings about how to use computers, not to the inherent capacities of the machines themselves. Indeed the statement about the computer gives the prevalent 'liberal' view of the modern situation which is so rooted in us that it seems to be common sense itself, even rationality itself. We have certain technological capacities; it is up to us to use those capacities for decent human purposes.

Yet despite the seeming common sense of the statement, when we try to think the sentence 'the computer does not impose on us the ways it should be used,' it becomes clear that we are not allowing computers to appear before us for what they are. Indeed the statement (like many similar) obscures for us what computers are. To begin at the surface: the words 'the computer does not impose' are concerned with the capacities of these machines, and these capacities are brought before us as if they existed in abstraction from the events which have made possible their existence. Obviously the machines have been made from a vast variety of materials, consummately fashioned by a vast apparatus of fashioners. Their existence has required generations of sustained effort by chemists, metallurgists, and workers in mines and factories. Beyond these obvious facts, computers have been made within the new science and its mathematics. That science is a particular paradigm of knowledge and, as any paradigm of knowledge, is to be understood as the relation between an aspiration of human thought and the effective conditions for its realization.

It is not my purpose here to describe that paradigm in detail; nor would it be within my ability to show its interrelation with mathematics conceived as algebra. Suffice it to say that what is given in the modern use of the word 'science' is the project of reason to gain 'objective' knowledge. And modern 'reason' is the summoning of anything before a subject and putting it to the question, so that it gives us its reasons for being the way it is as an object. A paradigm of knowledge is not something reserved for scientists and scholars. Anybody who is awake in any part of our educational system knows that this paradigm of knowledge stamps the institutions of that system, their curricula, in their very heart, in what the young are required to know and to be able to do if they are to be called 'qualified'. That paradigm of knowledge is central to our civilizational destiny and has made possible the existence of computers. I mean by 'civilizational destiny' above all the fundamental presuppositions that the majority of human beings inherit in a civilization, and which are so taken for granted as the way things are that they are given an almost absolute status. To describe a destiny is not to judge it. It may indeed be, as many believe, that the development of that paradigm is a great step in the ascent of man, that it is the essence of human liberation, even that its development justifies the human experiment itself. Whatever the truth of these beliefs, the only point here is that without this destiny computers would not exist. And like all destinies, they 'impose'.

What has been said about the computer's existence depending upon the paradigm of knowledge is of course equally true of the earlier machines of industrialism. The Western paradigm of knowledge has not been static, but has been realized in a dynamic unfolding, and one aspect of that realization has been a great extension of what is given in the conception of 'machine'. We all know that computers are machines for the transmitting of information, not the transformation of energy. They require software as well as hardware. They have required the development of mathematics as algebra, and of algebra as almost identical with logic. Their existence has required a fuller realization of the Western paradigm of knowledge beyond its origins, in this context the extension of the conception of machine. It may well be said that where the steel press may be taken as the image of Newtonian physics and mathematics, the computer can be taken as the image of contemporary physics and mathematics. Yet in making that distinction, it must also be said that contemporary science and Newtonian science are equally moments in the realization of the same paradigm.

The phrase 'the computer does not impose' misleads, because it abstracts the computer from the destiny that was required for its making. Common sense may tell us that the computer is an instrument, but it is an instrument from within the destiny which *does* 'impose' itself upon us, and therefore the computer *does* impose.

To go further: How are we being asked to take the word 'ways' in the assertion that 'the computer does not impose the ways'? Even if the purposes for which the computer's capacities should be used are determined outside itself, do not these capacities limit the kind of ways for which it can be used? To take a simple example from the modern institutions of learning and training: in most jurisdictions there are cards on which children are assessed as to their 'skills' and 'behaviour', and this information is retained by computers. It may be granted that such information adds little to the homogenizing vision inculcated throughout society by such means as centrally controlled curricula or teacher training. It may also be granted that as computers and their programming become more sophisticated the information stored therein may be able to take more account of differences. Nevertheless, it is clear that the ways that computers can be used for storing and transmitting information can only be ways that increase the tempo of the homogenizing processes. Abstracting facts so that they can be stored as information is achieved by classification, and it is the very nature of any classifying to homogenize. Where classification rules, identities and differences can appear only in its terms. Indeed the word 'information' is itself perfectly attuned to the account of knowledge which is homogenizing in its very nature. 'Information' is about objects, and comes forth as part of that science which summons objects to give us their reasons.

It is not my purpose at this point to discuss the complex issues of good and evil involved in the modern movement towards homogeneity, nor to discuss the good of heterogeneity, which in its most profound past form was an expression of autochthony. Some modern thinkers state that beyond the rootlessness characteristic of the present early stages of technological society, human beings are now called to new ways of being rooted which will have passed through modern rootlessness, and will be able at one and the same time to accept the benefits of modern homogenization while living out a new form of heterogeneity. These statements are not at issue here. Rather my purpose is to point out that the sentence about computers hides the fact that their ways are always homogenizing. Because this is hidden, questioning homogenization is closed down in the sentence.

To illustrate the matter from another aspect of technological development: Canadians wanted the most efficient car for geographic circumstances and social purposes similar to those of the people who first developed the mass-produced automobile. Our desire for and use of such cars has been a central cause of our political and economic integration and our social homogenization with the people of the imperial heartland. This was not only because of the vast corporate structures necessary for building and keeping in motion such automobiles, and the direct and indirect political power of such corporations, but also because any society with such vehicles tends to become like any other society with the same. Seventy-five years ago somebody might have said 'The automobile does not impose on us the ways it should be used,' and who would have quarrelled with that? Yet this would have been a deluded representation of the automobile.

Obviously, human beings may still be able to control, by strict administrative measures, the ways that cars are used. They may prevent the pollution of the atmosphere or prevent freeways from destroying central city life. It is to be hoped that cities such as Toronto will maintain themselves as communities by winning popular victories over expressways and airports. Whatever efforts may be made, they will not allow us to represent the automobile to ourselves as a neutral instrument.

Obviously the 'ways' that automobiles and computers can be used are dependent on their being investment-heavy machines which require large institutions for their production. The potential size of such corporations can be imagined in the statement of a reliable economist: if the present growth of IBM is extrapolated, that corporation will in the next thirty years be a larger unit than the economy of any presently constituted national state, including that of its homeland. At the simplest factual level, computers can be built only in societies in which there are large corporations. This will be the case whatever ways these institutions are related to the states in which they are incorporated, be that relation some form of capitalism or some form of socialism. Also those machines have been and will continue to be instruments with effect beyond the confines of particular nation states.

They will be the instruments of the imperialism of certain communities towards other communities. They are instruments in the struggle between competing empires, as the present desire of the Soviet Union for American computers illustrates. It might be that 'in the long run of progress', humanity will come to the universal and homogeneous state in which individual empires and nations have disappeared. That in itself would be an even larger corporation. To express the obvious: whatever conceivable political and economic alternatives there may be, computers can only exist in societies in which there are large corporate institutions. The ways they can be used are limited to those situations. In this sense computers are not neutral instruments, but instruments which exclude certain forms of community and permit others.

. . .

From *Understanding Media: The Extensions of Man*
Marshall McLuhan

Radio

The Tribal Drum

England and America had had their 'shots' against radio in the form of long exposure to literacy and industrialism. These forms involve an intense visual organization of experience. The more earthy and less visual European cultures were not immune to radio. Its tribal magic was not lost on them, and the old web of kinship began to resonate once more with the note of fascism. The inability of literate people to grasp the language and message of the media as such is involuntarily conveyed by the comments of sociologist Paul Lazarsfeld in discussing the effects of radio:

> The last group of effects may be called the monopolistic effects of radio. Such have attracted most public attention because of their importance in the totalitarian countries. If a government monopolizes the radio, then by mere repetition and by exclusion of conflicting points of view it can determine the opinions of the population. We do not know much about how this monopolistic effect really works, but it is important to note its singularity. No inference should be drawn regarding the effects of radio as such. It is often forgotten that Hitler did not achieve control through radio but almost despite it, because at the time of his rise to power radio was controlled by his enemies. The monopolistic effects have probably less social importance than is generally assumed.

Professor Lazarsfeld's helpless unawareness of the nature and effects of radio is not a personal defect, but a universally shared ineptitude.

In a radio speech in Munich, March 14, 1936, Hitler said, 'I go my way with the assurance of a somnambulist.' His victims and his critics have been equally somnambulistic. They danced entranced to the tribal drum of radio that extended their central nervous system to create depth involvement for everybody. 'I live tight inside radio when I listen. I more easily lose myself in radio than in a book,' said a voice from a radio poll. The power of radio to involve people in depth is manifested in its use during homework by youngsters and by many other people who carry transistor sets in order to provide a private world for themselves amidst crowds. There is a little poem by the German dramatist Berthold Brecht:

> You little box, held to me when escaping
> So that your valves should not break,
> Carried from house to ship from ship to train,
> So that my enemies might go on talking to me
> Near my bed, to my pain
> The last thing at night, the first thing in the
>   morning,
> Of their victories and of my cares,
> Promise me not to go silent all of a sudden.

One of the many effects of television on radio has been to shift radio from an entertainment medium into a kind of nervous information system. News bulletins, time signals, traffic data, and, above all, weather reports now serve to enhance the native power of radio to involve people in one another. Weather is that medium that involves all people equally. It is the top item on radio, showering us with fountains of auditory space or *lebensraum*.

From *Understanding Media: the Extensions of Man*, by Marshall McLuhan (New York: McGraw-Hill, 1964), 259–68.

It was no accident that Senator McCarthy lasted such a very short time when he switched to TV. Soon the press decided, 'He isn't news any more.' Neither McCarthy nor the press ever knew what had happened. TV is a cool medium. It rejects hot figures and hot issues and people from the hot press media. Fred Allen was a casualty of TV. Was Marilyn Monroe? Had TV occurred on a large scale during Hitler's reign he would have vanished quickly. Had TV come first there would have been no Hitler at all. When Khrushchev appeared on American TV he was more acceptable than Nixon, as a clown and a lovable sort of old boy. His appearance is rendered by TV as a comic cartoon. Radio, however, is a hot medium and takes cartoon characters seriously. Mr. K. on radio would be a different proposition.

In the Kennedy–Nixon debates, those who heard them on radio received an overwhelming idea of Nixon's superiority. It was Nixon's fate to provide a sharp, high-definition image and action for the cool TV medium that translated that sharp image into the impression of a phony. I suppose 'phony' is something that resonates wrong, that doesn't *ring* true. It might well be that F. D. R. would not have done well on TV. He had learned, at least, how to use the hot radio medium for his very cool job of fireside chatting. He first, however, had had to hot up the press media against himself in order to create the right atmosphere for his radio chats. He learned how to use the press in close relation to radio. TV would have presented him with an entirely different political and social mix of components and problems. He would possibly have enjoyed solving them, for he had the kind of playful approach necessary for tackling new and obscure relationships.

Radio affects most people intimately, person-to-person, offering a world of unspoken communication between writer-speaker and the listener. That is the immediate aspect of radio. A private experience. The subliminal depths of radio are charged with the resonating echoes of tribal horns and antique drums. This is inherent in the very nature of this medium, with its power to turn the psyche and society into a single echo chamber. The resonating dimension of radio is unheeded by the script writers, with few exceptions. The famous Orson Welles broadcast about the invasion from Mars was a simple demonstration of the all-inclusive, completely involving scope of the auditory image of radio. It was Hitler who gave radio the Orson Welles treatment for *real*.

That Hitler came into political existence at all is directly owing to radio and public-address systems. This is not to say that these media relayed his thoughts effectively to the German people. His thoughts were of very little consequence. Radio provided the first massive experience of electronic implosion, that reversal of the entire direction and meaning of literate Western civilization. For tribal peoples, for those whose entire social existence is an extension of family life, radio will continue to be a violent experience. Highly literate societies, that have long subordinated family life to individualist stress in business and politics, have managed to absorb and to neutralize the radio implosion without revolution. Not so, those communities that have had only brief or superficial experience of literacy. For them, radio is utterly explosive.

To understand such effects, it is necessary to see literacy as typographic technology, applied not only to the rationalizing of the entire procedures of production and marketing, but to law and education and city planning, as well. The principles of continuity, uniformity, and repeatability derived from print technology have, in England and America, long permeated every phase of communal life. In those areas a child learns literacy from traffic and street, from every car and toy and garment. Learning to read and write is a minor facet of literacy in the uniform, continuous environments of the English-speaking world. Stress on literacy is a distinguishing mark of areas that are striving to initiate that process of standardization that leads to the visual organization of work and space. Without psychic transformation of the inner life into segmented visual terms by literacy, there cannot be the economic 'take-off' that ensures a continual movement of augmented change of goods and services.

Just prior to 1914, the Germans had become obsessed with the menace of 'encirclement'. Their neighbours had all developed elaborate railway systems that facilitated mobilization of manpower resources. Encirclement is a highly visual image that had great novelty for this newly industrialized nation. In the 1930s, by contrast, the German obsession was with *lebensraum*. This is not a visual concern, at all. It is a claustrophobia, engendered by the radio implosion and compression of space. The German defeat had thrust them back from visual obsession into brooding upon the resonating Africa within. The tribal past has never ceased to be a reality for the German psyche.

It was the ready access of the German and middle-European world to the rich nonvisual resources of auditory and tactile form that enabled them to enrich the world of music and dance and sculpture. Above all their tribal mode gave them easy access to the new nonvisual world of subatomic physics, in which long-literate and long-industrialized societies are decidedly handicapped. The rich area of preliterate vitality felt the hot impact of radio. The message of radio is one of violent, unified implosion and resonance. For Africa, India, China, and even Russia, radio is a profound archaic force, a time bond with the most ancient past and long-forgotten experience.

Tradition, in a word, is the sense of the total past as *now*. Its awakening is a natural result of radio impact and of electric information, in general. For the intensely literate population, however, radio engendered a profound unlocalizable sense of guilt that sometimes expressed itself in the fellow-traveller attitude. A newly found human involvement bred anxiety and insecurity and unpredictability. Since literacy had fostered an extreme of individualism, and radio had done just the opposite in reviving the ancient experience of kinship webs of deep tribal involvement, the literate West tried to find some sort of compromise in a larger sense of collective responsibility. The sudden impulse to this end was just as subliminal and obscure as the earlier literary pressure toward individual isolation and irresponsibility; therefore, nobody was happy about any of the positions arrived at. The Gutenberg technology had produced a new kind of visual, national entity in the sixteenth century that was gradually meshed with industrial production and expansion. Telegraph and radio neutralized nationalism but evoked archaic tribal ghosts of the most vigorous brand. This is exactly the meeting of eye and ear, of explosion and implosion, or as Joyce puts it in the *Wake*, 'In that earopean end meets Ind.' The opening of the European ear brought to an end the open society and reintroduced the Indic world of tribal man to West End woman. Joyce puts these matters not so much in cryptic, as in dramatic and mimetic, form. The reader has only to take any of his phrases such as this one, and mime it until it yields the intelligible. Not a long or tedious process, if approached in the spirit of artistic playfulness that guarantees 'lots of fun at Finnegan's wake'.

Radio is provided with its cloak of invisibility, like any other medium. It comes to us ostensibly with person-to-person directness that is private and intimate, while in more urgent fact, it is really a subliminal echo chamber of magical power to touch remote and forgotten chords. All technological extensions of ourselves must be numb and subliminal, else we could not endure the leverage exerted upon us by such extension. Even more than telephone or telegraph, radio is that extension of the central nervous system that is matched only by human speech itself. Is it not worthy of our meditation that radio should be specially attuned to that primitive extension of our central nervous system, that aboriginal mass medium, the vernacular tongue? The crossing of these two most intimate and potent of human technologies could not possibly have failed to provide some extraordinary new shapes for human experience. So it proved with Hitler, the somnambulist. But does the detribalized and literate West imagine that it has earned immunity to the tribal magic of radio as a permanent possession? Our teenagers in the 1950s began to manifest many of the tribal stigmata. The adolescent, as opposed to the teenager, can now be classified as a phenomenon of literacy. Is it not significant that the adolescent was indigenous only to those areas of England and America where literacy had invested even food with abstract visual values? Europe never had adolescents. It had chaperones. Now, to the teenager, radio gives privacy, and at the same time it provides the tight tribal bond of the world of the common market, of song, and of resonance. The ear is hyperaesthetic compared to the neutral eye. The ear is intolerant, closed, and exclusive, whereas the eye is open, neutral, and associative. Ideas of tolerance came to the West only after two or three centuries of literacy and visual Gutenberg culture. No such saturation with visual values had occurred in Germany by 1930. Russia is still far from any such involvement with visual order and values.

If we sit and talk in a dark room, words suddenly acquire new meanings and different textures. They become richer, even, than architecture, which Le Corbusier rightly says can best be felt at night. All those gestural qualities that the printed page strips from language come back in the dark, and on the radio. Given only the *sound* of a play, we have to fill in *all* of the senses, not just the sight of the action. So much do-it-yourself, or completion and 'closure' of action, develops a kind of independent isolation in the young that makes them remote and inaccessible. The mystic screen of sound with which they are invested by their radios provides the privacy for their homework, and immunity from parental behest.

With radio came great changes to the press,

to advertising, to drama, and to poetry. Radio offered new scope to practical jokers like Morton Downey at CBS. A sportscaster had just begun his fifteen-minute reading from a script when he was joined by Mr Downey, who proceeded to remove his shoes and socks. Next followed coat and trousers and then underwear, while the sportscaster helplessly continued his broadcast, testifying to the compelling power of the mike to command loyalty over modesty and self-protective impulse.

Radio created the disk jockey, and elevated the gag writer into a major national role. Since the advent of radio, the gag has supplanted the joke, not because of gag writers, but because radio is a fast hot medium that has also rationed the reporter's space for stories.

Jean Shepherd of WOR in New York regards radio as a new medium for a new kind of novel that he writes nightly. The mike is his pen and paper. His audience and their knowledge of the daily events of the world provide his characters, his scenes, and moods. It is his idea that, just as Montaigne was the first to use the page to record his reactions to the new world of printed books, he is the first to use radio as an essay and novel form for recording our common awareness of a totally new world of universal human participation in all human events, private or collective.

To the student of media, it is difficult to explain the human indifference to social effects of these radical forces. The phonetic alphabet and the printed word that exploded the closed tribal world into the open society of fragmented functions and specialist knowledge and action have never been studied in their roles as a magical transformer. The antithetic electric power of instant information that reverses social explosion into implosion, private enterprise into organization man, and expanding empires into common markets, has obtained as little recognition as the written word. The power of radio to retribalize mankind, its almost instant reversal of individualism into collectivism, Fascist or Marxist, has gone unnoticed. So extraordinary is this unawareness that *it* is what needs to be explained. The transforming power of media is easy to explain, but the ignoring of this power is not at all easy to explain. It goes without saying that the universal ignoring of the psychic action of technology bespeaks some inherent function, some essential numbing of consciousness such as occurs under stress and shock conditions.

The history of radio is instructive as an indicator of the bias and blindness induced in any society by its pre-existent technology. The word 'wireless', still used for radio in Britain, manifests the negative 'horseless-carriage' attitude toward a new form. Early wireless was regarded as a form of telegraph, and was not seen even in relation to the telephone. David Sarnoff in 1916 sent a memo to the director of the American Marconi Company that employed him, advocating the idea of a music box in the home. It was ignored. That was the year of the Irish Easter rebellion and of the first radio *broadcast*. Wireless had already been used on ships as ship-to-shore 'telegraph'. The Irish rebels used a ship's wireless to make, not a point-to-point message, but a diffused broadcast in the hope of getting word to some ship that would relay their story to the American press. And so it proved. Even after broadcasting had been in existence for some years, there was no commercial interest in it. It was the amateur operators or hams and their fans, whose petitions finally got some action in favour of the setting up of facilities. There was reluctance and opposition from the world of the press, which, in England, led to the formation of the BBC and the firm shackling of radio by newspaper and advertising interests. This is an obvious rivalry that has not been openly discussed. The restrictive pressure by the press on radio and TV is still a hot issue in Britain and in Canada. But, typically, misunderstanding of the nature of the medium rendered the restraining policies quite futile. Such has always been the case, most notoriously in government censorship of the press and of the movies. Although the medium is the *message*,

the controls go beyond programming. The restraints are always directed to the 'content', which is always another medium. The content of the press is literary statement, as the content of the book is speech, and the content of the movie is the novel. So the effects of radio are quite independent of its programming. To those who have never studied media, this fact is quite as baffling as literacy is to natives, who say, 'Why do you write? Can't you remember?'

Thus, the commercial interests who think to render media universally acceptable, invariably settle for 'entertainment' as a strategy of neutrality. A more spectacular mode of the ostrich-head-in-sand could not be devised, for it ensures maximal pervasiveness for any medium what-ever. The literate community will always argue for a controversial or point-of-view use of press, radio, and movie that would in effect diminish the operation, not only of press, radio, and movie, but of the book as well. The commercial entertainment strategy automatically ensures maximum speed and force of impact for any medium, on psychic and social life equally. It thus becomes a comic strategy of unwitting self-liquidation, conducted by those who are dedicated to permanence, rather than to change. In the future, the only effective media controls must take the thermostatic form of quantitative rationing. Just as we now try to control atom-bomb fallout, so we will one day try to control media fallout. Education will become recognized as civil defence against media fallout. The only medium for which our education now offers some civil defence is the print medium. The educational establishment, founded on print, does not yet admit any other responsibilities.

Radio provides a speed-up of information that also causes acceleration in other media. It certainly contracts the world to village size, and creates insatiable village tastes for gossip, rumour, and personal malice. But while radio contracts the world to village dimensions, it hasn't the effect of homogenizing the village quarters. Quite the contrary. In India, where radio is the supreme form of communication, there are more than a dozen official languages and the same number of official radio networks. The effect of radio as a reviver of archaism and ancient memories is not limited to Hitler's Germany. Ireland, Scotland, and Wales have undergone resurgence of their ancient tongues since the coming of radio, and the Israelis present an even more extreme instance of linguistic revival. They now speak a language which has been dead in books for centuries. Radio is not only a mighty awakener of archaic memories, forces, and animosities, but a decentralizing, pluralistic force, as is really the case with all electric power and media.

Centralism of organization is based on the continuous, visual, lineal structuring that arises from phonetic literacy. At first, therefore, electric media merely followed the established patterns of literate structures. Radio was released from these centralist network pressures by TV. TV then took up the burden of centralism, from which it may be released by Telstar. With TV accepting the central network burden derived from our centralized industrial organization, radio was free to diversify, and to begin a regional and local community service that it had not known, even in the earliest days of the radio 'hams'. Since TV, radio has turned to the individual needs of people at different times of the day, a fact that goes with the multiplicity of receiving sets in bedrooms, bathrooms, kitchens, cars, and now in pockets. Different programs are provided for those engaged in diverse activities.

Radio, once a form of group listening that emptied churches, has reverted to private and individual uses since TV. The teenager withdraws from the TV group to his private radio.

This natural bias of radio to a close tie-in with diversified community groups is best manifested in the disk-jockey cults, and in radio's use of the telephone in a glorified form of the old trunkline wire-tapping. Plato, who had old-fashioned tribal ideas of political structure, said that the proper size of a city was indicated by the number of people who could hear the voice of a public speaker. Even the printed book, let alone radio, renders the political assumptions of Plato quite irrelevant for practical purposes. Yet radio, because of its ease of decentralized intimate relation with both private and small communities, could easily implement the Platonic political dream on a world scale.

The uniting of radio with phonograph that constitutes the average radio program yields a very special pattern quite superior in power to the combination of radio and telegraph press that yields our news and weather programs. It is curious how much more arresting are the weather reports than the news, on both radio and TV. Is not this because 'weather' is now entirely an electronic form of information, whereas news retains much of the pattern of the printed word? It is probably the print and book bias of the BBC and the CBC that renders them so awkward and inhibited in radio and TV presentation. Commercial urgency, rather than artistic insight, fostered by contrast a hectic vivacity in the corresponding American operation.

Technological Nationalism

Maurice Charland

In the opening sequence of the Canadian Broadcasting Corporation's production of the *National Dream*[1]—Pierre Berton's history of the Canadian Pacific Railway—the pristine majesty of the Rocky Mountains and a lone Indian are confronted with the technological dynamo of a locomotive.

This television image of a railroad as the 'national dream' heroically spanning the wilderness to fashion a state reveals in a condensed narrative the manifold relations between technology and a Canada which can imagine. Here, we are encouraged to see technology as constitutive of Canada, and as a manifestation of Canada's ethos. The *National Dream* highlights, of course, the role of space-binding technology in Canada's history. This CBC epic reminds us that Canada exists by virtue of technologies which bind space and that the railroad permitted a transcontinental economic and political state to emerge in history. Furthermore, the *National Dream* is an instance of the discourse of technology in Canada, of its rhetoric. The CPR is presented as the archetypal instance of Canada's technological constitution. More significantly, the CPR is offered as the product of political will. A nation and railroad were 'dreamt' of by Canada's architects and then consciously created. We see a Canada which imagined itself into existence.

Canada's imagination, a *Canadian* imagination, is manifest by the *National Dream* itself. Berton's televised history is a rhetorical epideictic for a technologically mediated Canada. This rhetoric of a technological nation, basing itself on a romantic interpretation of history, equates the construction of the CPR with the constitution of Canada and praises each with reference to the other. Canada is valorized as a nation because it is the product of a technological achievement, and the railroad is the great product of heroic individuals who dreamt a nation. Curiously, the *National Dream* rearticulates a rhetoric which gave rise to its own materialization. That rhetoric is offered through a product of itself, the CBC. The CBC exists by virtue of a discourse of technological nation-building, and reproduces the rhetoric which legitimates it and the Canadian state when it invites us to join Berton and dream of nationhood.

In this essay, I will explore what I perceive to be a rhetoric of technological nationalism in anglophone Canada which ascribes to technology the capacity to create a nation by enhancing communication. As I will show, the rhetoric of the CPR becomes the power-laden discourse of a state seeking to legitimate itself politically by constituting a nation in its image. This is a significant rhetoric, for it undergirds Canada's official ideology and guides the formulation of federal government policy, at least in the area of broadcasting: the CBC is legitimated in political discourse by the CPR. Furthermore, I will argue that the rhetoric of technological nationalism is insidious, for it ties a Canadian identity, not to its people, but to their mediation through technology.

Rhetoric and Ideological Discourse

This is, then, a critical theorization of the development of Canadian ideological discourse. With regard to the 'method' of ideology analysis, the study proceeds (1) by identifying how Canadian ideological discourse is grounded in the politics and economics of the early Canadian state; (2)

From *Canadian Journal of Political and Social Theory* 10, 1–2 (1986), 196–220. Reprinted by permission.

by tracing out the rhetorical effect—the consequence—of that discourse on the Canadian political, economic, and indeed popular mind, as it calls a certain Canada into being; and (3) by examining how this discourse creates the conditions of its own reproduction. I will demonstrate that the rhetoric of the CPR, seeking to constitute a state, becomes the rhetoric of the CBC, seeking to constitute a *polis* and *nation*. This rhetoric, the rhetoric of technological nationalism, is the dominant discourse of the official ideology of nation-building through state-supported broadcasting, and has been a significant (but not exclusive) determinant of the form of Canada's broadcasting system. It is also the dominant discourse of Canadian nationalism in anglophone Canada.

While my concern is with rhetoric and its significance, I will not simply study discourse. Such an approach would numb my critique, for rhetoric is precisely the form of discourse which projects outside of itself into the realm of human attitude and action. I will take a lead from Kenneth Burke who has rightly observed that while there exists a difference between things and words about things, words provide an orientation to things.[2] Thus, I will examine the relationship of words to things: specifically the relationship between two distinct but intertwined entities—the Canadian rhetoric of a technological nation, and the technology of the Canadian state. Both technology and rhetoric were necessary for Canada as a 'nation' coming to be, but they constituted a Canada within a spiral of contradictions. I will seek to identify these contradictions. Indeed, my claim is that the contradictions between these two have produced the recurring crises in Canadian broadcasting policy and in the quest for a Canadian 'identity'. Technological nationalism promises a liberal state in which technology would be a neutral medium for the development of a *polis*. This vision of a nation is bankrupt, however, because it provides no substance or commonality for the *polis* except communication itself. As a conse-

quence, technological nationalism's (anglophone) Canada has no defence against the power and seduction of the American cultural industry or, indeed, of the technological experience. Canada, then, is the 'absent nation'.

My analysis will take inspiration from James W. Carey and John J. Quirk's application of Innis in their study of the rhetoric of electricity in the United States.[3] I will consider how what Innis terms the 'bias' of communication technology undermines the promises of that technology's rhetoric, as Carey and Quirk put it:

> Innis uncovered the most vulnerable point in rhetoric of electrical sublime. . . . Innis principally disputed the notion that electricity would replace centralization in economics and politics with decentralization, democracy and a cultural revival. Innis placed the 'tragedy of modern culture' in America and Europe upon the intrinsic tendencies of both printing press and electronic media to reduce space and time in the service of a calculus of commercialism and expansionism.[4]

Following Michael McGee, I take rhetoric to be a necessary material condition of human social existence.[5] Indeed, rhetoric is a constitutive component of the social application of technology, for it guides its possible applications. Consequently, my aim is to consider the appropriateness of the rhetoric of technological nationalism in the face of Canadian exigencies.

Canada, Technology, and Technological Rhetoric

Canada is a technological state. This is just to say that Canada's existence as an economic trait is predicated upon transportation and communication technology. In addition, the *idea* of Canada depends upon a rhetoric about technology. Furthermore, we can understand the development of a Canadian nation-state in terms of the interplay between this technology and its rhetoric.

That Canada owes its existence to technologies which bind space is readily apparent. Canada is a sparsely populated territory in which rock, mountains, and sheer distance inhibit human contact between those who live in its several distinct regions. The telegraph and the railroad to a degree overcame these obstacles and permitted the movement of goods and information across what was, in the nineteenth century, an undeveloped wilderness. Indeed, as Harold Innis observes, '[t]he history of the Canadian Pacific Railroad is primarily the history of the spread of western civilization over the northern half of the North American continent.'[6] Through the CPR, Innis points out, western Canadian territories became integrated into the economic and political systems which had developed in eastern Canada.

And what is the nature of this 'civilization'? It is one based in the circulation or communication of commodities and capital. The civilization the railroad extended was one of commerce as the CPR extended Eastern economic interests. The railroad reproduced and extended a state apparatus and economy which concentrated power in metropolitan centres, permitting the incorporation and domination of margins. If the CPR was a 'national project', it was so first and foremost as an economic venture. The railroad was built with a combination of public and private capital for the advantage of the state and merchants, and the former, like the latter, saw its interests in terms of economic development. The nineteenth-century British-style state was, after all, a state of capitalists.

The railroad did more though than enhance trade. It permitted the development of a political state and created the possibility of a nation. It did so by extending Ottawa's political power: it permitted Ottawa to exclude a powerful American presence from western Canada and thus establish its political control over the territory.[7] Specifically, the CPR fostered immigration into the Western plain, effectively discouraging Minnesotans from moving northward and

annexing a sparsely populated area; the CPR permitted Ottawa to establish its military presence in the West, as it did when suppressing the Métis rebellion, and, of course, eastern Canadians no longer had to travel through the United States in order to reach British Columbia. Furthermore, this physical spanning of the country permitted Canadians, including those in Quebec, to unite in patriotic sentiment, as they did when militia from Nova Scotia, Quebec, and Ontario fought side by side against Riel's supporters in Saskatchewan.[8]

In a sense, the power the CPR extended could become the object of a 'national' experience; the CPR offered those in Canada the experience of a technologically mediated political unity as a common denominator.

My point here is that the CPR permitted more than the physical linking of a territory. Apart from joining the country to facilitate commercial intercourse and political administration, the CPR offered the possibility of developing a mythic rhetoric of national origin. Following McGee's arguments on the development of collectivities, I would argue that such a rhetoric is necessary to the realization of the project of Canadian nationhood.[9] That rhetoric is necessary both as a *legitimation* of a sovereign united Canada within the discursive field of parliamentary government, and as an *inducement* for those in Canada to see themselves as Canadian; for Canada to be legitimated, a myth is necessary. The CPR is well suited to such mythologization because (1) its construction in the face of political, economic, and geographic obstacles can be presented as an epic struggle; (2) the CPR was a state project and thus can be represented as the manifestation of a *Canadian* will to survive politically; and (3) the steam engine itself offers Canadians the opportunity to identify with a nationalized icon of power. In sum, the CPR is significant not only as a mode of transportation and communication, but also as the basis for a nationalist discourse. The technological nation is discursive as well as political. Furthermore, the very existence of the

CPR can be understood as a moment in the nationalist rhetoric it renders possible, for it was a symbolic strategy in the face of political exigencies.

To put it bluntly, the CPR's existence is discursive as well as material, for it stands as an articulation of political will. While the CPR proved economically profitable for its backers, the linking of Montreal to Vancouver was not a happenstance or the result of a private entrepreneurial venture, rather the road was built under the auspices of Canada's federal government for the explicit purpose of extending spatial control over a territory. That is to say, the determination of Canada to remain British in character rather than be absorbed by the United States preceded the railway's construction. Furthermore, the construction of the Pacific Railway was not even a necessary condition to British Columbia's entry into Confederation: that Pacific colony had demanded only that Ottawa build a wagon road. Thus, the CPR was part of a rhetorical ploy. Cartier and MacDonald offered more than was necessary, a rail link to the West Coast within ten years of British Columbia's joining the Dominion.[10] Consequently, the CPR cannot be viewed as the product or manifestation only of economy. The construction of the railroad was more than an overdetermined response to material and political exigencies; a will to statehood preceded it. It was an element of a strategy based in the belief that a nation could be built by binding space.

. . .

The myth of the railroad, or of the binding of space technologically to create a nation, places Canadians in a very particular relationship to technology.[11] In Kenneth Burke's language, this rhetoric privileges 'agency' as the motive force for Canada's construction.[12] Canada's existence would be based in a (liberal) pragmatism in which technology is more potent and more responsible for Canada's creation than the so-called 'Fathers of Confederation'. In the popular

mind, Canada exists more because of the technological transcendence of geographical obstacles than because of any politician's will. Thus, technology itself is at the centre of the Canadian imagination, for it provides the condition of possibility for a Canadian mind.

The import of 'agency' or technology in Canada's official popular culture also can be seen, for example, in Gordon Lightfoot's 'Canadian Railroad Trilogy', where the CPR fuses with an entrepreneurial spirit and heralds the truly modern project of expansion and 'progress':

> But . . . they looked in the future
> and what did they see?
> They saw an iron rail running
> from the sea to the sea . . .
> The song of the future has been sung,
> All the battles have been won.
> We have opened up the land,
> All the world's at our command . . .
> We have opened up the soil
> With our teardrops and our toil.

In the rhetoric and construction of the CPR, we see the genesis of technological nationalism as a component in the project of building the national state. This project has two components: one, physical, the other, discursive: (1) The existence of a transcontinental Canada required the development of a system of transportation facilitating territorial annexation, colonization, and the implantation of a military presence. (2) The existence of this Canada also required the development of a rhetoric which ideologically constituted those in Canada as Canadians, united in the national project and under the political authority of a national government.

For the moment, let us focus on the rhetorical component of technological nationalism. The Canadian tradition of parliamentary public address, which Canada inherited from Britain, places particular demands on the rhetoric of the Canadian state. In this 'Whig Liberal' tradition, political power is legitimated by a rhetoric of the 'people'.[13] That is to say, attempts to discursively secure legitimacy will argue that a national 'people' exists which authorizes the state's power. For Ottawa to successfully exercise the power the CPR extended, it must counter arguments in favour of provincial autonomy or, conversely, annexation by the United States by persuasively representing those in Canada as forming a Canadian people. Indeed, the existence of such a pan-Canadian collectivity was asserted by Georges Etienne Cartier in defence of Confederation.[14] Without such a persuasive rhetoric of 'national' identity and 'national' interest, Ottawa's power would dissolve.

In Canada, the constitution of a 'people' of individuals united under a liberal state requires that the barriers between regions be apparently transcended. As it permits mastery over nature, technology offers the possibility of that apparent transcendence. Consequently, in order to assert a national interest and unity, Ottawa depends upon a rhetoric of technological nationalism—a rhetoric which both asserts that a technologically mediated Canadian *nation* exists, and calls for improved communication between regions to render that nation materially present. In other words, Canada is a state which must constantly seek to will a *nation* in its own image, in order to justify its very existence. The CPR can be understood as one manifestation of this necessity, but as a form of *economic* communication, it gave rise neither to a common Canadian culture, nor to a Canadian 'public' of citizens capable of participating in the country's political will formation. At most, it offered those in Canada the possibility of jointly participating in the rhetoric of the national project. Primarily, the CPR enmeshed Canada within a series of networks of domination. As Innis observes and the suppression of the Métis uprising of 1885 makes manifesty clear, spacebinding technologies extend power as they foster empire. Because of the CPR's inability to create a people or nation, another technological instrument was necessary, an instrument

which would permit the representation and actualization of some form of Canadian 'public' and common Canadian culture. Both the rhetoric of national identity and the fact of a Canadian political community required a *cultural* rather than economic form of communication. Technological nationalism required radio, and the advent of the broadcasting era advanced the project of a technologically constituted nation.

Technological Nationalism in the Broadcasting Era

The development of electronic communication, and in particular broadcast technology, permitted a new articulation of the rhetoric of technological nationalism. Technological nationalism became a major factor in the development of the structure of broadcasting in Canada, as radio and television were enlisted into the national project. However, this rhetoric of a technologically mediated Canada is contradictory.

Significantly, Canada's first national radio network was established by a railway. While local radio had been pioneered by private entrepreneurs, national radio was the product of a state agency, the CNR. The national railway saw in radio a means to foster immigration, to enhance its own image, and to support the project of nationhood.[15] CNR radio, which initially broadcast to railroad parlour cars, developed in 1924 into a network of stations in major Canadian cities from Vancouver to Moncton. It offered symphony broadcasts, comic operas, special events, and in 1931, a dramatic presentation of Canadian history.[16] State-supported radio, following the railroad's path, presented those who live in anglophone Canada with an image of Canada.[17] CNR sought to bind Canada with information just as rail had bound Canada economically. Thus was forged the link in the official Canadian mind between railroad, radio, and national identity. As the official biographer of Sir Henry Thorton, the CNR's president and instigator of its radio services, writes:

As a direct result of Sir Henry's abilities to see the possibilities inherent in a new medium of expression, the railway did for Canada what she was too apathetic to do for herself. . . . He saw radio as a great unifying force in Canada; to him the political conception transcended the commercial, and he set out consciously to create a sense of nationhood through the medium of the Canadian National Railway Service.[18]

The rhetoric of technological nationalism had incorporated radio. It sought to enlist another space-binding technology in the project of constituting a nation in the image of the state. Furthermore, this vision of an electronically constituted Canada did not remain Thorton's, but became that of the national government. Thus, one of the first 'live' national broadcasts was a celebration of Canada. Prime Minister Mackenzie King's voice was heard across the country as he spoke from Ottawa on 1 July 1927, Confederation's anniversary. Commenting on that moment a month later at the Canadian National Exhibition, the prime minister presented radio, a gift of science, as the means whereby Canada would develop a 'people' or 'public' to justify its government:

On the morning, afternoon and evening of July 1, all Canada became, for the time-being, a single assemblage, swayed by a common emotion, within the sound of a single voice. Thus has modern science for the first time realized in the great nation-state of modern days, that condition which existed in the little city-states of ancient times and which was considered by the wisdom of the ancients as indispensable to free and democratic government—that all the citizens should be able to hear for themselves the living voice. [. . .][19]

King's statement preceded a national radio policy by five years. However, it can be understood as a charge to future policy makers. Certainly, it articulated the major themes of technological nationalism in the broadcasting era. In particu-

lar, it reveals the paradoxical promise of democracy and domination inherent to the rhetoric of technological nationalism. Mackenzie King's speech reduces Canada to a community or small city which does not suffer from the isolating effects of distance, regionalism, or cultural diversity. Here, technology would create a *polis* where the proximity of speaker to audience would promote 'freedom' and give rise to a 'democracy' of a public sharing a commonweal.[20]. . . As such, technological nationalism is a form of liberalism. It proposes the electronic *polis* and affirms no value save the communication of the people's voices as expressed in Parliament. However, this vision of a society in and through communication is undermined by technological nationalism's other goal, that of creating a *united* Canada. . . . Radio, if it offers community, also offers domination, as Innis observes in counterpoint to Mackenzie King:

The rise of Hitler to power was facilitated by the use of the loudspeaker and radio. . . . The radio, appealed to vast areas, overcame the division between classes in its escape from literacy, and favoured centralization and bureaucracy. A single individual could appeal at one time to vast numbers of people speaking the same language. . . .[21]

Mackenzie King's remarks capture the spirit of the rhetoric of Canadian government policy towards broadcasting as a means of binding space from his own time until the recent flirtations with cultural continentalism. As with rail service in Canada, broadcasting was consciously regarded as a means of *creating* a Canada with sufficient commonality to justify its political union, while simultaneously, it was also considered a means of simply enabling Canadians to be aware of each other and their already constituted values and identity. Such a contradictory role for broadcasting was articulated in various government reports dealing with the problems posed by broadcasting technology including the 1929 *Report of the Royal Commission on Broadcasting,* and the 1932 *Report of the Parliamentary Committee on Broadcasting*. These and subsequent reports offered a rhetoric which asserted the existence of a distinctly Canadian (and thus unitary) consciousness which required technological mediation and also charged broadcasting with the task of realizing that consciousness and its nation.

The Development of a Broadcasting Policy of Technological Nationalism

The 1932 Broadcasting Act followed rather than anticipated broadcasting's development. Canada's first commercial radio station was licensed in 1919. A decade elapsed before the Royal Commission on Radio Broadcasting, chaired by Sir John Aird, former president of the Canadian Imperial Bank of Commerce, issued a report calling for exclusive government control of broadcasting, including the nationalization of existing privately owned outlets.[22] The Commission's stance was one of 'defensive expansionism' as Margaret Prang would put it, for it pointed to the threat of Americanized airwaves and called for protective federal initiatives.[23] Of course, the Commission asserted that the airwaves must be protected from an American expansion driven by market forces. More significantly, the Aird Report also echoed Mackenzie King as it asserted that radio must become a means for developing Canadian hegemony and fostering a unified culture in the face of geography and regionalism:

At present the majority of programs heard are from sources outside of Canada. It has been emphasized that the continued reception of these had a tendency to mold the minds of young people in the home to ideals and opinions that are not Canadian. In a country of the vast geographical dimension of Canada, broadcasting will undoubtedly become a great force in imparting a national spirit and interpreting national citizenship.[24]

The official Canadian mind conceives of Canada as a nation which must come to be in spite of space. Thus, even though the Aird Commission did not seek to establish a repressive single Canadian discourse, but called for a broadcasting system in which programming would be provincially controlled, it sought to create an extended community in which common Canadian interests would be articulated and a shared national identity could emerge. The popular mind, like the land, must be occupied. Note, however, that technological nationalism only defines Canadian ideals and opinion by virtue of their not being from foreign sources. This is significant because, in its reluctance or inability to articulate a positive content to the Canadian identity—an identity still to be created—technological nationalism is a form of liberalism, privileging the *process* of communication over the substance of what is communicated. Consequently, if radio were to bring forth a nation by providing a common national experience, that experience would be one of communication, of sheer mediation. This is the first contradiction of technological nationalism: the content of the Canadian identity would be but technological nationalism itself.

. . .

The Contradictions of Economic and Cultural Communication

Canada did not end up with the exact broadcasting system these reports envisaged, of course, for the abstract principles of policy are not easily realized. In particular, the development of both communication and transportation infrastructures are based on technologies and economic forces which exist somewhat autonomously from the state. Indeed, from the outset, radio offered little promise of creating or strengthening the Canadian state or *nation*, since American signals penetrated Canada's borders far more easily than steel rails. By 1930, Canadians were more likely to receive American than

Canadian signals: nearly all Canadians were within reach of an American station, while only 60 per cent could receive a signal originating in Canada.[25] Furthermore, American-made programs were very popular among Canadians. At least 50 per cent of Canadian listening time was devoted to United States programming.[26] While the CNR at that time operated a national network service (albeit of limited scope), it could not compete with American programs, be they distributed in Canada by Canadian stations, or by powerful stations based in the United States. In consequence, Margaret Prang points out, as I observed above, that Canadian broadcasting policy has been characterized by 'defensive expansionism'. It has been sensitive to American expansion, and has called for a concerted state effort to use technology both as a form of defence and as a means of establishing Canadian hegemony over its territory. Canada had secured its western territory through space-binding technology; it had not, however, secured its cultural territory. Thus the Canadian Radio Broadcasting Commission, and its successor, the CBC, were instituted to occupy and defend Canada's ether and consciousness.

While various governments in Ottawa could rhetorically call for a technologically mediated *nation*, they were in no way assured of success, especially since radio, like rail, is an extension of an economic system dominated by American capital. In spite of Prang's 'defensive expansionism', and the conscientious work of broadcasters at the CRBC and CBC, anglophone Canada found itself saddled with a model of broadcasting as entertainment largely developed outside of the country, and with a timetable for its development over which Ottawa had little control. Canada was the subject of what Boyd-Barrett terms 'media [as opposed to cultural] imperialism'.[27] And, of course, both of these could only be countered through major government expenditures. Technological nationalism thus encountered its constraint.

In passing the 1932 Radio Broadcasting Bill,

Parliament sought to empower the discourse of technological nationalism. However, while talk may be cheap, its transmission by radio is not and Parliament was ultimately unwilling to advance the funds necessary for the new radio service, the Canadian Radio Broadcasting Commission (CRBC), to nationalize existing stations or establish many new facilities.[28] The federal government, under John A. Macdonald's leadership, had been willing to subsidize the CPR, but that project ultimately would promote Canadian commerce and the Canadian accumulation of capital. State radio, on the other hand, offered no financial benefits. On the contrary, state radio would always be a drain on the public purse, particularly if it were to avoid commercialization and seek to 'uplift' its audience, rather than transmit popular (and predominantly American) programs.

We see here a fundamental difference between the railroad and radio. While both were and are called upon to help create a nation, the railroad's nation is economic, while radio's is cultural and ideological. That the CPR would carry American goods, or that its Canadian cargo would be undistinguishable from American freight, was unimportant. Canadian commerce could be identical in content to its American counterpart and remain Canadian. Conversely, radio is not a common carrier and is thus quite unlike rail service. If radio were treated as a common carrier, like the railroad, its content would be irrelevant. Radio would be successful if it were profitable. However, radio is Canadian by its content, and is thus quite unlike the CPR. *Canadian* radio must create its own 'freight', and find a market for it as well. However, before Canadian radio had developed into a mature form, the nature of demand in the radio market had already been constituted by the distribution of American programs. Consequently, Canadian radio, unlike Canadian rail, could be either profitable or Canadian, not both. We see here then the second contradiction of technological nationalism: it identifies a medium ultimately based upon a foreign economic and programming logic as the site for Canada's cultural construction.

The CRBC's main failure was its inability to compete successfully with commercial broadcasters and so transform the airwaves into a medium fostering nationhood. This failure was not unique to the CRBC, but is endemic to Canadian broadcasting's history. The Canadian Broadcasting Corporation, established to succeed the CRBC in 1936, faced the same dilemma. From its creation until the advent of television in Canada in 1952, the CBC did, to a degree, offset the influence of American broadcasting in Canada. Certainly, without state-sponsored radio, the airwaves in Canada would have become but another market for American networks. In particular, the CBC did offer to Canadians a common experience and its popularity increased during the Second World War, as Canadians sought information on Canada's war effort. Nevertheless, American programming remained popular in Canada— Toronto and Montreal had US network affiliates, and the CBC's most popular programs were American productions such as 'Fibber McGee and Molly' and 'Edgar Bergen and Charlie McCarthy'.[29] Communication technology, heralded as the means of promoting Canadian statehood and nationhood, paradoxically offered those in Canada a common 'national' experience which included cultural commodities from the United States.

. . .

While, certainly, the Canadian economic state depends upon technology, we should question whether technology constitutes or regenerates a Canadian culture. Technological nationalism offers Canadians a common experience of signs and information in which culture is disembodied. Thus, technology promotes a cultural experience which is not grounded in a region or tradition, particularly if it is in the service of some 'national' interest. Because the state itself is the basis of a Canadian commonality, its nation-

al consciousness would be the product of a bureaucratic cultural apparatus. Once a culture is associated with television, and technology generally, the nature of the American subordination becomes clear. American culture (or, what's the same: intense commodification) is imposing itself on Canada through the very technologies which should be constitutive of the Canadian experience and essence. Furthermore, America's presence on Canadian screens is a curious form of subordination, for Canadians enjoy American cultural products, even while recognizing the cultural invasion, or what, in broadcast industry jargon, is referred to as 'market penetration'. It seems, then, more accurate to say that Canadians are being seduced by American cultural commodities designed for a technology capable of eliciting desire.[30] This points to the third contradiction of technological nationalism: the mediated culture which is imperative to Canadian statehood has within its logic the seduction of technology itself.[31] American television exploits the seductiveness of the technological experience.

Even in the ideal world of Canadian television envisioned by the CBC, the Canadian experience would remain an experience of technology, of the state, and of power. In its 1978 submission to the Canadian Radio Television Commission (CRTC), the CBC asserts that Canada's shared experience includes Paul Henderson's 1972 winning goal for Team Canada against the USSR, the televised drama of the Montreal Olympics, and Peter Kent's reporting of federal election results.[32] Note that each of these moments of experience are 'media events' where national identity is inscribed in a mythos of power, and where official state culture is celebrated. Each of these elements of our 'national experience' exists precisely as an absence of a non-technologized commonality. The Canadian imagination, according to technological nationalism, is a technologically mediated one which derives from the state and is in opposition to nature as well as regionalism. But, in the face of the American presence and regional cultures, traditions, and history the discourse of the Canadian state and its institutions can only offer mediation itself as the ground for unity, as I have earlier observed. Just as the CPR would be our 'national dream', so the CBC would be our common cultural ground. Thus, the CBC can assert that its purpose is 'the *creation* of our national consciousness' (my emphasis).[33]

As is obvious to even the casual observer of Canadian broadcasting, and as the CBC and CRTC have at times complained, electronic delivery systems cannot, in themselves, create a culture. As the 1956 Royal Commission on Broadcasting observed, what is important is the programming. In order to give rise to a Canadian identity, communication technologies must carry Canadian products. However, to simply berate Parliament for its unwillingness to better fund Canadian television, to criticize commercial interests for their unwillingness to sacrifice profit for the sake of a national culture, or to attack the CRTC for lacking the courage to halt the development of cable systems, is in large measure to miss the point. The failure of technological nationalism lies not in Parliament, CTV, or the CRTC, but in contradictions inherent to technological nationalism itself.

Conclusion

Rail and radio differ. The latter binds space much more efficiently than the former. The railroad depends upon the physical domination of geography to join distant points. Radio, on the other hand, does not so much bind space as annihilate it. The railroad binds space one-dimensionally as it links east to west; radio renders space insignificant across two or three dimensions as all points become proximate. Thus, radio, and electronic technology in general, will tend to ensnare Canada within an American web of information. The advocates of Canada's continual technological reconstitution seem to have intuitively, but naively, grasped what Innis observed, that technologies of communication extend and strengthen empires.

They sought to favour the Canadian (and British Empire) domination of a geographic and cultural territory, but they failed to realize that such technologies were not merely the tools of political will permitting control over a region. As Innis saw, space-binding technologies favour and transform existing centres of power. They are not the political, economic, and cultural equivalents of string and tape, which can patch together a territory. They are media which extend power, and for Canada in the twentieth century, power is based in the United States. Thus, as broadcasting developed in Canada, it adopted the form and content of American programs.

The Americanization of Canada's airwaves should hardly be surprising, for the American industry of cultural production has economic, technical, and human resources which Canada could not match. Sheer economic forces favoured the integration of English Canada's cultural market to the American one. This is particularly so because the penetration of American over-the-air signals into Canada during broadcasting's early years established the form of media in Canada. Broadcasting, the technology called upon to form a Canadian cultural identity, became a form of spectacle and entertainment.[34] American signals defined what radio and television would be in the popular mind. Thus, from the outset, radio and television were media dedicated to the distribution of cultural commodities. In the 'cultural' marketplace, a Canadian industry could hardly compete. Indeed, private broadcasters, acting with great economic rationality, largely contented themselves with distributing cultural products produced elsewhere rather than attempting to create their own.

. . .

To conclude: technological nationalism's promise is suspect because the commodified culture it would constitute would have no stability, and would be but another instance of the culture of technological society. As Innis observes: 'Stability which characterized certain periods in earlier civilizations is not the obvious objective of this civilization.'[35] Our space-binding culture, also a commodity culture, changes rapidly—fashions, music, politics, are celebrated and then their value is exhausted.[36] A technologically mediated Canadian culture, based in the experience of media commodities, would contribute little to a Canadian self-understanding. Rather than interpreting some supposedly Canadian experience, and offering 'a sense of balance and proportion',[37] technological nationalism can only offer itself in a constantly mutating form. We must develop new rhetorics about and for ourselves, and create our cultures otherwise and elsewhere. The national dream offers only the dark sun of alienation.

Notes

1 *The National Dream*, based on Pierre Berton's history of the CPR, was originally broadcast during the 1973–4 television season as an eight-part series. The series was rebroadcast in 1982 and 1985.

2 Kenneth Burke, *The Rhetoric of Religion: Studies in Logology* (Berkeley: University of California Press, 1961), 18; *Language as Symbolic Action: Essays on Life, Literature, and Method* (Berkeley: University of California Press, 1966): 362–73.

3 James W. Carey and John J. Quirk. 'The Mythos of the Electronic Revolution', *American Scholar* 39 (1, 1970): 219–51; 40 (2, 1970): 395–424.

4 Ibid., 238.

5 Michael Calvin McGee, 'The Ideograph: A Link between Rhetoric and Ideology', *Quarterly Journal of Speech* 66 (February 1980): 4–9.

6 Harold A. Innis, *A History of the Canadian Pacific Railway* (1923; rpt. Toronto: University of Toronto Press, 1971), 287.

7 I am subscribing to a 'metropolitan' interpretation of Canadian history. This perspective is central to Innis's analysis and is discussed in J.M.S. Careless, 'Frontierism, Metropolitanism, and Canadian History', *The Canadian Historical Review* 35 (March 1954): 1–21.

8 Quebec initially supported, albeit with some reservations, Ottawa's decision to put down militarily the 1885 Métis uprising. Popular support in Quebec for Riel developed subsequent to his defeat. See Robert Rumilly, *Histoire de la Province de Québec*, vol. 5 (Montreal: Editions Bernard Valiquette, 1942): 1–108.

9 Michael Calvin McGee, 'In Search of the 'People': A Rhetorical Alternative', *Quarterly Journal of Speech* 66 (February 1980): 1–16.

10 G.P. de T. Glazenbrook, *A History of Transportation in Canada*, vol. 2 (1934; rpt. Toronto: McClelland and Stewart Limited, 1964), 47.

11 Various rhetorics of technology are possible. Canada's rhetoric is rooted in its colonial origins and state-supervised development. In the United States, where local development preceded the federal state, a different rhetoric of technology arose. There, 'clean' electrical technology was heralded as a means to restore the pastoral ideals of a democratic community and harmony with nature. See Carey and Quirk, 226–35, *passim*.

12 Kenneth Burke, *A Grammar of Motives* (Berkeley: University of California Press, 1945), xv–xxiii, 275–317.

13 McGee, 'In Search of the "People"'.

14 Georges Etienne Cartier, address to the Assembly of Lower Canada, 7 February 1865, in *Le manuel de la paroles: Manifestes Québécois*, vol. 1 (Sillerey: Editions du boreal express, 1977), 53–61.

15 Frank W. Peers, *The Politics of Canadian Broadcasting 1920–1951* (Toronto: University of Toronto Press, 1969): 23–4.

16 Ibid.

17 CNR radio did offer some French-language programming on its network, much to the displeasure of many in western Canada who objected to the French language being on the air outside of Quebec. As Innis observes of radio: 'Stability within language units became more evident and instability between language units more dangerous.' Harold A. Innis, *The Bias of Communication*

(Toronto: University of Toronto Press, 1951): 82.

18 Darcy Marsh, *The Tragedy of Sir Henry Thorton* (Toronto: The Macmillan Company of Canada Limited, 1935): 115–16.

19 William Lyon Mackenzie King, address at the Canadian National Exhibition, July 1927, in *Signing On: The Birth of Radio in Canada* (Toronto: Doubleday Canada Limited, 1982): 190.

20 Ibid.

21 Innis, *Bias of Communication*, 82.

22 Canada. *Royal Commission on Broadcasting, 1929 (Aird Commission), Report*, 12–13.

23 Margaret Prang, 'The Origins of Public Broadcasting in Canada', *The Canadian Historical Review* 46 (1, 1965): 11–31.

24 Aird Commission, 6.

25 Prang, 3.

26 Ibid., 4.

27 Oliver Boyd-Barrett, 'Media Imperialism: Towards an International Framework for the Analysis of Media Systems', in *Mass Communication and Society*, edited by James Curran, Michael Gurevitch, and Janet Woollacott (London: Open University Press, 1977): 116–35.

28 The CRBC's funding problems are discussed in E. Austin Weir, *The Struggle for National Broadcasting in Canada* (Toronto: McClelland and Stewart, 1965): 173–7.

29 Ibid., 281; Peers, 283, 285.

30 For a discussion of the seduction of technological experience see Arthur Kroker, *Technology and the Canadian Mind: Innis/McLuhan/Grant* (Montreal: New World Perspectives, 1984 and New York: St Martin's Press, 1985), 53–74; and Max Horkheimer and Theodor Adorno, *Dialectic of Enlightenment* (New York: The Continuum Publishing Company, 1969): 138–47.

31 Ibid.

32 Canadian Broadcasting Corporation, *The CBC—A Perspective: Submission to the Canadian Radio-television and Telecommunications Commissions in Support of Applications of Network Licences*, May 1978, 1.

33 Ibid.

34 Of course, electronic technologies are in themselves spectacular. Radio's initial appeal, for example, lay not in its programming, but in its ability to invisibly and magically connect distant points.

35 Innis, *Bias of Communication*, 141.

36 For an enlightening exploration of the implications of the ephemerality and impermanence of 'space-bound' contemporary culture see James W. Carey, 'Harold Adams Innis and Marshall McLuhan', *The Antioch Review* (Spring 1967): 29–35.

37 Innis, *Bias of Communication*, 86.

Section II

Postal Systems
and Telecommunications

We are today awash in the rhetoric of 'communication revolution' and 'media convergence'. Personal computers, fibre-optic cables, cellular phones, satellite transmission, digital television, e-mail, and the World Wide Web enable personalized communication on multiple platforms in real time, all the time. Beyond the mass media model of 'one-to-many' communication, digital luminaries trumpet the virtues of 'one-to-one' communication, media systems tailored to our idiosyncratic desires and irregular schedules. Digital technology enables different media to perform similar functions. Telephones send text messages, computer monitors show television programs, and the Internet is used for long-distance calling. The 'content' of conventional mass media—newspapers, radio, television, and film—is married with 'carrier' technologies like cable, satellite, and telephone systems, which has spawned a number of corporate mergers and acquisitions. In Canada, BCE has bought CTV and the *Globe and Mail*, while printing giant Quebecor has snapped up Vidéotron, Quebec's largest cable provider, along with television stations and the Sun Media chain of newspapers. While stock market downturns have quieted some of the hoopla, media convergence—technological, corporate, and cultural—remains an animating feature of early twenty-first century communications.

But, as history shows, this kind of communication revolution is not an entirely new phenomenon. During the second half of the nineteenth century a number of communication innovations were as transformative, if not more, as those seen today. Postal systems, the telegraph, news wire services, and the telephone fundamentally altered people's perceptions of space, time, and being. They, too, carried—and mostly delivered—the promise of 'one-to-one' communication, in some cases in real time. Moreover, these communication advances occurred against the backdrop of sweeping historical change, as industrialization, urbanization, immigration, and secularization reconfigured the boundaries of North American societies and understandings of personhood.

Canada's postal system underwent a 'revolution in communications' in the latter half of the nineteenth century, Brian Osborne and Robert Pike argue. Higher literacy rates and improved road, water, and rail transportation formed the foundation for vastly improved mail delivery in Ontario and Quebec after the 1840s. Geographical mobility increased the demand for mail service, as larger numbers of people moved between regions or immigrated from abroad. Some settled in sparsely populated rural areas, where mail service was the main lifeline to kith and kin. Mail use grew fastest in urban areas, owing in part to its wholesale adoption by business: money orders and postal savings banks promoted financial transactions through the mails, and mailed advertisements, the forerunner of today's direct mail, appeared. Newspapers also travelled by mail, speeding the flow of news to outlying areas. In these and other ways postal communication facilitated modernization by augmenting personal mobility, individualism, privacy, bureaucracy, commerce, and the mass circulation of news and public commentary.

The telegraph was another key communication innovation in the mid-nineteenth century. As Dwayne Winseck shows, its development was closely tied to changes in market structure, the legal system, and involvement with newspapers, news agencies, and financial information services. Before telegraphic communication could become a profitable undertaking, cut-throat competition had to end, legal principles had to reflect the 'immaterial reality' of electronic communication, and 'common carrier' provisions needed to be in place. At various times, the telegraph converged and diverged with telephony, railway transportation, news wire services, and newspapers, with political and economic factors more than technological ones determining the course of events.

Like George Grant, Michèle Martin holds that technology—in this case the telephone—is not 'neutral' in design or application. Its emergence in the 1870s and later diffusion in Ontario and Quebec followed 'class contours' rather than 'mass' ones. Business executives, commercial operations, and middle- and upper-income earners in general were the prime beneficiaries of telephone service by the monopoly provider Bell Telephone Company, while telephone service in working-class areas was vastly underrepresented.

Technological convergence surfaced again during the late 1960s with the co-penetration of computers and telecommunication systems. Many believed that telephone and data transmission lines could bring the awesome calculating power of mainframe computers to institutions and citizens alike. As Laurence Mussio explains, the federal government sought to play a leading role in this area of convergence. Officials in the then recently formed Department of Communications envisioned the creation of a 'national computer utility', modelled on existing electrical and telephone utilities. This would represent a new National Dream, not made of rail ties or broadcast towers, but of computer power channelled into homes and businesses via telecommunications systems. By the mid-1970s, the idea of a national computer utility had crashed on the shoals of business opposition and policy makers' wariness for state activism.

Questions for Critical Reading

1. What accounts for the different levels of postal use in Ontario and Quebec between 1850 and 1910?
2. What social and economic consequences of an improved postal system were in evidence by the early twentieth century?
3. Why and how did telegraph companies and newspapers join forces? Are there similarities to media convergence today?
4. How did the business of telegraphy change from the mid- to late-1800s?
5. Why did telegraphy and telephony 'diverge' in the late nineteenth century?

6. In what ways was the telephone socially constructed for business purposes and the use of the bourgeois class?
7. How did women use the telephone? How did Bell and other telephone companies respond to this?
8. How did notions of privacy affect the development of the telephone?
9. What was envisioned by those who promoted the creation of a national computer utility? Why was this plan not realized?
10. Who opposed a strong state role in computer services? Why?

Further Readings

Armstrong, Christopher and H.V. Nelles. *Monoply's Moment: The Organization and Regulation of Canadian Utilities, 1830–1930.* Toronto: University of Toronto Press, 1988.
* This, in part, covers the development of the telephone as a government-regulated industry.

Babe, Robert. *Telecommunications in Canada: Technology, Industry, and Government.* Toronto: University of Toronto Press, 1990.
* Much of this covers the historical emergence of telephone and telegraph systems in Canada and their regulatory frameworks.

Goheen, Peter. 'The Impact of the Telegraph on the Newspaper in Mid-Nineteenth Century British North America'. *Urban Geography* 11, 2 (1990).
* The article explores the telegraph's impact on the speed of news dissemination in North America and Europe during the 1840s and 1950s.

Martin, Michèle. *'Hello, Central?' Gender, Technology, and Culture in the Formation of the Telephone Systems.* Montreal: McGill–Queen's University Press, 1991.
* This work is a theory-laden analysis of the rise of the telephone system in Ontario and Quebec between 1876 and 1920.

Mussio, Laurence B. *Telecom Nation: Telecommunications, Computers, and Governments in Canada.* Montreal: McGill–Queen's University Press, 2001.
* This thorough and nuanced overview of federal public policy regarding telecommunications covers the three decades after World War II.

Rens, Jean-Guy. *The Invisible Empire: A History of the Telecommunications Industry in Canada, 1846–1956.* Montreal: McGill–Queen's University Press, 2001.
* This is a detailed history of the telegraph from the first line between Toronto and Hamilton in 1846 until the American Bell System in 1956.

Lowering 'the Walls of Oblivion': The Revolution in Postal Communications in Central Canada, 1851–1911

Brian Osborne and Robert Pike

I

The continued development and implementation of telecommunications is a prominent feature of the late twentieth century. 'Telework', 'teleconferencing', 'telecommuting', and 'telecommunities' allow for the substitution of telecommunication for the physical movement of people and the face-to-face interaction characteristic of the traditional economic and social organization of our society. As such technological developments become widespread, they will have a considerable effect not only upon business and office organization, but the nature of home and family, and the quality of life of society. The potential impact of this telecommunications revolution upon individuals and society is increasingly recognized but an earlier, and in many ways analogous, revolution in distance communications has not been explored by social scientists in a formal way.

The introduction of a system of 'mass' public postal services in the latter part of the nineteenth century in the Western world was a significant innovation in communications which had certain similar effects. In Canada, the 1851–1914 period witnessed a major effort by the Canadian postal authorities to extend postal services to areas of new settlement as well as to improve existing services in relatively highly populated urban and rural areas. The system was 'mass' or widely accessible insofar as it 'made available to ordinary people, as an amenity of every day life, a facility which had been a luxury and privilege of rulers and elites'.[1]

The provision of a finer network of mail routes, the increased number of post offices, the increased frequency of the service, and the greater variety of postal and financial services offered, were all aspects of this change. Both the overall improvements in the system of written communication and the provision of new forms of commercial and social interaction served to decrease the need for face-to-face interaction which, in turn, had ramifications for traditional functions, agencies, and usages. Moreover, in the same way that a familiarity with computing is an essential prerequisite for the diffusion of electronic communications, so literacy was necessary for the development of a full use of the postal services.

In this paper, certain features of this early revolution in communications are discussed as they manifested themselves throughout the urban and rural communities of Ontario and Quebec between 1851 and 1911. The expansion and increased diversity of the postal system in Ontario and Quebec are presented, using data gathered from the annual reports of the postmaster general. . . . The development of the mass postal system constituted a revolution in communications. First and foremost, it facilitated private interpersonal communications, as well as making messages from a greater variety of organizational sources potentially more accessible. Easily accessible postal communications were thus widely perceived by more and more individuals and organizations to be a necessary public 'amenity of everyday life' both in newly settled areas and in the more established rural and urban communities. There were, however, substantial regional differences in the degree of

From *Canadian Papers in Rural History*, Vol. 4, ed. Donald H. Akenson (Gananoque, ON: Langdale Press, 1994), 200–25.

development of postal communications which may have been related to regional differences in social organization, public demand, urbanization, and economic growth.

II

Before 1851, the deputy postmaster generals in the Canadas and Maritime provinces were ultimately answerable to the postmaster general in London whose primary objective for the colonial postal service was to secure a profit to be remitted back to Britain.[2] Indeed, the 1846 Commission charged with inquiring into the affairs of the Post Office in British North America reported an inadequate administrative infrastructure, high postal charges, and insufficient numbers of post offices in some regions. Postal services were not yet perceived, at least by those who held ultimate responsibility for their development, as a major component in the expansion of settlement and commercial enterprise in a new colony.[3]

Any improvement in postal facilities associated with the advance of settlement and commercial development required advances in transportation technology which allowed the swift movement of mail, even to remote regions. In eastern and central Canada, the early improvement of roads, the establishment of regular stagecoach routes in the 1820s and 1830s, and the introduction of steamboats in the 1840s were all important elements in the early attempts to expand and speed the mail service. However, beginning in the 1850s, the creation of railway systems was the most significant technological advance which facilitated the development of a mass postal network. The ability of the Post Office to send the mails by rail to major communities located along the line for distribution to settlements off the line led to a dramatic reduction in the delivery times. For example, mail delivery between Quebec and Windsor which in 1853 had taken 10 1/2 days was reduced four years later, after the advent of the railway, to 49 hours. Between Quebec and Toronto, the reduction in

mail passage was from a week to 40 hours.[4]

In addition to these technical advances, the construction of a network of post offices developed in response to growing public demand. In turn, the improved efficiency of the postal service presumably acted as a stimulus to the further growth of that public demand. Before 1851, the high cost and limited availability of mail services and facilities deterred many would-be users of the official mails, who resorted instead to the use of private carriers.[5] Gradually, however, as the century wore on, the improved postal facilities acted in combination with a variety of social and demographic factors to produce a massive increase in the use of postal services in both Ontario and Quebec, although the latter province did not experience the same degree of expansion as did Ontario.

The official birth of the concept of a mass postal system in Canada can be traced to the year 1851 when the British government relinquished control to the several provinces of the postal offices in their territories. No longer a colonial system, therefore, the new indigenous control allowed for new emphases in policy and administration, and in the following half century there emerged an intimate interlinkage between the expansion of a mail network and the settlement process. In the words of William Smith, the only scholar to undertake detailed research on the early history of the Canadian post office:

> the principle governing the establishment of a postal system, and its expansion to meet local requirements, was fundamentally different in a new country from the principle by which they were guided at home [i.e. in Britain]. In a new country, a postal system was expected to afford the means of extending civilization, and to advance with equal step with settlement, whereas in a long-settled country, the postal system followed the train of civilization.[6]

This view summarizes the official philosophy of the postal system in the Canadas for 1851–67 and thereafter of the integrated system serving the new Dominion. In brief, the period between approximately 1851 and 1914 witnessed a major effort by the Canadian postal authorities both to extend postal services to areas of new settlement throughout the country and to improve services in populated urban and country areas where postal facilities were already in place. Thus, the number of post offices in existence almost quadrupled between 1851 and 1867, rising from 601 to 2,333. By 1911 there were 3,054. . . .

There was also consistent growth in the volume of post office business in Ontario and Quebec during the 60-year period between 1851 and 1911. During the initial 15 years—that is, between the time that the British government relinquished control over the Canadian Post Office and the year of Confederation—the volume of letters and postcards mailed annually by the inhabitants of these provinces increased seven-fold and then more than doubled again between 1867 and 1875. Thereafter, the expansion in all major spheres of post office business in both provinces continued steadily up to about 1900 and then showed a very large rate of growth during the first decade of this century. . . .

Besides the responsibility of moving the mails during this period, the Post Office also undertook the new function of facilitating financial transactions and banking facilities. Thus, from the 1840s on, the designation of certain post offices as money order offices assisted organizations and individuals to make the secure transfers of funds both within and over national borders. . . . Furthermore, the first Post Office Savings banks were established in 1868 with the expressed purpose of providing 'a means of promoting thrift among the people of low and moderate incomes.'[7] By 1911, 1,151 such savings banks were in operation across the Dominion with total deposits of over $43 million.[8]

. . .

That the advent of 'mass' postal services was attended by increased public use of the system is demonstrated clearly by the fact that on a per capita basis, as well as in terms of absolute volume, the increase in the use of post office services by the residents of Ontario and Quebec was very substantial. For example, the numbers of letters and postcards sent per resident of Ontario increased from approximately one every three weeks to almost two every week between 1881 and 1911. In Quebec, the flow of mail also increased, although it still amounted to only about one letter every week per resident in 1911. By the same token, on a per capita basis, the people of Ontario spent about 90 per cent more on post office services in 1911 than did those of Quebec.

But if the broad measures of increased volume of mail flows and increased per capita use of mail services suggest that there was a 'communications revolution' during this period, the social, demographic, and economic underpinnings of this significant development still need to be explored. Moreover, the macro-analysis must not be allowed to obscure significant regional variations in this process, and especially of the differences in the amplitude and form of mail flow exhibited by Ontario and Quebec.

III

During the last quarter of the nineteenth century, the Office of the Postmaster General received frequent petitions from both urban and rural communities complaining of the lack of adequate postal services. Nonetheless, the willingness of successive Canadian governments to regard the provision of postal services as a necessary concomitant of settlement, 'progress', and 'development' did result in constant efforts to improve ease of access to postal services; although, of course, the potential clientele had to be able to utilize such services, and be motivated to do so. The ability to make full use of the mail, as distinct from the money order system or savings banks, was obviously linked to the issue of literacy and education. Moreover, the burgeoning demand for the full range of all the postal services was associated with certain major social developments of the period: the expansion of settlement; urbanization and the associated development of manufacturing and commerce; and intra-regional and international migration. We shall refer briefly here to the relevance of each of these developments in order to obtain a better understanding of the changing patterns of public utilization of the postal system.

That the ability to read and write is an essential prerequisite for the full use of a 'mass' postal system is self-evident. In the second half of the nineteenth century, literacy could, in turn, be linked to the development of public elementary schooling. Thus, it is hardly coincidental that the gradual extension of public elementary education in the English-Canadian provinces from the 1840s on (with a high point being achieved in the attainment of free, compulsory, and universal elementary education in Ontario in 1871) occurred over approximately the same period as the rise of mass postal communications. Compulsory schooling did not guarantee literacy for all but it certainly helped to increase the numbers of the literate. In turn, the literate were able to send and receive letters directly, and—at least for some of them—the experience of schooling must have led to an acceptance of 'reading and writing' as a normal daily activity.

It is not suggested that the advancement of public education in Ontario was the prime cause of the expansion of mail communication but rather that it was an important institutional prerequisite. Likewise, while in Quebec, the often documented lack of adequate schooling opportunities for francophone youth[9] did not block an increasing use of the mail services, the relatively high illiteracy rates in that province certainly served to 'dampen down' the potential demand for such services. For example, in 1891, 20.3 per cent of the young men and 13.4 per cent of the young women in Quebec aged between ten and nineteen years were unable to read or write, compared with equivalent proportions in

Ontario of 5.1 per cent and 4.0 per cent respectively.[10] . . .

It would appear, therefore, that the ability to utilize the mails directly was more widespread among the population of Ontario than of Quebec. Furthermore, in Quebec country parishes, a related reason for people's limited use of the mails was probably that the culture of the parish had little place for the role of the written word. Hence, as Horace Miner wrote of the parish of St Denis in 1939:

> Until some fifty years ago literacy had but little utility in the parish . . . No commercial contacts necessitated reading or writing. The occasions when one was obligated to sign one's name were rare indeed—marriage contracts, records in the parish register and that was about all . . . Even today writing itself is left almost exclusively to the women, except for tradesmen.[11]

Thus, our general conclusion on the role of the post office in Quebec and Ontario respectively must be that Quebec citizens had less written communication with others, and *in toto* less ability and need to so communicate.

In the second half of the nineteenth century, the growth of the towns and cities, the influx of migrants, and the development of commerce influenced the growth of the post office as an essential public amenity just as public schooling was, in the context of settlement, perceived as an essential public amenity. For example, the proportion of the population of Ontario living in urban centres containing 1,000 inhabitants or more rose from 20.6 per cent in 1871 to 40.3 per cent in 1900 and 49.5 per cent in 1911. In Quebec, the comparable percentages were 19.9 per cent, 36.1 per cent, and 44.5 per cent,[12] although the province still contained far fewer larger urban centres than Ontario at the turn of the century.[13] Again, this process of urbanization was associated both with high levels of internal migration from the countryside to urban areas and also with an influx of immigrants from other lands which reached its peak during the great migration period of 1901–13. This latter period also witnessed an end to the world economic depression of the 1880s and early 1890s and a return to world prosperity. 'New markets opened up, money for investment flowed freely and immigrants looked to Canada as a land of promise.'[14]

Given these developments, it is hardly surprising that the business of the post office increased far more rapidly than the general increase in population. Nor is it surprising that the biggest per capita increase in mail flow and use of the money order system coincided with a period of massive immigration and economic prosperity (i.e. during the first decade of this century). The growth in trade and manufacturing in the expanding urban centres must have been associated with an expansion of commercial mail, including mailed advertisements and the early developments of the mail order system. Also, letter writing has long been used by individuals as a means of maintaining ties of kin and friendship with others and what better motivation for letter writing, especially in the absence of telephone communication, than separation from one's family and movement to a city or a new land? Finally, before the widespread provision of telephones and their 'mass' acceptance, communication with others living some distance away in the same large town or city would have been very arduous and time-consuming in the absence of the mails. Hence the phenomenon of 'drop mail' or 'city mail' posted and delivered on the same day within the same urban area became a widely used and valued public amenity in Canadian cities in the latter decades of the nineteenth century.[15]

During the last three decades of the nineteenth century, both Ontario and Quebec were still experiencing settlement extension into the marginal areas of the Ottawa-Huron tract and 'New Quebec' respectively. Such frontier areas experienced a transformation from isolation and subsistence to an integration and commercializa-tion of their activities, gradually acquiring the physical and social infrastructure of fully developed communities. In this process leading to 'mature' settlement, scattered families and their local service centres focused much attention on central functions such as stores, schools, churches, mills, and post offices. Apart from being symbols of 'progress', such facilities were important both for local integration and as connections with the wider society. Thus, while we have associated the increased use of postal services with urbanization and migration mainly to the urban centres, the role of the post office in 'linking' new outposts to well-established settlements and also in improving the communications between established settlements and the urban centres (not the least by means of newspapers) was clearly important as well.[16] Indeed, by the late nineteenth century, the services provided by the post office were a vital element in the commercial and business activities of enterprises at all levels of the developing settlement.

. . .

V

This paper has explored some dimensions of the 'postal revolution' as it occurred in central Canada during the period 1851–1911. The broad macro-social and economic trends associated with the development of mass postal services in Ontario and Quebec, and contemporary perceptions of the linkage between these trends and the role of the post office in community settlement and development, have been our main foci of analysis. The paper has concentrated rather more upon the causes and conditions which encouraged the growth of the mass postal system than upon the social consequences of that growth. Yet, as successive Canadian governments saw clearly, the expansion of post office facilities was itself an integral dimension of, and indeed, precondition for, the phenomenon which is sometimes referred to as 'modernization'. Without the spreading postal network, the development of large-scale state bureaucracy, of widespread commercial and industrial activity, and of the mass circulation of news would have been severely hampered. Without efficient postal services, the policy of opening up areas of new settlement, and the financial health of business enterprises in long-settled country towns, would have been severely at risk.

This theme of modernization in the period under review is of fundamental importance. In the introduction to our paper, we made an analogy between some aspects of advance in telecommunications and the advent of mass mail services. Like some of these advances, both the mail and the telephone have, as McQuail notes, an 'intimate connection with other features of modern society—with mobility, individualism, privacy and division of labour. They must encourage, facilitate and yet also act as antidotes to these tendencies. They make possible intercommunication and self-expression.'[17] Indeed, just as one can visualize a stage being reached where microcomputers situated in each home allow not only for communications with central data banks but also for new means of direct personal communications with other citizens, so too is it possible to perceive mail flow as a communications net expanding along spatial dimensions and increasing interactions between individuals and organizations. More specifically, the increasing ease of public access to postal services, and notably mail, led people to develop quite high expectations about the frequency and speed with which they could communicate with others over a distance, expectations which, in turn, had major social consequences. Three specific examples of such consequences would be appropriate to mention at this point, all underlining the importance of the postal system as 'a facilitator' of major demographic and institutional developments during the period under review.

First, we have already noted that prior to the development of the telephone system, even communication over relatively short distances became heavily dependent upon efficient mail services. In the absence of either telephones or well-organized mail services, as in the earlier decades of the nineteenth century, people with limited means who moved substantial distances away from their kin were likely to be completely cut off from home news. Indeed, perhaps the single most important social consequence for individuals of the postal revolution was that the fear of 'the walls of oblivion',[18] previously felt as a result of loss of contact with kin, was no longer the price exacted for moving from home. A contemporary writer, Harriet Martineau, could claim that, prior to the English postal reforms of the 1840s many young people of the English lower class who left home to become apprentices and domestics 'were cut off from family relations as effectively as if seas or deserts divided them'.[19] How much more cut off, before the postal reforms, were many Canadian settlers by seas and the great distances of the land? Thus, regular postal communications must have made migration to Canada, and within Canada, much less daunting than in earlier times, diminished the impact of distance and hence have facilitated the migration process. But more than this, letters sent home by those who had already migrated undoubtedly acted as travel brochures which then encouraged the movement of those who had stayed behind. This particular function of letter writing in Britain (and one assumes similarly in Canada) is nicely summed up in an observation from Charles Booth's monumental study of the people of London (1891), wherein it is noted that 'probably one of the most powerful and efficient migration agencies is that supplied by the letters written home by the country girl settled in domestic service in the great town'.[20] . . .

Second, the post office increasingly assumed the role of a 'mover of the public news', and, as such, became an important factor in the development of the Canadian press. As Paul Rutherford notes in his book on the Canadian media, not until the 1840s was the climate ripe for a daily press in Canada; by then, the new cities ensured a market for the wares of the daily journalist, the busy retail trade of these cities enhancing the all-important advertising revenues.[21] What Rutherford does not mention, however, is that in the cities, but still more in the country areas, the developing postal system became an important element in the wide spread dissemination of daily and weekly newspapers. . . .

For their part, Canadian newspaper publishers benefited from an absence of mail charges on newspapers for most of the 1890s[22] and in 1908 from the initiation of the free rural delivery system.[23] In the United States, newspaper publishers were indeed among the first people to see the advantage of free delivery to farm homes in the late nineteenth century, since in the words of US mail historian Wayne Fuller, 'They knew as well as they knew anything that farmers would subscribe to daily newspapers if they had a daily mail service.'[24] The increasing importance of newspapers cannot be separated, therefore, from the use of the postal service in the late nineteenth century.

Finally, in the continued diversification of the function of the postal system, its adoption as a distributing device for retail goods constituted a major development in the latter part of the nineteenth century. The economic and social consequences of the introduction of mail order by Sears-Roebuck, Eatons, and others have yet to be explored fully but it is clear that the universality and efficiency of the mail system was its cause. The convenience of mail advertising, mail order, and mail delivery was such that, paradoxically, it accelerated and ensured the demise of certain functions of the post office's early host, the general store.[25]

These three examples indicate some of the important social consequences of the advent of the mass postal system. However, since our comparative data for Quebec and Ontario show quite clearly that the system was used less intensively in Quebec, it is clearly important in our conclusions to look a little more closely at some of the possible reasons for the provincial differential in the rate of mail flow. The relative illiteracy rates and 'a non-writing culture' in Quebec has already been referred to. Also, we have observed that outside of Montreal the number of relatively large urban centres (i.e. over 4,000 inhabitants) were comparatively few. It was, however, in such centres that substantial commercial activity was focused, and in which—as our analysis of post office revenues indicates—the use of postal services was relatively high. Furthermore, in Ontario, the expansion of trade and commerce, as well as such public services as education, fostered the growth of a professional and commercial middle class which, located primarily in the urban centres, constituted a group whose members were likely to be major users, both for personal and business reasons, of the mail. In Quebec, at least amongst the francophone population, the middle class was smaller, professional rather than commercial and relatively ill-defined.[26] Finally, since we have counted international migration as an important stimulus to mail flow, it is relevant to note that, in 1901, 46.3 per cent of the foreign-born population of Canada resided in Ontario and only 12.7 per cent in Quebec. In 1911, after 10 years of very heavy immigration, the proportion of all the foreign-born residing in Ontario was 32.0 per cent and in Quebec, 9.3 per cent.[27] Most immigrants made for Ontario, and after 1900 for the West, leaving Quebec overwhelmingly populated by the native-born.

These factors probably account for some part of the difference between the two provinces in the use of post office facilities. Nonetheless, it is interesting that the relative volume of mail delivered even in the major urban centres of Quebec was considerably less than in the major urban centres of Ontario. This is apparent, for example, from postal statistics indicating the weekly flow of home delivered mail in various cities. Thus, in October 1891, the number of letters delivered weekly in Montreal averaged just under one per inhabitant, compared with nearly three in Toronto and 1.4 in Kingston.[28] Evidently, therefore, our earlier conclusion that Quebec citizens had much less communication with each other through the medium of the mails must be taken to include the flow of written communications into the large urban centres.

The above finding needs further detailed investigation as, indeed, do many other aspects of early post office development. For example, the Post Office Savings Bank and Money Order

system played an important role in the economic development of local communities and both certainly merit detailed study. Again, the interplay between mail and telephone services around the turn of the century has not yet received the attention it merits in either Canada or other advanced industrial societies. . . .[29]

Notes

1 D. McQuail, *Communications* (London: Longman, 1975), 87. The authors of the present study wish to acknowledge research support from Queen's University and from the SSHRC.

2 See A.W. Currie, 'The Post Office Since 1867', *Canadian Journal of Economics and Political Science*, vol. 24, no. 2 (1958), 241.

3 *Commissioners Appointed to Enquire into the Affairs of the Post Office of British North America: Report* (Montreal: Legislative Assembly, 1846), *passim.*

4 J. Dewe, *Canadian Postal Guide, 1863* (Toronto: R. and A. Miller, 1863), 13.

5 *Commissioners Appointed to Enquire into the Affairs of the Post Office of British North America: Report* (1846), 36.

6 W. Smith, *The History of the Post Office in British North America, 1639–1870* (Cambridge: Cambridge University Press, 1920), 264.

7 *Report of the Post Master General, 1964* (Ottawa: Queen's Printer 1964), 8.

8 *Report of the Post Master General, 1911* (Ottawa: King's Printer, 1911).

9 See, for example, R. Pike, 'Education, Class and Power in Canada', in R.J. Ossenberg (ed.), *Power and Change in Canada* (Toronto: McClelland and Stewart, 1980), *passim.*

10 Census of Canada, 1890–1, vol. 2, table 13.

11 H. Miner, *St. Denis, A French-Canadian Parish* (Chicago: University of Chicago, 1963), 73–4.

12 D. Kubat and D. Thornton, *A Statistical Profile of Canadian Society* (Toronto McGraw-Hill–Ryerson, 1974), 14.

13 In 1901, Quebec contained 17 centres with populations of 4,000 and over compared with 41 in

Ontario (see the Census of Canada, Bulletin IV, 1902).

14 R. Cook et al., *Canada: A Modern Study* (Toronto: Clarke Irwin, 1963), 142.

15 In the larger urban centres, the number of daily collections and deliveries were not uncommonly three or four during the later decades of the period under review.

16 For some comments on the relationship between the post office and the rise of the newspaper industry, see the conclusion to this paper.

17 D. McQuail, *Communications*, 87.

18 The phrase 'the walls of oblivion' is taken from E.C. Smythe, *Sir Rowland Hill: The Story of a Great Reformer told by his Daughter* (London: T. Fisher Unwin, 1907), 41.

19 Smythe, *Sir Rowland Hill*, 41.

20 C. Booth, *Labour and Life of the People of London* (London: Williams and Norgate, 1891), vol. 2, 460.

21 P. Rutherford, *The Making of the Canadian Media* (Toronto: McGraw-Hill–Ryerson, 1978), 7.

22 Smith, *The History of the Post Office in British North America*, 332.

23 Rural free mail delivery was initiated in Canada along the route from Hamilton to Ancaster in 1908 and apparently covered most of eastern Canada by 1914; see notably, G. Wilcox, *History of Rural Mail in Canada* (Ottawa: Public Affairs Branch, Canada Post, 1975), *passim.*

24 W.E. Fuller, *The American Mail* (Chicago: University of Chicago Press, 1972), 139.

25 Other uses include mail distribution and processing of film started by George Eastman with the

development in 1890 of roll-film, the mailable box camera, and, thus, 'mass photography'.

26 For commentaries on occupational structure in Quebec during the period, see J. Brazeau, 'Quebec's Emerging Middle-Class' and J.C. Falardeau, 'The Changing Social Structures of Contemporary French-Canadian Society', both in M. Rioux and Y. Martin, *French Canadian Society* (Toronto: Carleton Library, 1969).

27 Data from Kubat and Thornton, *A Statistical Profile of Canadian Society*, table M3, 74.

28 Details of weekly home deliveries taken from *The Report of the Post Master General, 1891*.

29 The first telephone exchange opened in Montreal in 1875. By 1925, there were 44.2 telephones per 100 households; see R.F. Latham, 'The Telephone and Social Change', in B.D. Singer, *Communications in Canadian Society* (Toronto: Copp-Clark, Second Revised Edition, 1975) for a discussion on the telephone and social change in Canada.

Back to the Future: Telecommunications, Online Information Services, and Convergence from 1840 to 1910

Dwayne Winseck

Contemporary discussions of new media, information services, and convergence proceed as if these are entirely new phenomena. In fact, as this paper shows, a similar pattern of events characterized the history of the telegraph, the rise of news and information services, and a kind of media convergence in the period between 1840 and 1910 in Canada, Britain, and the United States.

The historical account of telegraphy in Canada, Britain, and the United States in this paper emphasizes three processes: early growth typified by uncertain demand and 'methodless enthusiasm', followed by 'ruinous competition' and 'strategic consolidation;'[1] the close alignment of the telegraph, the press, news agencies, information services, and stock markets; and the transformation of classical legal concepts to accommodate the ephemeral nature of electronic media and information, which gave rise to the information commodity and modern conceptions of common carriage.

The paper shows that the new medium became commercially viable through close ties between the telegraph companies and the press, news agencies, information services, and changes in the law that recognized information as a commodity. These features also reflected a kind of media convergence in the era, as no rigid distinctions separated communications media along technological, functional, organizational, or legal lines. The paper highlights the collusive practices between telegraph and content providers during the phases of 'ruinous competition' and 'strategic consolidation' and shows how these led to the application of common-carrier principles to telecommunications. The paper also shows that the advent of key legal principles in telecommunications not only turned on collusive practices and government intervention but, more abstractly, a drawn-out process of modifying classical legal concepts to fit the new 'immaterial reality' of electronic communication. The 'fugitive and evanescent nature of information' and electronic communication required nineteenth-century legal systems to be changed before it was possible to establish information as a commodity and to regulate telecommunications according to common-carrier principles.[2] In the end, mapping how transformations in technology, market structure, and the law shaped the evolution of the telegraph can provide instructive insights for understanding the forces shaping the evolution of new media today.

Uncertain Demand and the Role of the State

The telegraph emerged without clear uses, social demand, or a system of organization. In Canada, the telegraph was relegated to the margins, despite the widely acknowledged need for speedier flows of information within the country, as well as to and from other countries. Indicative of this neglect of the telegraph, the Government Post Office published a report in 1863 that lamented the poor state of communication in the country and advocated efforts to improve transportation routes, to lower postal rates, and to grant more generous mail subsidies for the press. However, almost no mention was made of the telegraph.[3] This is surprising given the already

From *Media History* 5, 2 (1999), 137–53. Reprinted by permission of Taylor & Francis Ltd, http:/www.tandf.co.uk/journals.

well-developed state of the telegraph in Britain, the United States, France, and other European countries.

While the postponed introduction of telegraphy in Canada was unusually long, delayed introduction of new innovations in communication, or new technologies in general, was not unique to Canada. In Britain, Francis Ronalds demonstrated a feasible electric telegraph to the Royal Navy in 1816 but was turned away because of the Navy's recent investment in a semaphore telegraph network brought to England from France. Offers were also made to the French government but spurned for similar reasons and because the telegraph was seen as inferior to the semaphore system that had been in place since 1794.[4] Even though the United States was considered more hospitable to new innovations, Samuel Morse waited until 1843 and 1844 before his system was commercialized, despite having demonstrated its effectiveness in 1837.

The transition of the telegraph to an organized system of communication was tied to the advent of four other major agencies of nineteenth-century society: railways, the state, stock markets, and the press. It was not one set of interests alone that impressed themselves on the technology equally at all places and times, as Winston's (1995) claim that telegraphy emerged to serve the needs of the railway suggests.[5] Despite the persistent metaphor between transportation and communication, it was only in England during the boom years of the railway between 1837 and 1848 that the telegraph mainly served the railways. By the mid-1850s, English telegraph companies received most of their revenues from international communication and the press as well as from their own news and information services.[6]

In France and Germany, in contrast, the telegraph passed immediately into the hands of the state, serving to tie peripheral regions into the centre and to forge a national political culture with the state at its apex. As French Interior Minister Lacave-Laplagne declared in 1847, 'the telegraph is an instrument of politics, not of commerce.'[7] Morse's early efforts to develop a telegraph line in co-operation with a private French railway company were blocked and the telegraph reserved for the exclusive use of the government. Only in November 1850 were reforms introduced to liberalize French telecommunications and to open it up to the general public. The likely sources for such changes lie in the political revolution of 1848 and, more importantly, in the financial revolution that occurred as stock exchanges in Paris and London were connected by telegraph.[8]

Although England had chosen to allow the telegraph to be developed by private means, in 1863 legislation was enacted to allow the government to regulate the telegraph. In 1868 the scope of government intervention was expanded again by the introduction of an act that mandated nationalization of the telegraph system in 1870.

Government intervened less in telegraph matters in the United States than elsewhere. Subsidies given to privately owned telegraph companies were minuscule and of short duration. There was even a brief period of government ownership during early experiments with the new technique and later during the Mexican and Civil wars; however, private ownership was quickly restored after each war. A more influential impression on the telegraph occurred in 1844 when the two major political parties' conventions were reported by telegraph to an audience waiting at one end of the line in Washington and to a broader public via telegraphic news reprinted in the press. Likewise, the amount of information circulated by telegraph from the start of the Mexican War in 1846 reinforced perceptions of the telegraph's utility at a time when confidence in it was waning. Although such events highlighted the telegraph's importance, they did not facilitate government ownership or detailed regulatory intervention. The comparably weak role of the United States government was confirmed in 1844–5 when it rejected opportunities to buy exclusive rights to the Morse patents for $100,000. At the same time, the government privatized an experimental line it had operated between Baltimore and Washington after only one year of service, despite enduring calls by Morse, the Post Office, and others to operate the telegraph as a government monopoly and as an extension of the postal service.[9]

The role of the Canadian state in the development of the telegraph was somewhere between the model of the strong state projected by France and Germany and the less interventionist model of state-economy-communication relations typical in England and the United States. It was closer to the United States and English (before nationalization) examples insofar as takeovers of the telegraph for exclusive government use remained the exception rather than the rule and were typically short-term. However, the Canadian model was distinct from that of Great Britain and the United States in several respects. Acting between the poles of benign neglect and moderate doses of state intervention, Canadian governments limited themselves to establishing a general legal regime for telegraphy, granting charters to individual companies and resisting proposals such as that by the Atlantic and Pacific Telegraph and Transit Company in 1863 to license companies to build networks along certain routes in return for a guaranteed rate of profit (typically 4–5 per cent), annual subsidies, and a protected monopoly.[10] Circumstances differed between Canada and the United States, however, on the state's role vis-à-vis telecommunications policy, as indicated by the first Canadian telecommunications law, *The Electric Telegraph Companies Act of 1852* (hereinafter, referred to as the *Electric Telegraph Act*, Province of Canada).[11] The law predated similar efforts in England 11 years later, and in the United States, where it was not until 1911 that the government brought telecommunications under the *Interstate Commerce Act*. Moreover,

sections of the *Electric Telegraph Act*, although very liberal in overall orientation, did envision the possibility of government ownership of telegraphy.

The Telegraph, the News, and Media Globalization in the Nineteenth Century: From Methodless Enthusiasm to Strategic Consolidation

The passage of the *Electric Telegraph Act* signalled the emerging salience of telecommunications in Canada. Rens (1993) argues that the new law was so favourable that it ushered in a new wave of telegraph companies and rapid expansion of the telegraph network.[12] The new telecommunications law cleared the way for anyone to develop telegraph networks in Canada. Thereafter, three features in particular impressed themselves on the evolution of telegraphy in Canada: the close alignment between the growth of telegraph networks and the needs of the press in the United States; a shift from 'methodless enthusiasm' toward consolidation; and the mediation of developments in Canadian media by the competing pulls of continentalism, imperialism and, much later, nationalism.

Just prior to the Act, the telegraph system had begun to emerge in earnest; thereafter it began to explode along the corridor running from the Maritime provinces, Montreal, and Toronto. In 1846, several merchants from St Catharines, Hamilton, and Niagara Falls endeavoured to construct a telegraph system connecting Buffalo and New York to Toronto. A year later, Orton Woods, brother-in-law of Ezra Cornell, one of the leading figures in the Western Union company of the United States, began to organize the Montreal Telegraph Company to serve commercial and press interests in Canada.[13] Given the close ties between the new company and Western Union, the effort was also an early attempt by Western Union to extend its influence into Canada. In the same year, Frederick Gisborne established the British North

American Telegraph Company, with plans to link together Quebec, Nova Scotia, New Brunswick, and Newfoundland. The company, however, was unable to survive a cut-throat price war with the Montreal Telegraph Company, and in 1856 the British North American Telegraph Company was absorbed by the Montreal Telegraph Company. The latter was better connected, financially better endowed, and, crucially, able to subsidize competition with revenues gained from its monopoly lines.[14] A few years after Gisborne's failed venture, the Great North Western Telegraph Company obtained a charter, set up operations in Toronto, and harboured ambitions to initiate telegraphic communications west of Lake Superior.[15] Nonetheless, the scope of the telegraph system in Canada remained skeletal, with 1500 kilometres of network in place by 1852, in comparison to 36,000 in the United States, 3800 kilometres of line under the control of just one of the main companies in Britain, the Electric Telegraph Company, and 5000 in France in the same time period.[16]

The ties between the press and the telegraph were clear in the United States from the first attempts to commercialize the telegraph in the mid-1840s. Newspaper publishers were among the first and most generous investors in setting up telegraph operators, providing the largest source of revenue, and establishing organizations such as the Associated Press (AP) (1846) to exploit the potentials of electronic communication. In return, the press gained access to a relatively cheap, quick, and reliable means for distributing news, transmission privileges, and subsidized rates.[17] In short, the telegraph and the press were intimately intertwined through shared uses of a new technology, cross-ownership, functional interdependence, and, from about 1870 onward, a hybrid telecommunications/publishing legal framework—a point returned to later.

The obsession of the American press and telegraph organizations with the speed and volume of news and information flowing into and out of the United States drove each of these agencies up the Maritime coast and, from 1849 onwards, into Nova Scotia, New Brunswick, Newfoundland, and Prince Edward Island. Capturing the news in Canadian provinces and forwarding it by way of a patchwork of telegraph networks to the press and emerging news cooperatives, such as Associated Press, was up to 48 hours quicker than waiting for information from Europe to reach ports in the United States.[18] The emphasis on speed stemmed from the competitive nature of the media and, just as importantly, from the fact that the value of news did not yet reside in information *per se*. Because there was no copyright in news, its economic value lay mostly in the ability to arbitrage differences in time. Once differences in time were eliminated by the telegraph, the economics of newsgathering tilted from competition toward monopoly and to efforts to secure the commodity value of information. For the time being, however, news was not a commodity, and the idea that it could be covered by copyright laws remained a foreign one—a point returned to later.[19]

Under the competitive conditions prevailing in North America between roughly 1847 and 1855, many companies sprang up in the Canadian Maritime provinces.[20] Some were partially Canadian-owned, such as the New York, Newfoundland, and London Telegraph Company incorporated in 1854 in Newfoundland; the New Brunswick Telegraph Company; and the Nova Scotia Telegraph Company (1849), the first government-owned telecommunications network in Canada. By 1859, many of the small telegraph systems had combined to form the Great North Western Telegraph Company. Within a decade, the Dominion Telegraph Company (1868) started operations from Montreal and began challenging the larger Montreal Telegraph Company throughout Quebec, parts of Ontario, and much of the Maritimes for control of telegraphs and newswire services in Canada.[21]

However, strategic rivalry was already leading

to the absorption of smaller independent networks into more tightly knit organizations. On several occasions the New Brunswick Telegraph Company formed compromising alliances with Boston-based newspapers, as well as the Associated Press. Heavily reliant on these users for revenues and granting them privileged transmission rights as a result, the Canadian telegraph companies were both coveted by members of the United States press, Associated Press, and the larger United States telegraph companies as well as the target of anti-monopoly forces and rival news agencies trying to break Associated Press's stranglehold on foreign news. During the 1850s, a series of transactions eventually led to almost all companies in the Canadian Maritime provinces, including the government-owned Nova Scotia Telegraph Company, coming under the control of the American Telegraph Company (ATC).[22] In central and parts of eastern Canada, the Montreal Telegraph Company also went on an acquisitions spree, purchasing the Toronto, Hamilton & Niagara Electric Telegraph Company, the Vermont & Boston Telegraph Company, Prescott & Montreal Telegraphs (all in 1852), and a few years later, the British North American Telegraph Company (1856).[23]

Over a course of many twists and turns, the attempts of ATC and the Montreal Telegraph Company to consolidate control over telegraphy in North America became aligned with a broader effort to bolster AP's monopoly over information flows coming into North America. To this end, a far-reaching initiative was undertaken by ATC, the Canadian Frederick Gisborne, and the British and Irish Magnetic Telegraph Company to build a trans-Atlantic cable.[24] The initiative sought an unassailable monopoly over telegraphy and news in North America and to diminish the monopoly over foreign news held by Reuters in Britain. The result was the New York, Newfoundland, and London Telegraph Company. The new trans-Atlantic project linked together two of the largest telegraph companies in the United States and Britain, the Associated

Press, and a Canadian able to turn pressures on the Newfoundland legislature into one of the most favourable pieces of legislation to monopoly ever produced. In 1854, after a few ensuing machinations, the company emerged as the Anglo-American Telegraph Company, the company responsible for the first successful trans-Atlantic cable in 1865. The company was authorized to raise capital in Newfoundland, New York, and London. More importantly, the legislature barred anyone else from operating in, or landing a telegraph cable, at any point in Newfoundland for the next 50 years.[25] The company also received an annual subsidy of £14,000 from the British government.[26]

Over time the Anglo-American Telegraph Company came to own the telegraph system on Prince Edward Island. The influence of the company's efforts were delivered deeper into Canada through the Montreal Telegraph Company, whose line to Halifax was connected with the Anglo-American network by way of a complex web of relations between it, the American Telegraph Company (whose partial ownership of Anglo-American gave it exclusive rights to forward trans-Atlantic traffic through the Maritimes and into the United States), and Western Union. Throughout the 1850s and 1860s, the ties between the Montreal Telegraph Company, Western Union, and the American Telegraph Company became more intimate, not least because of their joint membership in the cartel-like arrangements of the North American Telegraph Alliance begun in 1857 (the Montreal Telegraph Company was admitted one year later), and became even more so in 1866 when Western Union finally swallowed the ATC.[27] By this time, Western Union had achieved an almost complete monopoly over the telegraph industry in the United States, except for a few small competitors scattered here and there.

Two companies that stood outside these arrangements were the American Union Telegraph Company and the Dominion Telegraph Company. Prevented from interconnecting with any of the other major telegraph companies in North America by the cartel arrangements of the North American Telegraph Association, American Union and Dominion Telegraph aligned themselves with each other, a competitive trans-Atlantic telegraph company, and, later, news services that had sprung up to challenge the AP monopoly. As links with the Dominion Telegraph Company in Canada and the Direct United States Cable Company (another trans-Atlantic cable operator) were put in place, American Union set out to challenge Western Union and AP's hold over telegraphy and news in North America and the 50-year exclusive landing rights that had been granted by the Newfoundland legislature to Anglo-American (by that time under the partial control of Western Union by way of its acquisition of the American Telegraph Company).[28]

In 1874, Direct United States Cable began offering services in competition with the Anglo-American system, a prospect made ever more difficult by costly and ultimately unsuccessful litigation against the latter's legislated monopoly over optimum areas of the Canadian coastline, as well as its exclusive interconnection rights with Western Union in the United States and the Montreal Telegraph Company in Canada. In the ensuing rivalry between the two transnational alliances, the Dominion Telegraph Company was given exclusive rights to carry Direct's traffic in Canada and also to distribute the National Associated Press news service linked to Direct and its United States–based counterpart, the American Union Telegraph Company. The arrangements completely united Canadian and American media interests; the Montreal Telegraph Company was allied with Western Union and Associated Press, whereas the Dominion Telegraph Company was attached to the American Union Telegraph Company and the nascent United Press.[29] Within Canada, a duopolistic telegraph industry had emerged between the Montreal Telegraph Company and Dominion Telegraph Company, with a smatter-

ing of companies continuing to offer services on the competitive fringes. Yet, even these arrangements subsided as the duopolistic rivalry between the Montreal Telegraph Company and Dominion Telegraph Company was brought to a head between 1878 and 1881.

During these years, the two companies engaged in ruinous price wars. This occurred not only as the companies were trying to expand the range of news and information services they offered but also as they were attempting to enter the nascent field of telephony. The ensuing price wars brought network expansion in telegraph to a standstill and led to a stillbirth in each company's efforts to provide telephone services. With respect to this latter point, the Montreal Telegraph Company had acquired rights to the Edison telephone patents and Dominion to the patent rights to Bell. Patents in hand and networks essentially already in place, competitive 'local telephone exchanges were opened in Montreal, Quebec City, Ottawa, Saint Johns (New Brunswick), Halifax and several other locations in Ontario'.[30] However, after exhausting themselves through competition, both companies were forced to abandon their telephone systems to the Bell Telephone Company in 1880. Another result of this bout of strategic rivalry was Western Union's acquisition of the Dominion Telegraph Company in 1881.

For the next three years Western Union and its close affiliate, the Great North Western Telegraph Company, enjoyed a near monopoly over telegraphy and delivery of Associated Press's 'online' news service, after which the entry of the Canadian Pacific Railway and Telegraph Company created another duopoly in transmission and news services. The new company acquired the rights of the former Dominion Telegraph Company to deliver the United Press's news service in Canada.[31] In addition, and crucially, given that each of these companies had been offering telephone services, the episode of ruinous competition between the Montreal and Dominion telegraph companies demonstrated that telegraphy and telephony were not separate arts requiring distinct systems of organization, but diverged as a result of strategic rivalry, the fruits of which accrued to the Bell Telephone Company of Canada. The possibility of dissolving these boundaries arose later that year when the Canadian Pacific Railway and Telegraph Company's (CP) enabling charter authorized it to operate in all areas of telecommunications. Rather than risk yet another bout of ruinous competition, however, Bell and CP promptly divided the field between themselves and shared their networks. This was the first phase of media divergence in Canada and it occurred *despite* the inherent compatibility between telephony and telegraphy and a legal framework that anticipated their interoperability, not separate development.

. . .

Media Convergence and 'Online Information Services'

Regardless of differences in scope of government intervention in telecommunications in Canada, Britain, and the United States, a remarkable commonality in each country was the close-knit ties between telegraph companies, news agencies, the press, and electronic information services. In each country, there were no legal, organizational, or technical grounds for distinguishing between communications media during the period, roughly, from 1840 to 1910.

In Canada, neither the *Electric Telegraph Act* (1852), nor any of the charters granted to new telegraph companies, prevented companies from operating across media boundaries. This point was illustrated by the fact that neither of the charters granted to the Bell Telephone Company (1880) or the Canadian Pacific Railway and Telegraph Company (1881) prevented them from operating in all spheres of electronic communication.[32] . . . In this context, it is not surprising that telegraph operators doubled up as journalists and reporters and that telecommunications providers provided news and informa-

tion services from the outset. In his history of the Canadian Press wire service, Nichols (1948) refers to the fact that the Montreal Telegraph Company (1846) and Great North Western Telegraph Company (1847) provided newswire services to the press from their inception. As he states,

> . . . the newspapers and the telegraphs were closely knitted in mutually advantageous business; they were complementary to each other. The newspapers needed the telegraph companies' services, the telegraph companies not only needed the business but found they could carry it at a fraction of commercial rates and show some profit.[33]

The two companies also began offering the Associated Press newswire service by the early 1850s, if not sooner, in Canada.[34] The same was true for an 'online' information company known as Gold and Stock, a company that Western Union became affiliated to by 1868. By 1871, Gold and Stock delivered an 'online' information service of stock quotes, gold prices, and other data pertinent to commodity trading to 800 subscribers from banks and brokerage houses.[35] References in leading Canadian court cases involving the telegraph also identified the long-standing news reporting and information services being offered by the Dominion Telegraph Company, affiliates of Western Union, and other independents.[36] Also, as mentioned earlier, the Dominion Telegraph Company distributed the wire services of the United States–based National Associated Press (the precursor to United Press) for a short period between 1874 and 1881, when it was acquired by Western Union. A few years later (1884), Canadian Pacific (CP) began carrying the United Press newswire service, only to drop it a decade later on learning it was actually under the control of Associated Press. After dropping the counterfeit agency, CP and Associated Press signed (on 2 January 1894) a contract to 'collect, distribute, and exchange news for publication in newspapers in the United States [and] Canada, . . . and to deliver news reports to no other party for use within . . . Canada, the British provinces of North America, [or] the United States'.[37] CP obtained the rights to the Associated Press news service after the ties between Associated Press and Western Union were loosened during the late 1870s and 1880s, as a consequence of the financial collapse of the Montreal Telegraph Company, and because only CP's telegraph system crossed the country, whereas the Western Union/Great North Western Telegraphs system reached only to Winnipeg in the west.[38]

The intimate connections between the telegraph, press, and information services also affected the development of laws that came to govern the telegraph. Whereas the courts had initially accepted analogies between the telegraph and railways to elaborate the concept of common carriage, by the 1870s this approach, and the analogy underlying it, were rejected. Between the 1870s and the turn of the century, the courts gradually adopted the view that 'telegraph companies cannot be treated as analogous to or coextensive with that of a common carrier'.[39] Common carriage fell from favour for two reasons. First, the analogy between telegraphs and transportation was seen as inappropriate. . . . Second, common-carrier principles were rejected on the grounds that they arbitrarily distinguished between separate aspects of an integrated system of communication. The modern newspaper was seen to be so much the combined product of telegraphy, newswire services, and the press that any legal distinctions drawn between them would not only be dubious but, more importantly, likely give licence to irresponsible journalism and the circulation of libellous content.

. . .

Constructing the Information Commodity

One of the important new information services to be developed in England was that by the Exchange Telegraph Company. In 1872 the Exchange Telegraph Company (Extel) was licensed to run a private network over the Post Office system for the purpose of offering specialized information, news, and entertainment services to subscribers mainly from the financial community, but also from the press and various clubs, news rooms, and so on. The new company distributed prices, quotes, and other stock-related data obtained under exclusive licence from the London Stock Exchange to brokers, traders and other subscribers. Over time the company established connections with the New York Stock Exchange and Paris Bourse (1874), Dow Jones (1885), and various others. By the mid-1880s Extel offered its information services to over 600 subscribers.[40]

Of course, Extel was not the only 'online' information service provider. An 1876 Post Office Select Committee Report identified a burgeoning information market, and other sources corroborated this with references to companies such as the Electric News Company, Central News, MacMahon's Telegraph News Company, Cochrane News Service, Gregory News Service, the Howard, London, and Manchester Press Agency, and so on. During the period between 1879 and 1881, the Post Office liberally licensed new content providers, as MacMahons, Central News, and a few other services were brought into existence. Such liberality did not, however, extend to all aspects of the burgeoning new field of 'online' service providers, as certain companies were prohibited by the Post Office from offering stock market quotes, most likely to protect Extel.[41] Thus, the Post Office was regulating the content of 'online' service providers, although not directly on political grounds but on commercial ones.

Although the Post Office encouraged some competition, Extel complained bitterly that it 'had now licensed [too] many rival institutions'. Given that the Post Office's policy had caused Extel 'to fight for its living', the company reasoned that it could petition for lower telegraph rates.[42] After failing to get the Post Office more involved in regulating competition, Extel began eliminating competitive threats on its own terms. One effort of this ilk was the attempt to create a cartel arrangement among the dominant telegraph-news agencies.[43] Another more ambitious method was the elimination of competition through mergers and acquisitions. This path was pursued vigorously by Extel in the early 1880s, as it acquired MacMahons (1882), Central News (1884), and Electric News (1884). The Post Office stood idly by, stating that it would only require Extel to revise its licence to take account of its new possessions.[44]

Another enduring impact on the development of telegraph-news agencies stemmed from the London Stock Exchange's and Extel's efforts to create a monopoly over news and information flows from the Stock Exchange. This was not necessarily unusual, as similar efforts had been used in the United States by the New York Stock Exchange to impose a time-delay on telegraph news agencies to ensure that local traders retained an advantage over others outside the city.[45]

While many tried to erode the information monopoly held by Extel, either by establishing competing services, or by piracy or legal challenges, they failed to get Extel and the Stock Exchange to yield their control over information. The courts were also unhelpful in the matter, as they validated monopoly information rights, outlawed information piracy, and embarked on a radical program to reconstruct and expand copyright law to ensure that property rights to information became inviolate. In a precedent-setting case, the Court of Appeals stated unequivocally that telegraph news agents 'had a common law right of property in information'. Moreover, the Court claimed that the Stock Exchange and Extel were 'entitled to limit the supply of . . . information . . . as they thought fit'.[46] As such, information scarcity, not abundance, had become the source of profit, and the courts wasted no time in reinforcing this trend, despite the fact that government ownership of the telegraph, press subsidies, and universal service policies was sup-

posed to increase access to the means of communication and information, not limit it.

Events in North America took a similar turn. In fact, the precedent-setting case by the United States Supreme Court, *International News Service v. Associated Press* (1918), referred to the English cases just mentioned as support for recognizing information as 'quasi property'.[47] The Court recognized that copyright did not cover news and that information was 'too fugitive and evanescent to be the subject of property'.[48] However, seeking to obtain a practical solution to information piracy, the Court created a new category of property rights rooted in the *commercial value of things* as opposed to the *nature of things*. The classical concept of property based on *absolute dominion* over *tangible things* had changed. Vandevelde (1980) refers to this as the 'dephysicalization of property', a process that created a new expanse of property rights in intangible things such as trademarks, goodwill, and news.[49] This development completely transformed existing notions of property and made determining a 'valuable interest' dependent on the appraisal of the courts. While this lent itself to a pragmatic approach to business disputes and policy issues, it did not present firm and obvious grounds as to why the *commercial value* of information property rights should be prioritized over the *public-good values* associated with the free flow of information, or whether or not the courts were even the proper place for deciding such matters. Essentially, law was transformed into a system of tradeoffs—between the commodity and public-good values of information and between the courts and policy-makers in determining that balance. This was highlighted by Justice Brandeis in his dissent, as he argued that the decision

> . . . would effect an important extension of property rights and a corresponding curtailment of the free use of knowledge and ideas; and the facts of this case admonish us of the danger involved in recognizing such a property right in news,

without imposing upon news-gatherers corresponding obligations. . . .[50]

Media Divergence and the Birth of Common Carriage

The Extel and INS cases in Britain and the United States, respectively, highlighted the extent to which law played a role in constructing the foundations of commercially viable information markets. They also illustrated that the confrontation between classical legal categories and electronic communication beget a new and expansive role for the courts and policy-makers in devising methods to deal with the new media. In a fundamental way, it was from within this broad transformative process that the modern conception of telecommunications policy in particular and communications policy in general emerged. Nowhere was this more evident than in the events leading to the advent of common-carrier principles and to separation between telecommunications and publishing.

As noted above, the idea that common carriage could be applied to telecommunications was rejected by the courts. This, however, changed in North America at the turn of the century. The notion that content providers should be able to access the distribution networks of telecommunications carriers according to rates and terms that were non-discriminatory and 'just and reasonable' was formally recognized in the United States at the federal level by the Supreme Court in 1901 and built into legislation by the way of the *Interstate Commerce Act* in 1911 and the *Communications Act* in 1934.[51] Events in Canada were also pointing in the same direction at this time, although a regulatory solution was deferred until 1910. The following and last section of this paper recounts these events.

The fact that relations between the telegraph companies and the press in Canada were breaking down was signalled by the Canadian Press Association's call for government ownership of the telegraph system in 1901. This dramatic call

was no doubt related to the history and perception of abuses stemming from the duopolistic nature of the telegraph industry shared, by this time, between Canadian Pacific Telegraphs (CP) and Great North Western Telegraphs (GNWT) (the latter controlled by Western Union) and that CP had exclusive rights to distribute the Associated Press newswire service in Canada. Moreover, the fact that the Canadian government was in the midst of completing its end of the colonial-inspired 'All Red' global telegraph network, and that government ownership of the telegraph in Britain had lavished subsidies on the press, demonstrated to the press that the state could play a useful role in developing a national telecommunications system.[52] Yet, despite this confluence of factors, another decade passed before rivalry between the press and the telecommunications industry, combined with regulatory decisions by the recently formed Board of Railway Commissioners (BRC) (1903), led to GNWT and CP abandoning newswire services and to the implementation of common-carrier principles.

The antagonistic relationship between the press and CP was ultimately brought to a head on account of actions taken by CP between 1907 and 1910. The crisis was precipitated by CP's announcement, in 1907, that it would no longer provide Western newspapers with its combined AP/Canadian news service directly from Montreal. . . .[53] The proposal created significant disparities between the Eastern and Western press, as it added considerably to the cost of news production for the Western papers.

The Western press responded by devoting substantial energies to developing an alternative news service and distribution system. Even though the presence of the competing telegraph systems of GNWT and the more marginal Canadian Northern Telegraphs suggested that it might be possible to break the CP/AP monopoly, these two companies' networks did not extend beyond Manitoba. As a result, rival news services could not avoid dependence on the CP system, a factor the company exploited by charging commercial rates (as opposed to press rates) for the would-be rivals, . . . and by raising rates between 65 per cent and 233 per cent.[54]

On the one hand, these actions rendered attempts to establish alternative newswire services futile. On the other hand, though, the abuse of network dominance broadened and galvanized calls for government ownership, or at least for stronger regulation of tariffs and telegraph companies' ability to control the flow of news and information. More importantly, CP's actions helped translate esoteric arguments steeped in technology, law, and economics into a readily understood and far-ranging debate over freedom of the press. Welding together themes of corporate abuse, public ownership, telecommunications, and media freedoms, the tenacious critic of corporate wealth and power W.F. Maclean wrote an article in the *Toronto World* lambasting 'attempts on the part of public service companies to muzzle free expression of opinion by withholding privileges that are of general right'.[55]

CP responded by threatening to cut back services even further to those publishers offering news space to such malcontents and by continuing to offer different terms for members of the press depending on whether they were subscribers to the AP service or one of the rival services. CP argued that such differences were legitimate because of the financial burden of the press subsidies and, furthermore, that the rates charged for its news services were beyond the purview of the new regulatory agency, the Board of Railway Commissioners. . . .

Although CP argued that the BRC had no regulatory powers to compel telegraph companies to separate costs for news services and for transmission, the BRC rejected this. The BRC responded that the *Railway Act* compelled it to ensure that rates were 'just and reasonable' and that unless transmission rates were separate, explicit,

and equitable, 'telegraph companies could put out of business every newsgathering agency that dared to enter the field of competition with them'.[56] Consequently, all telegraph companies were required to submit separate tariffs for distributing news services, and all newspapers, regardless of where they were located had to be treated equally. . . . The BRC insisted on unbundling telecommunications charges from news service charges. Shortly thereafter, CP and GNWT abandoned the field of newswire services and newsgathering altogether. Such activities became the preserve of the newspaper industry and other content providers. As such, telecommunications had diverged from publishing and a key prop in twentieth-century telecommunications policy, common carriage, instituted.

Conclusion

The analysis offered by this paper has tried to further understanding of the influences on the evolution of electronic communication and telecommunications policy in the period from 1840 to 1910. The four trends identified—progression of the telegraph through stages of methodless enthusiasm, ruinous competition, and strategic consolidation; media convergence; the transformation of law; and media divergence—offer conceptual tools for understanding changes in the media today. Together, these processes winnowed down an array of potential options for media development to one or two dominant 'models' and set the foundations for the information commodity and telecommunications policy in the twentieth century. If recognizing historical patterns provides any guidance for the present, perhaps the history of electronic communication presented in this paper can provide some insights into the nature of media evolution today.

Notes

1 R.L. Thompson, *Wiring a Continent: The History of the Telegraph Industry in the United States, 1832–1866* (Princeton: Princeton University, 1947).

2 *International News Service v. Associated Press*, Supreme Court, 39, *Supreme Court Reporter* (1918), 73.

3 J. Dewe, *Canadian Postal Guide: Containing the Chief Regulations of the Post Office* (Montreal: E. Pickup, 1863).

4 J. Kieve, *The Electric Telegraph: A Social and Economic History* (Newton Abbot: David and Charles, 1973), 16–17.

5 B. Winston, 'How are Media Born and Developed', in J. Downing, A. Mohammadi and A. Sreberny-Mohammadi, eds, *Questioning the Media*, 2nd edn (London: Sage, 1995), 68–9.

6 Kieve, *The Electric Telegraph*, 47–9.

7 Kieve, *The Electric Telegraph*, 46 (author's translation).

8 J. Attali and Y. Stourdze, 'The Birth of the Telephone and Economic Crisis: he slow death of the monologue in French society', in I.S. Pool, ed., *The Social Impact of the Telephone* (London: Massachusetts Institute of Technology, 1977), 101.

9 M. Blondheim, *News Over the Wires: the telegraph and the flow of public information in America, 1844–1897* (London: Harvard University, 1994), 32–4; Thompson, *Wiring a Continent*, 33–4.

10 Colonial Office and the Authorities in Canada and British Columbia, *Telegraphic Communication between Canada and the Pacific (Continuation of Parliamentary Paper, No. 438, of Session 1863)* (Correspondence relating to the affairs of Canada, Irish University Press series of British Parliamentary Papers), (Shannon, Ireland: Irish University, 1864–6), 12–16; H.A. Innis, *A History of the Canadian Pacific Railway* (Newton Abbot: David and Charles, 1923/1972), 39–43.

11 Province of Canada, 'Electric Telegraph Companies Act, 1852', *Statutes of the Province of Canada*, 16 Vict., Cap. 10. (Quebec: Stewart Derbishire and George Desbarats, 1852).

12 J.G. Rens, *L'empire invisible: histoire des télécommunications au Canada, de 1846 à 1956* (Sainte-Foy, Québec: Presses de l'Université du Québec, 1993).

13 Thompson, *Wiring a Continent*, 241, 253.

14 R.E. Babe, *Telecommunications in Canada* (Toronto: University of Toronto, 1990), 38.

15 Innis, *A History of the Canadian Pacific Railway*, 38–9; M.E. Nichols, *The Story of the Canadian Press* (Toronto: Ryerson, 1948), 10.

16 P. Flichy, *Dynamics of Modern Communication: the shaping and impact of new communication technologies* (London: Sage, 1995), 52; Kieve, *The Electric Telegraph*, 53; Thompson, *Wiring a Continent*, 241.

17 Blondheim, *News Over the Wires*, 41–5; Thompson, *Wiring a Continent*, 217–25.

18 Thompson, *Wiring a Continent*, 299.

19 INS v. AP, 1918; Nichols, *The Story of the Canadian Press*; Post Office, *Report for the Select Committee on Post Office (Telegraph Department)* (London: HMSO, 1876), 190–2.

20 Thompson, *Wiring a Continent*, 259.

21 Babe, *Telecommunications in Canada*, 47; Nichols, *The Story of the Canadian Press*, 10.

22 Blondheim, *News Over the Wires*, 151–63; Thompson, *Wiring a Continent*, 226–40.

23 Babe, *Telecommunications in Canada*, 45.

24 Kieve, *The Electric Telegraph*, 106–10; Thompson, *Wiring a Continent*, 299–301, 306–7, 335.

25 *Direct United States Cable Co. v. Anglo-American Telegraph Co. et. al.*, *Newfoundland Law Review*, 6 (1876/7), 1–52, affirmed House of Lords, Judicial Committee of the Privy Council, February 14, 1877.

26 Kieve, *The Electric Telegraph*, 108.

27 Thompson, *Wiring a Continent*, 310–30.

28 *Direct United States Cable Co. v. Anglo-American Telegraph Co. et. al.*, 1877.

29 Blondheim, *News Over the Wires*, 163–4; Rens, *L'empire invisible*, 32.

30 Rens, *L'empire invisible*, 32 (author's translation).

31 Nichols, *The Story of the Canadian Press*, 10–12; Rens, *L'empire invisible*, 53–5.

32 D. Winseck, *Reconvergence: A Political Economy of Telecommunications in Canada* (Cresskill, NJ:

Hampton, 1998), ch. 4.

33 Nichols, *The Story of the Canadian Press*, 10–11.

34 Nichols, *The Story of the Canadian Press*, 5–11.

35 Thompson, *Wiring a Continent*, 444–5.

36 *Dominion Telegraph Co. v. John Silver and Abraham Martin Payne, Reports of the Supreme Court of Canada*, 10 (1882/3), 238–9.

37 Contract reproduced in full in Board of Railway Commissioners, 'The Western Associated Press v. The Canadian Pacific Railway Company's Telegraph and the Great Northwestern Telegraph Company of Canada', *Sessional Papers of the Parliament of Canada* (Ottawa: J. De Labroquerie Tache, Printers to the King's Most Excellent Majesty, 1910), 270 (author's emphasis).

38 Nichols, *The Story of the Canadian Press*, 12; Rens, *L'empire invisible*, 48.

39 *Baxter v. Dominion Telegraph Co., Upper Canada Queen's Bench*, 37 (1874/5), 470.

40 Post Office, *Exchange Telegraph Company: royalties and applications for reductions* (File VI). From: *Exchange Telegraph Co. License: Part 1* (London: British Telecom Archives, 1882-1907), post 30/253B, 1–3; J.M. Scott, *Extel 100: The Centenary of the Exchange Telegraph Company* (London: Ernest Benn Ltd., 1972), 15–25.

41 Post Office, *MacMahon's Telegraphic News Agency: royalties and extracts from correspondence* (File 1). From: *Exchange Telegraph Co. License: Part 1* (London: British Telecom Archives, 1879–81), post 30/253B, 6.

42 Post Office, *Exchange Telegraph Company*, 18.

43 Scott, *Extel 100*, 29–34.

44 Post Office, *Exchange Telegraph Company*, 4.

45 J. Carey, *Communications as Culture* (Boston, MA: Unwin Hyman, 1989), 219.

46 *Exchange Telegraph Company Limited v. Gregory & Co.*, 155, 157.

47 J. Boyle, *Shamans, Software and Spleens: law and the construction of the information society* (Cambridge, MA: Harvard University Press, 1996), 37, 71.

48 Boyle, *Shamans, Software and Spleens*, 73.

49 K.J. Vandevelde, 'The New Property of the Nineteenth Century: the development of the modern concept of property', *Buffalo Law Review*, 29 (1980), 333–45.

50 INS v. *Associated Press*, 1918, 81–2; J. Brandeis dissenting.

51 E. Noam, 'Beyond Liberalisation II: the impending doom of common carriage', *Telecommunications Policy*, 18, no. 6 (1994), 437.

52 The 'All Red' route was a British-inspired project to link together its present and former colonies by a global telegraph system.

53 Nichols, *The Story of the Canadian Press*, 20.

54 This and the following paragraphs are derived mainly from Nichols, *The Story of the Canadian Press*, 38–41.

55 Quoted in Nichols, *The Story of the Canadian Press*, 41.

56 The *Railway Act* (1903) and the mandate of the BRC were extended to encompass telecommunications regulation in 1906. Board of Railway Commissioners, 'The Western Associated Press v. The Canadian Pacific Railway', 275.

Communication and Social Forms: The Development of the Telephone, 1876–1920

Michèle Martin

This paper is concerned with the political-economic development of the Bell Telephone Co.'s telephone system in the Canadian provinces of Quebec and Ontario from 1876 to 1920, and the cultural practices which its expansion created. The telephone should not be seen as a 'neutral' technology, for its diffusion creates a structure of opportunities which may become a matter of interest to different social groups and classes. Since telephone use involves minimal skills, issues of control centred mainly around physical access to this medium and also around attempts by Bell Telephone Co. to plan the development of its distribution and possible uses. This paper discusses how the telephone system developed by Bell Company produced a type of communication which influenced the social forms already existing in Canadian society.

Some Theoretical Concepts

Williams in *Problems in Materialism and Culture* (1982) and Mattelart in *Communication and Class Struggle* (1979) complain that most of the theoretical models related to social studies in communication are one-dimensional. For that reason, each suggests a two-dimensional model that involves not only a relationship with the capitalist process of production, but also with the cultural formation. However both models, although two-dimensional, fail to integrate the two dimensions they examine. Marx avoids this problem particularly in the *Grundrisse* (1953) and in the three volumes of *Capital* (1981) where he recurrently relates the development of means of communication to the process of circulation/exchange of capital. For him, there is no

accumulation of capital without communication. Not only do the means of communication reproduce capitalist relations of production, but ever more rapid systems of communication are at the basis of an accelerated circulation and, hence, accumulation of capital. On the other hand, the desire of capitalists in the sphere of communication to make profit contributes to accelerate the development of systems of communication. Thus there exists a dialectical relationship between the processes of production and consumption of communication. . . .

This paper focuses on how the development of one means of communication, the telephone, influenced cultural practices. It looks at the way public and private interests involved in the process of exchange/circulation are transformed into concern about private and public aspects of systems of communication.[1] The determination of the public and private aspects of communication is not only based on economic and political structures, but also on ideology and cultural practices. . . .

On these premises, I have divided this analysis into two main sections: the structure of diffusion of the telephone system in Ontario and Quebec, and its impact on the cultural activities it created.

Diffusion Strategies: Profits and Class

This section outlines the development of the telephone in Quebec and Ontario between 1876 and 1920 and focuses on its developers' concern with maximizing profits in the short term and establishing a monopoly position in the long term. It examines how private interest was

Abridged from *Antipode* 23, 3 (1991), 307–33. Reprinted by permission of Blackwell Publishing.

served given the role of the telephone in capital-ist production during that period. I look at dis-criminatory pricing and its effect on the avail-ability of telephone service, particularly in Montreal, and on its rates of spread among dif-ferent classes. I also discuss the spread of tele-phone use among different social classes. . . .

Of note, Brown's 'market and infrastructure perspective' is concerned with the supply aspect of the diffusion process. Brown focuses on how innovations are made available to individuals or households, and argues that opportunities for adoption are 'purposely unequal' (Brown, 1981: 7). Inequality is created by diffusion agencies which establish discriminatory strategies of adoption of an innovation. Although, as Blaut (1987) argues, people may be equal in inven-tiveness, Brown suggests that the mechanisms through which an innovation is made available make the process of diffusion discriminatory. The developers of innovation are the source of control of diffusion and of discrimination. Centralized, decentralized, or decentralized with co-ordination loci of decision making may lead to hierarchical diffusion whether it is based on minimizing costs or maximizing profits, and to a more equitable diffusion when it is based on maximizing sales. Discrimination is created through different mechanisms of supplying an innovation, when the manipulation of that process entails conditions of diffusion detrimen-tal to some social groups (Brown, 1981).

Brown's model speaks to the development of the telephone in Ontario and Quebec, controlled by Bell Telephone Co. This was not a 'natural' development as some of the company's managers and politicians suggested, but a discriminatory diffusion organized by the developers to maxi-mize profit. This strategy favoured business to the detriment of the working class. However, maximizing profit was a short-term strategy tem-pered by the company's aim to build and main-tain a monopoly position in the long term. Although these two objectives were generally complementary, there were situations in which

they were contradictory. This engendered activi-ties which seemed irrational to a logic of simple capitalist accumulation. Since the telephone business was not meaningfully regulated by the state before the end of the 1800s, these contra-dictions were the creation of Bell Telephone Co.'s internal policies. To unveil these characteristics of telephone development, this paper discusses not only the spread of telephone networks, but also the political aspect of its system and its uses. It is my contention that an interaction between all of these elements led to a spatial distribution of the telephone system which did not follow the distribution of population, but which rather fol-lowed its class contours.

In Montreal, five telephone exchanges were opened between 1880 and 1903 to accommo-date business and bourgeois areas. The first exchange, the Main office, opened in 1880 in the centre of the business district. Seven years later, in 1887, the second office, Uptown, was built in the wealthy English area of Montreal. Then, the other exchanges came successively: East, 1888; South, 1890; Westmount, 1898. In July 1900, Montreal had 8,120 stations.[2] In 1903, there were 3,622 subscribers, less than 1 per cent of Montreal residents. The total number of residen-tial telephones was 941, a little less than 26 per cent of the total subscriptions.[3]

The telephone lines connecting the five offices had to cross the working-class districts in order to reach either the industrial or the ruling-class residential areas, but only public tele-phones were made available in these districts.

The telephone system in Toronto took a sim-ilar structure to that in Montreal. There were four exchanges in 1894: two serving the busi-ness areas, and two in wealthy residential areas. By 1915, there were 57,304 stations in Toronto; 47 per cent of these stations were business con-nections, and only 6.3 per cent of all city resi-dences had a telephone. In Montreal, there were 51,201 stations, half of which were business connections, and 3.6 per cent of residences had a telephone. In 1922, these percentages had increased to 10.4 per cent in Toronto, and 5.6 per cent in Montreal.[4] Most of these telephones, however, were distributed in sparsely populated wealthy areas and industrial and business districts rather than in the most populated areas. These numbers show that almost fifty years after its commercialization, the price of the telephone strictly limited its accessibility, domestically, to the dominant and part of the middle classes. The other classes, in Montreal and Toronto, were said to be served by public telephone.

It seems, then, that the expansion of the telephone by Bell Telephone Co. supports certain assumptions in the debate on diffusionism. For instance, the policy of maximizing profit may have contributed to a hierarchical distribution of the telephone. Private interests did not serve the collective interest. In 1922, 90 per cent of the communities 'served' by a telephone system were limited to a partial access to its use through public telephone offices, whereas less than 10 per cent of the same population had the service of one or more private lines in their households. Although Bell Telephone Co. has consistently claimed that the telephone system developed 'naturally', the system was planned in fact to make a profit. The working class did not have the means to pay for telephone services. The social distribution of the telephone was class-specific, its access limited to particular classes for economic reasons. In a 'natural' expansion, its geographical distribution would have been available to all people in the areas crossed by its lines.

A cheap collective telephone line erected in these areas for working-class families could have lessened the burden of their misery. There were many uses for telephones in a working-class household, and a telephone company manager even recognized that it would have been cheaper for the company to furnish working-class families with cheap telephones than to cross their areas without leaving any other installations than public telephones. At five cents per call, public telephones were very expensive. Five cents was the price of half a pound of butter in 1892 in

Montreal. The use of a public telephone also meant that a member of the family had to go out to make the call, which produced a considerable delay in emergencies.

Thus, although the company saw itself as generously putting public telephones at their disposal, working-class families did not use them. Bell Telephone Co. interpreted this as evidence that the working classes did not understand the utility of the telephone and did not need its service.

But the opening of the Beaches exchange in Toronto, however, belied this argument. In 1902, the local manager of the Beaches area canvassed the territory in order to urge people who desired a telephone in their households to sign a list. At that time, the Beaches area was mainly inhabited by farmers, working-class families, and, during the summer, by a small group of bourgeois families. According to the manager, 'it was an easy thing to get a large number of people to sign the petition.' Clearly, this group of people thought that the telephone could be of some utility to them. However, Bell charged the prohibitive price of $100 per year for installation, so that only a few of the signatories could afford it. Facing such uncertain promises, the company claimed it 'received no encouragement', and decided to offer a summer telephone service to accommodate the bourgeois (BCHC, Dunstan Letter 1902). The criterion for opening an exchange was thus not the needs of the majority of the residents of an area. Low-income groups in the cities were not a serious market for the telephone industry. . . .

A closer look at the economic condition of the working classes in Montreal during the period studied shows the reality of this statement. Towards the end of the nineteenth century, Montreal was well on its way to becoming an industrial city. In 1899, a large portion of male and female labourers were working in factories. Women and children, in particular, were hired in low-paying jobs, which constituted a necessary contribution to households whose major concern was survival.

Most workers experienced seasonal unemployment so that in 1899, the average annual household wage was between $170 and $558, up to 65 per cent of which was necessary for food alone. For a family that was earning about $0.45 per day, butter at $0.35 per pound, eggs at $0.20 per dozen, and flour at $2.25 per hundred pounds were almost out of reach (see DeBonville, 1975; Copp, 1974). The telephone at about $50 per annum, payable in advance, was financially out of the question, though it was technically possible since the lines passed through working-class districts.

Telephone rates, however, were not standardized. Local managers constituted the barometers of the consumers' attitude to prices set by the company, and wrote regularly to the general management in Montreal which repeatedly adjusted rates according to diverse criteria—geographical, social, numerical, etc.[5] One of these criteria was the number of subscribers in an exchange. Further, the general state of the economy had some effect on the rise and fall of the number of consumers and, therefore, on the price. An average price of the telephone for the period 1876–86 cannot be determined due to the large variation in rates from user to user.[6] In addition to the previously mentioned factors, variations were also due to the lack of organization of the company and to the fact that the telephone apparatus was sold in detached pieces with different models sold at different prices. Rates also varied according to the type of connections, for example residence as opposed to business stations. . . .

Montreal and Toronto, despite their difference in population, had similar telephone rates. In the mid-1890s, when the 'long-distance telephone' was put on the market, the commodity reached prices as high as $55 per annum for residences, and $75 per annum for businesses. In addition, subscribers had to pay a $10 extra charge 'for each half-mile or fraction beyond first mile from exchange'. When subscribers wanted to use the phone for long-distance calls, they had to pay another extra fee (BCHC, document # 803). All of these charges made the telephone a very expensive commodity. In 1901, rates went down a little—$60 per annum for businesses, $40 for residences—and the extra mileage charges were abolished within the city limits (BCHC, 'Toronto Rates 1877–1909'). None-the-less, Pike and Mosco (1986) assert that, in 1900, the rate for a residential telephone was 'equivalent to about two weeks' pay for a male public schoolteacher, three weeks' pay for a skilled crafts-person, and five weeks' starting pay for a female Bell telephone operator' (1986: 23). At that price, the diffusion of the telephone in low-income group areas was sharply restricted. . . .

The diffusion of the telephone system coincided with a period of rapid capitalist industrialization in Canada. Small entrepreneurial businesses became big capitalist industries competing in national and international markets. This competition created increased pressures for technical means of communication by which each capitalist could rapidly get relevant information on market conditions. A network of telegraphic communication already existed which had considerably shortened the circulation time of capital. However, the telegraph often required several days for the completion of a commercial transaction and also required the mastery of complex skills. The telegraphic system also required the employment of operators, threatening the privacy of telegraphed transactions.

The telephone presented a means through which business transactions could be made directly from person to person. But the telephone was also accessible in principle to all who could master the relatively simple skills involved. In central Canada, Bell Telephone Co. concentrated its efforts on developing a telephone system for rapid, private business communications. This development involved the expansion of a long-distance network. This raised the price of the telephone beyond the reach of some social groups, and encountered resistance (see below).

Long-distance service was indispensable because it guaranteed Bell a measure of control of telephone networks organized by smaller companies. Control of long-distance service also secured the only class of subscribers in which the company was seriously interested at that time: businessmen. Since long-distance lines between big cities were the most profitable, the company emphasized their development to the detriment of those in rural areas (BCHC, *Montreal Gazette* 1905b). . . . Considering that people in rural areas were the most remote from doctors, fire departments, police, etc., and thus most likely to find a telephone system useful, one might expect that a company which had been confirmed as a 'public utility' would have supported its development in these areas. . . .

The telephone system was developed for and on the basis of the business clientele. The utility of the residential telephone was considered by Bell Company to be the link it afforded between the businessman's office and his home. Conversation on telephone lines for any purpose other than business was seen as a waste of time and money for the telephone company and its subscribers (BCHC, document #30114).[7] The telephone interested this particular class of subscribers because it allowed them to save time and labour. In all Canadian and American cities, the first exchanges to be opened were situated in the business districts. . . .

Bell's refusal of cheap telephone services to low-income groups can be understood in two ways. First, the company was afraid that furnishing the telephone to these groups at low rates would create a precedent that would have negative consequences for the whole system— subscribers asking for cheaper prices for other types of service. Second, it was not seen as a good policy to furnish these populous and 'infamous' areas with a means of communication which, according to Bell's managers, they did not need and of which they did not know the value (BCHC, document #17958). . . .

Brown's argument that the opportunities for adoption of an innovation are 'purposely unequal' is supported by the case of the development of the telephone by Bell Telephone Co. in Montreal and Toronto. The centralization of decision making by capitalist interests led to the establishment of strategies of diffusion and adoption incompatible with a 'universal' distribution of the service. To maximize profit, Bell management purposely planned to implement, maintain and expand the telephone in wealthy urban areas, and to join such areas by long-distance lines.

Private and Party Lines Vis-à-vis Cultural Activities

While access to the telephone, especially in cities and towns, differed according to class, accessibility was not a sufficient condition for wealthy classes to pay for telephone service. Businessmen also demanded privacy on the lines. In fact, one of the arguments sustaining Bell's demands for increased telephone rates was that of obtaining the capital necessary for the transformation of party lines into the private lines very much in demand among businessmen. The working classes complained that there was a contradiction in the managing of a 'public utility' by a private company and that this was demonstrated by the fact that 'Bell would rather furnish high-priced telephone service to a small group than cheap party lines to a majority' (BCHC, *La Presse* 1918b).

Telephone development by Bell Telephone Co. in central Canada led to the transformation of party lines into private lines. For telephone users, different cultural practices were possible on party and private lines. The cultural practices of telephone users were, however, influenced not only by technological characteristics of the telephone system but also by other elements such as the gender and social location of the users themselves. I turn now to a discussion of the transformation of the telephone from a party to a private line system, and of the way consumers, particularly female consumers, were oriented towards what became standardized telephone uses, suggested by the telephone companies in accordance with their conception of essential and 'futile' uses.

The adoption of private lines produced types of interaction between users which differed from those occurring on party lines. Together such practices, some of which were quite unexpected by telephone companies, constituted a telephone culture. Telephone activities related to recreational uses were introduced slowly as the telephone developed, and were popular with women. They were placed in a telephone system shaped by men from the ruling classes, who prescribed *rational* activities governed by an ensemble of rules and procedures which specified what were thought to be appropriate uses. Female consumers did not necessarily agree.

Telephony for daily activities appeared in cities and towns towards the end of the 1890s. Very specific telephone practices were prescribed by the companies: the use of the telephone for shopping and making appointments during daytime, for personal conversations during the evening, and for protection during the night (BCHC, *Quebec Daily Telegram* 1911). By the early 1900s, however, bourgeois and petty bourgeois women were already using the telephone extensively for social purposes, at all times of the day (BCHC, *Saturday Evening Post* 1907). Telephone activities became part of some women's social practices in urban areas, not only changing the notion of 'acceptable' uses developed by Bell Company, but also affecting the development of the system. Women's extensive use of the telephone obliged Bell to take domestic development into account. Urban residential sectors began to look attractive to the company, and houses were later equipped with extensions or supplementary lines in order to allow both the husband's business calls and the wife's social calls. Most of these changes were due to practices unforeseen by Bell's management. The

'social' aspect of telephone technology had not been anticipated by the early capitalist developers of the telephone system.

Independent telephone companies, finding niches in areas to which Bell refused to extend its system, were thriving in rural areas from the early 1890s. In Ontario alone, between 1892 and 1905, 83 independent telephone companies were created, and between 1906 and 1915, 676 mainly rural independent telephone companies were established (Babe, 1988: 17–18). Several rural telephone companies were co-operatives whose structure was determined by the users themselves. This contrasted with the more rigid systems installed by Bell in urban areas. Independent companies had much cheaper rates, so that in many areas almost everyone could afford a telephone. At the same time, they applied much looser rules to the use of their telephones. . . . Co-operative control, general distribution, and familiarity among users generated types of telephone activities which were considered rude and 'unethical' in the rules which Bell published specifying approved uses of the telephone. However, they were often seen as participation in community life in the informal code of rural party-line practices. These represented a complete reversal of the standard uses; so much so that big company managers were scandalized by the practices allowed on rural party lines. Yet, some small-company managers thought that 'the party line was a necessity and ha[d] come to stay' (BCHC, *Telephony* 7(6): 1904). Some managers themselves eavesdropped and participated in subscribers' conversations (BCHC, document #29909).

An important activity on party lines was that of 'meeting on the lines'. For isolated women in rural areas, the telephone was a means of remaining connected with the rest of the community. 'Meetings on the line' were used to break their isolation and enhanced the use value of their telephone. These activities practised by women over the party lines influenced the companies' conception of the value of the telephone, as a technology whose system had been conceived exclusively for business seemed to have alternative uses worth considering. However, private companies were constrained to maximize profits. Collective calls, regularly practiced by women on party lines, were not part of that strategy, and these lines were gradually replaced by private lines and 'twosome' telephone calls.

The replacement of party lines by private lines, especially in urban areas, was partly engendered by pressure from business classes for more privacy on the lines. In spite of the high price involved initially (due to their limited supply), Bell's managers claimed that the majority of their subscribers demanded private lines (BCHC, document #1173). High rates did not deter the wealthy class of subscribers. The structure of the telephone system and its mode of communication were determined by the social requirements of dominant classes for private lines, notwithstanding those of other social groups. However, telephone companies could meet these demands only in so far as the technology permitted it. In the 1880s, private line technology was not practicable, because 'open' iron wires did not allow privacy (BCHC, no source, 1938). . . .

The demand for privacy in telephone calls grew over time. In 1877, privacy was not much of an issue as the telephone systems involved a few 'domestic lines', relating a small group of friends' and relatives' households and businesses. The telephone networks constituted a supplementary link in an already entrenched social group (BCHC 'The Telephone', G.G. Hubbard, May 1877). Privacy became more problematic when these domestic lines were connected together through an exchange, and when different groups of subscribers were indiscriminately distributed on party lines. People could no longer choose those with whom they shared their line (BCHC document #12016), and telephone exchanges limited the capacity of the telephone to reproduce the privacy already existing in the social practices of the ruling classes. In late-Victorian society, these classes had a highly developed sense of privacy and, to many of their members, the idea of having a conversation overheard by eavesdroppers was in itself a limitation to 'freedom of speech'. . . .

The new mode of communication produced by the telephone system reproduced some social activities and modified others in the creation of a telephone culture. A characteristic feature of the telephone system was its speed. The effect was multi-dimensional. The telephone was developed in a context of capitalists' demands for faster means of communication and it had accelerated transactions. Its capacity for long-distance contacts led some to argue that it had strengthened the nation (Carty, 1922) and eliminated class differentiation (Carty, 1926). In fact, telephone contacts between members of the working classes and ruling classes were governed by a prior, rigid system of etiquette. Users of the telephone system were expected to comply with the dominant moral order, and working-class morality was often questioned by the dominant and middle classes (see *Rapports pastoraux*, 1843–1935, Diocese of Montreal Archives). Wealthy women on party lines often complained of the bad manners of the working-class people, such as maids, occasionally using the system, and urged the telephone companies to provide private lines.

While Brown (1981) suggests that people passively adopt an innovation when they have been selected as a market by the diffusion agencies, the initiative of consumers was important in determining both the diffusion of an innovation and the uses to which it is put. The exclusion of rural areas from Bell's market diffusion strategies did not prevent people in them from building their own cheap systems adapted to their financial and social needs. Further, women's telephone practices forced the company to change its view of the use of a telephone, and also its patterns of distribution. While this study better supports Blaut's stress on 'equality of inventiveness' translated into technological modifications, it suggests that innovation is not limited to the mechanical transformation of a technology, but also extends to its use. Women gave the telephone use new dimensions which had the effect of revealing new possibilities of this technology. This is not to say that the telephone would never have been used for social purposes, but women were the first to discover its utility for this and, in giving this particular characteristic to the innovation, they influenced its pattern of diffusion. This suggests that a study of the diffusion of an innovation should take the social and cultural practices of its users into consideration. Such activities play a vital role in the realization of the technological possibilities of an innovation. This, however, does not eliminate the hierarchical effect of the diffusion of an innovation based on 'maximizing profit'. In spite of these 'deviations' in the expected expansion of the telephone, its accessibility remained limited to small privileged groups.

. . .

Conclusion

The diffusionism debate suggests that the diffusion of an innovation is based on a process in which the opportunities for its adoption are purposely unequal. The reason for this inequality is said to be the manipulation of the process of diffusion of an innovation by its developers, and a certain passivity on the part of its adopters. Very little thought is given to the social context in which an innovation is adopted and *used*. As Blaut (1987) stresses, it is a myth to suppose innovations are diffused into empty (social) spaces. These spaces are areas in which cultural practices already exist. The Marxist model used in this paper helps to look at the social conditions under which an innovation develops.

Even the telephone, whose use required no particular skills, did not develop 'naturally' in a capitalist society. Telephone expansion was related to the general mechanism of production and exchange, and to the fact that, as such, its distribution created a structure of possibilities chosen by the groups that controlled its development. Its use was not dictated by nature but became a matter of interest to different social groups and classes. Unlike the model of diffusionism, however, I show how this difference of interests created certain kinds of opposition and resistance. This opposition was translated into forms such as unexpected uses, which sometimes forced the telephone industry and state agencies to modify some elements of expansion of the system. Thus, while political and economic factors influenced the formation of the system, its structure and practices, in turn, were responsible for some changes in the political economy of its development.

This model constitutes a useful conceptual framework for studies of the diffusion of a communication innovation. It helps to locate the process of communication within the process of production, and to situate systems of communication within the specific conditions in which they expanded. It also allows one to study the dialectical relation between private and public interests, which enables one to make a real link between diverse levels of analysis, a link which was missing in other studies. From the perspective of consumption of means of communication, it is considered from an ideological point of view, and corresponds to the private and public aspects of systems of communication, where it contrasts the form of 'privacy' conceived by male capitalists, with 'group interaction' practised by other groups. From the production side, the economic underpinnings of private and public interests are considered, suggesting that industry profits have priority over an equitable social distribution in the capitalist development of communication systems. These two aspects of the consumption/production process are interrelated, because 'privacy' in communication is supported by the dominant ideology and culture.

Notes

1   In this paper, public interest means the interest of the majority, while private interest means the interest of private capital. Private aspects refer to privacy or secrecy of communication, whereas public aspects refer to collective communication.

2   A station corresponded to one telephone line and their number was not equivalent to the number of subscribers, as some users had more than one line. South was closed a few years later and the few subscribers, mostly industries, were connected to the other exchanges.

3   Bell Canada Historical Collection (hereafter BCHC), 'Telephone History—Montreal', no date.

4   BCHC, 'History of Toronto Telephone Develop-ment'; 'Bell Telephone Co. of Canada in Cities, 1915–1922'.

5   See, for example, BCHC, Letter from J. Stewart to L.B. McFarlane, 24 Feb. 1880; Letter from P.W. Snider to L.B. McFarlane, 23 Feb. 1880; Letter from G.P. Dunlop to L.B. McFarlane, 24 Feb. 1880; Letter from H.C. Baker to L.B. McFarlane, 18 Oct 1880.

6   For instance, two Ontario lessees who rented a telephone at intervals of about two months faced a $20 difference in price (BCHC, Lease to C.D. Cory and H.C. Baker, Hamilton, 18 Oct. 1879; lease to J.R. Lee, Toronto, 18 Dec. 1879).

7   Marvin (1988) elaborates on this particuliar issue.

References

Primary sources

Diocese of Montreal Archives:
Rapports pastoraux, 1843–1935

Bell Canada Historical Collection (BCHC):
Documents
#803, Montreal Telephone Directory, Aug. 1890.
#1059, Letter from a subscriber to Wadland, 20 Dec. 1879.
#1069, 45–6 Victoria (1880) ch. 71, sec. 2. 'The Bell Telephone Co. Act Incorporation'.
#1069.4, 1 Edward VII (1902). 'The Bell Telephone Co. Act of Incorporation and Amendments'.
#1173, Letter from L.B. McFarlane to T. Swinyard, 9 Feb. 1880.
#3379, 'Lecture on the telephone business: the regulation of telephone rates'. J.E. MacPherson, Bell Telephone Co.
#3536.1, 'Statistics—Montreal', 1911–19.
#7966, Letter from E.C. Baker to C.F. Sise, 1 Jan. 1892.
#9710, Letter from C.F. Sise to Mr. Smith, 7 Nov. 1888.
#12015, 'The Telephone Unmasked', *The Peterborough Times*, 2 Nov. 1877.
#12016, 'Quiet Telephone', no source, 1884.
#12016.1, 'Prescription by Telephone', *Daily Herald*, 10 Jan. 1880.
#12016.2, 'Telephone Exchanges', W.H. Harper, 1880.
#12016.3, 'Across the wires', *Montreal Witness*, 21 Mar. no date.
#17958, 4–5 Edward VII (1905). *Report of the Select Committee on Telephone Systems*, minutes of evidence, appendix 1, pp. 805–6.
#18485, 'Relation Between Bell Telephone and Population in Cities over 50,000 population'. AT&T, 1912–19.
#20144, Letter from C.P. Sclater to M. Seaborn, 16 Jan. 1884.
#24092, 'Circular' to managers, 17 Aug. 1914.
#24096, Letter from L.B. McFarlane to L. Irwing, 12 Jan. 1884.
#24874, Letter from L.B. McFarlane to K.N. England, 16 Jan. 1882.
#24894, Letter from C.F. Sise to J.E. Hudson, 5 July 1893.
#29144, Letter from C.P. Sclater to C.F. Walsh, 16 Jan. 1884.
#29870, Letter from C.F. Sise to H.M. Douglas, 3 September 1880.
#29909, 'The life-saving line of a country doctor',

Family Herald, 2 Feb. 1918.

#30114, 'The Druggiss "Dread"', *Montreal Gazette*, 11 Sept. 1965.

#30744, Letter from E.C. Baker to C.F. Sise, 4 Aug. 1880.

Letters

from Baker, E.C. to C.F. Sise, 1 Jan. 1892.

from Dunstan, K.J. to local manager in Hamilton, 2 Jan. 1902.

———— to Bell Telephone Co., 22 Jan. 1902b.

from McFarlane, L.B. to T. Swinyard, 24 Feb. 1880.

———— to R.N. England, 16 Jan. 1882.

———— to J. Gilmour, 25 Jan. 1892.

———— to J. Gilmour, 25 Jan. 1904.

Newspapers and journals

Bloor Watchman, 'The telephone', 30 May 1929.

La Presse, 'Un ultimatum des pharmaciens à la cie de téléphone Bell', 23 Nov. 1918.

———— 'Le téléphone pour tous', 26 Nov. 1918a.

———— 'Le peuple contre le trust qui l'exploite', 27 Nov. 1918b.

———— 'Le téléphone ne doit pas être tenu comme un luxe', 28 Nov. 1918c.

———— 'Des nécessiteux qui thésaurisent', 6 Dec. 1918d.

———— 'Le téléphone progressif', 14 Dec. 1918e.

Mail, "Phone Co's pact is ratified', 20 Nov. 1913.

Montreal Gazette, 'Telephone Rates', 25 Mar. 1897.

———— 'Telephone Inquiry', 10 Mar. 1905.

———— 'Telephone Inquiry', 23 Mar. 1905a.

———— 'Telephone Inquiry', 26 Mar. 1905b.

———— 'Telephone Inquiry', 26 May 1905c.

Montreal Star, 'Telephone Rates', 25 Mar. 1897.

News, 'Girls were never greater blessing than when they entered phone exchanges', 4 Nov. 1916.

No source, 'This brave new world', Aug. 1938.

Quebec Daily Telegram, 'Advertisement', 9 Sept. 1911.

Saturday Evening Post, 'The diary of a telephone girl', 19 Oct. 1907.

Star, 'For telephone girls are educating subscribers', 13 Sept. 1913.

———— 'Usually the public fault', 4 Oct. 1919.

Telephone Gazette, no title 2(6), 1910.

———— 'Responsibility of Toll Operators', 2(9), 1911.

Telephony, 'The "hello" girls and "central"', 9(1): 32–42, 1901.

———— 'The party line controversy', 7(6): 452–3, 1904.

———— 'Heard on party line', 8(3): 211, 1904.

Sise, C.F. 'logbooks', #2: 1887, #3: 1888, #4: 1889, #7: 1892, #18: 1903.

Telephone directories: Montreal, 1883; Toronto, 1899.

Secondary sources

Abler, R. (1977) 'The Telephone and the Evolution of the American Metropolitan System'. In I. de S. Pool (ed.) *The Social Impact of the Telephone*. Cambridge: MIT.

Amstrong, C. and H.V. Nelles (1986) *Monopoly's Moment*. Philadelphia: TUP.

Attali, J. and Y. Stourdze (1977) 'The Birth of the Telephone and Economic Crisis: The Slow Death of the Monologue in French Society'. In I. de S. Pool (ed.) *The Social Impact of the Telephone*. Cambridge: MIT.

Babe, R.E. (1988) 'Control of Telephones: The Canadian Experience'. *Canadian Journal of Communication* 13(2): 16–29.

Blaut, J.M. (1987) 'Diffusionism: A Uniformitarian Critique'. *Annals of the Association of American Geographers* 77(1): 30–49.

Brown, L.A. (1981) *Innovation Diffusion*. New York: Methuen.

Carty, J.J. (1926) 'Episodes in Early Telephone History'. *Bell Telephone Quarterly* 5(2): 59–70.

———— (1922) 'The Telephone Development'. *Bell Telephone Quarterly* 1(1): 23–37.

———— (1922) 'Ideals of the Telephone Service'. *Bell Telephone Quarterly* 1(3): 1–11.

Copp, T. (1974) *Anatomy of Poverty*. Toronto: McClelland & Stewart.

DeBonville, J. (1975) *Jean-Baptiste Gagnepetit*. Montreal: Aurore.

Fischer, S.C. (1988a) 'The Revolution in Rural Telephony, 1900-1920'. *Journal of Social History* 21(1): 5–26.

———— (1988b) 'Touch Someone: The Telephone

Industry Discovers Sociability'. *Technology and Culture* Jan., pp. 32–61.

Harvey, D. (1985) *The Urbanization of Capital*. London: Basil Blackwell.

Jewett, F.B. (1936) 'The Social Implication of Scientific Research in Electrical Communication'. *Bell Telephone Quarterly* 15(4): 205–18.

Martin, M. (1988) 'Rulers of the Wires? Women's Contribution to the Structure of Means of Communication'. *Journal of Communication Inquiry* 12(2): 89–103.

——— (1987) 'Communication and Social Forms: A Study of the Development of the Telephone System, 1876—1920'. Unpublished Ph.D. thesis, Department of Sociology, University of Toronto.

Marvin, C. (1988) *When Old Technologies were New*. Cambridge: Oxford.

Marx, K. (1981) *Capital I, II, III*. Montréal: Nouvelle Frontière.

——— (1953) *Grundrisse*. New York: Vintage.

Mattelart, A. and S. Seigelaub (Eds) (1979) *Communication and Class Struggle*, vol. 1. New York: International.

Mattelart, M. (1976) 'The Feminine Version of the Coup d'Etat'. In J. Nash and H. Icken Safa (eds) *Sex and Class in Latin America*. New York: Preager, pp. 225–45.

Ogle, E.B. (1979) *Long-Distance, Please*. Toronto: Collins.

Perrine, J.O. (1925) 'The Development of the Transmission Circuit in Communication'. *Bell Telephone Quarterly* 4(2): 114–31.

Pike, R.M. (1989) 'Kingston Adopts the Telephone'. *Urban History Review* 18(1): 32–7.

——— and V. Mosco (1986) 'Canadian Consumers and Telephone Pricing'. *Telecommunications Policy* March, pp. 17–32.

Rhodes, F.L. (1923) 'Development of Cables Used in the Bell System'. *Bell Telephone Quarterly* 2(2): 94–106.

Smythe, D.W. (1981) *Dependency Road*. Norwood: Ablex.

Spofford, H.P. (1909) 'A Rural Telephone'. *Harpers Magazine* 118: 830–7.

Williams, R. (1982) *Problem in Materialism and Culture*. London: Verso.

Prophets Without Honour? Canadian Policy Makers and the First Information Highway, 1969–1975

Laurence B. Mussio

Introduction

The fusion of computer and communications technology has received a great deal of attention in recent years. The phenomenon of convergence of once distinct technological systems—computers and telecommunications—has attracted commentary from an array of regulators, policy makers, analysts, tractarians, and futurists intent on 'redeeming the promise of confluence', in the suggestive phrase of W.T. Stanbury.[1] . . . Technological innovation has summoned policy makers to an exceptional historical moment. Major political and economic decisions about the architecture of regulation and policy will have to be made. Public policy will have to define and defend the state's own objectives, mediate between competing private interests, and ensure that decisions taken will promote maximum system development.

These same questions were very much on the minds of Canadian policy makers during the 1970s. Industrial organization of the sector, the importance of national social and economic objectives, and even the vision of what was then called a National Computer Utility motivated the state to consider the implications of the intersection of computers and communications. The conviction that computer/communications had common property resource qualities produced doubt that the market could equitably diffuse its benefits. That judgment led federal policy makers to try to define the technological moment by applying traditional models of state intervention. But the divergent interests of the players—the common carriers and domestic and US computer industries—would make an aggressive national computer/communications policy impossible to achieve. In the end, circumstance, will, and inertia imposed strict limitations on federal policy in this sector.

Perhaps seduced by the forward-looking nature of the 'theatre of revolutionary technology' and by their concentration upon the challenge of determining public policy, many of the participants in today's debate over confluence seem unaware of the historical context in which the Canadian state has handled transformations of a technological nature. How did policy makers respond to technological change during the 1970s? What characterized Canadian thinking about technology? How does the institutional memory of government affect its apprehension of technological change? Through examining these questions, I hope to provide a historical context for the current debate on technological change in communication. By resurrecting an awareness of how the state dealt with similar issues, we can identify another type of convergence—that of past actions and future directions in a critical area of public policy. At the very least, that context will provide current participants with an understanding of the state's experience in dealing with the embryonic convergence of telecommunications and computers in another era. . . .

The initial responses of the federal state to computer/communications is the subject of the next section of this chapter. The one after that examines the development of government policy in computer/communications policy between 1972 and 1974, while . . . the following section

From Chapter 14 of *Perspectives on the New Economics and Regulation of Telecommunications*, ed. W.T. Stanbury (Montreal: Institute for Research on Public Policy, 1996), 257–81. Reprinted by permission of IRPP.

contains a more general discussion of Ottawa's computer/communications policy by 1975. . . .

The Initial Responses of the State to Computer/Communications, 1968–1970

The creation of a federal government department, a major decision about the industrial organization of the sector, and the promotion of a national computer utility was dramatic proof that computer/communications had engaged the efforts of policy makers between 1968 and 1970. To provide some context, I will begin with a discussion of how the state perceived technological changes in communications.

By the late 1960s, the federal state could point to the emergent computer communications field as an area in which public policy could exert its influence. Time-sharing computers (large, mainframe type) could offer multiple connections, streamline accessibility of computing power, and eliminate the problem of distance.[2] The spread of digital transmission capacity over the public telephone network improved its efficiency.[3] If it was too late for the state to have a major impact on the configuration of the computer equipment industry, the government could enter on the 'ground floor' with the marriage of computers and communications. After all, regulatory control over communications was already firmly established. . . . The attributes assigned to telecommunications—its economic importance, its relevance to national unity and sovereignty, and its important implications for Canada's international position—were easily enlisted to describe the intrinsic value of the marriage of computers and communications. . . . The integration of the state's historic aims in telecommunications—notably universal service and coverage of distance—were grafted onto new technologies that promised speed. . . .

In Canada, linking computers and communications struck a resonant chord, for two reasons. First, the Canadian experience with traditional utilities (hydro-electricity, telephones, railroads)

had imprinted the state's thinking about the import and potential extent of new technologies. On this terrain, the familiar could meet the future: the public utility could meet the computer. 'Five years from now,' *The Financial Post* reported in 1967, 'many Canadian companies may buy their computing power just as they buy their electricity or gas today—from a utility supplying service from a big central computer . . . The day of the computer utility is here.'[4] Perhaps the day of the computer utility would belong to Canadians as computer technology had not.

The event that provided the entry point for federal government intervention was the takeover of Computer Sciences Canada by CN/CP[5] in March of 1969. Canadian National and Canadian Pacific each paid $500,000 for the controlling interest of the Canadian subsidiary of Computer Sciences Corporation of Los Angeles. The acquisition was made to promote data communications and establish a stronger national link between capital and technology in a Canadian-based computer service company.[6]

The details of the acquisition were innocuous enough, but the implications were instantly recognized by the telecommunications and computer titans. IBM did not see the development as a threat, but took pains to stress that any cross-subsidization should be prevented from occurring. Bell Canada protested that it was shut out of the new business owing to the restrictions imposed by Parliament on the company in its newly minted charter in 1968.

Ottawa's intention to deal with communications issues had assumed a new vigour with the creation of the Department of Communications (DOC) in 1968. Its first minister, Eric Kierans, suggested it signalled the growing importance of communications and the recognition that 'communications has moved to the forefront of our national affairs' and was now 'the nerve system of a nation in search of itself'.[7] The state had become quite aware that information retrieval would be an important component of national technological progress. An industry–government partnership would be needed to anticipate the transformation of society.[8] Internationally, this 'information explosion' was based on the availability of increasing telecommunications services. It resulted in expanding activity of global agencies charged with regulating such linkages.[9] The time seemed to be right for the creation of a comprehensive policy. The DOC would lead the way in creating an environment in which industry could implement technology and diffuse its benefits across society.[10]

Opportunities to apply the state's new-found resolution about technological progress would come in rapid succession between 1969 and 1975. Once distinctly separate areas, telecommunications and computers were becoming intertwined, forcing the government to consider the implications. What social and political product would emerge from the regulation of these new econotechnical systems? Clearly, new areas of public interest were opening. . . . The state had not yet staked its regulatory claim in an area of considerable importance and activity. The department anticipated that within a decade, computer service centres would provide computer power 'in a manner analogous to the distribution of electric power' on an information processing and distribution grid.

The DOC was concerned that data processing and telecommunications were being brought into 'unprecedented intimacy',[11] and would encourage Canadian common carriers to attempt market entry into a new utility market. The acquisition of Computer Sciences (Canada) Limited (CSC) by CN/CP, approved by Order-in-Council in January 1969, signalled that the transformation was at hand.[12]

The elements surrounding the purchase of CSC typified the Canadian technological problem. CSC's American parent firm, Computer Sciences Corporation, was one of the giants in the information science field. The only way that CN/CP could readily enter the market was to acquire the subsidiary and contract for the technology.[13] How could Ottawa stop the continentalization of the computer/communications field? One option was the use of the members of the Trans-Canada Telephone System (TCTS),[14] principally Bell Canada, to provide competition in the computer utility field. But that cure might be worse than the disease. Allowing the (then) telecommunications monopolies to enter the field would create truly frightening concentrations of economic power.

This was the dilemma presented to Cabinet in the spring of 1969. The marriage of computers and telecommunications would create a massive advantage for telecommunications companies who owned the means of transmission. The advantages of this alternative were tempting: large pools of raw computer power would lead to reduced cost and divert American penetration by consolidating East–West links. One Cabinet document warned that 'computer utilities are developing much in the fashion that power utilities evolved 50 years ago.'[15] The new utilities also promised to have a phenomenal rate of growth and become 'as much a part of everyday life as the telephone is today'.[16] . . . Further, cross-ownership could spur innovation in switching and terminal apparatus, not to mention the diffusion of these technological innovations.[17] . . . It was also clear that the birth of a new utility would require some regulatory expansion. Regulatory oversight of private wire services was the beginning: computer utilities might be next.[18] In face of the evidence, the Cabinet agreed that the time had come for renovating the regulatory architecture in communications.[19]

The purchase of CSC Ltd. elicited a flood of advice about how to handle the apparently rapid formation of information utilities.[20] In July 1969 several computer service companies sought to focus the federal government's attention on the 'serious implications' that had issued from the CSC-CN/CP deal.[21] . . . Domestic computer service firms were convinced that the marriage between communications common carriers and the computer service industry should be annulled. The only hope for the Canadian situation was the removal of the common carriers, who were often laggards in technological advances. To them, the greatest challenge to public policy makers was the maintenance of competition and innovation. . . .

The Cabinet finally met to formally consider participation by telecommunications carriers in public data-processing in February 1970 after considerable pressure was brought to bear on Kierans and on the minister of Industry, Trade, and Commerce, Jean-Luc Pépin. The telecommunications common carriers, especially Bell, were anxious to enter the field and 'make the computer as much a part of everyday life as the telephone is today'. CN/CP already had, in January of the previous year. Since then, the company had been developing an aggressive promotion of the utility. The independent data-processing industry feared the worst.[22]

Kierans and Pépin suggested to their Cabinet colleagues that inaction would have grave implications for Canadian sovereignty. The country had been traditionally unwilling to submit to the impact of market forces on essential links. 'Historically', one Cabinet memorandum explained, 'Canada has been unwilling to submit to the unconstrained effects of market forces on its essential services. In the development of railroads, telecommunications, highways, and air services, the vital importance of establishing an East–West axis has been recognized at some cost. A parallel can be drawn with the present need for a policy that will facilitate the establishment of a national Computer Utility network owned and controlled in Canada.'[23] Innovation had sired a new utility; policy would have to shape it in a Canadian direction. The state had to hardwire the country before transnational lines were imposed on it. . . .

The Cabinet was thus faced with the challenge of giving a new utility its pattern, if not its fundamental thrust. This new utility could be the anchor for a Canadian computer industry, strengthening the export potential of the telecommunications sector as it developed. The political dimensions were not as promising. Allowing carrier entry would be interpreted as capitulating to pressure from Bell, and cutting loose the data-processing companies that worked on the margins. To exclude the carriers and the government would be selling out to IBM and General Electric.

The response of the common carriers to even the hint of reciprocal provision of data processing and communications was predictable and fierce. The Trans-Canada Telephone System insisted that proliferation of telecommunications facilities would result in duplication, interrupt 'continuity of service under conditions of natural disaster or acts of war',[24] and undermine efficiencies gained by economies of scale. TCTS argued that the public would be ill-served by having to deal with a number of companies for its communications needs. 'The future need', TCTS contended, 'is for simultaneous voice, data computer, and visual interaction.'[25] CN Telecommunications argued that the present number of carriers was more than enough for the demands of Canadian business. . . .

In any case, industry on both sides of the issue paid homage to the protection of the competitive market for data processing. This was certainly ironic given the dominance of IBM on the data processing side and Bell on the telecommunications side. But the pre-empting of intrusive government regulation was a concern shared by large and small. State regulation would retard technological progress in the field and mar industry flexibility.[26] Most were agreed, however, that the state should regulate security and privacy concerns, as well as standards. Ultimately, however, the Cabinet decided that too much concentration would result in allowing telecommunications carriers to engage in data processing. As a result, the carriers were ultimately denied entry into the computer/communications and data-processing fields. . . .

Government Policy and Computer/Communications, 1970–1974

The development of federal computer/communications policy in the early 1970s began with great aspirations. The government sought to implement some of its initiatives in this period, but found that the diversity of sectoral interests at stake in any initiative and waning political interest reduced its ability to coordinate national policy.

The establishment of the Canadian Computer/Communications Agency (CCCA) was proof that the Cabinet had taken computer/communications technology seriously. . . . Five million dollars had already been earmarked among the Economic Sovereignty High Priority Expenditures for 1971–2[27] for the creation of a national computer/communications network. The ambition of its promoters was the prevention of total foreign domination of the computer and communications industries. More urgently it seemed, the Cabinet expressed the keen wish to ensure that computer centres and information were kept in Canadian hands and under Canadian law.[28]

The proposals were grounded in the traditional concerns of public policy. Concerns that fastened telecommunications and other utilities to the common weal would also guide the state in navigating computer technology. The DOC wanted to ensure that the advantages of computer power were properly disseminated throughout the country in the most cost-effective fashion.[29] Only then would technology meet the state's social and economic development objectives.

The government's best predictions about the growth of the computer services industry were truly astounding. Forecasts suggested that the computer services industry would 'equal or surpass the auto industry' in size and contribution to GNP. It would also carry vital consequences for Canada's social and political structure, although those consequences were usually left undefined. The marriage of computers and communications was setting the stage for a 'veritable quantum jump in human capabilities'.[30]

Inevitably, that jump would be powered in Canada mainly by foreign-owned companies.

Over 80 per cent of the domestic data-processing market was supplied by foreign companies. Losing any control over what might become the largest industry in Canada and 'the most important determinant of the future quality of Canadian life' would be a major disaster. The very viability of Canada would come under question. On the other hand, the promise of the merger of computers and telecommunications was that the country would become 'one great information system' with the computer as common as the telephone had been. The levels of creativity and leisure time unleashed would be added to the economic and social health of the polity.[31]

But, as policy makers were finding out, talking about a national computer/communications policy and acting on a plan were different things. Not only would the policy have to be assessed on the contribution it made to the achievement of government aims, but it would also have an impact on the traditional (and powerful) monopoly public communications services. . . .

Pressure to clarify the state's interests led to yet further DOC studies under the aegis of the Canadian Computer Communications Task Force. The CCCTF chairman, Dr H.J. von Baeyer, was to direct a series of studies that were to form the basis for a new technology policy. Several months later, in May of 1972, von Baeyer presented a two-volume report entitled *Branching Out*.[32] The task force emphasized the need for governments at all levels to recognize computer/communications as a key area of social and industrial activity. The report stressed that competition was the most effective vehicle for the development of the data-processing industry and that the federal government should play a role as 'Focal Point'.[33]

The concept of a computer utility, extensively discussed two years before in Cabinet, was dismissed: low demand and the variety of services offered did not fit the utility model. Despite this, the idea of a national computer utility persisted for a few years. Decision makers were especially reluctant to relinquish the 'utility' model. What really killed the idea of a 'computer utility' were suspicions that such a 'utility' meant a radical change in the way business was done, and more state interference.[34] . . . Lack of confidence (well placed, in retrospect) in the long-term survival of commercial systems operators that provided raw computer power was also an important factor in business attitudes. The lack of a clear jurisdiction in computer/communications at any regulatory level, however, was one of the more obvious institutional problems.[35] Government policy was developing into little more than the desire to respond to innovation and to keep data flows within Canada. The gulf was slowly widening between the stated importance of computer/communications and concrete actions by the state. . . .

There was little agreement about who exactly would lead the government charge in implementing computer/communications policy. The Department of Communications felt it was the natural place for such discussions. The Department of Finance had different ideas. It believed that the Ministry of State for Science and Technology would have been a more appropriate place to perform coordination, since it was established to perform such a role.[36] The issues were daunting: competition, regulation, national control. The prime aim in computer/communications was to direct the technology to 'promote economic and social aims, emphasize national identity, and maximize Canadian influence and control and providing appropriate services'.[37] The dissent within the state illustrates the difficulties associated with the direction and control of computer industry development.

Apart from dealing with the carriers, higher-level policy considerations presented themselves quickly in the development of the thinking within the federal government. The impact of the traditional monopoly in public communications had to be considered, as did the interests of the common carriers generally. Competition in the form of new carriers constructing new transmission facilities would be undesirable. In the long-haul communications field, the DOC considered the effectiveness of competition limited by the nature of the service. Policy makers believed that the integrity of the monopoly services must be safeguarded. In any event, extending competition would undoubtedly incite serious provincial opposition.[38]

It was believed that open competition in computer/communications could potentially involve further foreign penetration and harm existing carriers. The carriers considered any competition to come only at their expense. The benefits of competition were believed to increase with traffic density, but would have adverse effects upon both regional distribution of computer services and between firms. Though gains in network efficiency would be achieved, the DOC concluded that the effects on competition, especially between the TCTS and CN/CP, would not improve the Canadian computer services situation. The market could not meet the social and economic objectives of the state.[39]

Meanwhile, the diffusion of computer technology between 1970 and 1973 confirmed its economic importance.[40] The government had to reconcile the irreconcilable: it had to protect the country's economic and social fabric while preserving private initiative and innovation. Ministers responsible in Communications and Industry assured their Cabinet colleagues that the new computer/communications technologies would not be allowed to override the older telecommunications configuration.[41]

By 1974, several things were made clear by Ottawa's attempts to develop a national computer/communications policy. The complexity of the technology was matched by the diversity of interests at stake in any federal initiative. The problems of computer/communications, moreover, did not attract the political interest it had once generated. Finally, the centrepiece of federal initiatives—the computer utility—did not have much hope of achieving any consensus.

. . .

Dissent and Default: Federal Computer/Communications Policy, 1974–1975

. . . The idea of a National Computer Utility died hard, in spite of the recommendations of *Branching Out*.[42] But if the idea of a computer utility found resonance with policy makers in Ottawa, the private sector was far more suspicious of the idea. Many reacted negatively to the very term, especially given the lack of familiarity with the new technology most businessmen possessed. Some were convinced that the term described a covert intent by the state to change the operational environment of computer operations from a competitive, unregulated field into a franchised monopoly service such as other utility-sector undertakings.[43]

By 1975, computer/communications had installed itself in the Canadian communications infrastructure. That installation first generated ambitious plans, then disillusionment on the part of policy makers. Aspirations of using the administrative capacities of the state in this field ultimately faltered.

This outcome might have been disappointing, but it was not surprising. Internal and external pressures for state action were more than offset by those who held an interest in preserving the status quo. Perhaps most important, large corporate interests prevailed over smaller concerns, particularly of the domestic computer service industry. A lack of policy protected the position of the well-established enterprises, at the expense of the newcomers. Advocates of a vigorous policy in computer/communications, moreover, could not mobilize authority within the state to the cause of directing this technological transformation. That blockage further weakened the state's attempts to put its imprint on this technological innovation. . . .

The failure of the Canadian state to develop a policy had consequences. . . . First, hopes that national and public priorities would figure prominently in computer/communications were

frustrated. In spite of the aspirations of the more determined policy makers, national policy had confronted the new technology with a mixture of naïveté, ambition, confusion, then resignation. The result was that Canadian priorities were subordinated to other concerns.

Second, the attempts to frame the historical model drawn from the state's experience with utilities surrendered to the pressures and experience of the day. Even if the technology could support something approaching a national computer utility, the political and economic impetus crucial to its implementation existed but in traces. Instead, another model imposed itself upon the new technology. In place of a utilities development model, the nature of federal involvement in the computer/communications field reflected the compromise reached between state and corporate power as well as between federal and provincial interests.

Third, the notion of computer/communications as a common property resource like telephony and electricity was subordinated to market prerogatives. Market distribution of computers and computer communications accentuated regional disparity; Toronto and Montreal were the principal beneficiaries. Economically marginal provinces like Saskatchewan instead relied on the state to distribute technological blessings. The new technology was diffused in a remarkably rapid fashion across the commanding heights of the Canadian economy, but without the application of utility-based principles.

The Canadian experience with this technology provides an interesting insight into the way governments viewed the introduction of innovation. The technologies were sanctioned by their 'revolutionary' potential to transform economic and even political relationships for the better. Intentionally or not, the advertising was misleading: the revolution did not happen. The technological transfiguration of society would happen in a diffuse manner, not in a highly focused way.

The state's experience in the field ultimately revealed its ambivalence in the face of the convergence of computers and communications. On the one hand, it harboured deep suspicions over whether the market could satisfy the national interest. On the other hand, advocates of reform could not mobilize the full authority of the state to effect serious reforms. The consequence was disjointed policy and an inept choice of tools. In the process, it exposed the limits of the state's capacity to act. The role of technology was important, but not determining. . . .

Conclusion

Ambitious Canadian policy makers in the late 1960s and early 1970s perceived that seizing the moment would require an expansion of the administrative capacities of the state. The creation of a government department, the proposal of a National Computer Utility, the establishment of a body of government dedicated to ushering in the 'millennium' were all attempts to graft the state's interest onto new, emerging technologies. Grand policy schemes failed because those policy makers could not mobilize authority within the state, because of the disinterest of the market, and not least because of monopolists anxious to preserve the status quo. Instead of developing a limited but cogent set of policy objectives, lack of effective coordination resulted in the failure of a national computer/communications strategy. The state was simply not strong enough to define the

field. Direct conflict between national economic and cultural imperatives on the one hand and the exigencies of the market on the other was quietly resolved in favour of the latter.

There may be some lessons to be drawn from the experience of the federal state with the fusion of computers and communications during the 1970s. The Canadian experience seems to suggest that Canadian policy makers considering an information highway policy should, to the greatest extent possible, favour market mechanisms to diffuse its benefits. Policy makers in 1970 favoured significant state intervention in promoting computer/communications, and perhaps even state control. Attempts at such a policy faltered because of the inability to galvanize the different parts of the state to coordinate and agree upon a course of action. The unpredictability of the direction of technological change also plagued policy makers. Policy stalled, while technology evolved. The market is a much more effective instrument in predicting and implementing technological change. Although there does not seem to be the same enthusiasm for extensive state participation today, those formulating policy might be motivated by similar assumptions regarding the importance of public policy in ensuring social and economic objectives. This would also seem to apply to questions of universal and affordable access.. . .

Notes

1   W.T. Stanbury, 'Redeeming the promise of Confluence: Analysis of Issues Facing the CRTC', in Steven Globerman, W.T. Stanbury, and Thomas A. Wilson (eds), *The Future of Telecommunications Policy in Canada* (Toronto: Bureau of Applied Research, Faculty of Commerce and Business Administration, University of British Columbia, and Institute for Policy Analysis, University of Toronto, April 1995).

2   For a thorough description of the technical details of time sharing, see Bryan Dewalt, *Building a Digital Network: Data Communications and Digital Telephony, 1950–1990* (Ottawa: National Museum of Science

and Technology, 1992), 20–3.

3   Dewalt, *Building a Digital Network*, 22.

4   'In Five Years, Computer Time Will Be Sold as Public Utility', in *The Financial Post*, vol. 61, 27 May 1967. See also 'Telephones Will Permit Users to Share Computer Operation'.

5   CN/CP Telecommunications later became Unitel Communications after Rogers Communications Inc. acquired CN's share in 1989.

6   Ian Rodger, 'CNCP Rocking Computer Boat', *The Financial Post*, vol. 63, 8 March 1969.

7   National Archives of Canada, Records of the Department of Communications, RG 97, vol. 185,

file D-2, 'Nerve System of the Nation, Communications Belong to the Public', in *Electronics and Communications/IEEE* (December 1968).

8 Eric Kierans, quoted in Hal Winter, 'Computerese Coming Easy, Says Kierans', *Montreal Gazette*, 11 November 1968.

9 National Archives of Canada, Records of the Department of Communications, RG 97, vol. 74, file 83; and F.G. Nixon, 'The Establishment of BTI', 6 September 1968.

10 National Archives of Canada, Records of the Department of Communications, RG 97, vol. 71, file 41, Memorandum, Task Force on the Organization of the Department of Communications—Purpose and Organization of National Policy Group, 10 September 1968.

11 National Archives of Canada, Records of the Department of Finance, RG 19, Interim Box 139, vol. 4963, file 4170-02, Part 2, Memorandum to the Cabinet, *Amendment to the Railway Act Concerning the Regulation of Telecommunications*, 30 April 1969.

12 Order-in-Council, Privy Council 1969-187, issued 28 January 1969.

13 National Archives of Canada, Records of the Department of Finance, RG 19, Interim Box 139, vol. 4963, file 4170–02, Part 2, Memorandum to the Cabinet, *Amendment to the Railway Act Concerning the Regulation of Telecommunications*, 30 April 1969, 2.

14 Trans-Canada Telephone System was renamed Telecom Canada in 1983 and reorganized as the Stentor Alliance in January 1992.

15 National Archives of Canada, Records of the Department of Finance, RG 19, Interim Box 139, vol. 4963, file 4170-02, Part 2, Memorandum to the Cabinet, *Amendment to the Railway Act Concerning the Regulation of Telecommunications*, 30 April 1969, 2.

16 Privy Council Office Records, Cabinet Document 13/18/70, Memorandum to Cabinet Re: Canadian Computer/Communications Agency, 15 September 1970, revised 15 October 1970.

17 National Archives of Canada, Records of the

18 National Archives of Canada, Records of the Department of Finance, RG 19, Interim Box 139, vol. 4963, file 4170-02, Part 2, Memorandum to the Cabinet, *Amendment to the Railway Act Concerning the Regulation of Telecommunications*, 30 April 1969, 4.

18 National Archives of Canada, Records of the Department of Finance, RG 19, Interim Box 139, vol. 4963, file 4170-02, Part 2, Memorandum to the Cabinet, *Amendment to the Railway Act Concerning the Regulation of Telecommunications*, 30 April 1969, 10.

19 National Archives of Canada, Records of the Department of Communications, RG 97, vol. 187, file I-11, 'Some Policy Questions Relating to Wired City', 5 May 1969.

20 Privy Council Office, Cabinet Document 543/69. Confirmation of the Decisions of Cabinet Committee, 26 May 1969.

21 National Archives of Canada, Records of the Treasury Board, RG 55, accession 198687/259, box 32, file 7148-02(1) FP, 'Brief on Public Policy and the Marriage of Communications Services with Computer Services', the Computer Group, 23 July 1969.

22 National Archives of Canada, Records of the Department of Communications, RG 97, accession 1989–90/185, box 13, file 5635-1, Part 1. Memorandum to the Cabinet, 'Participation by Telecommunications Carriers in Public Data-Processing', 23 February 1970, 1.

23 National Archives of Canada, Records of the Department of Finance, RG 19, vol. 4963, file 4170-02, Memorandum to the Cabinet on Participation by Telecommunications Carriers in Public Data-Processing, 23 February 1970, 2.

24 National Archives of Canada, Records of the Treasury Board, RG 55, accession 1986–7/359, box 33, interim 2, file 7148-06; and National Archives of Canada, Records of the Department of Finance, RG 19, vol. 4963, file 4170-02, Memorandum to the Cabinet on Participation by Telecommunications Carriers in Public Data-Processing, 23 February 1970, 5.

25 National Archives of Canada, Records of the Department of Finance, RG 19, vol. 4963, file

4170-02, Memorandum to the Cabinet on Participation by Telecommunications Carriers in Public Data-Processing, 23 February 1970, 5.

26 National Archives of Canada, Records of the Treasury Board, RG 55, accession 1986–7/359, box 33, interim 2, file 7148-06, Annex C to Memorandum to Cabinet, 23 February 1970. Summary of Responses to Questions 5 and 8 of the 'Study of the Relationships Between Common Carriers, Computer Services Companies and their Information and Data Systems', 1.

27 Privy Council Office, Cabinet Document 442-70, 9 April 1970.

28 Privy Council Office, Cabinet Document 13/18/80, Memorandum to Cabinet, Canadian Computer/ Communications Agency, 15 September 1970, revised 15 October 1970, 2.

29 Privy Council Office, Cabinet Document 13/18/80, Memorandum to Cabinet, Canadian Computer/ Communications Agency, 15 September 1970, revised 15 October 1970, 2–3.

30 National Archives of Canada, Records of the Department of Communications, RG 97, vol. 78, file 6900-10-3, D.F. Parkhill, 'Computer/ Communications Policy Options for Canada', speech to the Toronto Chapter of the Canadian Information Processing Society, 2 February 1971.

31 Parliament of Canada, House of Commons, Standing Committee on Transport and Communications, Parliament XXVIII, 3rd Session, *Minutes of Proceedings and Evidence*, no. 5, Respecting Estimates 1971–2, Department of Communications, 11 March 1971. Evidence of Minister of Communications, Hon. Eric Kierans.

32 Department of Communications, *Branching Out: Report of the Computer/Communications Task Force*, 2 volumes (Ottawa: Queen's Printer, 1972).

33 *Branching Out*, vol. 1, p. 80, passim pp. 183 and 197.

34 National Archives of Canada, Records of the Department of Communications, RG 97, vol. 407, file 7500-1031-2-A-4, Part 1; and H.H. Brune, 'The Feasibility of the National Computer Utility', November 9, 1973.

35 *Branching Out*, vol. 2, 18.

36 National archives of Canada, Records of the Department of Finance, RG 19, vol. 4934, file 3710-02(1), Accession Box 35, Economic Development, Division Computer/Communications General Series Policy Development Memorandum Re: Draft Memorandum to Cabinet Computer/Communications Policy; Memorandum from T.K. Shoyama to S.S. Reisman, February 6, 1973; and Memorandum from S.S. Reisman to A.E. Gotlieb, February 6, 1973.

37 National Archives of Canada, Records of the Department of Communications, RG 97, interim 117, accession 1985–1985/507, Box 001, File 1465-16; and B.A. Walker, 'Data Communications. Aspects of a Policy on Computer/Communications', January 15, 1972, p. 1.

38 National Archives of Canada, Records of the Department of Communications, RG 97, interim 117, accession 1985–1985/507, box 001, file 1465-16; and B.A. Walker, 'Data Communications. Aspects of a Policy on Computer/Communications', January 15, 1972, p. 4.

39 Walker, 'Data Communications'.

40 OECD, Study Panel on Policy Issues of Computer/Telecommunications Interaction, DAS SPR 71.63. Cited in Records of the Treasury Board, National Archives of Canada, RG 55, Accession 1986–87/359, Box 32, File 7148-02 (1) FP, Cabinet Memorandum on Computer/Communications Policy, 28 February 1973.

41 National Archives of Canada, Records of the Treasury Board, RG 55, accession 1986–7/359, box 32, file 7148-02 (1) FP, Cabinet Memorandum on Computer/Communications Policy, 28 February 1973.

42 National Archives of Canada, Records of the Department of Communications, RG 97, vol. 407, file 7500-1031-2-A-4, Part 1; and H.H. Brune, 'The Feasibility of the National Computer Utility', 9 November 1973.

43 Brune, 'The Feasibility of the National Computer Utility', 6.

Print Mass Media

Newspapers have long relied on institutions, not readers, to support their operations. Early newspapers in British North America, like the *Montreal Gazette* (started in 1793), turned to government patronage for the bulk of their finances. In the nineteenth century, newspapers aligned more closely with political parties, papers like George Brown's Reformist *Globe* (launched in 1844) and the Tory *Mail* (started in 1872). In most cities, two rival newspapers, one Liberal or Reform-affiliated, the other Tory, competed for readers—and voters at election time. The reliance on governments and parties waned as advertising revenues grew. By the early 1900s, about 75 per cent of revenues at large urban dailies came from advertising. Newspapers were beholden to a new set of organized interests, now commercial as opposed to political. When medical and state officials campaigned in the early 1900s to tighten controls on harmful patent medicines, newspapers were largely silent, fearful of alienating a key source of advertising. Similarly, Toronto newspapers for many years reported little unfavourable about Eaton's, a prominent newspaper advertiser.

While they are commercial operations, newspapers also embody disinterested ideals. As conveyers of news and commentary, they are said to educate and inform the public, performing an important democratic function. Freedom of the press is protected in Canada's Charter of Rights and Freedoms, part of a centuries-long tradition depicting a free press as a guardian of liberty and the rule of law, in opposition to arbitrary power and state tyranny. The newspaper is a civic institution, a sounding board and message board for local community and sprawling metropolis alike. When the commercial and civic natures of newspapers clash—as, for example, when a chain closes one of its papers or scales back local coverage to save money—the resulting controversy underscores the awkward blend of materialism and idealism constituting the modern newspaper.

Colonial newspapers redefined themselves in the early 1800s, Jeffrey McNairn argues. Weekly newspapers in Upper Canada (present-day Ontario) shifted their focus from commercial news and 'polite sociability', and themes like morals and manners, to 'democratic sociability', in which they functioned to reflect and mould public opinion. By the 1830s, an 'imagined' political community of readers came into being, abetted by the common practice of reading newspapers aloud in social settings and by the predominance of non-local news coverage. Provincial politics and international events were brought home and mediated by the weekly newspaper. Subscription levels grew rapidly, aided by the low subsidized postal rates newspapers enjoyed. By 1840, widespread newspaper readership fostered a nascent 'public sphere' in Upper Canada, a shared community embracing hamlet and metropole.

The public service creed of newspapers, as Minko Sotiron highlights, began to wane in the late nineteenth century. The era of the editor-publisher was replaced by that of the big city daily, whose high overhead and printing costs required mounting revenues, which came increasingly from advertising. To attract advertisers, newspapers worked to boost circulation, which meant dampening, though not eliminating entirely, their political outlook so as not to alienate readers. 'Objectivity' was the new journalistic creed, the 'inverted pyramid'—with its priority on the essential details—its signature style. News became a commodity, and not just political news but a hearty diet of 'human interest' stories designed to broaden circulation. The doctrine of readership trumped partisanship by the 1910s, resulting in widespread changes to the production, content, design, and marketing of newspapers, which by then shared little in common with their predecessors of the 1880s.

The modernization of newspapers coincided with the consolidation of the advertising industry. Russell Johnston, in his essay, examines the rise of the advertising agent, an intermediary between advertisers and newspapers selling ad space. The early ad agents were primarily space buyers, who developed detailed knowledge of the hundreds of daily and weekly newspapers and magazines in Canada—their circulation levels, political orientation, advertising rates, and publishing schedules. Initially aligned more closely with newspapers, the ad agents gradually shifted their primary allegiance to advertisers. Their fortunes rose with the upswing in national advertising, beginning in the 1890s, seen first with patent medicines and then with firms specializing in packaged goods, like Wrigley's Spearmint gum. As trademarked, nationally marketed goods proliferated, the need for national advertising grew, as did the skill sets of advertising agents like Anson McKim and J.J. Gibbons.

Beginning in the early 1900s, media owners and advertising agencies pursued scientific validations of the merits of advertising. Statistical and social-scientific methods were used to demonstrate advertising's effectiveness. By the 1920s, these methods included the use of representative sample surveys of consumers and media audiences. These marketing surveys, Daniel Robinson tells us, gauged people's buying habits, demographic features, and media use. As advertising's share of media revenues grew, so did the need for newspapers and magazines to demonstrate that their readers matched the consumer profiles of interest to prominent advertisers. Typically, these were middle- and upper-income earners, urban dwellers, and married women. Ad agencies and market research firms conducted dozens of surveys for advertisers and print and electronic media, notably for Maclean Publishing—owner of *Maclean's* and *Chatelaine*—which formed its own research department in 1943.

Alongside advertising, a prominent feature of the modern newspaper industry is concentrated ownership. Newspaper chains, like those of the Southam and Sifton families, began around the turn of the last century. By the mid-1900s, the Thomson family had built its newspaper empire. More recently, Conrad Black's Hollinger chain assumed national dominance. Today, Quebecor controls the Sun Media newspapers and French-language dailies like *Le Journal de Montréal*. Broadcaster CanWest Global Communications operates Southam, the country's largest newspaper chain. Media owners argue that consolidation creates operating efficiencies, freeing up resources for more features and local reporting.

Critics say it places profits before readers, much less the public interest, and typically results in cost-cutting and layoffs. As Richard Keshen and Kent MacAskill discuss, newspaper concentration was a hot-button issue in 1980 when the Trudeau government appointed Tom Kent to head a Royal Commission on the matter. Kent's recommendations to minimize newspaper concentration were lambasted by publishing interests and largely ignored by governments. Recently, however, there has been renewed interest in the Kent report as Canadians grapple with the democratic implications of media concentration.

Until recently, Canadian magazines have had a troubled history. Since the early 1900s, competition from American magazines has often been severe. In 1925, estimated sales of US magazines in Canada outpaced Canadian titles by a ratio of nearly 8:1, prompting Canadian magazine owners to lobby, largely unsuccessfully, for import restrictions on US publications. By the mid-1950s, American titles accounted for 80 per cent of the Canadian magazine market. The Canadian 'split-run' editions of *Time* and *Reader's Digest* (in essence, the US editions with modest additions of Canadian content) alone accounted for 37 per cent of all general-interest magazine ad revenues in 1955. Canadian magazines started to fold, beginning with the *Canadian Home Journal* in 1958, and followed two years later by *Mayfair*. In 1965, Ottawa made advertising expenditures in foreign-owned, split-run editions ineligible for tax deduction; however, it exempted *Time* and *Reader's Digest*, two of the largest players in the Canadian market. Only after these exemptions were lifted in 1976 did the situation improve for Canadian magazines. *Maclean's* moved to its current weekly format in 1978, and *Harrowsmith* and *Report on Business* were launched in 1976 and 1984 respectively. Ad revenues for Canadian magazines jumped 66 per cent between 1976 and 1980. Circulation rates for Canadian titles rose from 30 per cent of the total in 1971 to 68 per cent in 1992. While still vulnerable to US competition, the Canadian magazine industry stands on much firmer ground today than a generation ago.

Though not as old as newspapers, Canadian magazines have a long pedigree, as Peter Desbarats recounts. The first offerings in the early 1800s were short-lived affairs, but by century's end a number of magazines, like *The Week*, *Canadian Magazine*, and *Saturday Night*, had generated multi-year production runs. Literary in nature, they combined moral crusading with social and political commentary, appealing to relatively small numbers of upscale readers. Mass magazines at the turn of the century, like the American *Munsey's* and *Ladies Home Journal*, challenged this model. They spawned Canadian imitators, notably *Maclean's* and *Canadian Home Journal*, and, importantly, they enabled US competitors to capture broad shares of the Canadian market. Magazines were vulnerable to American competition in ways that newspapers were not. They targeted national, sometimes international, audiences, while newspapers were local in nature. As weeklies or monthlies, they had longer shelf lives, minimizing the effect of travel time. Advertised goods in US magazines were also available in Canada. The general interest content of consumer magazines meant they could be enjoyed by people of a different nationality. American dominance of the magazine market in Canada was a perennial topic of concern for domestic magazine publishers and government officials throughout much of the twentieth century.

More than a business operation, magazines promote cultural expression and collective self-consciousness among readers. In the case of *Chatelaine* during the 1960s, as Valerie Korinek highlights, readers sought to fashion their own 'cultural community of Canadian women', which at times was at odds with the 'preferred' meanings of the magazine's editors. The magazine's annual 'Mrs Chatelaine' contest, whose winners and finalists were mostly upper-middle-class, stay-at-home mothers, ignited a spark of opposition among some readers. In a letter to the editor, one reader proposed her own 'Mrs Slob' contest, and subsequent letter-writers spotlighted the absence of lower-income and working women from the 'Mrs Chatelaine' rosters. These women believed that Canada's only women's magazine needed to represent them, especially at a time when traditional notions of domesticity were giving way to feminist ideas and greater female participation in the workforce.

Questions for Critical Reading

1. What type of people were most likely to be newspaper readers in the 1830s? In what venues were newspapers read, and what sort of political community arose from this practice?
2. Discuss the relationship between newspaper publishing and the postal system in the 1820s and 1830s.
3. What key changes in content and design occurred in newspapers between the 1880s and 1920? What caused these changes?
4. How did newspaper readership change from the 1880s to 1920?
5. What social and economic factors account for the emergence and spread of advertising agencies in the late nineteenth century?
6. What different functions did the advertising agent perform between 1880 and 1920?
7. What social and economic trends contributed to the rise of sample surveys of media audiences and consumers?
8. What types of readership surveys did magazines and newspapers sponsor? How were they used?
9. What problems does newspaper concentration present to Canadian democracy?
10. What were the main findings and recommendations of the Kent Commission? Are they relevant to today's newspaper market?
11. What tensions exist between definitions of the newspaper as an 'important community institution' and as a commercial enterprise?
12. How did the Canadian magazine industry respond to American imports? Why were US magazines so successful in Canada?
13. Outline the various responses of the federal government to the American magazine presence in Canada. How effective were these?
14. Discuss the role that letter writing played in shaping *Chatelaine*'s community of readers. How does this work with today's women's magazines?
15. How might one reconcile the many feminist-related articles in *Chatelaine* with the ubiquitous 'service material' promoting domestic consumption?

Further Readings

Brennan, Patrick H. *Reporting the Nation's Business: Press-Government Relations During The Liberal Years, 1935–1957*. Toronto: University of Toronto Press, 1994.
   • This is the definitive account of relations between the press and the Liberal government during the King and St Laurent years.

Buxton, W.J., and C. McKercher. 'Newspapers, Magazines and Journalism in Canada: Towards a Critical Historiography'. *Acadiensis* 28, 1 (Autumn 1998), 103–26.

- This article provides a useful historiographical overview of recent works on newspapers and magazines.

Keserton, W.H. *History of Journalism in Canada*. Toronto: McClelland & Stewart, 1967.

- A dated but useful account of the history of journalism, this book deals extensively with newspaper operations.

Magder, Ted. 'Franchising the Candy Store: Split-Run Magazines and a New International Regime for Trade in Culture'. *Canadian–American Public Policy* 34 (April 1998), 1–66.

- Part of this deals with the history of split-run magazines in Canada, which is very informative and well written.

Rutherford, Paul. *A Victorian Authority: The Daily Press in Late Nineteenth-Century Canada*. Toronto: University of Toronto Press, 1982.

- This is the most authoritative history of nineteenth-century newspapers, including the popular press.

Spencer, David R. 'Bringing Down Giants: Thomas Nast, John Wilson Bengough and the Maturing of Political Cartooning'. *American Journalism* 15, 3 (1998), 61–88.

- This article discusses the satirical magazine *Grip*, whose political cartoons by Bengough and others lampooned elected officials.

Sutherland, Fraser. *The Monthly Epic: A History of Canadian Magazines 1789–1989*. Toronto: Fitzhenry & Whiteside, 1989.

- This book offers a descriptive, though not very analytical, overview of the Canadian magazine scene.

'The Most Powerful Engine of the Human Mind': The Press and Its Readers

Jeffrey L. McNairn

. . .

Little is yet known about what Upper Canadians read, how they understood it, and its impact, but most of their political information ultimately came from colonial newspapers. From the 1820s, their nature, number, distribution, and regular reports of parliamentary intelligence reflected their centrality to the public sphere. Physically, their readers met most obviously in newsrooms and taverns, but collectively they formed the colony's largest and most important voluntary association.

The author of 'Domestic Recreations', a series of essays published in 1819 by the *Kingston Chronicle*, described his move to the area as being 'transplanted from the midst of a lively circle into the woods'. He 'first felt like one who is suddenly struck dead and dumb.' Relieved only by the arrival of the newly established *Chronicle*, he announced his intention 'through its medium to talk to the public by *proxy*.' Such talk would lessen his sense of isolation. More important, it would allow him to participate in a cornerstone of polite sociability.

The man living in a city was 'blessed with the means of daily communicating his opinion to his fellow-mortals', making him feel that he 'has a vote in the general concerns of the world.' This 'reciprocal communication of sentiments and ideas' was 'one great subordinate principle upon which the existence of society depends'. It induced men to congregate and develop 'sympathy, friendship, or cordiality'. It broadened horizons, tempered selfishness and 'the desire of exhibiting himself to advantage, and communi-

cating importance to his opinions, induces him to cultivate his mind, and enlarge his ideas, by the acquisition of knowledge.'[1]

These claims on behalf of polite conversation echoed those of such eighteenth-century British commentators as the Third Earl of Shaftesbury. In the wake of the civil and religious strife of the previous century, polite conversation was thought capable of taming partisanship and bigotry. The principles of a new political order could be found in the measured exchange of opinion among gentlemen and in the cultural institutions and practices that promoted that exchange, rather than in a monarchical court or established church.[2] The British coffeehouse epitomized these principles. Similar associations, such as the Upper Canada Club or its short-lived predecessor, the Toronto Club House, devoted to 'kindly intercourse, and intellectual conversation', began to appear at the provincial capital by the end of the 1830s.[3] In 1819, however, the author of 'Domestic Recreations' was surely right to insist that other means were required in a colonial setting.

He found them in newspapers as 'organs of sentiment, and theatres for discussion'. Four positive consequences were to flow from an expanded colonial press. First, by diffusing knowledge, more newspapers would spark readers' curiosity and awaken 'that intelligent spirit, which will urge men to seek deeper sources of information'. Second, they would reduce apathy by calling attention to topics of common concern. Newspapers helped define those issues, furnished the necessary information, and encouraged readers to act. Third, newspapers,

Abridged from *The Capacity to Judge: Public Opinion and Deliberative Democracy in Upper Canada, 1791–1854*, by Jeffrey L. McNairn (Toronto: University of Toronto Press, 2000), 116–34. Reprinted by permission of University of Toronto Press.

much like agricultural societies, held up models worthy of emulation. They 'celebrate the bravery of the hero—they display the eloquences and genius of the orator—they communicate to mankind all over the world a mutual knowledge of the local and general concerns of each other, and encourage an emulation in arts, sciences, elegances and accomplishments.'

Finally, a flourishing press had important political implications. If free, newspapers became 'the organs through which the public feelings are manifested'. From the number of newspapers on each side of a public question 'a pretty correct estimate of the state of public opinion may generally be formed.' By disseminating information and argument, newspapers helped to create, not just reflect, public opinion. By exposing misdeeds, newspapers were also able 'to check the abuses which are often exercised by those who hold office.' Moreover, 'when a government encourages political discussion, the people are inspired with a confidence in their rulers,' who thereby appeared to have nothing to hide, but 'when public discussion is fettered . . . the people begin to be suspicious.'[4]

Writing in 1819, this essayist stood at a threshold in the history of the colonial press. Previously, most of the colony's handful of newspapers had provided their limited readership with commercial and foreign intelligence mixed with 'the opportunity to participate imaginatively in' what David Shields characterizes as 'a discursive analogue of genteel company'.[5] Frequent essays, letters, and copied articles on morals and manners, history, and literature, and the arts and sciences mimicked the form and content of polite conversation. A reader of the *Chronicle*'s predecessor complained of the frequent use of Greek and Latin, revealing much about the content and assumed readership of the early colonial press.[6] The essayist's first three goals—sparking curiosity, defining issues of common concern, and encouraging emulation—were evident in the earliest colonial newspapers.

The author of the 'Domestic Recreations'

added a fourth, explicitly political, role for newspapers. With a couple of notable exceptions, earlier newspapers had been wary of commenting on provincial politics. With the expansion of the periodical press called for by these essays soon under way, the political role threatened to engulf the other three. By the 1820s, diffusing the norms and content of polite sociability was nearly eclipsed as most newspapers became political weapons to create and reflect public opinion. Concurrently, most became less genteel in readership, tone, and intent. Democratic sociability was replacing its polite precursor.

Even if this essayist was right to think that newspapers could substitute for polite conversation, there were still significant differences between publication and verbal transmission or private correspondence.[7] Oral conversation reached only those in range of the speaker. The identity of the speaker influenced how his or her words were received. Conversation also demanded an immediate response, which might come from passion or insufficient reflection. In print, opinions could be abstracted from the person of their original author and could reach countless others. Authors might be unknown and could thus exercise influence only by their words, not their identities. The resulting conversation could appear as general in location and universal in applicability.

Not only did publication differ from oral communication, but publication predominantly in newspapers or pamphlets, rather than books, was also significant. The periodic and more ephemeral nature of newspapers, their increasing number, often clearer biases and errors, and fierce attacks on each other, fostered critical distance between reader and text. For some readers, surrounded by abundant publications, active choice was possible, even required. Other forms of public communication, such as sermons or charges to grand juries, were authorized by social superiors for consumers who were to be largely passive. They spoke to their audience. Colonial readers were increasingly faced with competing and combative newspapers, divorced from formal state or devotional practices. Few originated from obvious social superiors. They conversed with their audience. Readers were thus encouraged to adopt a more casual and skeptical attitude towards printed texts.[8] Finally, newspapers integrated their readers into a common political community. They participated in public debate by talking with each other and their readers. As Michael Warner argues, 'The reader does not simply imagine him- or herself receiving a direct communication or hearing the voice of the author. He or she now also incorporates . . . an awareness of the potentially limitless others who may also be reading. For that reason, it becomes possible to imagine oneself, in the act of reading, becoming part of an arena of the national people that cannot be realized except through such mediating imaginings.'[9]

The growth of the provincial press is the single best indicator of the size of that arena.[10] The first newspaper printed in Upper Canada, the *Upper Canada Gazette*, appeared in April 1793 as the official, subsidized organ of government. The first privately owned paper, the *Canada Constellation*, appeared five years later at Newark, after the *Gazette* had followed the government to York. By 1819, papers had been published in six towns, but only three (Niagara, Kingston, and York) could sustain a paper for any length of time. Thirty years later, 39 communities had supported at least one local newspaper. Some supported several; others saw repeated failures.

Ten of these communities boasted at least one newspaper between 1820 and 1829. Nine (excluding the capital) accounted for 19 different titles in this decade. Five (Brockville, Kingston, Markham, Niagara, and York) sustained at least two newspapers simultaneously at some point during the 1820s. The number of communities with a local press more than doubled during the next decade (from 10 to 23) while the number sustaining two or more simultaneously doubled

(from 5 to 10). Competitive local markets could be found in both the eastern (Cobourg, Prescott, Belleville, and Kingston) and western (Hamilton, St Catharines, St Thomas, London, and Niagara) sections of the colony as well as at the capital. Five of these ten supported more than two newspapers simultaneously at some point during the 1830s. In all, 73 newspapers were published in Upper Canada outside the capital between 1830 and 1839; 51 lasted at least a year. At the capital, 20 newspapers survived from the 1820s or were established during the following 10 years. Of these 20, at least 14 appeared regularly for a year or more during the 1830s. Of course, not all 65 papers (51 plus 14) lasting at least one year during the decade were published at the same time.

Comparing two specific years, 1828 and 1836, reveals more. In 1828, the colony faced a heated election after prolonged conflict over the rights of former American citizens then resident in Upper Canada. In July, at the time of the election, 8 communities had at least one paper and accounted for at least 14 titles (and perhaps as many as 16). Competition existed in at least 4 local markets (Brockville, Kingston, Niagara, and York). By 1836, these figures more than doubled: from 8 communities with at least one newspaper to 18; from approximately 18 different titles by the end of 1828 to 46 published some time in 1836; and from 4 competitive markets to 9 or 10. In the same period, the colony's population barely doubled. By the election in July 1836, the radical *Constitution* had been founded by William Lyon Mackenzie, joining 34 newspapers already in existence. It was the seventh in Toronto alone. In November, the *Statesman* appeared at Brockville and, with the addition of the daily *Royal Standard*, 8 newspapers were published at Toronto. The capital's population had yet to reach 10,000.

Impressive as they are, such figures can mislead. As we shall see, readers were not restricted to the place of publication. The number of titles also says little about the numbers of readers—except that, given the remarkable stability of printing technology across these decades, successful expansion was largely driven by demand. Such demand fuelled competition, which in turn further broadened the market.[11] Living at or near a competitive market could be important. Alternative interpretations of local issues and events were more likely from newspapers published in the region. The expansion and decentralization of the newspaper press to non-metropolitan centres provided not only local sources of information and a sense of connectedness to the larger community, but also the potential to produce pamphlets, broadsheets, and books locally. Editors frequently doubled as local booksellers and agents for other newspapers or bookstores. The nature and ideals of their profession also made them prominent promoters of libraries, newsrooms, schools, literary and agricultural societies, and mechanics' institutes. A disproportionate number also appear to have been Freemasons. Cultural production in the hinterlands was a key component of what David Jaffee aptly calls the 'village enlightenment'.[12]

The amount of purely local material in any colonial newspaper was, however, relatively small. Notices or minutes from local associations and coverage of local officials or local candidates for the assembly were fairly common, but most communities were still small enough that any community-based news was already known before it could appear in the local weekly. Newspaper editors usually found out about local events at the same time and in much the same way as fellow residents. To be sustainable, newspapers had to provide what was not otherwise readily available. That meant non-local material. In the days before the telegraph transformed them into vehicles for the rapid transmission of 'news', newspapers were especially suited to reproducing lengthy documents and commentary. Subscribers might bind their copies to form reference works.[13] Thus, much of what was printed at one location was relevant to readers elsewhere. This was particularly true of newspapers at the capital, where editors had easier

and more timely access to political news and documents. The number of presses at the capital underlines the importance of politics to readers throughout the colony. Shortly after founding the *Globe*, George Brown solicited 'communications' from an acquaintance at Brockville—'anything spicy—accounts of meetings—interesting trails—but especially political news'.[14] Nonetheless, a rigid division of labour had yet to develop between metropolitan and local papers or between papers serving sizeable market segments and those aimed at the public as a whole. By the 1830s, community papers were dominated by provincial politics, including reports of parliamentary debates, not local matters. There was no paper of record in Upper Canada like *The Times* of London. None approached such dominance during these decades.

Geographical diffusion was not just a matter of more communities sustaining a local newspaper. It also involved agents, private carriers, and the post office.[15] The *Weekly Post* was printed at York, but had agents in 19 other communities. Brockville's small conservative paper, the *Gazette*, was primarily intended to counter the moderate reform *Brockville Recorder*. Its agents were concentrated in eastern Upper Canada, but they could also be found at York, Hamilton, and Niagara, communities with one or more conservative organs of their own. In 1835, *The Reformer*, a radical Cobourg paper, had agents in at least 42 communities in Upper Canada. With the exception of the largest and most prestigious newspapers, most concentrated on their immediate hinterland, but sill sought subscribers further afield.[16]

Newspaper agents fulfilled a variety of roles.[17] Some were largely passive, merely forwarding subscriptions to the editor. Others were energetic salesmen. William Lyon Mackenzie mailed out the *Colonial Advocate* to people he hoped would subscribe. He then depended upon his agents to keep track of the individuals who took, refused, or returned these early issues. A few agents, including Marshall Spring Bidwell, distributed copies themselves. Charles Duncombe forwarded the names of 45 subscribers to Mackenzie and ordered 8 copies of each issue for himself. The acting agent at Ancaster tried to arrange for a prominent London merchant with a branch store in Ancaster to 'take at your office 150 or 200 Advocates weekly' for the Thames region, thus saving Mackenzie the postage.

Agents also had the daunting task of trying to collect payment from subscribers. Some forwarded advertisements, reported on local opinion and reaction to the newspaper, discussed editorials with Mackenzie, or relayed concerns about the ease and regularity of delivery. Agents also helped to distribute pamphlets and books published by newspaper editors, an especially valuable service for those readers without easy access to a bookseller.[18]

In return, agents might get a free subscription. A few, like Charles Duncombe, advanced their own political careers by distributing supportive newspapers, but this was far from typical. Most were motivated by confidence in the paper. Charles McDonell, Mackenzie's agent at Cornwall, told his fellow Scotsman, 'I feel really proud of a countryman conducting such an independent paper as the Advocate.' In 1825 Henry Lasher, agent at Bath, congratulated Mackenzie on the appearance of a new series of the *Advocate*. It could not 'be denied to be superior in every respect to any circulating newspaper ever yet published within this Province and which has therefore enabled me to procure the names annexed as subscribers.' In the same year, Jacob Keefer of Beaverdam was less fawning: 'If your political statements had not been such as I admired and approved I should not have taken that interest in the circulation of the Advocate for which you are pleased to express your satisfaction.'[19] Active agents believed in the newspaper they represented to their neighbours. By helping to construct a network of readers beyond its place of publication, they were vital to its survival.

Several newspaper agents and a few editors doubled as postmasters. The connection made considerable sense since many papers flowed through the mails. Despite frequent, not always unjustified, complaints about slow or irregular delivery, the expansion of the postal system remains impressive. There were seven postmasters in Upper Canada in 1791. By 1817 there were still only about a dozen but, by the end of 1831, more than a hundred post offices had been established in the province. A further 127 were added by 1841, roughly mirroring population growth. By then, there was a post office for about every 1800 Upper Canadians.[20] About ten communities had a post office for every one that had a newspaper.

Until 1841, the standard postal rate, set by British statute, failed to distinguish inland letters from newspapers or pamphlets. Determined on the basis of distance and the number of sheets, the rate would have effectively prohibited the dissemination of newspapers by post. It never appears to have been enforced. Instead, a highly preferential rate was arranged whereby the sender of a weekly newspaper was charged four shillings currency a year per copy or one pence per issue to mail it anywhere in the colony. The postage for an average letter was estimated to be eight or nine times higher. While critics charged that any postage was a 'tax on knowledge', editors from smaller centres had no interest in free postage. It would only allow papers from larger centres to swamp their smaller, local market. Thus, the preferential rate was low enough to encourage the distribution of colonial newspapers outside of their place of publication, but high enough to offer some protection to local markets.[21]

Editors could also send a copy free of charge to their colleagues. The resulting exchange of newspapers was the primary method of newsgathering. It created a free pool of material from which to copy and increased the number of potential readers for a copied item. As Anna Jameson noted, 'Paragraphs printed from English or American papers, on subjects of general interest, the summary of political events, extracts from books or magazines, are copied from one paper into another, til they have travelled round the country.'[22] If some editors copied only to criticize, they still informed their readers that other opinions were being expressed, what some of those opposing arguments were, where to find such analysis, and, finally, that readers of other newspapers were part of the same discursive community. Editors could also compare reports of the same event or issue in several papers and often commented on discrepancies.

Apparently editors often failed to pay all the postage they owed. They declared the number of issues being mailed and were 'seldom afterward questioned'. Postmasters had little incentive to count through bundles of newspapers. An official report concluded that the sums collected 'fall considerably short' of what the regulations suggested. 'In many cases, indeed, it appears that a fixed sum is paid under an old agreement, without any reference to the number of papers now mailed.'[23]

Thus in three ways—with a preferential rate, by supporting the exchange system, and through lax enforcement—the postal system subsidized the diffusion of newspapers. In the two Canadas, the system generated a gross revenue of £62,400 for the fiscal year ending July 1840. Only about £3,000 or less than 5 per cent came from distributing newspapers. For the same period, Deputy Provincial Postmaster General Thomas Stayner estimated that the number of newspapers and pamphlets circulated was slightly higher than the number of chargeable letters. Since newspapers were bulkier and heavier than most letters and often constituted about half of the items handled by postmasters, the preferential rate combined with its lax enforcement meant that the post office's other business heavily subsidized the transmission of newspapers.[24]

The existence of a network of agents and post offices meant that a colonial newspaper was potentially available to any Upper Canadian living close to one of these conduits. But to what extent did newspapers actually circulate beyond their own locality? How many Upper Canadians could afford to subscribe to a colonial newspaper even if its diffusion was subsidized by the post office? Of those who could afford to, how many actually subscribed?

Several contemporaries tried to use postal records to answer these questions. According to Anna Jameson, 427,567 papers circulated through the mails in 1836 among a population of about 370,000. Almost a quarter were transmitted free of charge, and, of those with postage paid, almost half originated in the United States or elsewhere.[25] This suggested a newspaper per week for as few as one family in seven. The proportion receiving a provincial paper and paying postage comes out as low as one in fifteen or sixteen. Jameson herself was impressed, but did so few families have direct access to a provincial newspaper? The *Christian Guardian* was rightly skeptical. In its review of *Winter Studies and Summer Rambles*, it asserted that 'in Upper Canada there is twice the number of newspapers read, in proportion to the population than there is in any country, city, town or village, in England.'[26]

If Jameson had read William Lyon Mackenzie's *Sketches of Canada* before leaving Britain, she missed the footnote in which he noted that, to avoid paying postage, colonial newspapers sent as many copies as possible by other means.[27] Yet Mackenzie had himself used the amount of postage paid by 19 colonial papers in 1831 to compare their circulation to his claimed printing of 1,000 to 1,250 *Colonial Advocates*. There is no way of knowing how many actually went to paying subscribers or if his claim was inflated, and, if so, by how much.[28] In 1831, the *Advocate* paid the second highest amount of postage, £57, or enough for about 265 yearly subscriptions. Mackenzie probably mailed more copies than he paid for; others were sent free of charge or by other means. Nonetheless, if we can give any credence to his figures, the post office transmitted as little as a third of his print run. . . .

Postal records give little sense of the overall number of readers. Guesses ranged wildly from one in ten in the Niagara area to one copy for almost every family in Hamilton.[29] In 1824, Mackenzie tried to be more systematic. He listed the print runs of his six competitors as follows: *Gazette* 300, *Observer* 290, *Chronicle* 350, *Upper Canada Herald* 420, *Brockville Recorder* 300, and *Gleaner* 190, for a total of 1,850. Mackenzie boasted a rapidly expanding readership 'and will now print upwards of 1,000 copies of the *Advocate*, weekly, being more then one third of all the papers printed in the Province.' Again, these figures cannot be verified. Marshall Spring Bidwell wrote from Kingston to add one hundred copies to Mackenzie's total for the *Upper Canada Herald*. The *Niagara Gleaner* accused Mackenzie of attempting to steal advertisers by pegging its circulation at only 190, claiming to have printed an average of 300 copies a week for the past seven years.[30]

While Mackenzie's individual numbers were disputed, the average, just over 300, seems reasonable. If the seven papers in 1824 printed no more than 2,500 copies a week, only about one family in ten had direct access to a newspaper each week. The proportion in Toronto (where the *Gazette*, the *Observer*, and shortly the *Advocate* were published) and Kingston (home to the *Chronicle* and the *Herald*) was probably higher. Others had indirect access, but totals remained small.

Five years later, in 1829, when Thomas Dalton established the *Patriot* at Kingston (the fourth local paper), Mackenzie forecast that 6,000 issues would soon be printed by 18 colonial papers, which would 'average a number a week among every five families'.[31] In the five years from 1824 to 1829 the population had increased by only a quarter, but the number of families receiving a weekly paper had probably doubled. During the next decade, the newspaper press continued to grow faster than the population, although far less dramatically. Mackenzie

was not alone in noticing the sudden expansion at the close of the 1820s. The St Catharines *Farmers' Journal* fretted that many of the new publications could not be sustained 'and yet all seem to prosper . . . Should these, together with the older Journals . . . receive as liberal support as present appearances indicate, it will auger well for the moral and intellectual improvement of their patrons, and the rising generation.'[32] The *Journal* thought it saw the dawning of a new era for the colony. It saw the beginnings of the public sphere.

During the 1830s, several papers, especially those at the capital, printed considerably more than the average of 300 to 350 copies per week used here for the previous decade. By 1831, the *Christian Guardian* was paying to mail at least 1,000 copies per week and claimed 1,900 subscribers, up almost 300 from the year before.[33] The *Correspondent & Advocate* claimed 1,400 subscribers in 1834, and two years later Mackenzie claimed that 1,250 subscribed to the *Constitution*. Given that these were among the leading papers, such figures are not incredible. Newspapers outside the capital may still have averaged around 350 copies, although several claimed substantially higher print runs: in 1832 the *Brockville Antidote* and the *St Thomas Liberal* claimed 645 and 600 subscribers respectively.[34]

There is no entirely satisfactory way to compare the proportion of families receiving their own weekly newspaper in 1829 (about one in five) with the proportion in 1836. To be cautious, if we assume that four of the newspapers at the capital had a circulation of three times our base average of 350 (or 1,050—still well below each of their claims), and that three other papers had twice that average, almost 16,000 newspapers would have been printed each week.[35] While a conservative estimate, this is still well over four times Anna Jameson's conclusion from postal records and translates into a weekly paper for about one in four families. The press continued to expand. According to the *Christian Guardian*, by 1841 the more than 50 newspapers and journals printed in Upper Canada had a combined weekly circulation of at least 40,000. This was the equivalent of one copy for every two families. Some families subscribed to several journals, but any over-counting this may represent is compensated for by using all families as our universe rather than only those families who *could* have subscribed (that is, minus those that were too isolated or in which none could read). Regardless, the community of newspaper subscribers had outgrown the electorate.[36]

The ability to join this community was partially set by income, although for many geography and family priorities were probably greater determinants. Who could afford the fifteen or twenty shillings a year that most weekly newspapers charged in the 1830s?[37] The lowest advertised wage rate for craftsmen Douglas McCalla found in that decade was about five shillings per day; it could reach almost twice as much. Thus, artisans and some journeymen could subscribe to a colonial newspaper for about three days' wages. Again relying on McCalla, with a bushel of wheat selling for five shillings in 1832, a year's subscription was the equivalent of three or four bushels. The conversation rate was important since subscribers often paid in kind.[38]

Newspaper subscriptions still represented a considerable investment or unattainable luxury for many. For male farm labourers earning fifty to sixty shillings a month or for shantymen in the Ottawa Valley timber trade earning as little as forty shillings a month, the price of a subscription was measured by the week rather than by the day.[39] Many subscribers were constantly in arrears. They paid only what and when they could—to the constant complaint of proprietors. It was not uncommon for papers to threaten to stop sending copies to subscribers only when they were more than a year behind in payment— a standard feature of the colony's credit system and one that created opportunities to receive numerous copies without incurring the expense.[40]

A profile of potential subscribers emerges.

Merchants and professionals, clerks and shopkeepers, skilled artisans and journeymen, and most relatively established farm families could afford a newspaper subscription. Within this disparate group, inclination was probably crucial in determining whether or not to subscribe for any given year. Few women probably subscribed independent of their fathers or husbands.[41] William Lyon Mackenzie counted Mississauga Natives at Credit River among his subscribers[42] and a paper was established for unilingual Germans at Berlin in 1835. Only the most isolated or transient, unskilled wage labourers and others with highly unstable employment, marginal farmers, and families in which no one could read were largely absent from the community of newspaper *subscribers*.

Neither members of these groups nor those who chose not to subscribe were thereby excluded from the community of newspaper *readers*. Each copy probably had multiple readers. Mackenzie was informed that non-subscribers were reading copies of the *Advocate* 'for by their appearance they must have made the tour of Brockville half a dozen times.'[43] Such indirect access was possible through family and friends, at local stores, inns and taverns, and through voluntary associations, especially libraries, newsrooms, and mechanics' institutes. Some may also have found newspapers at their place of work or where they boarded. Anne Hales of Kingston insisted that '*they* only take the *Christian Guardian* for the servants to read.'[44] While the Hales family may have enlisted the Methodist organ to provide moral instruction for their domestic help, they also provided them with some of the most extensive reports of parliamentary debates. Finally, Michael Katz found boarders in mid-century Hamilton predominantly in the homes of the relatively affluent—those most able to subscribe to newspapers—not in the homes of the poor.[45]

Joseph Howe claimed that everyone who desired it had access to his *Novascotian*. 'The merchant reads it to his customers round the

counter; the smith drops his hammer for a reference to its pages; and it passes from hand to
hand, around each farmer's fire all over the broad
bosom of the country whose name it bears.' A
subscriber to one of Howe's competitors found
himself at the centre of a micro-public.
'Generally on the evening after the paper comes
to hand, a few of the neighbours assemble in my
house . . . a reader is appointed, who after drawing his chair up to the head of the table, trim-
ming the candle, coughing, and clearing his
throat, unceremoniously bawls out *"Silence"*—
and immediately all are attention. After the reading is over, then come the remarks.'[46] Reading
aloud and otherwise sharing newspapers encouraged critical discussion.

Patterns of community and family reading in
Upper Canada await their historian. John
Howison, one of the more caustic travellers to
the colony, recorded the scene when the landlord
entered the parlour of his tavern 'and having
seated himself among the seamstresses [includ-
ing his wife], began to read articles of foreign
intelligence. His female auditors listened with
undivided attention until he had got through a
paragraph and then they all broke silence at once
and commented with much prolixity upon what
it contained.'[47] If Howison, like everyone else,
thought some were less suited to the effective use
of their reason in public than others (French
seamstresses in this case), the reading aloud and
discussion of newspapers in mixed audiences
did not itself strike him as unusual.

The *Artisan*, founded in 1848, may have been
the colony's first nonreligious paper to appeal
explicitly to women as well as men in its prospectus. Some classes of women may also have had
fewer points of direct access to newspapers than
did their male relations with greater recourse to
certain types of taverns and voluntary associations. Yet women had long read and commented
on the colonial press. While political commentary was usually written as if its readers were

male, the goods and services advertised on the
same page acknowledged women as readers as
well as consumers. Wives might also manage
newspapers during the absence of their editor-
husbands and retain ownership as widows.[48]

If women were not systematically excluded
from the community of readers, neither were the
illiterate. The best estimates suggest that, by
1840, about 80 per cent of Upper Canadian
adults could read and write, compared to only
about two-thirds of British men and half of
British women. (Earlier colonial patterns probably varied considerably and are far less clear.[49])
The high rate by 1840 was partly the product of
individual and family initiative combined with
private academies and an increasingly state-
directed system of elementary schools. Considerable work had, however, also been done by hundreds of free Sunday schools devoted to basic literacy. Almost all were products of local, interde-
nominational, voluntary associations—yet another contribution of voluntary associations to
the public sphere.[50] Reflecting its appreciation of
the impact of these efforts to school the young,
the *Brockville Recorder* urged the illiterate to put
newspapers 'into the hands of your children,
direct them to read their contents aloud'.[51]
Reading aloud in non-familial settings further
mitigated against inadequate literacy.

Despite its impressive reach, the community
of newspaper readers was not universal. Access
was easier for some groups than others.
Subscribers formed an even smaller, if partly
self-selected, association. Editors exaggerated
and assumed a community of interest when they
spoke of 'the people' rather than the public of
newspaper readers. Yet for those who had lived
through the exponential growth of the press
over less than two decades, it must have been
easy to extrapolate from that recent past to a
future possibility that already seemed visible on
the horizon.

. . .

Notes

1 'Domestic Recreations', *Kingston Chronicle*, 5 Feb. 1819; 5 and 19 March 1819.

2 Lawrence E. Klein, *Shaftesbury and the Culture of Politeness: Moral Discourse and Cultural Politics in Early Eighteenth-Century England* (Cambridge: Cambridge University Press 1994), 96–101; Marvin B. Becker, *The Emergence of Civil Society in the Eighteenth Century: A Privileged Moment in the History of England, Scotland, and France* (Bloomington: Indiana University Press 1994), 43–4, 55–6, 69; and Dena Goodman, *The Republic of Letters: A Cultural History of the French Enlightenment* (Ithaca: Cornell University Press 1994), 5, 114, 120–2.

3 *Royal Standard*, 9 and 11 Nov. 1836.

4 'Domestic Recreations', *Kingston Chronicle*, 5 Feb. 1819; 5 and 19 March 1819.

5 David S. Shields, *Civil Tongues: Polite Letters in British America* (Chapel Hill: University of North Carolina Press 1997), 12.

6 Timothy Peaseblossom (?), *Kingston Gazette*, 23 March 1816.

7 See Roger Chartier, *The Cultural Origins of the French Revolution*, trans. Lydia G. Cochrane (Durham: Duke University Press 1991), 26, 31–2, 65–6; Michael Warner, *The Letters of the Republic: Publication and the Public Sphere in Eighteenth Century America* (Cambridge, MA: Harvard University Press 1990); and Richard D. Brown, *Knowledge Is Power: The Diffusion of Information in Early America, 1700–1865* (New York: Oxford University Press 1989).

8 David Jaffee, 'The Village Enlightenment in New England, 1760–1820', *William and Mary Quarterly*, 3rd Ser., 47, no. 3 (July 1990), 342–3. For contrasting evaluations of the theory of an eighteenth-century 'reading revolution', see Chartier, *Cultural Origins of the French Revolution*, 89–90, and David D. Hall, 'The Uses of Literacy in New England, 1600–1850', in William L. Joyce, D.D Hall, Richard D. Brown, and John B. Hench, eds., *Printing and Society in Early America* (Worcester: American Antiquarian Society 1983), esp. 21–34.

9 Warner, *Letters of the Republic*, xiii.

10 Statistics in the following paragraphs were calculated from Brian J. Gilchrist, *Inventory of Ontario Newspapers, 1793–1986* (Toronto: Micromedia 1987).

11 David Vincent, *Literary and Popular Culture: England, 1750–1914* (Cambridge: Cambridge University Press 1989), 11, 210.

12 Jaffee, 'The Village Enlightenment', 333, and Richard D. Brown, 'The Emergence of Urban Society in Rural Massachusetts, 1760–1820', *Journal of American History* 61, no. 1 (June 1974), 43–4.

13 Peter G. Goheen, 'The Changing Bias of Interurban Communications in Nineteenth-Century Canada', *Journals of Historical Geography* 16, no. 2 (1990), 183, and Brown, *Knowledge Is Power*, 36–8. The *Western Herald*, 10 Feb. 1838, encouraged more of its readers to preserve their copies in bound volumes.

14 National Archives of Canada, George Brown Papers, Brown to W.B. Richards, 8 March 1844.

15 The role of peddlers in the transmission of texts has not been studied, but see Brian S. Osborne, 'Trading on a Frontier: The Function of Peddlers, Markets, and Fairs in Nineteenth-Century Ontario', in Donald H. Akenson, ed., *Canadian Papers in Rural History*, 2 (Gananoque, ON: Langdale Press 1980), 61–8. Critics charged that itinerant preachers increased the speed of delivery and geographic reach of the *Christian Guardian*.

16 *Weekly Post*, 1 March 1821; *Brockville Gazette*, 22 Aug. 1828; and *The Reformer*, 24 Feb. 1835.

17 Information on agents is from Archives of Ontario, Mackenzie-Lindsey Papers, especially the letters to Mackenzie from M.S. Bidwell, 19 June 1824; G. Tiffany, 6 Jan. 1825; Henry Lasher, 11 Dec. 1825; Charles McDonell, 20 Feb. 1826; Jacob Keefer, 25 Feb. 1825; Matthew Crooks, 9 June 1826; and Charles Duncombe, 15 April 1831.

18 E.g. *The Reformer*, 29 Dec. 1835.

19 George Brown Papers, Brown to W.B. Richardson,

8 March 1844.

20 *Report of the Commissioners*, app. F, no. 16.

21 *Report of the Commissioners*, esp. app. D and O. The Province of Canada experimented with free transmission but reverted to a preferential rate. American newspapers mailed to Canadians were charged a fairly nominal rate of one penny per issue, while, after 1834, British newspapers arriving by the Halifax Packets travelled to their Canadian destination free of charge.

22 Jameson, *Winter Studies and Summer Rambles*, 153.

23 *Report of the Commissioners*.

24 Ibid.

25 Jameson, *Winter Studies and Summer Rambles*, 153. For the *Report of the Commissioners* Stayner estimated that postage was paid on 600,000 sheets (newspapers and pamphlets) by their printers in both Canadas and a further 50,000 were sent by someone else. Non-printers also paid to import 210,000 sheets from the US. He estimated that a further 596,000 sheets were posted free of charge, including 320,000 sheets from Britain via the Halifax Packets.

26 *Christian Guardian*, 20 Feb. 1839. See also *Colonial Advocate*, 1 Nov. 1832.

27 Mackenzie, *Sketches of Canada*, 451n.

28 *Colonial Advocate*, 19 Sept. 1833.

29 *Niagara Gleaner*, 16 March, and A Subscriber, *Western Mercury*, 11 April 1833. I have adopted an average household size of six. For the household size of 5.8 in Hamilton and 6.4 in Peel in 1851, see Michael B. Katz, *The People of Hamilton, Canada West: Family and Class in a Mid-Nineteenth-Century City* (Cambridge, MA: Harvard University Press 1975), 221, and David Gagan, *Hopeful Travellers: Families, Land, and Social Change in Mid-Victorian Peel County, Canada West* (Toronto: University of Toronto Press 1981), 69.

30 *Colonial Advocate*, 5 Aug. 1824; Mackenzie-Lindsey Papers, Bidwell to Mackenzie, 24 Aug. 1824; and *Gleaner*, 21 Aug. 1824.

31 *Colonial Advocate*, 8 Oct. 1829. Mackenzie was using the reasonable averages of about 330 issues per newspaper and 6.7 people per household. When considering relaunching the *Western Herald*

at Sandwich, the publisher refused to 'incur the risk of another publication, till we are possessed of at least three hundred and fifty subscribers'.

32 *Farmers' Journal*, 23 Dec. 1829.

33 *Christian Guardian*, 16 Nov. 1831, and 11 Dec. 1830.

34 J.J. Talman, 'The Newspapers of Upper Canada a Century Ago', *Canadian Historical Review* 19, no. 1 (March 1938), 12, and Mary Lucinda MacDonald, 'Literature and Society in the Canadas, 1830–1850', Ph.D. thesis, Carleton University (1984), 68–9.

35 Thus, only about one-quarter to one-third of newspapers were transmitted by the post.

36 *Christian Guardian*, 27 Oct. 1841.

37 Macdonald, 'Literature and Society', table 1, 62. Most early papers charged a similar amount; Carl Benn, 'The Upper Canadian Press, 1793–1815', *Ontario History* 70, no. 2 (June 1978), 100. Thus, absolute cost remained stable despite economic fluctuations.

38 Douglas McCalla, *Planting the Province: The Economic History of Upper Canada, 1784–1870* (Toronto: University of Toronto Press 1993), 114–15, 336–7. As late as 12 December 1838, the *Chronicle & Gazette* advertised its need for firewood for the benefit of those who paid their subscription in that commodity.

39 McCalla, *Planting the Province*, 55, and Terry Crowley, 'Rural Labour', in Paul Craven, ed., *Labouring Lives: Work & Workers in Nineteenth-Century Ontario* (Toronto: University of Toronto Press 1995), 24.

40 McCalla, *Planting the Province*, 144 and *Gleaner*, 24 April 1830.

41 Of the original 33 subscribers to the *Colonial Advocate* at York, only one, a tavern owner, was a woman. Mackenzie-Lindsey Papers, W. Beggins to Mackenzie, 31 Aug. 1824.

42 Mackenzie, *Sketches of Canada*, 133.

43 Mackenzie-Lindsey Papers, Thomas S. Maitland to Mackenzie, 8 March 1825.

44 Egerton Ryerson to Samuel Junkin, 30 March 1838, in C.B. Sissions, *Egerton Ryerson His Life and Letters*, 1 (Toronto: Clarke, Irwin 1937), 438.

45 Katz, *People of Hamilton*, 36–8, 77, 231–2.

46 *Nova Scotian*, 1 March 1832 and *Colonial Patriot*, 28 March 1828 in J.S. Martell, 'The Press of the Maritime Provinces in the 1830s', *Canadian Historical Review* 19, no. 1 (March 1938), 47.

47 Howison, *Sketches of Upper Canada*, 207–8.

48 *Artisan*, 12 Oct. 1848; Kathleen Wilson, *The Sense of the People: Politics, Culture and Imperialism in England, 1715–1785* (Cambridge: Cambridge University Press 1995), 41n; and H.P. Gundy, 'Publishing and Bookselling in Kingston since 1810', *Historical Kingston* 10 (Jan. 1962), 26, on Hugh Thomson's wife managing their Kingston newspaper while he attended the assembly at York. She assumed ownership after his death.

Thomas Dalton's widow retained the *Patriot*.

49 Gordon Darroch and Lee Soltow, *Property and Inequality in Victorian Ontario: Structural Patterns and Cultural Communities in the 1871 Census* (Toronto: University of Toronto Press 1994), 119. For a summary, see Susan E. Houston and Alison Prentice, *Schooling and Scholars in Nineteenth-Century Ontario* (Toronto: University of Toronto Press 1991), 84–5.

50 Allan Greer, 'The Sunday Schools of Upper Canada', *Ontario History* 67, no. 3 (Sept. 1975), 173.

51 *Brockville Recorder*, 17 Jan. 1834. How were the illiterate to read such advice? See also Bird, *English Woman in America*, 317.

Public Myth and Private Reality
Minko Sotiron

By the end of the nineteenth century the commercialization of Canada's English-language press had spread from Montreal and Toronto to other cities. This caused a growing difference of opinion between the public, which believed that the press's role was to educate and to guard society's freedoms, and the publishers, who thought that the prime purpose of newspapers was to make money by attracting more readers and thus more advertisers. Publishers increased their readership by making newspapers more sensational and by adding women's, sports, and entertainment features, which resulted in a dilution of the press's educative function. The public held on to the nineteenth-century reality of the press as political advocate and champion of a better society, while the publishers believed in the twentieth-century reality of newspapers as enterprises driven by business considerations.

The concept of the press as a servant of the public interest had begun to appear in the 1860s and blossomed under the 'civic populism' movement of the late Victorian era. In this period, newsmen and others increasingly assigned the newspaper altruistic roles for the benefit of the public. Indeed, it was claimed that the formation of the Canadian Publishers' Association (CPA) in 1859 was 'to promote the influence of the press as a factor in the welfare of the State'.[1]

The idea of the newspaper as public educator grew in popularity in Canada during the latter part of the nineteenth century. In 1876 the *London Advertiser*'s William Cameron spoke to a CPA convention about the newspaper's 'power to educate'.[2] The concept of the newspaper as teacher also became intertwined with the concept of the press as public defender. In 1880, for example, A.J. Matheson of the *Perth Expositor* described the recently assassinated George Brown as a believer 'in the newspaper as a public educator and as a power to defend the rights and privileges of the people'.[3] The popular belief in the press's responsibility to educate the public stemmed from the partisan nature of nineteenth-century Canadian newspapers. 'Responsible government' was the nineteenth-century editor's greatest concern. An emphasis on the editorial role of newspapers and on their function as a public record of legislative proceedings contributed to the idea of the press as a 'public utility' to educate the people. Joseph Howe's libel trial, in which he successfully played the role of defender of the public interest against the depredations of Family Compact favouritism, and William Lyon Mackenzie's adoption of a similar stance in Ontario helped to further the notion of the press as a 'Fourth Estate'. Thus, the idea arose that the press had a public responsibility and was more than a mere commercial enterprise.

By the 1890s, however, this vision of the educative function of the press was threatened. Contemporary observers were concerned that the growing emphasis on boosting circulation and the increasing dependence on advertising signalled an increase in sensationalism, trivial news, and entertainment at the expense of editorial opinion, social analysis, and serious commentary. Others believed that the decline in importance of the editorial indicated that the newspaper was losing its power to do good and its educative purpose. They pointed to the

Abridged from *From Politics to Profit: The Commercialization of Canadian Daily Newspapers, 1890–1920,* by Minko Sotiron (Montreal and Kingston: McGill–Queen's University Press, 1997). Reprinted by permission of McGill–Queen's University Press.

famous dictum of celebrated *Manchester Guardian* editor C.P. Scott: 'A newspaper has two sides to it. It is a business like any other, and has to pay in the material sense in order to live. But it is more than a business; it is an institution; it reflects and influences the whole community . . . its primary office is the gathering of news. At the peril of its soul, it must see that the supply is not tainted.'[4] Mindful of this danger, Toronto *Globe* business manager J.F. Mackay noted in 1903 that the 'press as presently constituted is a commercial venture', which meant it was 'weakening in its social role' as the watchdog of the public interest. Its increasing dependence on advertising, he warned, was leading to a fear of taking 'strong stands', which in turn would lessen its social influence. Mackay contended that 'so soon as the newspaper has become entirely commercialized so soon will the press have fallen from its high estate.'[5]

Indeed, some feared that the newspaper industry was falling under the sway of the huge trusts and corporations that dominated other industries. A.H.U. Colquhoun warned in 1902 that the 'danger is not imaginary' of a 'newspaper trust which might be organized by persons with large selfish ends to serve in gaining the ear of the public'.[6] Echoing these fears in 1905, Goldwin Smith expressed concern about the changing nature of the press: 'Is it succumbing to the omnipotence of wealth? Is the Tribune of the people becoming the slave of the millionaire?'[7]

The daily press itself addressed this issue. In a story headlined 'Does Capital Threaten Liberty of the Press?' the *Toronto Star* commented on the public's fear that newspapers had come under the influence of monopolistic business concerns. According to the *Star*, people believed that this state of affairs was leading to conflicts of interest, and that newspapers now were being run like any other commercial enterprise. The newspapers' 'sole object [was] . . . making money for the proprietors,' who in turn depended on the advertisers for the greater proportion of their revenues. Although the *Star* dismissed

public fears of a corporative threat to press freedom as a 'bugaboo', it admitted that there were grounds for suspicion, especially since newspapers had become assets of immense value. If a newspaper came onto the market, the *Star* noted, 'it [was] impossible on account of the magnitude of the enterprise for anyone but a millionaire or a company of men with large means to become the purchaser.' The *Star* added that 'the day of the editor-proprietor, running a paper solely for the opportunity of expressing his own opinions', was gone. 'A man may be willing sometimes to pay a lot to see his composition in print, but he is not likely to pay two or three hundred thousand dollars for it.'[8]

The *Star* put its finger on the dramatic transformation of the daily newspaper from a small undertaking, published more for political influence than commercial gain, to a valuable property operated for profit. As newspapers everywhere grew in size and value between 1890 and 1920, publishers adopted business methods and goals, first to encourage the newspaper's growth and to protect the successful newspaper's competitive edge, and then to sustain the owner's increasingly valuable financial interest in the enterprise.

A parliamentary exchange in 1898 between Sir Charles Tupper and John Ross Robertson, founder of the *Toronto Telegram* and a pioneer of the popular and commercial press, illustrated the significant gap between the public understanding of the press's primary role and that of the publishers. Tupper, a supporter of the press, argued in favour of the subsidies that substantially reduced newspaper postal rates, which Postmaster General William Mulock was attempting to cancel. Speaking against the subsidies, Robertson dismissed the idea of the newspaper as public educator and pointed out that a 'newspaper is published to make money, and its educational influence is merely an incident in the business of making money'.[9] . . .

Despite these pragmatic views, the idea of the newspaper as educator grew during the twentieth century. Several contributors to the 1901 collection of essays on *Journalism and the University* emphasized the newspaper's educational function. Joseph Flavelle bought the Toronto *News* in 1902 because he believed in the 'service' the newspaper would render to the 'administration of public affairs'.[10] The newly purchased *News* proclaimed that its 'province' was to educate the public. On this account, said the *Canadian Printer and Publisher* (CPP), Flavelle should be considered a public benefactor, because 'Mr Flavelle has made a great deal of money, far more than a man of his quiet but liberal tastes can ever use. He might have endowed universities or established free libraries, but he has adopted the far more practical policy of educating the people. He endows newspapers; good newspapers are the universities of the people.'[11]

The two most prominent Canadian editors of the time, J.W. Dafoe and J.S. Willison, certainly believed that it was their mission to educate the people and improve society. Willison considered the press 'necessarily and legitimately an agitator, very often a voice crying in the wilderness always, if it performs its true functions, seeking to better social and material conditions'. Furthermore, 'it is the business of the journalist to develop public opinion, to liberalize and energize the social and industrial forces, to utter the voice of the people.'[12] . . .

The press's view of itself as a kind of public utility persisted after World War I. In 1922 the *Ottawa Journal*'s P.D. Ross stated that the newspaper's function was 'to guide and mould public opinion' and 'to support all good causes . . . and fight wrongs or rank injustice'.[13] Celebrating its ninetieth anniversary on 5 March 1934, the Toronto *Globe* trumpeted its tradition of championing public rights and 'honesty in administration' and of waging 'war against privilege and corruption'.[14] . . .

It is significant that the men who discussed the inevitable contradiction between public and industry perceptions of the press's function were those who either owned a newspaper or were involved with the management of one. The *Toronto Star*'s Joseph Atkinson astutely observed that the public laid stress on the educational side of the press, while 'the commercial is left entirely out of sight, as though there was nothing to be done but for the editors to write instructive articles which would be eagerly bought by the public.' Atkinson underlined the economic reality of newspaper publishing, since 'this everlasting question of subsistence lies at the root of journalism.' He admitted, however, that a newspaper may be so far 'governed by the question of profits that it may become a trading concern without other aims than dividends. Or a newspaper may make mere circulation its god, sacrificing everything to boast of figures.'[15]

Atkinson's managing editor, John R. Bone, considered that commercialism posed the greatest danger to freedom of the press, and that advertising was the spearhead of this danger. '"I will take my advertisement out" is a threat which confronts the editor almost every day he picks up his pen. The threat does not need to be spoken, the editor knows it is there. It takes courage to disregard it.'[16] J.S. Willison likewise warned of the 'growing power of corporations and the influence of great aggregations of capital in a few hands'. This state of affairs presented a 'real danger' to the press, which had no 'mission in the world except as the articulate voice of the plain unorganized and unsubsidized people'.[17]

These fears of a growing commercialization of the press were not illusory. Beginning in the 1890s publishers and their business managers reduced the role of the editorial page and decreased the amount of political coverage and social commentary in their newspapers. More space was devoted to news and entertainment. The amount of sensational and trivial material, such as 'human-interest' stories, increased. By 1917 *Manitoba Free Press* editor John Dafoe disapprovingly noted that 'publishers had dropped into the notion that editorial opinion was a sort of luxury, perhaps a useless luxury in the paper. They looked doubtingly at the editorial page, begrudging the space given to mere opinion, and figuring out how many comic features or other "real" circulation builders they could accommodate in that space.'[18]

The decline, in the 1880s, of the editorial page in the more popular big-city dailies such as the *Star* in Montreal and the *Telegram*, *News*, and *World* in Toronto presaged an industry-wide diminution of its importance in the twentieth century. By 1898 many papers had abandoned the practice of printing verbatim accounts of parliamentary debates, another sign of the shift away from an ethos of public service towards an emphasis on entertainment and profitability. The *Toronto Star* commented in 1905 that 'the debates of the House . . . have become a comparatively unimportant news feature.'[19]

The declining importance of the editorial page perhaps explains why Hugh Graham of the *Montreal Star* toyed at one time with the idea of getting rid of his newspaper's editorial page.[20] F.A. Acland, the Toronto *Globe's* business manager, figured that in the 1890s the paper could have doubled its profits without its editorial columns.[21] In 1909 an eastern daily dropped its editorial page because its management believed that the public was more interested in a 'straight, unvarnished news service than in the opinion of the editors on the issues of the day'.[22] At the CPA's convention in the same year, a sign of the lessening importance of the editorial pages was that the association actually took up the question whether the editorial page was necessary.[23]

Even such resolutely partisan newspapers as the *Winnipeg Free Press* began to de-emphasize the editorial page in favour of increased news coverage. In 1904, for example, editor Dafoe added commentary on international events to his editorial pages, which formerly had included only expressions of political partisanship and anti-imperial rhetoric. When publisher Clifford Sifton resigned from the federal cabinet the next year, the *Free Press* began to move even more determinedly away from political polemic and hard news.[24]

Stewart Lyon, the Toronto *Globe's* managing editor, remarked on a similar trend in the newspapers of his city. He compared a week of editorial pages from 1889 with others from 1916 in both the *Globe* and its archrival Tory daily the *Mail* (later amalgamated with the *Empire*). In 1889 the *Globe* contained 21 articles on politics and public affairs. This number fell to 8 in 1916, another 6 articles addressed religious subjects, and 1 covered miscellaneous affairs. In 1916 the *Globe* ran 10 articles on the war and another 12 on a variety of non-political issues. The trend at the *Mail* was roughly similar. In 1889 it published 15 political articles, 1 on a religious subject, and 4 on other subjects. In 1916 the *Globe* had 10 articles on the war and 12 on miscellaneous subjects. Lyon concluded that the 'opinion-making side' had declined between 1889 and 1916 because readers were no longer interested in the views of newspaper editors.[25] Lyon realized that newspaper readers had become more interested in features such as the comics, advice columns, sensational crime stories, and human-interest stories than in news columns that preached and enlightened.

The decline of the editorial page was tied to the rising costs of operating a newspaper, which compelled publishers to attempt to increase readership by resorting to more aggressive promotional strategies. In the process, the way the news was deployed changed. Before the 1890s most newspapers, perhaps with the exception of such pioneers of the popular press as Toronto's *Telegram* and *World* and the *Montreal Star*, emphasized the informational aspects of news. News reports may have been politically biased, but their main purpose was either to persuade or to inform. A newspaper's physical appearance was not important. The news was generally set in a small, crabbed typeface and crammed onto the pages with little regard for graphic organization. Newspapers were meant to be read and studied, not to attract the attention of large numbers of readers.

By the 1890s, however, news was being transformed from a source of information into a commodity that could be sold to a larger readership, which in turn would attract more advertising revenue. *Saturday Night*'s E.E. Sheppard observed in 1893 that the publisher's role was not to be a 'moulder of public opinion' but 'to make the paper pay and to mould it in such a way as to make the most money out of it'.[26] More and more this meant that the news had to be enticingly written and attractively presented. As Michael Schudson observes, newspapers increasingly had to advertise their product—the news—and this led to self-promotion and sensationalism. All aspects of newspaper policy and design were affected (with the exception of basic news-gathering routines). Newspapers were now designed to attract the eye and pocket-change of readers.[27] The new strategy of self-promotion included extensive and sensational coverage of local affairs and crime, scandal, natural disasters, and war; vigorous touting of the newspaper's circulation status, advertising gains, and news-gathering prowess; self-advertisement of special and exclusive features and correspondence (for example, the *Montreal Star* promoted its correspondent during the Boer War in South Africa on its front pages); an end to front-page advertising; greater use of illustrations and white space; and the addition of bolder, blacker, multi-column headlines. Newspapers discarded the traditional way of telling a news story, which presented events in chronological order and ended with a dramatic conclusion. Instead, they adopted the new inverted pyramid style that led off with a reference to the most important aspect of the event in question.

To sell newspapers the news had to be attractively displayed. Successful newspapers increasingly used photographs and design changes to make the news easier to read and thus more saleable. Information was packaged like merchandise in department store display cases with local news separate from provincial, national, and international news, and sports separate from business or women's news. Getting the news out as speedily as possible became the order of the day. Less and less emphasis was placed on the context of news; newspapers strove more often to highlight the spectacular and the unusual than to explain the significant.[28]

Based on a random sample of Canadian daily newspapers from 1890, 1895, 1898, 1899, 1900, 1902, 1904, and 1905, it is clear that the changes in content and layout that gave rise to today's omnibus newspaper (serving as wide a readership as possible) occurred, in the main, between 1895 and 1905. In 1890 most of the newspapers in the sample were not organized around separate sections confined to specific areas of interest, such as news or sports. News stories and other items were scattered throughout the newspaper. Small-size type filled the page and was organized into ruled columns broken only by short, neutral heads. Rarely, if ever, were the newspapers enlivened by illustrations. With the exception of the *Telegram* and *World* in Toronto and the *Star* in Montreal, newspaper content was dominated by political news, verbatim reports of parliamentary debates, dry commercial information, and accounts of events in foreign places.[29]

By 1905, however, the newspapers had undergone significant change. Their front pages were mostly ad-free. The newspapers employed streamer headlines that crossed columns; they were often stacked with vivid, descriptive headlines and they used illustrations and photographs to dramatize the news stories. The papers were organized into separate sections devoted to finance, sports, drama, literature and entertainment, women's concerns, and other areas.

The Canadian newspapers of 1905 resembled those of the United States. Indeed, in the 1890s Canadian publishers had only to look across the border to see that visually exciting newspapers meant increased profit. They were aware of Joseph Pulitzer's innovative journalistic methods of the 1880s, and of how his turn-of-the-century circulation war with William Randolph Hearst had led to spectacular circulation gains for Pulitzer's *World*. Canadian publishers and editors, despite their occasional denunciations of sensationalism and 'yellow journalism', were clearly influenced by developments in the American newspaper industry. Their trade journals regularly reprinted articles from American trade journals such as *Editor and Publisher* and *Newspaperdom*. In addition, Canadians attended American newspaper conventions and belonged to American associations. In the early twentieth century newsman Orlo Miller observed that more and more American methods were being adopted, both in the writing of news and in its display tradition, following the lead of the big New York dailies.[30] A typical piece of American advice from 1902 recommended the use of methods that would 'make a paying paper'. It suggested the inclusion of an index and news summaries, the publication of bulletins, the subdivision of the paper into departments, and a list summing up all advertised bargains.[31]

With readership, rather than partisanship, becoming progressively more important, newspapers had to be made more appealing to readers. Front-page news began to be presented in a more dramatic fashion and more weight was given to local events. Greater attention was paid to the importance of the front page as an advertising window for the newspaper. As well, placement of the news became important, as John Dafoe argued in his 1895 piece 'Where the Best News Should Be'. Dafoe criticized the old-fashioned habit of putting abbreviated telegraph reports on the front page and relegating sensational but local news to the inside pages. His advice was: 'First page for the best news . . . the best news is that which will interest the greatest proportion of readers. That is the modern, sensible plan. Four times out of five the best news, under this rule, will be local news.'[32]

More and more newspapers removed advertisements from the front page, which shows that publishers had become aware that front-page news lured customers. The editor of Gaven, Saskatchewan's *Prairie News* called the front page 'the display window of his store of news, [which] must be well filled with good samples'. He added that 'the front page of a local newspaper is the parade to the circus. Interest is created. Those who have the money follow, place their money on the ticket counter, and pass inside.'[33] Similarly, the Toronto *Globe's* business manager J.F. Mackay called for 'better make-up on the front page so as to better promote circulation'.[34]

Despite some assertions to the contrary by newspapermen of the time, yellow journalism in Canada was widespread because it made money for the newspapers. In 1894 the *Montreal Herald's* new evening edition was condemned for its sensationalism, although one critic realized 'that this is the kind of news that takes with the masses'.[35] John Cameron, editor of the Toronto *Globe* from 1882 to 1890, recognized that yellow journalism did exist in Canada. He mentioned the existence of 'flaring headlines, out of proportion of the matter following'. He cited the 'coarse caricatures' and the 'too large space given to murders and other crimes, often with details that simply pointed out to everybody how crime could be committed'. Other hallmarks of yellow journalism in Canada included 'the tearing open of private wounds of families for sensational ends, and the unfair appeals to mere demagogic prejudice'.[36]

For some newspapers, especially those facing strong competition, the temptation to sensationalize must have been irresistible. Quality newspapers such as the *Montreal Gazette* and the Toronto · *Globe*, whose financial status was secure, remained aloof from sensationalism. But newspapers in desperate circumstances, such as the *Montreal Herald* in the mid-1890s and the *Toronto Star* at the end of the century—when the new owners fought for survival in a crowded and extremely competitive market—had little choice but to sensationalize the news.[37] The

Halifax Herald was a case in point. Locked in a circulation standoff with its rival, the *Halifax Chronicle*, it lost the financial advantage of federal patronage after the Laurier election victory of 1896. To boost circulation, publisher William Dennis adopted modern business methods and shifted the news focus towards local news, with an emphasis on crime, scandal, and fires.[38]

Sensational accounts of events increased, and more newspapers adopted the practice. In 1894 the Toronto grand jury denounced the Toronto press's extensive and descriptive coverage of several trials involving assaults on women and girls.[39] The Montreal papers' coverage of the murder of a young girl in 1906 was deemed so sordid, according to one commentator, that 'the dailies were hardly fit to be picked up with a pair of tongs.'[40] The *Vancouver Province*, while denying charges by its rival, the *Vancouver World*, that it was 'yellow', ran lurid stories of murders and other mayhem and was fond of references to the alleged depredations of 'wily Mongolians' or 'slit-eyed Chinks'.[41] It took the Boer War, however, to bring to full flower all the eye-grabbing, attention-getting tactics of yellow journalism—the bold streamer headlines, the loud promotion of special war coverage. . . .

Fears that newspapers were retreating from their public responsibilities prompted concerned citizens—educational reformers, women's groups, and the clergy—to protest the introduction of comics strips. When the *London Free Press* began carrying 'The Yellow Kid', the famous weekly coloured comic strip, the newspaper drew a barrage of public criticism. The *Free Press* was called a 'corrupter of the young' and the furor reached such heights that the newspaper was forced to suspend the feature. It was some years before the *Free Press* again offered its readers a comic strip, and this time it chose the far less controversial 'Buster Brown'.[42] In Ottawa the Women Teachers Association asked the city newspapers not to publish comic strips because, the teachers said, they failed to teach accuracy in drawing, politeness, or

deportment. But the *Ottawa Journal's* P.D. Ross was unmoved; the comics would stay.[43] No publisher could ignore the importance of comic strips in attracting readers. The *Gazette's* R.S. White made this clear when he complained about how 'degrading' it was to be forced to rely on those 'frightful monstrosities' to increase circulation.[44] W.J. Darby, the Toronto *Mail and Empire's* circulation manager, concluded that the comic strips would be valuable 'so long as advertisers make the circulation of a paper . . . the sole standard of the newspaper's merit as an advertising medium'.[45]

The success of publisher Joseph Atkinson's *Toronto Star* was attributed by his long-time employee J.H. Cranston to his understanding of the publisher's view that what the average Canadian wanted in a paper was not 'instruction in the more serious aspects of the news, but entertainment and amusement. And since his objective was a large circulation, he must seek the tastes and preference of this wider audience. He must win favour in every section of the community large enough to provide a sizeable body of readers.'[46]

In Canada, the *Star* led the way in rejecting the florid, embroidered style characteristic of nineteenth-century newspapers with their heavy emphasis on partisan editorializing. By the early years of the first decade of the twentieth century the *Star* had adopted the streamlined style and more 'objective' approach to the news that present-day readers are familiar with. In 1905 the *Star's* advice to its reporters was 'Boil it down'.[47] Other newspapers followed suit. Gone were the homespun moralizing and leisurely style where the reporter ended with a dramatic conclusion. Triple-decker narrative-style headlines were abandoned for shorter, more sensational headlines that set forth only the highlights of a story.

Some people gave wire services the credit for inventing the inverted pyramid style, because the expense and constraints of the telegraph demanded brevity. But according to the *Toronto*

Star's sports editor W.A. Hewitt, who around the turn of the century was the first to use the inverted pyramid style in Canada, the reason for its use really lay in the overriding needs of advertising. Because Hewitt never knew how much space an advertisement would require, he instructed his reporters to 'tell the result of the contest in your first paragraph, then if your report has to be cut for an advertisement, the readers will at least know who played, where, and who won, and the score.'[48]

By the start of twentieth century, partisan shrillness and heavy doses of political news began to give way to 'human-interest' news stories and other features designed to turn as many family members as possible into devoted newspaper readers. It became plain that success rested on the publisher's ability to shift the newspaper's emphasis from political news and advocacy to entertainment. The contrasting fortunes of the *Toronto Star* and its rival, the Toronto *News*, certainly demonstrated this. While both were taken over by new owners at roughly the same time (the *Star* in 1899 and the *News* in 1902), their subsequent histories could not have been more different. While the *Star* became the Canadian newspaper success story of the twentieth century, the *News*, despite vast amounts of investor money, remained in the red until it was closed down in 1920.

In 1906 Charles Clarke, an ex-*Toronto Telegram* newsman working for Hearst's *New York Journal*, wrote to the *News*'s publisher, Joseph Flavelle, pinpointing the reasons for the *News*'s lack of success and suggesting that it could solve its problems by adopting Hearst's journalistic methods. He categorized editor J.S. Willison as 'helplessly a pupil of the old Toronto school', whose editorials were 'picayune, hair-splitting, temporizing,' and 'replete with classical allusions comprehensible to no one but a university man'. What was needed, Clarke advised, was to give readers 'something in short sentences, and short words, with a bunch of ideas, instead of a hazy idea spread out to fill so much space with no regard to the value of space. It is far better to bring out an edition of your paper without an editorial than to inflict a fixed quantity of drivel on your readers every week.' Clarke also suggested focusing on Toronto news rather than British stories, since 'Toronto is big enough to furnish the story that leads the paper every edition, except in case of very important outside happenings.' He concluded that Willison did not understand how to present news to modern readers. 'The comparative value of news is a sealed book to him. He goes on the old-fashioned English plan that a good editorial column (in his eyes) is all that is needed, and is ignorant of the fact that proper display of news attracts the people, and that circulation comes from giving the news, first, last, and all the time.'[49]

Flavelle's response provides an interesting contrast between the new journalism of profit and the old journalism of political advocacy. He confessed to being 'old-fashioned enough to believe that a newspaper proprietor has some other duty to the public than to make money, and some other responsibility to society than seeking to inflame prejudice and passion'.[50] Flavelle represented the waning reality of the publisher as educator and moral instructor. The need for profit had become paramount and the way to achieve it was through the adoption of sensationalistic news coverage and the introduction of entertainment features such as the comic strips. . . .

Notes

1 John R. Bone, Joseph T. Clark, A.H.U. Colquhoun, and John F. Mackay, *A History of Canadian Journalism in the Several Portions of the Dominion with a Sketch of the Canadian Press Association 1859–1908* (New York: AMS Press, 1976), 4.

2 Ibid., 83.

3 Ibid., 92.

4 C.P. Scott, 'On Journalism', in *C.P. Scott, 1846–1832: The making of the 'Manchester Guardian'* (London: F. Muller, 1946), 161.

5 J.F. Mackay, 'Journalism', *Canadian Printer and Publisher (CPP)* (12 April 1903), 4.

6 A.H.U. Colquhoun, 'Canadian Universities and the Press', in *Journalism and the University*, ed. John R. Bone (Toronto: Copp Clark, 1903), 23.

7 'The Canadian Publishers' Association Annual Meeting', 27.

8 'Does Capital Threaten Liberty of the Press', *Toronto Star* (26 August 1905).

9 House of Commons, *Debates*, 13 May 1898, 5543, 5550.

10 Queen's University Archives (QUA), Joseph Flavelle Papers, case 1, J.W. Flavelle to J.S. Willison, 8 April 1903.

11 'The News and Its Promoters', *CPP* (January 1903), 5.

12 John S. Willison, 'A Lecture on Journalism', *CPP* (January 1900), 4.

13 I. Norman Smith, *The Journal Men: P.D. Ross, E. Norman Smith and Grattan O'Leary of The Ottawa Journal: Three Great Newspapermen and the Tradition They Created* (Toronto: McClelland and Stewart, 1974), 60-1.

14 Archives of Ontario, C.H.J. Snider Papers, 1934.

15 Quoted in J. Macdonald Oxley, 'What the University Can Do for the Journalist', in Bone (ed.), *Journalism and the University*, 90-1.

16 Bone et al., *History of Canadian Journalism*, 293.

17 Richard T. Clippingdale, 'J.S. Willison, Political Journalist: From Liberalism to Independence', Ph.D. dissertation, University of Toronto (1970), 408.

18 John W. Dafoe, 'The Press Blamed for National Paralysis', CPP (July 1917), 39.

19 'The Largest in Canada', *Toronto Star* (26 August 1905), 2.

20 National Archives of Canada (NAC), MC 30, D45, J.W. Dafoe Papers, reel M-74, George Iles to Dafoe, 22 December 1924.

21 F.A. Acland, 'Beacon of Light', Toronto *Globe* (5 March 1919).

22 'The Relation of the Press to National Life', CPP (December 1909), 42.

23 'Is the Editorial Page Necessary?' CPP (May 1909), 32.

24 Murray Donnelly, *Dafoe of the Free Press* (Toronto: Macmillan, 1968), 50.

25 Stewart Lyon, 'Shall the Editor or the Business Manager Reign?' Toronto *Globe*, 17–18.

26 CPP (March 1893): 7.

27 Michael Schudson, *Discovering the News: A Social History of American Newspapers* (New York: Basic Books, 1978), 95.

28 J. Herbert Altschull, *Agents of Power: The Role of the News Media in Human Affairs* (New York: Longman, 1984), 66.

29 The following newspapers were examined: *Manitoba Free Press; Montreal Star; Ottawa Journal; Regina Leader*; Toronto *Empire, Globe, Mail, News, Star, Telegraph*, and *World*; and *Vancouver Province*.

30 Orlo Miller, *A Century of Western Ontario: The Story of London, 'The Free Press', and Western Ontario, 1849–1949* (Westport, CT: Greenwood Press, 1949), 244.

31 CPP (December 1902): 6.

32 John W. Dafoe, 'Where the Best News Should Be', CPP (December 1895), 10.

33 Sam J. Latta, 'A Clean Front Page', CPP (February 1910), 23.

34 HD, 9 October 1907.

35 CPP (July 1894): 7.

36 John Cameron, 'University Chairs in Journalism', in Bone (ed.), *Journalism and the University*, 214.

37 See G.L. Spalding, 'The Toronto Daily Star as a Liberal advocate, 1899–1911', MA thesis, University of Toronto (1954), 15.

38 William March, *Red Line: The Chronicle-Herald and The Mail-Star 1875–1954* (Halifax: Chebucto Agencies, 1986), 68.

39 CPP (November 1894): 20.

40 CPP (April 1906): 26.

41 See front page of *Vancouver Province*, 11 March 1900.

42 Miller, *A Century of Western Ontario*, 248.

43 NAC, MG 30, D98, P.D. Ross Papers, vol. 1/1, undated editorial (c. 1910).

44 R.S. White, 'Newspapers of the Past and Present', CPP (June 1905), 10.

45 W.J. Darby, 'The Comic Supplement', CPP (June 1906), 20.

46 J.H. Cranston, *Ink on My Fingers* (Toronto: Ryerson Press, 1953), 61.

47 'City Edition Net for News', *Toronto Star* (26 August 1905), 11.

48 W.A. Hewitt, *Down the Stretch: Recollections of a Pioneer Sportsman and Journalist* (Toronto: Ryerson Press, 1958), 37.

49 QUA, Flavelle Papers, case 1, Chas. B. Clarke to Flavelle, 21 June 1906.

50 QUA, Flavelle to Chas. B. Clarke, 25 June 1906.

Newspapers, Advertising, and the Rise of the Agency, 1850–1900

Russell Johnston

'You run your newspapers to make money. You are not running newspapers to mould public opinion. That is all guff. That makes me sick.' (Laughter)
—*Roy V. Somerville, speaking to the Canadian Press Association in 1893*[1]

James Poole was probably a typical mid-nineteenth-century Canadian publisher. In 1860, in the rural countryside of eastern Ontario, Poole owned and operated the Carleton Place *Herald*, a four-page weekly paper upholding the Liberal cause. It carried his reports of local people and events, stories from around the world brought in by telegraph, and—on every single page— advertisements. He had a good variety of ads. Local people with produce to sell, personal ads, out-of-town financial houses offering investments and insurance, and railways and steamship operators running their monthly schedules all found a spot in his pages. Far more frequent, however, were local retailers and artisans notifying readers of recently acquired goods. Out-of-town advertisers might have come and gone, but the bread and butter of Poole's advertising were the shops within his own community.[2]

Why was Poole typical? Because in the early 1860s, there were some 150 other weekly papers in villages across the province, and another 79 throughout the rest of British North America. By contrast, there were only some 23 dailies. Few of them, weeklies and dailies alike, had circulations over one thousand readers.[3] Journalists such as Poole were more than simple publishers. They were editors, business managers, and pressmen

all rolled into one. Newspapering was more than a career for souls such as these with ink in their blood. It was a way of life, like farming or the clergy.

Forty years later, rural journalism found itself the backward cousin of the urban press. As the European demand for wheat and the American demand for pulpwood and minerals grew after 1880, Canada became a favoured destination for hundreds of thousands of immigrants. With them came a host of manufacturers providing consumer goods to a growing working-class population. With these consumer goods came an ever-increasing volume of advertising.

Two groups encouraged this growth in advertising: publishers and advertising agents. Publishers slowly adapted to the emerging industrial economy and left behind the nineteenth-century world of personal journalism. Circulation drives boosted readership and revenues and prompted ever greater investment in new technologies. Much of their new revenue was achieved by increasing the volume of advertising they carried in their pages. What was once a secondary source of income fast became a primary source, and more resources were dedicated to its cultivation among local and out-of-town businesses.

The publishers' enthusiasm for advertising was matched by a new cadre of businessmen, the advertising agents. However, while the publishers were developing a latent economic potential within their own businesses, the agents were essentially outsiders poaching on the publishers' trade. Many had formerly been salesmen in the publishers' employ. As freelance agents, they

Excerpts from Chapter 1 of *Selling Themselves: The Emergence of Canadian Advertising*, by Russell Johnston (Toronto: University of Toronto Press, 2000), 18–51. Reprinted by permission of the publisher.

were still selling publishers' white space, but now they accrued a portion of the profits from this trade to their own accounts.

. . .

1895: A Turning Point?

The Canadian economy changed dramatically between 1880 and 1914, and publishers were very much attuned to these developments. From 1871 to 1901 the aggregate value of capital invested in Canadian manufacturing rose more than five times, from $78 million to $481 million, and hundreds of plants opened in the Maritimes, Quebec, and Ontario. Most were located in Ontario.[4] In their wake, thousands of Canadians migrated to the industrializing urban centres, and for good reason. The number of jobs increased with the pace of investment. Between 1891 and 1901, while the rural population of Canada grew by roughly sixty thousand, its cities and towns grew by around half a million. At the same time, the annual value of wages more than doubled from $41 million to $113 million. Retailers and marketers were keenly attuned to these developments. On paper, at least, the country seemed flush with disposable income.[5]

With the increase in goods and markets came a perceived increase in the volume of advertising, particularly in the period 1895–1905. Although no statistics exist from this period for the advertising trade, several items offer corroborative evidence. Agents identified 1895 as a turning point because that year reputable firms began to outnumber patent medicines as foreign advertisers.[6] Using the balance sheets of five Toronto dailies, economist Thomas Walkom has calculated that total advertising receipts had already eclipsed other sources of newspaper revenue by 1898, when they accounted for 73 per cent of gross revenue.[7] The establishment of American branch plants brought a raft of new consumer goods into the country, and these companies already knew the value of advertis-

ing. Since Toronto was at the centre of the country's growth in manufacturing, its papers would have benefited first from increased advertising budgets.

As distribution networks extended outward, advertising followed suit. The establishment of new papers and the improvement of existing ones could be used to gauge investor confidence in local trade conditions. The Fort William *Times-Journal* was an apt case, but so too was the experience of the entire Prairie west. There, the number of dailies and weeklies tripled between 1891 and 1904. These start-ups may have been inspired by the immigrant boom, but readers alone would not have sustained them. Rather, advertisers expanded their publicity with the population, seeking new markets among the new settlers. An officer of the Canadian Press Association estimated that advertising revenue overtook subscriptions as the primary source of income at almost every Canadian paper by the First World War.[8]

Trade paper publishers were also quick to capitalize on the growing interest in advertising. Between 1898 and 1908 at least five new journals began serving the advertising trade in Canada. There was a decided novelty in the focus of their news coverage. When an earlier venture appeared in Toronto in 1893, its subtitle declared that it was 'an aid to all interested in advertising'. Nonetheless, its lead article addressed only retailers, the traditional source of local advertising. Manufacturers, the core group of foreign advertisers, were nowhere mentioned. The reverse was true of *Economic Advertising* when it began 15 years later. Its editors purposefully set out to attract a readership composed of manufacturers and rarely ran articles on retailing. For agencies, the turning point appears to have been 1902. That year, McKim Limited opened its first branch office in Toronto, and its most aggressive rival there promptly responded with an office in Montreal. Toronto adworkers noted a surge in interest in their work, and two new journals appeared in Montreal. A third started in 1905.[9]

While their industrial counterparts formed trade associations, established standards, and contemplated mergers, publishers remained decidedly individualistic. Their day-to-day operations often involved ruthless competition with crosstown rivals, and they were relatively isolated from the experience of publishers elsewhere. On the surface, it might have appeared that nothing had changed among the rural weeklies. Few publishers could imagine their trade reduced to an impersonal process reorganized like sugar, steel, or cigarettes to fit within the system of mass production. A newspaper was not a standardized product, but an expression of the editor himself and a reflection of the community he served. Newspapers were far too intimate and local to contemplate corporate consolidation.[10]

In their business practices the publishers also evaded standardization. The frequency of publication and the number of pages per issue were entirely dependent on a paper's revenue. More subscriptions and advertising meant that more pages could be run. When George Brown expanded the *Globe* from a weekly to a tri-weekly in 1849, it was not because there was an increase in newsworthy events in Toronto. He was satisfying an increased demand for advertising space. As ad content increased, editors increased their pages to accommodate it. They then increased their editorial content to maintain a respectable ratio of news to ads.[11]

Just as the frequency and page count of each paper could vary, so too could the page size and column width of each paper. This was not a problem for local advertisers since their typesetting was done by the paper itself—note James Poole's work for the Wylies. Alternatively, if the town was large enough to support a job printing plant, an advertiser could get its ad made to order in plate form before sending it to the paper. Foreign advertisers who used several papers and wanted a consistent 'look' for their advertising relied on print shops. However, the lack of standardization among papers increased the cost of plate-making dramatically; each new column size required its own setting.

The rate paid by the advertiser for the space in the paper was open to negotiation. This could vary according to the size of the ad, the frequency of its insertion, and the circulation of the paper. One of James Poole's correspondents avoided all of these questions and simply trusted him to use his best judgment, asking: 'Please advertise the following to the amount of one dollar . . .'[12] The value of a publisher's white space was a complex issue. Publishers could have as many as four rates: one for local business, a second for foreign business, a third for government notices, and a fourth, rarely acknowledged but generally understood, for family and friends. To call these 'rates' may be misleading. They were guidelines within which a paper's business manager would operate.[13]

One group of entrepreneurs saw a tremendous opportunity in this chaos: the advertising agents. So long as the papers retained their idiosyncratic production standards and rates, there existed a niche for someone who could assist advertisers in the placement of their notices. This is the opportunity that the agents seized.

. . .

Agency Models

In 1865 changes altered the trade in the United States. That year, George P. Rowell established an agency in Boston with a new rate structure. Competitive pressures were lowering returns from commissions as more agencies were entering the field. Most frequently, agents would rebate part of their commissions to their clients in order to lower the price of their services. Subsequently, their profit margins steadily shrank. Rowell found a way to avoid this problem. Other agents secured their clients first, and then placed their ads; Rowell contracted large amounts of space in one hundred New England papers, and then sold this list complete to advertisers. In short, he became a wholesaler of publishers' white space, a 'space jobber'. He possessed the lowest rates available for those papers, and he could attract advertisers on that basis. Imitators soon appeared who specialized in the papers of other regions and other types of periodicals. Such agents included Lord and Thomas, who contracted space in religious periodicals, and J. Walter Thompson, who did the same with general magazines. Thompson took the new system a step further by securing exclusive access to the publications on his list. Exclusive or not, commissions became irrelevant. Profits were made from the resale value of the white space the agents controlled.[14]

American advertisers eventually questioned the 'closed' contracts of these space jobbers. The papers on an agency list were not selected with an individual advertiser in mind. Rather, they were merely the papers with which the agency had contracts. A.J. Ayer, the founder of N.W. Ayer and Son, exploited this resentment with the introduction of an 'open' contract in 1875. Each advertiser would be offered a judicious selection of media sensitive to its product and distribution network. In so doing, Ayer introduced the concept of advertiser-oriented service into the agency's operations. The agency would not simply be a publishers' representative, nor a wholesaler, but an expert providing the advertiser with objective media counsel. To pay for this service, Ayer readopted the commission system. Despite the allure of service, no agency would have survived had it relied on that alone to amass clients. Advertisers still sought cheap rates, and the agencies that offered them won the contracts.[15]

In Canada, there is insufficient evidence to state which model the agencies followed, be it Rowell's wholesale agent, Thompson's closed contract, or Ayer's open one. . . . However, it might be ventured that the space jobbers never held sway in Canada to the same extent that they did in the United States. Few companies apart from patent medicine makers advertised beyond their immediate locales before 1890. Since advertising was traditionally the forte of retailers, most manufacturers were probably happy to

leave this expense to them. Further, as previously mentioned, Canadian manufacturers did not produce trademarked goods in great quantities until the mid-1890s. Without recognizable trademarks, most goods could not be advertised effectively.[16]

The Agent as Broker: Anson McKim

To describe Anson McKim's beginning, it is necessary to describe the circumstances surrounding his entry. In 1872 Sir John A. Macdonald surveyed the newspaper field in Toronto and decided that the local Tory organ, the *Leader*, was no match for George Brown's formidable *Globe*. At his suggestion the Toronto *Mail* was formed, which won the support of local Conservatives and forced the *Leader* out of business. Still, the paper was not an immediate financial success. In 1877 it was sold to its chief creditor and a partisan Tory, John Riordan. Riordan set out to re-create the *Mail* with an impressive new building, new presses, new type, and an editorial policy that made it a paper of record to rival the *Globe*. With these changes accomplished, the paper then did something that no one foresaw: it declared its editorial independence from the Conservatives. Rival newspapermen grudgingly acknowledged that the paper's period of 'splendid isolation' represented the best journalism of the day. Readers apparently agreed. By 1892 it had the largest circulation of any paper in Toronto, second only to the *Montreal Star* across the country.[17]

T.W. Dyas was the paper's advertising manager. While Riordan and his editor, Edward Farrer, expanded the paper's plant and influence, Dyas made the paper profitable through its advertising columns. Since all of the Toronto papers competed for the same local advertisers, he decided to look beyond the city itself. Dyas knew that many American papers had branch offices in other major centres. Such offices gave remote advertisers a personal link to the paper and won substantial contracts. Dyas thought this a good idea, and in 1878 he created a *Mail* office in Montreal. It was staffed by a young man, then 26 years old, who had worked at the paper for six years: Anson McKim.

Hired as a special representative, McKim gradually transformed the office into an independent advertising agency. When he arrived in Montreal, he discovered a rival from the *Globe* had preceded him. Neither man found many opportunities in the city, and McKim sometimes went weeks without landing a new contract. His fortunes changed when he reorganized the office along agency lines. Several advertisers wanted to place notices in Ontario centres outside of Toronto. If McKim could secure contracts with several papers at once, he would gain a decided advantage for the *Mail* itself. The *Mail* agreed to this arrangement, as did other Ontario papers. In exchange for this service, McKim took a commission from each paper, part of which was rebated to the *Mail*. By 1889 the other papers were convinced of the value of this operation, but had grown tired of surrendering a commission to the *Mail*. With their encouragement, McKim left the *Mail* and became an independent solicitor.[18]

Incidentally, McKim's success in Montreal inspired Dyas to open a similar office in Toronto. McKim was not only selling the *Mail*, he was selling a service. There was no reason to believe that advertisers in Ontario would not appreciate this service as well. Instead of hiring another special representative, however, Dyas took the next logical step and opened an 'independent' advertising agency in 1882: the Mail Advertising Agency. Although still connected to the paper, and staffed by one of its former solicitors, it too placed ads in any number of Ontario papers, and sent agents throughout British North America looking for clients.[19]

McKim's success has been credited to his own daring and imagination, but it should not be forgotten that his agency grew out of one of the most respected papers of his day. . . . McKim began with the prestige and credit of the *Mail*

behind him, a publisher who was willing to take chances, and a capable mentor in Dyas. Only after 17 years at the *Mail*, and with the backing of several other papers, did McKim sever this connection. (Even then, the 'Mail' name remained above his storefront until the late 1890s.[20]) However, the apparent success of his agency, and those of men such as Pettingill, Ayer, and Thompson in the United States, inspired other men to go into the trade. Not surprisingly, without the same corporate support that McKim had enjoyed, few succeeded in Canada. City directories for Montreal and Toronto listed agencies throughout the 1870s and 1880s. There were usually four or five in each city in any given year, but few made more than a single appearance.[21] After 1895, however, when the volume of advertising increased, agencies began to survive in most of the regions with rapidly developing mercantile and industrial centres—cities such as Halifax, Ottawa, Hamilton, London, Winnipeg, Edmonton, and Vancouver.

Agency Services

The expanding volume of foreign advertising after 1895 opened many opportunities for new entries into the agency field. Once again, competition sparked innovation, and once again Canadian adworkers would look south for new ideas. Starting in 1900 new types of agency service would transform the typical agency from a small office operation into a modern, departmentalized company employing dozens of staff.

At the root of the agency business remained the solicitation of new clients and space-buying. 'First and foremost and all the time', McKim's newspaper directory declared, 'it is the business of an advertising agency to promote and facilitate newspaper advertising.'[22] It was their job to solicit supra-local advertisers for the papers. Insofar as the agency system had evolved out of the advertising departments of actual newspapers, this must have seemed self-evident. Regardless, the commission system was based on this premise, and agencies were paid commission on every contract placed, whether new or not. This could be justified because the solicitation process was undertaken at the agency's expense. Long before any ad was placed, before any bill was submitted, the agency was hustling clients on its own time and account. Toronto agent J.J. Gibbons boasted that, in his own shop: 'A corps of intelligent and high-salaried solicitors are constantly working on the non-advertising manufacturers and others, persuading them to become regular advertisers, offering experienced direction to their campaigns, and doing everything in their power to induce them to take up newspaper advertising.'[23] Few newspapers had anything comparable to attract new business.

No matter how much time and effort an agent put into this process, there was always the possibility that nothing would come of it. At times, business could simply be slow. At other times, agencies had to deal with the realities of the market: a competing agency could get the account. A.R. Coffin, an executive with a Nova Scotia printing house, painted a third possible scenario: 'A general advertiser who, in these days, wishes to start in advertising with a fair amount of success has a complete advertising campaign laid out for him, by an agency, which must include all detail . . . Then after all the whole proposition may be laid on the shelf for another year, or it has been known that the advertiser would not say thank you to the agency but get a clerk in his office to put into effect the agency's scheme and hold up the papers for the agency's commission.'[24] Coffin knew more than one manufacturer had tried this trick. Understandably, he did not name them in print.

Again, after solicitation, space-buying was the core service agencies provided to their clients. An extensive knowledge of the periodical market was required to do the job effectively, and this became the responsibility of 'media departments'. There were three main groups within such departments: researchers, space-buyers, and checkers. The researchers' task was to know everything about every periodical in the country: where it was published and by whom, its tone and reputation, what market it served, its circulation, its political or religious affiliations, whether or not it carried advertising, and its line rates if it did. Space-buyers would then use this information to maximize the value of each advertiser's appropriation by reaching as many readers as possible at the lowest possible expense. Once the ad was run, it was then the checkers' task to ensure that everything appeared according to contract.[25]

The most difficult information to obtain was invariably the paper's circulation. Most companies wanted their advertising placed in papers that would reach as many readers as possible. In areas with more than one paper, this generally meant they would only select the paper with the highest circulation. Competition among publishers for lucrative advertising contracts led them into a cycle of ballooning estimates and mutual recriminations. Gibbons related the following experience while speaking before the Canadian Press Association: 'I went into one newspaper office in Ontario and inquired about their circulation. One partner told me 1,200, while the other a few hours later told me they were printing 600 and seemed to think they were making splendid progress. In another town the people said the local paper had a circulation of 300; the pressman after thinking it over placed the circulation at 600, while the publisher assured me on his word of honour that the circulation was 900.'[26] Caught between their clients and publishers, agencies had to draft their own estimates. Sometimes, as Gibbons's comments suggest, this was done simply by chatting with the locals and getting a sense of the paper's popularity. The agents requested verified numbers but were resisted by most publishers. It took the combined effort of Canada's top advertisers to change their minds. That would not happen until the 1910s.

Space rates provided a second bone of contention between publishers and agents. Many publishers had rate cards that they issued once a year for the benefit of their patrons, but they did not strictly follow their stated rates. Competing publishers entered a dangerous spiral of price-cutting to attract agencies looking for the best deal. Agents exploited this practice unabashedly. It was a talking point in their solicitations. An article in McKim's directory was exceptionally frank when it stated that a good agency 'must know the rock bottom rates . . . of every publication'. Maxwell R. Gregg claimed to possess 'special facilities for inserting advertisements at the lowest possible rates', while W.F. Carrier and Company simply stated: 'Our Rates are the lowest procurable.'[27] Clients expected no less, and expected agencies to compete for their business. The Sun Life Assurance Company is a case in point. It wanted to run a brief campaign in 1911 and requested estimates from two different agencies, for the exact same ad in the exact same list of cities. One agency could do it for $2,330.65, the other for $2,011.17. Naturally, Sun Life hired the second agency.[28]

Taken together, solicitation and space-buying were the two core services provided by agencies at the turn of the century; the first was essentially sales, the latter purchasing. Other conveniences were provided to clients, but these were ancillary in nature: having plates made, sending them out, checking the insertions after publication, and paying the bills.

Copywriting and illustration were not a part of the typical agency's repertoire. It was assumed that clients knew their products best and would prepare their ads themselves. Advertisers who wanted help with creative tasks could find qualified help in two different places. For illustrations, an advertiser could readily call upon a print shop, the bastion of the commercial artist. For ad copy, an advertiser could hire a self-styled 'advertising specialist'. A demand for expert copy services led some fledgling authors to compose ads on a freelance basis. Most would not place the ad they wrote. Rather, they were hired by advertisers who wanted more polished notices

than the run-of-the-mill stuff that appeared in the papers, and who placed their ads 'direct'. Thomas Bengough, a veteran Toronto pressman, placed the start of this trend in 1891; three years later he wrote, 'even the old-timers are falling into line.' Some agencies were also known to hire specialists for specific jobs.[29]

The story of Wilson P. MacDonald is interesting in this light. In the 1920s MacDonald was known for a brand of romantic poetry that critics scorned but adoring fans embraced. While developing his craft, he earned his keep as a freelance copywriter. MacDonald travelled throughout much of Canada and the United States between 1900 and 1918, stopping in towns for two or three months at a time. He rarely stayed longer. He carried with him a stock of pre-written advertisements, which he resold in every new town. When his stock was nearly empty, he moved on. A bachelor, living in hotels or boarding houses, MacDonald never had a secretary, let alone a full-service agency under his care.[30]

When the finished ad was needed in plate form, most agencies did not have the facilities to create them themselves. This task too was farmed out to job-printing plants. The 1890s witnessed the flowering of these firms in Canada, and Toronto was home to several. Among the better known were Toronto Lithography, Copp Clark, Brigden's, and Grip Limited. Firms of this calibre maintained the skilled labour and equipment necessary to produce a broad range of printed goods, from tickets and handbills to full-size posters. Agencies contracted them for many of these goods, but the most common items sought were plates.[31]

Given the range of expertise at their command, print shops were well positioned to enter the agency business themselves. Since they already illustrated and set advertisements, it was only logical to place them as well. One shop that did so was Diver Electrotype, owned by Frederick Diver. Founded in 1878, it enjoyed a close relationship with the Toronto *World* and produced ready-prints for several weekly papers.

These sheets carried a high volume of foreign advertising. About 1897 Diver capitalized on this business by entering the general agency field; he hired a former *Mail* salesman to act as his manager and renamed his firm the 'Central Press Agency'. By 1899 the agency was placing ads nationally for companies such as R.S. Williams Pianos, Salada Tea, and Sleeman's Ale.[32]

The Agent as Corporate Consultant: J.J. Gibbons

The agency scene changed dramatically after 1900, thanks to John J. Gibbons. Like Dyas before him, Gibbons drew upon American expertise to introduce new services in Canada. While still a teenager he was hired by the Toronto *News* to become its special representative in New York City. The opportunity acquainted him with several agencies there that offered copy and art services to their clients. They charged nothing for them. Rather, the agencies believed the expense was necessary to enhance the client's advertising—and by extension, to enhance their own reputations within a competitive trade. Gibbons realized that no Canadian agency did this, and in 1899 he returned to Toronto to open a new agency on these lines. In so doing, he established the first copy and art departments to be found at any agency in Canada, and he staffed them with experienced personnel raided from newspapers, advertisers, and other agencies.[33]

Gibbons was not the first to offer these services to Canadian advertisers, but he was the first to bundle them with solicitation and space-buying under one roof. This gave him much greater influence over all aspects of his clients' campaigns. Within three years, his staff was designing plans that achieved thematic and stylistic continuity through every part of a product's marketing, from trademark design and packaging to newspaper ads and display cards. The agency's successes were numerous, and culminated in one set of ads designed for Lever Brothers'

Sunlight Soap in 1902. Lever found them so attractive, it used them in Great Britain and the United States as well. Lever's contract with Gibbons had been a coup in itself; previously, Lever had worked exclusively with McKim. Gibbons similarly won the McClary contract from J.S. Robertson, a Toronto freelancer.[34] The conversion of these high-profile clients was a portent of things to come. J.J. Gibbons Limited set the pace in Toronto for the next three decades, selling the wares of companies such as Neilson's Chocolates, Northern Electric, Pear's Soap, White Star Steamships, Canada Life Assurance, and Packard Motor Cars. . . .[35]

Every agency that sought to expand its stable of clients with prestigious, national accounts was compelled to adopt the full-service approach. At least two other agencies opened in Toronto between 1900 and 1904 offering creative services, and the established agencies quickly took note. The Desbarats Advertising Agency of Montreal admitted as much in 1912: 'In our own advertising business, changes have been the order of the day. The more or less perfunctory service has given way to a really highly specialized one, and we look back to the times that we thought we were giving our customers good service much in the same way perhaps as we will be looking back in another ten years on our efforts today.'[36] It was a costly undertaking, as Edouard Desbarats knew. He decided to incorporate in 1901, after ten years in business. With fresh capital in hand, he immediately acquired greater office space and filled it with copy and art men. McKim began hiring artists after 1900. Four years later he too incorporated his agency and similarly expanded his physical plant.[37]

The increasing costs incurred by these new services led to a desire for greater security among agency owners. A full-service agency had significant capital tied up in personnel and plant. By 1904 two agencies were listed in R.G. Dun and Company's credit reference book for Canada. Desbarats was listed with $10,000 to $20,000 in capital assets, and Frederick Diver's print shop and agency was listed at \$35,000 to \$50,000. Fifteen years later, the Montreal offices of McKim Limited and the Canadian Advertising Agency also appeared, and both rated at \$35,000 to \$50,000.[38] Freelancers could not say the same. Gibbons had very little patience with men such as Wilson P. MacDonald. MacDonald's entire approach to the trade was antithetical to its long-term interests. Whether or not his clients succeeded might have made no difference to him; he would be off to the next town regardless. Further, with no capital investment in the trade, he could afford to undercut the commission charged by other agencies. He tapped the system for its wealth while contributing little of lasting value, and for this he was thoroughly scorned by the full-service agencies. Gibbons decried these 'men that had no office other than their hats'. McKim argued that freelancers were not true agents in comparison with the 'legitimate advertising agency, possessing large capital, thorough equipment, and a staff of trained employees.'[39]

. . .

The newspaper world that James Poole had known was not completely forgotten, but its sun was setting. Urban papers such as the *Star* and *La Presse* in Montreal and the *Telegram* in Toronto reached over 75,000 readers daily by 1900. Rural and small-town papers were now, more than ever, thrown to the mercy of a marketplace dominated by out-of-town advertisers and agencies with no personal relationship with individual publishers. Businessmen such as

these had little patience for the small circulations of rural papers. At the same time, the largest dailies could command the respect and patronage of advertisers due to the sheer size of their circulations. Weekly publishers could not do the same, and they felt that control of their papers was slipping away to strangers and outsiders.

After 1900, as the number of papers in Ontario peaked and competition reached an all-time high, publishers realized they would have to co-operate to harness the changes that had overtaken them. In time, both the advertisers and the agents agreed that certain restrictions would have to be imposed for the good of the trade, and they participated in the creation of a more stable business environment. Their choices did not hearken back to a previous time, but reflected an acceptance of new conditions and practices. Primary among these was the fact that revenue from foreign advertising would soon surpass that from any other source of income the newspapers enjoyed, including reader subscriptions.

In facing these problems, adworkers were forced to assess their roles in this growing trade. Over time, the field became populated by a wide assortment of companies, with innumerable backgrounds and vastly different services for sale. Out of this diversity, there emerged a core group of agents who became spokesmen for the 'new' trade. All of them were connected with full-service agencies. Their desires, both economically and psychologically, would play a large role in the construction of the modern advertising trade in the years to come.

Notes

1   *Printer & Publisher* 2:3 (March 1893), 10.

2   William Meikle, *The Canadian Newspaper Directory* (Toronto: Blackburn's, 1858), 26.

3   A. McKim & Company, *Canadian Newspaper Directory*, 1st edn (Montreal: McKim, 1892), 59; Meikle, *Canadian Newspaper Directory*, Appendix A. See also Paul Rutherford, *A Victorian Authority: The Daily Press in Late Nineteenth-Century Canada*

(Toronto: University of Toronto Press, 1982), 37.

4   Canada; Department of Trade and Commerce, *The Canadian Industrial Field*, 2nd edn (Ottawa: King's Printer, 1933), 9; Kenneth Buckley, *Capital Formation in Canada* (Toronto: McClelland & Stewart, 1974), 10–11; T.W. Acheson, 'The National Policy and the Industrialization of the Maritimes, 1880–1910', *Acadiensis* 1:2 (1972), 3–28.

5　HSC, 2nd edn, A68–A69; Department of Trade and Commerce, *Canadian Industrial Field*, 2nd edn, 9; O.J. Firestone, *Canada's Economic Development, 1867–1953* (London: Bowes & Bowes, 1958), 76–97.

6　See J.J. Gibbons, 'The Weekly Section', *Printer & Publisher* 18:4 (April 1909), 21; Bertram Brooker, 'Forty Years of Canadian Advertising [Pt 4]', *Marketing* 21:5 (6 September 1924), 134–6; H.E. Stephenson and C. McNaught, *The Story of Advertising in Canada: A Chronicle of Fifty Years* (Toronto: Ryerson, 1940), 75.

7　Thomas Walkom, 'The Daily Newspaper Industry in Ontario's Developing Capitalistic Economy: Toronto and Ottawa, 1871–1911' (unpublished Ph.D. dissertation, University of Toronto, 1983), 344–404.

8　*Canadian Newspaper Directory*, 1st edn (1892); *Canadian Newspaper Directory*, 4th edn (1905); W.J. Taylor, 'Advertising the Real Backbone of the Business', *Printer & Publisher* 27:6 (June 1918), 22. Two recent studies have come to the same conclusion; see Jean de Bonville, *La Presse Québécoise de 1884 à 1914: Genèse d'un media de masse* (Quebec: Presses de l'Université Laval, 1988), 326–9, and Minko Sotiron, *From Politics to Profit: The Commercialization of Daily Newspapers, 1890–1920* (Montreal: McGill–Queen's University Press, 1997), 10–22.

9　*Canadian Advertiser* 1:1 (June 1893); *Economic Advertising* 1:1 (September 1908), 3–4. On the growth of business, see 'The Advertising Men', *Printer & Publisher* 11:6 (June 1902), 6; W.A. C[raick], 'Brief Interviews', *Printer & Publisher* 11:7 (July 1902), 17; C.G.H., 'American Advertising', *Printer & Publisher* 11:10 (October 1902), 17; 'Advertising Arena', *Printer & Publisher* 12:1 (January 1903), 15; 'Advertising in Montreal', *Printer & Publisher* 12:5 (May 1903), 16; Brooker, 'Forty Years [Pt 5]', *Marketing* 21:10 (15 November 1924), 274. The three papers were *Ad World* (1902), *Points of the Star* (1902), and *Publicité-Publicity* (1905).

10　A.R. Fawcett, 'The Country Editor', *Printer & Publisher* 2:10 (October 1893) 6–7; 'Co-operation among Local Publishers', *Printer & Publisher* 4:4 (April 1895), 4–5; 'The Circular on Foreign Advertising', *Printer & Publisher* 13:12 (December 1904), 12–13; S.D. Scott, 'The Newspaper of 1950', *Printer & Publisher* 10:3 (March 1901), 17; J.H. Cranston, *Ink on My Fingers* (Toronto: Ryerson, 1953), vii–viii; Rutherford, *Victorian Authority*, 190–227; Michael Bliss, *A Living Profit: Studies in the Social History of Canadian Business, 1883–1911* (Toronto: McClelland & Stewart, 1974), 33–54; Tom Traves, *The State and Enterprise: Canadian Manufacturers and the State, 1917–1931* (Toronto: University of Toronto Press, 1979), 30–3.

11　J.M.S. Careless, *Brown of the Globe*, vol. 1 (Toronto: Macmillan, 1959), 100; M.E. Nichols, *(CP) The Story of the Canadian Press* (Toronto: Ryerson, 1948). For a different view, see Peter G. Goheen, 'The Changing Bias of Inter-Urban Communications in Nineteenth-Century Canada', *Journal of Historical Geography* 16:2 (1990), 177–96.

12　Poole papers, v. 2, f. January 1864, W. Riddell to J. Poole, December 1864.

13　Brooker, 'Forty Years [Pt 1]', *Marketing* 20:9 (3 May 1924), 281.

14　George P. Rowell, *Forty Years an Advertising Agent, 1865–1905* (New York: Franklin, 1926); James W. Young, *Advertising Agency Compensation* (Chicago: University of Illinois Press, 1933), 23–5.

15　Young, *Agency Compensation*, 25–8; Ralph M. Hower, *The History of an Advertising Agency: N.W. Ayer & Son at Work* (Cambridge, MA: Harvard University Press, 1939); James Playsted Wood, *The Story of Advertising* (New York: Ronalds, 1958), 242–5.

16　Stephenson and McNaught, *Story of Advertising*, 49–75; David Monod, *Store Wars: Shopkeepers and the Culture of Mass Marketing, 1890–1939* (Toronto: University of Toronto Press, 1996), 99–148, especially 140–1.

17　Carman Cumming, *Secret Craft: The Journalism of Edward Farrer* (Toronto: University of Toronto Press, 1992); *Canadian Newspaper Directory*, 1st edn (1892), 222–3; see also Hector Charlesworth, *Candid Chronicles* (Toronto: Macmillan, 1925), 75;

Donald Creighton, *John A. Macdonald: The Old Chieftain* (Toronto: Macmillan, 1955), 115–20.

18 Anson McKim, 'Advertising Agencies—Whose Agents Are They?' *Printer & Publisher* 24:11 (November 1915), 17–19; Brooker, 'Forty Years [Pt 1]', 281–2; Stephenson and McNaught, *Story of Advertising*, 18–35.

19 Brooker, 'Forty Years [Pt 1]', 282; 'Started in Canada', *Printer & Publisher* 15:5 (May 1906), 20; George French, *20th Century Advertising* (New York: Van Nostrand, 1926), 224–5.

20 'A Tribute to Anson McKim', *Printer & Publisher* 16:9 (September 1907), 37.

21 *Montreal Directory* (Lovell: Montreal, [1870–90]); *Toronto City Directory* (various publishers: Toronto, [1871–90]).

22 'The Business of the Modern Newspaper Advertising Agency', *Canadian Newspaper Directory* 2nd edn (1899), 26; see also 'The System and Equipment of the Modern Newspaper Advertising Agency', *Canadian Newspaper Directory*, 3rd edn (1901), 25–6.

23 J.J. Gibbons, 'The Agent's Standpoint', *Printer & Publisher* 14:4 (April 1905), 20–1; see also W.A. C[raick], 'Brief Interviews', *Printer & Publisher* 11:9 (September 1902), 18–19.

24 A.R. Coffin, 'The Advertising Agency', *Printer & Publisher* 15:3 (March 1906), 13.

25 'The Business', *Canadian Newspaper Directory* 2nd edn (1899), 26.

26 J.J. Gibbons in *Printer & Publisher* 13:12 (December 1904), 12–13.

27 'The Business', *Canadian Newspaper Directory*, 2nd edn (1899), 26; *Toronto City Directory* (Toronto: Might, 1890), 1363; *Toronto City Directory* (1900), 990.

28 Sun Life Corporate Archives (SLA), Acc. 00480, b. 84, f. 'Early Advertising Ideas', Lawrence G. Cluxton, 23 February 1911; Desbarats Advertising Agency, 23 February 1911.

29 Thomas Bengough, 'Improvements in Advertising', *Biz* 1:2 (January 1894), 2. On artists, see *Canadian Newspaper Directory*, 2nd edn (1899), 29; W.A. C[raick], 'Brief Interviews with Advertising Men', *Printer & Publisher* 11:9 (September 1902), 18–19;

Joan Murray, 'The World of Tom Thomson', *Journal of Canadian Studies* 26:3 (Fall 1991), 5–51; on copywriters, see Stephenson and McNaught, *Story of Advertising*, 102–5.

30 National Archives of Canada (NAC), MG30 D279, Wilson MacDonald papers, v. 10, f. 10–11, 'Notes on W.M.'s Life'; Cheryl MacDonald, 'A Shakespeare for Canada', *Beaver* 67:2 (1987), 4–8.

31 *Canadian Newspaper Directory*, 3rd edn (1901), 23–4; Angela E. Davis, 'Art and Work: Frederick Brigden and the History of the Canadian Illustrated Press', *Journal of Canadian Studies* 21:2 (Summer 1992), 22–36; Angela E. Davis, *Art and Work: A Social History of Labour in the Canadian Graphic Arts Industry to the 1940s* (Montreal: McGill–Queen's University Press, 1995).

32 *Printer & Publisher* 8:11 (November 1899), 4; *Printer & Publisher* 12:5 (May 1903), 16; *Economic Advertising* 3:8 (August 1910), 18; CPA records, v. 2, Recognition Committee, 'Minute Book 1910–19', 21 June 1910; Brooker, 'Forty Years [Pt 3]', *Marketing* 21:3 (9 August 1924), 68, 95; Walkom, 'Daily Newspaper Industry', 39–40.

33 'The Value of Expert Aid', *Printer & Publisher* 9:1 (January 1900), 16–17; 'Advertising Arena', *Printer & Publisher* 11:6 (June 1902), 13; 'Advertising Arena', *Printer & Publisher* 11:11 (November 1902), 18; 'People Who Do Things', *Saturday Night* 51:10 (11 January 1936), 16.

34 W.A. C[raick], 'Brief Interviews', *Printer & Publisher* 11:9 (September 1902), 18; 'Advertising Arena', *Printer & Publisher* 12:11 (November 1903), 12; Brooker, 'Forty Years [Pt 5]', 272–4.

35 NAC, MG27 II D7, George E. Foster papers, v. 17, f. 1570, J.J. Gibbons to E.O. Osler, 4 August 1915; *Lydiatt's Book*, 9th edn (1922), 227–43; Brooker, 'Forty Years [Pt 5]', 272–4, 278.

36 Desbarats Advertising Agency, *The Desbarats Newspaper Directory*, 2nd edn (Montreal: Desbarats, 1912), 4. The two Toronto agencies were run by J.E. McConnell and J.H. Woods; C[raick], 'Brief Interviews', *Printer & Publisher* 11:9 (September 1902), 18; *Toronto City Directory* (1905), 975.

37 'An Agency Incorporated', *Printer & Publisher* 10:4

(April 1901), 20; *Canadian Newspaper Directory*, 3rd edn (1901), 23; McKim, 'Advertising Agencies', 17–19; 'Advertising in Montreal', *Printer & Publisher* 12:5 (May 1903), 16; 'The System and Equipment of a Modern Newspaper Advertising Agency', *Canadian Newspaper Directory*, 3rd edn (1901), 21–6; *Printer & Publisher* 16:10 (October 1907), 35; *Printer & Publisher* 16:6 (June 1907), 30; Stephenson and McNaught, *Story of Advertising*, 99–109; French, *20th Century Advertising*, 226–8.

38 R.G. Dun & Company, *The Mercantile Agency Reference Book* (Toronto: Dun, 1904), 265, 423; R.G. Dun & Company, *The Mercantile Agency Reference Book* (Toronto: Dun, 1919), 311, 507, 512, 526.

39 J.J. Gibbons, 'The Arrangement between the Agents and Publishers', *Printer & Publisher* 17:2 (February 1908), 32f–g; *Canadian Newspaper Directory*, 3rd edn (1901), 21–2.

Polling Consumers: The Rise of Market Research Surveys in Canada, 1929–1941

Daniel J. Robinson

Consumer surveys, the progenitor of public opinion polling which began in Canada in 1941, appeared in the late 1920s as a response to the perceived business 'problem' of marketing. Production methods, assisted by business statistics and scientific techniques, were significantly more rationalized and efficient by the 1920s, especially among large manufacturers. But comparable improvements in the marketing of goods were largely absent. Consumer sample surveys offered a means of gauging and anticipating consumer wants, thus enabling better production planning. More importantly, they were a powerful tool for advertisers to penetrate the desires and behaviour of Canada's 'market segments', securing data to improve the effectiveness and reliability of advertising itself. Two main groups spearheaded the development of this commercial technique: advertising agencies and market research firms, and magazine and newspaper owners seeking reader demographic profiles to showcase their publications' advertising potential.

By the late 1930s, market researchers had acquired the capacity to conduct national representative sample surveys, but rarely did such polls mirror the composition of the general population. Conceived and conducted not as a democratic or an egalitarian undertaking, consumer survey research targeted specific socio-economic groups thought most likely to purchase the product in question. Accordingly, most, though not all, surveys over-represented middle- and upper-income earners, city dwellers, and married women. Such surveys, indicative as they were of advertiser and manufacturer depictions of preferred or 'typical' consumers, call into question historical accounts of mass marketing emphasising broad-based popular participation. Daniel Boorstin, for example, argues that a salutary feature of American consumerism was manufacturer and advertiser efforts to 'democratiz[e] the market by inventing ways for the consumer to vote his preferences', which encompassed a 'new science for sampling the suffrage of consumers'.[1] More recently, Richard Tedlow praised the emergence of American mass marketing for 'making products available to the masses all over the nation', in essence 'democratizing consumption'.[2] From the standpoint of inter-war Canadian marketers, however, 'mass' consumption constituted less a universal phenomenon than a variable and stratified one.

Canada's economy experienced massive quantitative and qualitative changes in the two decades preceding the Great War. The GNP grew 112 per cent from 1900 to 1910, from $1.06 billion to $2.24 billion, making the early years of 'Canada's century', on an aggregate level, decidedly prosperous ones.[3] Staple products—wheat, wood, minerals, and other natural resources—fuelled much of this economic 'Great Boom', but there were also important structural changes in manufacturing, the result of concomitant industrial and managerial innovations beginning in the 1890s. In some industrial sectors, the drive to lower costs through longer, more efficient production runs gave rise to large, multi-unit enterprises, many horizontally or vertically integrated, and where hierarchies of salaried managers over time supplanted individual entrepreneurs in the office and on the shop floor. Operations were centralized, manufacturing methods stan-

Abridged from *Journal of the Canadian Historical Association* 8 (1997), 187–211. Reprinted by permission.

dardized, and national and international markets replaced local ones. Such Canadian and foreign-owned companies as Algoma Steel, Canadian General Electric, Canadian Westinghouse, Ford of Canada, and Canada Foundries typified this 'Second Industrial Revolution'.[4] . . .

An emergent feature of the ideology and operation of economies-of-scale manufacturing was the use of business statistics, most of which were supplied by Ottawa. The 1901 census of manufacturers was 'improved immeasurably' from earlier versions, containing broader classifications of industries and inaugural and comprehensive figures on material costs, wages, and miscellaneous expenses.[5] In 1905 the Census and Statistics Office was established—the first semi-permanent federal statistics agency.[6] Reflecting the growing importance of commercial statistics, the office was transferred from the Ministry of Agriculture to Trade and Commerce in 1912. Most significantly, the first annual census of production was conducted in the midst of the Great War in 1917, which provided detailed data on a wide range of economic activity in the manufacturing, construction, fisheries, forestry, and mining sectors. When established in 1918, the Dominion Bureau of Statistics' (DBS) mandate underscored the growing interconnection of state-sponsored statistics and the marketplace, seen as especially crucial for wartime industrial mobilization. The Bureau's purpose was to 'collect, abstract, compile, and publish statistical information relative to the commercial, industrial, social, economic, and general activities and condition of the people.'[7] . . .

While, by the 1920s, statistical knowledge of production processes was well advanced, far less was known about the product's passage from factory gate to purchasing consumer.[8] As one advertiser underlined in 1928: 'Distribution is the most important problem of modern business.'[9] . . . There were scant or non-existent statistical data in most marketing fields, including wholesale and retail practices, product packaging, sales methods, advertising, and consumer behaviour.

. . . When American officials moved to combine a census of distribution with the 1930 decennial census, Canadian businessmen—including manufacturers, advertisers, board of trade members, and bankers—seized on this precedent and lobbied for a similar Canadian venture to be part of the 1931 census. Ottawa consented, and a census of wholesaling and retailing, according to one DBS official, was launched 'with the blessings of representative bodies in the business world'.[10]

A watershed in Canadian marketing history, the Census of Merchandising and Service Establishments represented the first extensive and systematic overview of wholesale and retail operations in Canada and was a vital source of market research information from the early 1930s on. Lists of wholesale, retail, and service establishments were compiled by population enumerators and from other sources. These businesses were then mailed questionnaires soliciting such information as the commodities they handled, sales totals, employee wages, and supply channels. In total, 125,003 retailers, 13,140 wholesalers, and 42,223 service and amusement establishments were enumerated, along with 4,958 hotel operations;[11] only 5 per cent of eligible businesses were missed, the DBS estimated. In 1933, the Bureau began an annual survey of wholesale and retail operations, employing a sampling method that used the 1931 decennial census figures as a benchmark. As well, using smaller samples, monthly surveys of department stores, chain stores, and some independent retailers were initiated.[12] . . .

Government marketing statistics were a powerful, and for many, indispensable tool for navigating the vast and unpredictable empire of merchandizing. But for marketers seeking greater control and profitability of product distribution and sales, DBS figures were only a partial solution, for they revealed little about the consumer purchasing process. Questions that had long preoccupied business planners lacked definitive answers: who bought the product—young or old, male or female, rich or poor? Why did they buy it, and from where did they get the idea? Were they likely to keep on buying it? What kinds of appeals could get them to buy more of it? In providing answers, sales figures and price trend data were of limited use; rather, one had to ask consumers directly. And commencing in earnest in the late 1920s, a variety of interests began doing just that: conducting interviews with consumers, usually employing a sampling method, that probed the meanings and associated behaviour of mass consumption. Two groups were closely associated with this project to harness consumer opinions for commercial ends: advertising agencies and market research firms who hoped to enhance the effectiveness and 'scientific' authority of advertising; and magazine and newspaper owners wanting socio-economic profiles of reader audiences to furnish advertisers in their publications. By the early 1940s, this branch of market research—interview-based consumer research—was well developed, both methodologically and conceptually, evolving into a 'mass feedback technology'[13] that functioned to anticipate, rationalize, and ultimately increase consumer purchasing. It was, in part, the demand-side corollary of mass-production techniques long underway.

Credited as Canada's first full-time market researcher when hired in 1929 by the advertising firm Cockfield, Brown & Company, Henry King attributed his appointment to vice-president Warren Brown's interest in American market research, which he viewed as 'the coming thing' to Canada.[14] And indeed Americans were well advanced in consumer research by the late 1920s. The first systematic market research operation was started by Charles Coolidge Parlin in 1911, when he took charge of the newly formed research department at the Curtis Publishing Company, publisher of the *Saturday Evening Post* and *Ladies' Home Journal*. His 1912 four-volume study *Department Store Lines* was a seminal work in the new marketing 'science'. Parlin conducted 1,121 interviews and logged 37,000 miles visiting America's largest 100 cities

to compile the most detailed report of merchandising in department, dry goods, and men's ready-to-wear stores. The study, coupled with another three years later which in part analyzed consumer attitudes towards automobiles, was an early example of consumer feedback techniques: information gleaned from consumer surveys was fed back to producers and designers planning future products, and simultaneously fed forward to copywriters devising ads for current goods.[15] By 1916 the *Chicago Tribune* was conducting house-to-house interviewing to determine the socio-economic composition, buying habits, and newspaper reading traits of Chicago consumers, and in 1922 the *Milwaukee Journal* undertook a similar survey, repeated annually, for the Milwaukee area.[16] Such studies were used to convince consumer goods manufacturers of newspaper advertising's efficiency—it could target specific reading 'publics' or consumer markets—and effectiveness: it could employ the most persuasive selling techniques. Total advertising volume in the United States increased dramatically in the early twentieth century, rising from $256 million in 1900 to nearly $3 billion in 1929.[17] To ensure these advertising dollars targeted likely buyers and that ads used the most compelling sales appeals, questionnaire surveys on consumer preferences and the purchasing decision-making process took on increased importance.

In light of advertising's close links to market research, it is not surprising that advertising agencies developed extensive expertise in this materializing field. The most notable example was the advertising colossus J. Walter Thompson, particularly after 1916 when Stanley Resor became president. Resor, a disciple of nineteenth-century positivist philosopher Thomas Buckle, who proclaimed that aggregate human behaviour was observable and predictable only by statistical laws, insisted that advertising be empirically grounded. Soon after assuming office he created a market research department, and in 1920 added the renowned behavioural psychologist John B. Watson to the company payroll. By the early 1920s, Resor had recast JWT into a 'university of advertising', with its intensive consumer research and employee training programs based on social-scientific methods. . . .

As noted earlier, Cockfield, Brown & Company was the first Canadian advertising agency to acquire a market research capacity. The Montreal firm was formed in early 1929, when Warren Brown of National Publicity merged operations with Harry Cockfield's Advertising Service. In the late 1920s, Brown became concerned about the paucity of available statistics for advertising research. Most DBS data dealt with manufacturing and population demographics, and Brown championed the need for a 'self-contained operation', capable not only of analyzing data, but of collecting them too.[18] In late 1928, just before the merger, he hired William Goforth of McGill's Economics and Political Science Department as a part-time adviser on 'commercial research'. As Goforth was not available on a full-time basis until the end of the 1928–9 academic year, Henry King, an Oxford-educated classicist with prior advertising experience, was hired in January 1929 to oversee the firm's research operations. Soon after, other university-trained professionals appeared on the company payroll. Hubert Kemp, a marketing professor in the Political Economy Department at the University of Toronto, worked in the Montreal office during teaching breaks. Other economists offering their consulting services included Gilbert Jackson of the University of Toronto, Burton Hurd of the University of Manitoba, and McGill's John Culliton. Of the four full-time staff members of the recently formed Commercial Research and Economic Investigation Department in 1930, outside of King and Goforth, two were Harvard MBA graduates and another had an MA in economics. By 1930, the department was conducting a wide range of market studies for advertising clients.[19]

Judging by the rapid growth of research clientele, Cockfield, Brown had struck a reso-nant chord in the business community. In 1929, the firm conducted 6 major and 80 minor research assignments; during the first six months of 1930 alone it contracted for 30 major research commissions.[20] A cumulative list of completed market research studies, circa 1936, lists 68 major surveys spanning a broad range of fields, with such titles as 'Canadian Market for Surgical Dressings and Kindred Products', 'Rubber Footwear and Tire Market', 'Canadian Market for Canned Soup, Beans, and Spaghetti', and 'Canadian Market for Swimming Suits and Other Knit Goods'. Such firms as the Campbell Soup Company, Molson's Brewery, Kenwood Mills, Imperial Oil, and the Dominion Rubber Company counted among the many research clients of Cockfield, Brown.[21] One of its most thorough studies was done in 1932 for the soda maker Orange Crush. It investigated potential retail outlets by analyzing local business and weather conditions, and included a consumer sample survey of beverage preferences and drinking habits. Unfortunately, the latter's methodology was not discussed.[22] Cockfield, Brown's extensive research program, broadening the advertiser's traditional role beyond that of space buyer and copywriter, was championed by Harry Cockfield as early as 1931 as a 'highly important and even essential factor in effective agency work'. Relying on 'pretty pictures and clever copy' at the expense of research was a 'fundamentally unsound' advertising practice.[23] . . .

Many consumer research survey reports done in the 1930s by J. Walter Thompson's Canadian office have been preserved. From yeast cake to ammonia use, from garment tag reading to newspaper browsing, the ad firm's consumer surveys probed intently the thoughts and behaviour of the buying public. Taken together, they provide the most concerted and systematic Canadian effort to penetrate and harness consumer opinions for advertising purposes. In the late autumn of 1929, New York–based JWT opened an office in Montreal. Office manager Robert Flood, during a briefing of branch operations to JWT executives in New York, described how the firm had conducted 'the first Dominion-wide market survey' for the food manufacturer Standard Brands in December 1929 and January 1930. Although few methodological details were revealed, the survey covered seven food products sold in 29 cities and some 12,000 retail outlets. Flood reported that 'three out of every four women' bought Magic brand baking powder, and subsequent advertising had increased its sales by 5 per cent. As well, one of four 'housewives' made coffee in 'old-fashioned' pots, the rest in percolators. Sample size, survey method, and field interview systems were not discussed.[24]

While the above survey, probably JWT's first, was only mentioned, more than a dozen consumer surveys exist in the company's archives, documenting the range and increasing sophistication of the firm's research program. A December 1930 report on magazine readership was based on a nationwide sample survey of 1,688 people, comprising a 'representative cross-section of the urban population'.[25] Interviews were 'divided among families of different economic classes in relation to the estimated proportion of population in each class'. The report did not disclose sex distribution, how class stratification was determined, or how interviewing was conducted, but it did reveal a tidy amount about Canadians' magazine tastes and reading habits. Fifty-eight per cent read American magazines regularly, seven per cent more than read Canadian magazines, with *Maclean's* and *Canadian Home Journal* being the two most popular. Thirty-eight per cent read both Canadian and American publications, and reader 'duplication' rates for Canadian magazines were highlighted, information that could help advertisers more efficiently target reader-consumer markets.

Again, with a January 1931 report on household ammonia use by '1,040 housewives in 21 representative cities across Canada', there was little reporting of survey operation. 'Proportionate numbers from all economic class-

es' were said to comprise the sample, and in Quebec both English and French speakers were 'given adequate representation'.[26] The focus here, as with the earlier Standard Brands survey, on urban, married women was typical of many JWT consumer surveys and those of other organizations. During the 1920s and 1930s, women were thought to control 80 per cent or more of consumer spending; wives were typically considered by marketers and advertisers as the family's 'purchasing agent'.[27] City dwellers on average were more affluent than town or rural residents, who were also more expensive to interview owing to greater travel time. The result was a polled preponderance of urban, married women and the oftentimes conflation of homemaker, consumer, and respondent.

Accompanying this bias towards urban wives was a class bias. The first JWT report to provide class breakdown figures was a 1933 survey for Standard Brands on use of baking powder by Toronto, Kingston, Montreal, and Sherbrooke housewives. The sample was divided into three economic groups, of which the upper- and middle-income sections constituted 81 per cent of the 832 respondents.[28] A more pronounced class bias was found with a 1938 survey on breakfast cereal use in Ontario and Quebec. A JWT analysis of occupational statistics indicated that in a survey divided into four income groups, the top two—'A' and 'B'—should not exceed 30 per cent of the sample. However, 'to permit an adequate upper-class sample for tabulation', it was decided to use the following income quotas: 10 per cent for the 'A' homes (annual income above $5,000); 25 per cent for 'B' ($3,500 to $5,000); 50 per cent for 'C' ($1,500 to $3,500); and 15 per cent for 'D' (under $1,500). These categories, however, grossly inflated Canada's income distribution. Listed below are the average annual salaries by occupation group for 1931, the most recent census year: labourer ($480); semi-skilled ($791); skilled ($1,042); clerical-commercial-financial ($1,192); professional ($1,924); and managerial ($2,468).[29] Without significant sources of secondary income, none of these average wage-earning families even came close to the 'B' range. All but professionals and managers would fall into the 'D' group, which comprised just 15 per cent of the survey. Presumably, only plutocrats filled the 'A' quota.[30] Of course, consumption of breakfast cereal, like that of many other commodities, was not a democratic phenomenon; 'A' cupboards on average contained three times the cereal as 'D' ones. Understandably, market researchers here and on other occasions targeted consumer markets or 'universes' with disproportionate numbers of the 'buying' public, while simultaneously under-representing other groups among the 'general' public.

Witness the unorthodox 1938 survey of adolescent newspaper reading habits which deliberately oversampled upper-income children. Some 495 Toronto youths aged 8 to 16 were given questionnaires to complete in small groups at Sunday schools, settlement houses, and Boy Scout meetings. Boys and girls, at 54 and 46 per cent respectively, were included in near proportionate numbers. But the sampling framework fixed the A-B group ('those whose fathers earn $3,000 a year or over') at 30 per cent, even though JWT officials estimated 'that only 15 per cent of the population [came] under the AB classification'. Class determination was 'judged by the neighbourhood in which the interviews took place'. Two-thirds of respondents were 12 years or older, which 'correspond[ed] roughly to the potential appeal advertising can make on the adolescent', since older children were thought more receptive to advertising. The 25-question survey probed reading interests and routines for various Toronto daily and weekly newspapers. Part of the questionnaire adopted a fact-quiz format for comic-strip, editorial, and advertising items, including questions like, 'Where did Donald Duck try to take a bath in last Sunday's *Telegram*?' and 'What product in the *Star* was advertised by an umbrella and the headline "Under the Weather?"' Comic strips proved the

hands-down reading favourite; nearly three-quarters of children could recall and describe the plot of interviewer-selected strips in their previous day's paper. Only 39 per cent remembered the front-page headline. While just 15 per cent recognized prominently displayed ads from yesterday's paper, a remarkable 59 per cent identified products promoted by comic-strip advertising.[31] The implications of such findings for youth-directed advertising were obvious.[32] . . .

Along with J. Walter Thompson and Cockfield, Brown, another firm assumed prominence in the consumer surveying field. Founded in 1932, Canadian Facts was not an advertising agency, but a 'research house' which performed specialized market research services for corporate, and later government, clients. Still operating today, it endures as Canada's oldest market research firm. Its origins date back to a 1932 meeting between Cockfield, Brown executive Frank Ryan and Ethel Fulford, a Bell Telephone operator supervisor. Ryan sought a telephone-based survey method to measure the size and composition of radio program audiences in order to develop advertising strategies for this new medium. Fulford recruited some of her operators into a newly formed business which conducted telephone surveys of Toronto residents to gauge their radio listening. Known as the 'coincidental telephone method', respondents were asked which station, if any, they were tuned to when called. Demographic information was also solicited. Canada's pioneer radio 'ratings' service (or 'audience research',[33] as it later was known), it counted Procter & Gamble and Lever Brothers among its early clients, both major sponsors of daytime radio soap operas.[34] The firm's early operations focussed on radio audiences, but by the late 1930s it had moved into other areas of market research. . . .

Of extant Canadian Facts surveys, the most ambitious was a December 1940 readership poll for *Maclean's* magazine.[35] A 1,438-person sample of magazine readers were shown two recent issues and asked to select editorial items they had read. Interviewing was restricted to cities and, significantly, targeted upscale readers: 'No attempt was made to match proportionate income levels in the various cities, calls being concentrated primarily in middle- and high-income areas. . . .' The A-B income group ($1,800 and up) formed 60 per cent of the sample. Among occupational categories, executives and professionals totalled 40 per cent, unskilled labourers just 3 per cent. The survey was highly unusual in one respect: men comprised 53 per cent of the sample, one of the few instances in which adult males outnumbered women. A public-affairs magazine with a sizeable male readership, the *Maclean's* survey conferred 'consumer' status and sampled inclusion to this characteristically (and ironically) under-represented group. Indeed, many of the survey's findings highlighted male–female reading differences. Of the 46 editorial items listed, men on average read (or claimed to have read) 18.2, women 15.3. Men preferred articles and editorials over fiction, women generally the reverse; more women than men tackled crossword puzzles. Both groups judged 'topical subjects' as better cover photos than 'pretty girls'. A surprise finding, no doubt reassuring to *Maclean's* officials, was the higher-than-thought average number of readers—4.03—for each copy sold. The report included 100-plus pages of cross-tabulations by age, sex, class, region, city, and item reading. Such data, according to *Maclean's* associate editor Arthur Irwin, could serve as a guidepost to 'market demand, i.e. the interest and tastes of our reader constituency', and 'the degree to which our editorial contents meet that demand'. While editorial decisions could not be made 'solely on the basis of a chart', survey data could be 'extremely useful to a good editor'. [36]

It was also 'extremely useful' for advertisers to learn of survey findings revealing greater-than-expected readership rates, especially among upper-income audiences. On 15 April 1941, the Maclean Publishing Company hosted a reception for advertising executives, during

which presentations were made on the Canadian Facts survey. *Maclean's* editor H. Napier Moore called it the first time that a 'publication [had] revealed the result of a factual test showing each and every [editorial] item' and corresponding reader interest. The data, Moore stated, were 'going to be a guide to us in our editorial planning and they either confirm or revise our editorial judgment.' Irwin, who had earlier corresponded with American magazine publishers about their reader survey experiences,[37] was more lukewarm to this numerative standard: surveys allowed 'scientific methods' to become a planning feature of the editorial process, but the editor's job still remained more an art than a systematic technique. But advertisers, who for over a decade had been exposed to the research doctrine of statistics and scientific investigation, were perhaps more receptive to president Horace Hunter's concluding comments: survey research should function as an 'external audit' of business or marketing practices, mirroring the 'intelligence departments of any army' seeking to 'get at the real facts'.[38] Besieged by advertising competition from American magazines and radio, the company promoted the survey's findings to win back lost advertising dollars. Throughout the war years, Canadian Facts continued to poll *Maclean's* and *Chatelaine* readers annually,[39] and in 1943 Maclean Publishing established its own research department.[40]

Canadian newspaper owners similarly strove to take the pulse of reader-consumers to bolster advertising revenue, which by the 1930s had become the financial cornerstone of the daily press. Mirroring related trends in other industries, newspaper publishing was transformed by mergers and economies-of-scale production, beginning in the 1910s. The number of Canadian dailies peaked at 138 in 1913, but by 1931 this had dropped to 111, and by 1941 only 90 remained. Meanwhile, average circulation rates rose from 5,000 in 1901 to over 25,000 in 1940. In the same period, spurred on by higher rates of literacy and urbanization, total daily newspaper circulation grew from 600,000 to 2,165,000.[41] By the late 1930s, two newspaper chains, Southam and Sifton, controlled nearly 20 per cent of the Canadian market. Whereas Victorian-era newspaper publishers required moderate financial outlays and derived much of their revenue from subscriptions or political patronage, the typical post-war daily was a heavily capitalized, advertising-dependent operation. Subscription and newsstand revenues lagged well behind the large sums needed to meet burgeoning payrolls or operate the photo-engraving plants and faster presses of the 'mass' dailies. By 1918, most profitable newspapers required 60 to 65 per cent of their space to be filled by advertising.[42] A key consequence of 'the industrialization of the press and its dependence upon advertising', according to Carlton McNaught, was the emphasis on broadening circulation, 'not primarily to enlarge a newspaper's influence upon the minds of its public, but to enhance the value of its space to advertisers',[43] without whom accelerating production costs could not be met.

The earliest known newspaper reader survey was a *Toronto Star*–commissioned survey in 1930, the results of which were trumpeted in a *Star* promotional. The poll, done by a little-known organization, the Library Bureau of Canada, comprised a cross-section of the 'newspaper reading habits' of members of Toronto homes. Sample size and survey methodology were not disclosed. Claiming the *Star* was read in 50,110 Toronto homes (and disproportionately so among home- and car-owners), the survey constituted 'proof' of the *Star*'s advertising superiority over the *Telegram* and the *Mail and Empire*: 'The mass of buying in Toronto is done by families of the kind who were found to be readers of the Star.'[44] Its publishers would later claim in 1934 that 'repeated surveys' had confirmed the *Star*'s widespread penetration of 'the homes of people of means, or those able to buy the produce or service advertised'.[45] In 1938, the *Winnipeg Free Press* released the results of its 'Independent Survey of the Winnipeg Market'.

According to the advertising trade magazine *Marketing*, the questionnaire survey revealed not only the number of *Free Press* readers, but 'how many of these families [had] automobiles, radios, electric refrigerators', and owned homes. Copies of the report were distributed among consumer goods advertisers and ad agencies.[46]

A more centralized and systematic program of newspaper market research was launched in the mid-1930s by the Canadian Daily Newspapers Association (CDNA). Here again, the primary objective was to augment advertising revenue, which the Depression and magazine and radio competition had rendered more tenuous. In 1936, the CDNA established a Research Committee, which worked closely with the Dominion Bureau of Statistics to compile data on newspaper buying and consumer markets. The following year the committee released *The Canadian Market*, a compilation of census and marketing statistics elucidating consumer purchasing power in regional and local markets served by newspapers. Its promotional campaign stressed the strengths of the daily newspaper as an advertising vehicle. As well, the committee conducted a study of the food industry, a sector making up one-quarter of total retail sales and a heavy print advertiser.[47] In 1939, CDNA researchers published *The Consumer Survey*, a statistical overview of consumer brand buying in newspaper markets, based on the results of questionnaires printed in 70 CDNA member dailies. Respondents who completed and mailed back the surveys were eligible for gifts and prize money, and some 20,000 questionnaires were reportedly returned. National advertisers and ad agencies were also involved with the project.[48]

While none of this research incorporated sample survey interviews, this would change with the activities of the Bureau of Advertising, which succeeded the Research Committee in late 1938. Possessing a larger budget and broader mandate than its predecessor, the Bureau also benefited from formal affiliation with an American partner, the Bureau of Advertising of the American Newspaper Publishers Association (ANPA). Ties to the American Bureau, CDNA officials asserted, would grant Canadian publishers access to American head-office executives who made advertising decisions for their Canadian branches. As well, since 1935, the ANPA had been spearheading a 'United Front' campaign among newspaper owners seeking to win back advertising lost to radio, magazine, and billboard advertising.[49]

Consumer and advertising research figured prominently in the United Front campaign, best exemplified by 'The Continuing Study of Newspaper Reading'. Launched in July 1939 in co-operation with the Association of National Advertisers and the American Association of Advertising Agencies, the Continuing Study encompassed a series of newspaper reader surveys conducted by the Publication Research Service, formerly the Gallup Research Service. The supervisor of field operations was Harold Anderson, a partner of George Gallup and co-founder of the American Institute of Public Opinion. The survey method used was pioneered by Gallup in the 1920s and was known among market researchers as the 'Gallup method'. Selected samples of individuals were presented copies of the previous day's newspaper and asked to mark editorial, advertising, and other items they had read. By 1941, such surveys had been done for some two dozen American newspapers, and, in Canada, *Hamilton Spectator*, *Windsor Star* and *Montreal Star* readers were similarly polled.[50] The combined survey results revealed that 75 per cent of men and 93 per cent of women read advertisements, excluding the classifieds. Countering conventional wisdom, left-page ads were read more often than right-page ones. Local ads registered more with readers than did national ones, a fact which privileged newspaper advertising, as one speaker at the 1940 CDNA annual meeting highlighted: 'Each individual man or woman is most interested in the things that immediately concern him, his neighbour, his town, his county . . . the newspaper is the only

medium which is hand-tailored to fit exactly this interest in every market.'[51]

Though the study's composite data were mostly American, CDNA officials actively publicized its findings to Canadian advertisers. In 1940 and 1941, the Advertising Bureau gave presentations on Continuing Study results to 19 different groups of advertisers and ad agency executives. Firms like General Foods, Campbell Soup Company, Kellogg, and Pepsi-Cola were supplied with survey results. Large companies seen as underemploying newspaper advertising, or those which had recently curtailed print advertising, were specifically targeted. Indeed, promotional work for the Continuing Study was deemed the Bureau's 'foremost activity' in 1941.[52] The research program, in the words of Bureau executive Duncan MacInnes, worked to foster a 'new and more constructive concept of media'. Newspapers could now advance beyond a preoccupation with circulation figures and concentrate on 'the potentialities of the markets reached . . . [and] the manner in which people read'.[53] Such research provided fact-based assessments of reader-consumer habits and functioned, asserted one newspaper market researcher in 1940, to 'make the newspaper an adviser, friend, and counsellor to [ad] agencies and manufacturers, rather than the space-chaser it largely is today'.[54]

No doubt, some corporate advertisers and ad firm executives cast skeptical glances on newspaper-sponsored surveys trumpeting the merits of daily press advertising. Any claims of 'objectivity' were obviously compromised by economic self-interest. But the significance of the CDNA research program lies less in its impartial credibility than in its very presence. Aware that magazine publishers and radio owners were using sample surveys to shore up advertising revenue, newspaper publishers followed suit, believing quantitative analyses were necessary to maintain or boost ad dollars—the *sine qua non* of the modern daily. By 1941, the Advertising Bureau's research activities had grown considerably from their mid-1930s origins; procuring newspaper advertising and conducting market research were increasingly coterminous.

By 1941, consumer surveys were a familiar, if not ubiquitous, feature of Canadian marketing and advertising. The advance of this commercial technique was a manifestation of a deeper drive for rationalization and efficiency characterizing large-scale manufacturing in Canada. Since the early 1900s, census manufacturing statistics had helped facilitate economies-of-scale production systems. The Census of Merchandising and Service Establishments of 1931, along with other DBS marketing data, were conceived and championed as statistical tools to replicate this feat for distribution and sales. Such data, however, fell short of procuring 'facts' about consumer attitudes and the purchasing decision-making process. Consequently, firms like Cockfield, Brown, J. Walter Thompson, and Canadian Facts turned to quota sample surveys in order, in the words of one contemporary, to determine 'the *what* of manufacturing, the *where* of advertising, and the *how* of selling'.[55] The market researcher's frequent invocation of 'science' to distinguish the consumer survey from rule-of-thumb practices served more as an appropriation of an authoritative symbol than as a bona fide display of experimentally derived predictive 'proof'. But market research polling by the early 1940s, nonetheless, had become a powerful and singular technique for quantifying and correlating consumer opin-

ions, tastes, and behaviours, a fact supported by the willing adoption of consumer surveys by advertising-dependent newspaper and magazine publishers.

It is useful to reiterate James Beniger's by now self-evident point that specific business interests were the impetus and locomotion for early market research surveys, which were definitely not the result of 'consumers looking for new ways to "speak their minds"'.[56] 'Enfranchising' consumers or expanding 'consumer sovereignty' via opinion surveys did not factor into the market researcher's schema.[57] The goal was to penetrate and exploit for profit consumer worries, fancies, and longings. But not necessarily all consumers. While, as Susan Strasser observes, 'twentieth-century rhetoric has conflated democracy with an abundance of consumer goods,' business decision making operated mainly on a 'one dollar–one vote basis'. The poor were and are effectively disenfranchised.[58] Converse similarly underscores that early American market research samples were disproportionately 'cross-sections of the prosperous'.[59] The same was also true for most Canadian consumer polls before 1941. As the poor went mostly undetected, so too did men. 'Woman is a shopper,' pioneer marketer Charles Parlin proclaimed in 1912,[60] and in inter-war Canadian consumer surveys so she largely remained, most likely married, a city dweller, and drawn from middle- to upper-income ranks.

Notes

1   Daniel J. Boorstin, *The Americans: The Democratic Experience* (New York, 1973), 148.
2   Richard S. Tedlow, *New and Improved: The Story of Mass Marketing in America* (New York, 1990), 16.
3   M.C. Urquhart and A.H. Buckley, eds, *Historical Statistics of Canada* (Toronto, 1965), 141.
4   Robert Bothwell, Ian Drummond, and John English, *Canada 1900–1945* (Toronto, 1987), 74; Graham D. Taylor and Peter A. Baskerville, *A*

Concise History of Business in Canada (Toronto, 1994), 309–12, 336–8.
5   M.C. Urquhart, 'Three Builders of Canada's Statistical System', *Canadian Historical Review* 68 (September 1987), 423.
6   Canada. *Dominion Bureau of Statistics: History, Function, Organization* (Ottawa, 1952), 9.
7   *Dominion Bureau of Statistics*, 10; Urquhart and Buckley, eds, *Historical Statistics*, 454; Urquhart,

'Three Builders', 428; R.H. Coats, 'Beginnings in Canadian Statistics', *Canadian Historical Review* 27 (June 1946), 127–9.

8   Few historical works examine marketing in Canada. On retail chains, see Joy L. Santink, *Timothy Eaton and the Rise of His Department Store* (Toronto, 1990). See also, David Monod, 'Bay Days', and especially his *Store Wars: Shopkeepers and the Culture of Mass Marketing, 1890–1939* (Toronto, 1996), 102–8.

9   Ian H. Macdonald, 'USA Makes Census of Distribution', *Canadian Advertising Data* (February 1930), 78.

10 Herbert Marshall, 'The Statistical Basis of Marketing Policy', in *Canadian Marketing Problems*. H.R. Kemp, ed. (Toronto, 1939), 13; 'The Reasons for Taking Census of Merchandising in Canada', *Canadian Advertising Data* (July 1931), 8.

11 Dominion Bureau of Statistics, 20, 47.

12 Canada. *Census of Canada, 1931*, vol. 10, *Merchandising and Services, Part I*, and vol. 11, *Merchandising and Services, Part 2* (Ottawa, 1934); Marshall, 'The Statistical Basis of Marketing Policy', 13–20; Urquhart and Buckley, eds, *Historical Statistics*, 562–3.

13 James R. Beniger, *The Control Revolution: Technological and Economic Origins of the Information Society* (Cambridge, MA, 1986), 20.

14 Henry King, 'The Beginning of Marketing Research in Canada', in *Marketing Research in Canada*. W.H. Mahatoo, ed. (Toronto, 1968), 20–2. See also, A.B. Blankenship, Chuck Chakrapani, and W. Harold Poole, *A History of Marketing Research in Canada* (Toronto, 1985), 28.

15 Charles Parlin, *The Merchandising of Automobiles, An Address to Retailers* (Philadelphia, 1915); Douglas B. Ward, 'Tracking the Culture of Consumption: Curtis Publishing Company, Charles Coolidge Parlin, and the Origins of Market Research, 1911–1930', Ph.D. thesis, University of Maryland, 1996; Beniger, *The Control Revolution*; Jean Converse, *Survey Research in the United States: Roots and Emergence 1890–1960* (Berkeley, 1987), 89; Robert Bartels, *The Development of Marketing Thought* (Homewood, IL,

1962), 109.

16 Lawrence C. Lockley, 'Notes on the History of Market Research', *Journal of Marketing* 14 (April 1950), 735; Converse, Survey Research, 90.

17 Daniel Pope, *The Making of Modern Advertising* (New York, 1983), 26.

18 Blankenship, Chakrapani, and Poole, *History of Marketing Research*, 18–19.

19 W.H. Poole, 'Marketing Research in Canada', *Commerce Journal* (February 1957), 21; King, 'Beginnings of Marketing Research', 21.

20 National Archives of Canada (NAC), MG 32 G9, H.E. Kidd Papers, vol. 26, Goforth to Kidd, 17 June 1930.

21 NAC, Kidd Papers, vol. 25, file 14, 'Partial List of Market Surveys'.

22 'Orange Crush Base Campaign on Nation-Wide Survey', *Canadian Advertising Data* (May 1932), 3.

23 H.R. Cockfield, 'Trend in Advertising Agency Practice (Part II)', *Canadian Advertising Data* (January 1931), 19.

24 Duke University, Special Collections Library, J. Walter Thompson Papers [JWT], Box 2, Minutes of Representatives Meetings, 14 May 1930; 'Montreal Office Growing Rapidly' *J.W.T. News* (June 1930): 3.

25 JWT Papers, Reel 223, 'Facts on Canadian Media', December 1930.

26 JWT Papers, Reel 223, 'Survey of the Canadian Market For Household Ammonia', January 1931.

27 Roland Marchand, *Advertising the American Dream: Making Way for Modernity* (Berkeley, 1985), 66.

28 JWT Papers, Reel 224, 'Survey of the Baking Powder Market in 4 Canadian Cities', June 1933.

29 Urquhart and Buckley, eds, *Historical Statistics*, 96.

30 JWT Papers, Reel 232, 'A Consumer Survey of the Canadian Market for Ready-to-Eat Cereals', August 1938.

31 JWT Papers, Reel 224, 'Survey of Newspaper Reading Habits of Adolescents', July 1938.

32 On comic strips and advertising, see 'Boom in Comics', *Canadian Advertising* (March 1935), 27–8; Spalding Black, 'Adapting Colored Comics to Advertising', *Canadian Advertising* (April 1937), 11–12; and 'Even the Politicians Go for the Strip',

Canadian Advertising (October 1937), 22.

33 On this subject, see Ross A. Eaman, *Channels of Influence: CBC Audience Research and the Canadian Public* (Toronto, 1994).

34 Canadian Facts (Toronto) company records, 'Canadian Facts at Fifty', circa 1982. Blankenship, et al., *History of Marketing Research*, 22; Eaman, *Channels of Influence*, 50.

35 Archives of Ontario [AO], Maclean-Hunter Papers, vol. 403, file 'Surveys', Canadian Facts Survey, 'Report of a Readership Study on Maclean's Magazine in Twenty-three Canadian Cities', December 1940; Irwin memo, 'Notes on Survey of Reader Reaction to Maclean's Magazine, December 1940', n.d. Since the early 1930s, *Maclean's* had conducted or sponsored small-scale, *ad hoc* surveys of its readers. Blankenship, et al., *History of Marketing Research*, 23.

36 Ibid. Irwin memo, 'Notes on Survey of Reader Reaction . . .' On journalists' complaints in the early 1980s about the use of marketing surveys to determine editorial content—derided as 'Pablum Canada' by one reporter—see Canada, *Report of the Royal Commission on Newspapers* (Ottawa, 1981), 172.

37 Maclean-Hunter Papers, vol. 402, file 'W.A. Irwin—correspondence, 1941', Irwin to McLaughlin, 5 April 1941; Irwin to Robinson, 5 April 1941; McLaughlin to Irwin, 8 April 1941.

38 Maclean-Hunter Papers, vol 402, file 'W.A. Irwin—notes, drafts' 'Special Conference—Royal York Hotel, Reader Survey of *Chatelaine* and *Maclean's*', 15 April 1941.

39 Maclean-Hunter Papers, vol. 402, file 'Surveys—Chatelaine', 'Second Readership Study of Editorial Items in Chatelaine, October–November 1941', December 1941; 'Report of Item-by-Item Study of Readership of Two Consecutive Issues of Chatelaine', 17 January 1944. Vol. 404, file 'Maclean's Readership Survey 1941–42', 'Study of Readership on an Item-by-item Basis of Two Consecutive Issues of Maclean's Magazine', 24 December 1942; 'Survey of M.M. Readership, 1944', n.d.; file 'Survey Audience 1944', 'Report of Results of Study of Canadian Publication Audiences', 6 June 1945.

40 Floyd S. Chalmers, 'Canada A New Market', *The Commerce Journal* (April 1944), 54. Since 1925, Maclean Publishing had produced the annual *Financial Post Business Year Book, Canada & Newfoundland*, which compiled manufacturing and marketing statistics for business audiences.

41 H.R. Kesterton, *A History of Journalism in Canada* (Toronto, 1967), 71; Carlton McNaught, *Canada Gets the News* (Toronto, 1940), 9–10, 24; Rutherford, *Making of the Canadian Media*, 48–9; Canada, *Report of the Royal Commission on Publications* (Ottawa, 1961), 245; *Report of the Royal Commission on Newspapers*, 65.

42 Vipond, *Mass Media in Canada*, 17.

43 McNaught, *Canada Gets the News*, 19; see also Harold Innis, *The Press: A Neglected Factor in the Economic History of the Twentieth Century* (London, 1949), 12; Rutherford, *Making of the Canadian Media*, 50–2; and Minko Michael Sotiron, 'From Politics to Profit: The Commercialization of Canadian English-Language Daily Newspapers 1890 to 1920', Ph.D. thesis, Concordia University, 1990, 4–12.

44 'Star Strength in Toronto', (ad) *Canadian Advertising Data* 3 (March 1930), 47.

45 'Still Bigger value for your advertising dollar' (ad) *Marketing* (4 August 1934), 5. For similar promotional ads by the *Montreal Daily Star* propounding reader purchasing power, see 'Logic!', *Marketing* (10 February 1934), 3; and 'Are You Keeping Step With This Market?', *Marketing* (29 May 1937), 3.

46 'Survey of Buying Power', *Marketing* (10 December 1938), 9.

47 Canadian Daily Newspapers Association (CDNA), Toronto, 'Report of Nineteenth Annual Meeting of the Canadian Daily Newspaper Association', 22 April 1938, 37–9; W.A. Craick, *A History of Canadian Journalism*, vol. II (Toronto, 1959), 210–12; 'Canadian Markets Shown in Volume of Vivid Charts', *Canadian Advertising* (October 1937), 23. See too CDNA, *The Canadian Market: 1938 Supplement; A Graphic Summary of Canadian Statistics, and an Analysis of Retail Trade* (Toronto, 1938).

48 CDNA, 'Report of the Twenty-First Annual Meeting of the Canadian Daily Newspapers Association', 30–1 May 1940, p. 40; 'CDNA Market Study Ready in September', *Marketing* (22 July 1939), 8. Canadian data on newspaper markets were available in the American trade publications *Editor and Publisher: Market Guide* and *Editor and Publisher: The Fourth Estate*. Also noteworthy was the annual *Lydiatt's Book of Canadian Market and Advertising Data*.

49 CDNA, 'Report of Nineteenth Annual Meeting of the Canadian Daily Newspaper Association', 22 April 1938, p. 42; Craick, *History of Canadian Journalism*, 213.

50 Duncan MacInnes, 'What of Newspaper Advertising?' *Quarterly Review of Commerce* 8 (Spring 1941), 230–9.

51 CDNA, 'Report of the Twenty-First Annual Meeting of the Canadian Daily Newspapers Association', 30–1 May 1940, pp. 52–3. Wilder Breckenridge was the speaker.

52 Ibid., 46–7; 'Report of the Twenty-Second Annual Meeting', 7 March 1941, pp. 8–9.

53 MacInnes, 'What of Newspaper Advertising?' 230–1.

54 Elmer P. Resseguie, 'Newspapers and Market Research', in *Marketing Organization and Technique*. Jane McKee, ed. (Toronto, 1940), 68.

55 Douglas J. Wilson, 'Psychological Aspects of Market Research', *Quarterly Review of Commerce* 3 (Winter 1936), 67.

56 James R. Beniger, 'The Popular Symbolic Repertoire and Mass Communication', *Public Opinion Quarterly* 47 (Winter 1983), 482.

57 See also Sally Clarke, 'Consumer Negotiations', *Business and Economic History* 26 (Fall 1997), 109.

58 Strasser, *Satisfaction Guaranteed*, 288.

59 Converse, *Survey Research*, 92, 445 fn 35.

60 Cited in Boorstin, *The Americans*, 152. On this point, see also William R. Leach, 'Transformation in a Culture of Consumption: Women and Department Stores, 1890–1925', *Journal of American History* 71 (September 1984): 319–42; and Marchand, *Advertising the American Dream*, 66–9.

'I told you so': Newspaper Ownership in Canada and the Kent Commission Twenty Years Later

Richard Keshen and Kent MacAskill

'I told you so' was part of Tom Kent's reply when asked recently about the state of the newspaper industry in Canada (Cobb 1996b, A1). Kent, chairperson of the 1980 Royal Commission on Newspapers, might be forgiven his expression of self-satisfaction. Deprecated and dismissed when the Commission's report first appeared, Kent and his report are now being cited for their prescient analysis. Shelved as either dangerous or impracticable, the Commission's recommendations are now being seriously debated. This paper aims to explain this renewed interest in the Kent Commission.

Background

The Royal Commission on Newspapers, popularly known as the Kent Commission, was created in 1980 in response to allegations of collusion following the same-day closings of the Thomson-owned *Ottawa Journal* and the Southam-owned *Winnipeg Tribune*. These closings left each company—Southam in Ottawa and Thomson in Winnipeg—with monopolies in their respective cities. The closings were followed by expressions of public concern over newspaper concentration in Canada and worries that the fourth estate was not fulfilling its democratic function. The Commission's mandate was to explore these concerns and make recommendations for improvement.

At the time of the Kent Commission, these two newspaper chains, Thomson and Southam, were dominant. Together, they accounted for 77 per cent of the 117 dailies in Canada. Significantly, this proportion was up from 58 per cent just 10 years previously, when the first gov-

ernment inquiry on newspapers had been established under Senator Keith Davey. In 1980 Thomson owned the largest number of Canadian newspapers. As well as publishing the *Globe and Mail*, Canada's only national newspaper at the time, Thomson owned 40 other dailies. The Southam chain, on the other hand, had the largest total daily circulation, capturing 32.8 per cent of the English-Canadian newspaper-buying public (Canada, Royal Commission 1981, ch. 1).

The Kent Commission was generally critical of Canada's newspaper business, confirming the fears that instigated the Commission. Kent reserved his harshest criticism, however, for the Thomson newspaper chain. While praising Thomson for maintaining the quality of the *Globe and Mail*, the Commission saw the Thomson-controlled smaller dailies as epitomizing the worst aspects of corporate ownership in the print media. The Kent Commission argued that Thomson was squeezing the quality from most of its newspapers in exchange for higher profits. As well, the Thomson conglomerate owned large assets outside the newspaper business. Kent argued that Thomson ran its newspapers much the way it operated its other businesses—profit was its dominant goal. By contrast, Southam (then owned by the Southam family) was focused primarily on newspapers, and quality was not necessarily sacrificed to profit. As Kent put it, Southam still had a 'newspaper conscience': 'They spend, on the contents of their newspapers, many millions of dollars a year that are by the simple criterion of the bottom line, entirely wasted' (Kent 1982). A paper bought out by Thomson, on the other hand, inevitably 'becomes a little thinner and the share of

Abridged from *American Review of Canadian Studies* 30, 3 (Autumn 2000), 315–25. Reprinted by permission.

advertising increases as a percentage of the newspaper's total space' (Kent 1982). Cost-cutting measures are frequently introduced, especially with regard to editorial and news space. These cost-cutting measures occur in an already highly profitable industry, Kent argued. The Thomson conglomerate was (and is) owned by Ken Thomson. But the philosophy behind Thomson newspapers seems to have come from Roy Thomson, Ken's father and founder of the Thomson empire. Roy Thomson famously said that owning television stations and daily newspapers in Canada is like owning money-making machines—only with newspaper ownership, unlike television, one doesn't need a licence (Siegel 1996, 123). Focusing on ownership, the Kent Commission predicted conglomerate ownership would increase in the 1980s and 1990s. The Commission produced evidence that chains like Southam—those with a 'newspaper conscience'—would become ripe for a takeover if the political situation were not changed. As we will see, this prediction has been fulfilled.

Based on evidence compiled over a 10-month period, the Kent Commission laid out a set of dramatic recommendations to improve the industry. The Commission proposed a tax incentive designed to increase news and editorial content. Any newspaper spending more than the industry average on news content, in proportion to its total revenue, would be rewarded with a substantial tax credit. In order to balance this incentive, 'since there is no reason to subsidize the industry as it is, a 25 per cent surtax would be imposed on papers spending less than the industry average on news and editorial content' (Kent 1985, 20).

In a direct attack on conglomerate ownership, Kent proposed a number of measures to block both further newspaper concentration and further cross-media ownership. Such recommendations included prohibiting ownership of a national newspaper if a company owned other newspapers, prohibiting extreme geographic concentration (no monopolies in a province, for example),

and, finally, the two largest chains should be made to divest some of their dailies and other media holdings.

Kent believed that his most important long-run recommendations were those designed to open newspapers to public scrutiny. A newspaper is an important community institution, he argued, yet its affairs are normally hidden behind the boardrooms of conglomerate companies. Kent proposed that the editorial unit of a newspaper be required to issue a public statement of its purpose and policy. The content of the statement would be entirely up to the newspaper; it would simply be putting on public record what it stands for. The newspaper would then be required to publish an annual report detailing what it has been doing to fulfil its stated purpose. An advisory committee, consisting of two representatives of the owners, two members of the journalistic staff, and three outside members chosen by the first four, would evaluate the annual reports, and the evaluations would be made public. Finally, as a further countervailing force, there would be a Press Rights Panel within the Human Rights Commission that would comment on both the annual report and the advisory committee's evaluation.

The negative reaction that met the Kent Commission on publication was unprecedented in the history of Canadian Royal Commissions. 'Idiot's delight', 'monstrous', 'vindictive', 'unacceptable and dangerous' were typical of the insults hurled at the Commission (*Saskatoon Star-Phoenix* 1981). Innumerable references were made to 'Big Brother' and to the end of press freedom. Personal attacks were levelled at Tom Kent. He was said to be 'authoritarian' and a dupe of the Liberal party. Often, the Commission was simply treated as a joke. Fred Hagel, editor-in-chief of the two Irving newspapers in Saint John, proclaimed that its report 'reads a bit like a psychedelic dream' (*Saskatoon Star-Phoenix* 1981). Through the Canadian Daily Newspaper Publishers Association (CDNPA), the newspaper owners flexed their political muscle in Ottawa. In the end, the government decided Kent's recommendations were unsaleable to the Canadian public, and the report was shelved. The concern over newspaper ownership, which had flared up so quickly, died down almost as quickly.

. . .

The Re-emergence of the Kent Commission

Whereas the publication of the Kent Commission in 1981 provoked cries of 'big brother' and 'monstrous', recent comments on the Commission are almost always commendatory. Typical of this new attitude is the change of view between editions of Arthur Siegel's standard text, *Politics and the Media in Canada*. In the first edition, published in 1983, Siegel issued a harsh indictment of the Kent Commission, stating that its recommendations were 'produced in haste' (Siegel 1983, 146). He particularly condemned Kent's proposal for a government ombudsperson and wondered whether the deeper issue wasn't really a struggle between big business and big government with Kent leading the charge on behalf of big government. With the publication of the second edition in 1996, however, Siegel's view of the Commission has undergone a dramatic change. Though Siegel still worries about government intervention, he acknowledges that Kent's concerns over conglomerate ownership were justified (and Siegel's second edition was written before Conrad Black finalized his sole ownership of Southam). Siegel now respectfully lays out for consideration the Commission's proposals (Siegel 1996, 250).

Recent general political science textbooks have also revived their interest in the Kent Commission, almost always commending it. For example, Rand Dyck, in his *Canadian Politics*, praises the Kent Commission for its recommendations to curb newspaper concentration and to protect editors' independence from corporate owners. He further describes how corporate pressure was partly responsible for shelving the

report when it first appeared (Dyck 1996, 318–19).

Kent's own public entry into the debate during the Conrad Black era occurred as early as 1993 when Black first became a shareholder in Southam. Kent wrote an article in the *Montreal Gazette* criticizing Black's previous newspaper ventures both at home and abroad for 'their poverty of journalistic content and penny pitching style of management' (Kent 1993, A11). He noted that when Black takes over a newspaper, the political slant of the paper nearly always shifts to reflect Black's right-wing views. Kent was pessimistic about the Chrétien government's will to take the needed action: 'If the Trudeau government wasn't prepared to face a row with publishers, I'm sure this government isn't going to' (Flavelle 1996, C1).

If the government is not considering action in the direction Kent would wish, nevertheless Kent's concerns are sometimes being voiced, often in his own words, from other quarters. In an article in the *Windsor Star*, Chris Cobb worried that Southam had come under the control of Conrad Black. Cobb cites Tom Kent's remark that the takeover 'marks the end of Southam as we know it'. He then discusses the recommendations of the Kent Commission, stating that 'not only have those recommendations been ignored, but, in many cases the opposite has occurred.' Cobb cites Florian Sauvageau, a Laval University media specialist, who writes that 'perhaps we should look at the Kent report again, and begin giving editors contracts that guarantee independence' (Cobb 1993, A7).

The Royal Commission on Newspapers was invoked when the Maclean-Hunter media empire was taken over by Rogers Communication in 1994. The result of this transaction was a virtual monopoly for Rogers Communication in some fields of publishing, cable systems, television stations, and magazines. In his article 'Consumers Will Pay a Price for Decline in Competition' Rod Ziegler of the *Edmonton Journal* wrote about the dangers of this type of monopoly. Ziegler expresses his fear that the prominent business imperative of today is that 'you have to be big to compete'. He then cites the Kent Commission and expresses sympathy with Kent's lament over the demise of competition in the media (Ziegler 1994, B4).

The renewed interest in the Kent Commission has occurred largely from 1996 onward. Probably not coincidentally, this was when the issues raised by the Commission were again brought to the forefront by Black's acquisition of 19 small Thomson dailies and by his purchase of Paul Desmarais's stake in Southam. Dana Flavelle of the *Toronto Star* reported in 1996 that 'Tom Kent feels vindicated 15 years after he warned that ownership of Canada's daily newspapers was drifting into the hands of a few powerful corporate interests at the public's expense.' Flavelle quotes Kent as saying he believes the Commission's recommendations are still relevant today even though he doubts the government has the 'political will to do anything about this', and then describes in detail the history of the controversial Commission (Flavelle 1996, C1). . . .

When the state of Canada's newspapers is spotlighted, Tom Kent's opinion is sought. For example, in his essay on the *National Post*, 'Public Reaction Split on New Paper', Richard Foot of the *Hamilton Spectator* features remarks by Tom Kent: 'One welcomes competition, but one wishes it weren't being done by someone who already owns much of the press' (Foot 1998). When Rob Ferguson and John Honderich of the *Toronto Star* write demanding a review of newspaper ownership laws, they refer positively to the Kent Commission's recommendations and cite Kent as describing the current situation as 'a tragedy' (Ferguson 1998a, C1).

Even when commentators defend the principle of corporate takeovers or express admiration for Black, there is none of the sneering dismissal

of Kent so typical of the early 1980s. Thus, for example, Christopher Dornan, director of the Carleton University School of Journalism, defends the role of big corporations in the newspaper business, while granting that the Kent Commission had given a thorough airing to the anxieties rife in the industry (Dornan 1998, B2). Similarly, Duart Farquharson of the *Edmonton Journal* defends letting the market work itself out in the newspaper industry even when this means increased corporate concentration. At the same time, he grants that the worries expressed in the Kent Commission represent a legitimate point of view (Farquharson 1999, F3).

Conclusion

Buried at its birth by abuse and neglect, the Kent Commission and its report have experienced a resurrection. The report and its chairperson are key reference points wherever there is debate about media concentration in Canada. At stake are questions fundamental to democracy: What is the role of the media in a well-functioning democracy? Are newspapers more important to democracy than other media? Does democracy suffer when the media are owned by a relatively few conglomerates? Do privately owned newspapers have an obligation to provide balanced coverage of news events and a broad spectrum of editorial comment? If the answers to the last two questions are *yes*, is it ever appropriate for a democratic government to enforce divestment or to set up an ombudsperson to ensure fair coverage and commentary? Two decades ago, the Kent Commission boldly raised and, according to its own lights, answered these questions. But the debate invited by the Commission did not occur at that time. Now developments predicted by the Commission itself have made its report central to the current debate on newspaper ownership.

References

Black, Conrad. 1995. 'Accusation of Milking Newspapers Offends Conrad Black'. *Ottawa Citizen*, 4 March.

Canada, Minister of Supply and Services. 1981. *Royal Commission on Newspapers*. Ottawa.

Cobb, Chris. 1993. 'When the Rich Sit Down to Deal: Who Wins When Newspapers Are Concentrated in the Hands of the Elite'. *Windsor Star*, 12 April.

Dornan, Christopher. 1998. 'The Case for Corporate Ownership of Newspapers'. *Montreal Gazette*, 31 October.

Dyck, Rand. 1999. *Canadian Politics: Critical Approaches*. 2nd edn. Scarborough: Nelson Canada ITP.

Farquharson, Duart. 1999. 'In the Newspaper Game, Size Is the Prize'. *Edmonton Journal*, 9 January.

Ferguson, Rob. 1998a. 'Review Newspaper Ownership Rules'. *Toronto Star*, 21 May.

———. 1998b. 'Critics Crank up Pressure over Black's Newspaper Play'. *Toronto Star*, 23 May.

Flavelle, Dana. 1996. 'Media Critic Says Black Is Proving Him Right'. *Toronto Star*, 2 June.

Foot, Richard. 1998. 'Reaction Split on New Paper'. *Hamilton Spectator*, 9 April.

Kent, Tom. 1982. 'The Newspaper Problem'. Atkinson Lecture, Ryerson Polytechnic Institute, Toronto. 18 May.

———. 1985. 'The Significance of Corporate Structure in the Media'. April.

———. 1993. 'Conrad Black Has Put Profit before Quality'. *Ottawa Citizen*, 4 March.

McCarthy, Shawn. 1996. 'Black Fallout: Free Market or Muzzled Freedom?' *Toronto Star*, 1 June.

Saskatoon Star-Phoenix. 1981. 'Newspaper Editorial Writers Debunk Kent Criticisms'. (August).

———. 1981. 'Government and Press'. Editorial. (August).

Siegel, Arthur. 1983. *Politics and the Media in Canada*. Whitby, ON: McGraw-Hill Ryerson.

———. 1996. *Politics and the Media in Canada*. 2nd edn. Whitby, ON: McGraw-Hill Ryerson.

Ziegler, Rod. 1994. 'Consumers Will Pay Price for Decline in Competition'. *Edmonton Journal*, 10 March.

The Special Role of Magazines in the History of Canadian Mass Media and National Development

Peter Desbarats

. . .

'A magazine appeals to the miscellaneous imagination,' according to Fraser Sutherland's 1989 history of Canadian magazines. 'From the beginning, magazines were that way.'[1]

Although the British are inveterate publishers and readers of magazines, it was the French who invented the format. The first periodical other than a newspaper is generally considered to be the *Journal des Scavans* launched in Paris in 1665, 209 years after Gutenberg's Bible began the era of print.[2] It was a monthly review of new books, interested particularly in the natural sciences, and was the inspiration for the *Philosophical Transactions of the Royal Society* published in London the same year. Within a few decades, periodicals of such sober character were joined by more popular journals such as the *Weekly Memorials for the Ingenious*,[3] followed by question-and-answer magazines that were like catechisms on current events and general knowledge. . . .

In the fifty years after the appearance in 1789 of *The Nova-Scotia Magazine and Comprehensive Review*, Canadian magazines made what historian Wilfrid Kesterton describes as a 'token beginning'.[4] Most magazines of the period lasted for only a few years at most, often for only a few months, although there were exceptions, such as *La Bibliothèque Canadienne* published from 1825 to 1830 by the journalist, historian, and poet Michel Bibaud, and John Lovell's *Literary Garland*, which lasted from 1838 to 1851 and first published Susanna Moodie's classic description of life in the bush of Upper Canada.[5]

The pace of publishing activity of all kinds accelerated in the second half of the century. By 1865, there were almost 400 newspapers publishing in British North America, including 35 dailies.[6] In retrospect, knowing what we do about the trials of Canadian publishing in the following century, the ambition of Canadian magazine publishers of the period was breathtaking. When George Desbarats[7] launched his 16-page *Canadian Illustrated News* in 1869 and followed it with a French-language edition, the population of Montreal was about 130,000. There were only 3,300,000 people in the entire country. The *Canadian Illustrated News* survived until 1883, by which time Desbarats had also launched the *Daily Graphic* in New York, the first newspaper in the world to use photographic illustrations, the product of advanced Canadian technology.

Like other Canadian publishers of his time, Desbarats closely identified the *Canadian Illustrated News* and his other magazines with an emerging sense of Canadian nationalism. In his prospectus for the new magazine, he promised that, 'by picturing to our own people the broad dominion they possess,' the illustrated periodical would help its readers 'to feel still prouder of the proud Canadian name.'[8]

During this period, Canadian magazines multiplied in number and showed more durability. One of the most popular and longest-lived was *Grip*, an illustrated satirical weekly established in 1872 by John W. Bengough, the most prolific and influential political cartoonist of his day. It survived for more than twenty years, all the more surprising in light of the failure of humorous magazines in recent times to attract

From *Communications in Canadian Society* (5th edn), ed. Craig McKie and Benjamin D. Singer (Toronto: Thompson Education Publishing, 2001), 57–66. Reprinted by permission of the author.

and hold a large Canadian audience, at least in English-speaking Canada. . . .

Magazine editors of a century ago were often as colourful and grandiloquent as their Victorian prose. Edmund Sheppard, a flamboyant journalist from St Thomas, Ontario, who spent a short time as an American cowboy and subsequently adopted boots, chewing tobacco, and the pen name 'Don' as his trademarks, started *Saturday Night* in 1887, the only magazine of that period which still publishes.[9] Goldwyn Smith, the expatriate British author and academic who married a widowed heiress and adopted Toronto as his home, not without some condescension, edited *The Week* from 1883 to 1896 and helped to make it the most influential periodical of its time.[10]

The Struggle for Survival against US Competition

Goldwyn Smith produced his magazine towards the end of a period when Canadian magazine publishers had managed to co-exist with foreign periodicals and even, in the earlier days, to benefit from them. Distance and lax copyright regulations enabled Canadian publishers of the nineteenth century, before the overseas telegraph brought instant communication with Europe, to scalp stories from British and French periodicals. Reprints from US periodicals were also available to Canadian magazines at little or no cost. At a time when magazines were relatively expensive and provided an elite readership with political, business, and cultural information, Canadian magazines had enjoyed something of the natural monopoly that protected Canadian newspapers from American competition. This began to change towards the end of the nineteenth century, as Goldwyn Smith noted in his own magazine in 1894. 'In the field of periodical literature,' he wrote, 'what chance can our Canadian publishers have against an American magazine with a circulation of a hundred and fifty thousand, and a splendour of illustration such as only a profuse expenditure can support?'[11]

Goldwyn Smith and his contemporaries in the fledgling Canadian magazine industry were beginning to feel the effects of a shift in North American magazine publishing from class to mass. In the years just before and after the turn of the century, the success of the 10-cent magazine created a revolution in the industry. The decision of *McClure's* magazine to go to 10 cents in 1893 forced most of its chief competitors to follow suit—*Munsey's*, *Peterson's*, *Godey's*, and *Cosmopolitan*. By 1903, the publisher Frank Munsey estimated that 10-cent periodicals comprised about 85 per cent of the total circulation of magazines in the US. Some magazines, such as the *Saturday Evening Post*, dropped to 5 cents per copy, and a few publishers even experimented with magazines selling for 1 cent or 2 cents.[12]

As prices dropped and readership increased dramatically, the largest and most profitable magazines were those that carried entertainment in the form of fiction and light features, or service information such as recipes and other types of household intelligence. Unlike political or cultural information, this type of content carried little national bias. Deprived of the protection from competition that their distinctive content had provided in the days of elitist magazine publishing, and dependent on a relatively small readership and advertising base, it was almost impossible for Canadian magazines to compete with a growing number of American publications coming across the border. The best-selling US periodicals in Canada in the 1920s were *Saturday Evening Post*, *Pictorial Review*, and *McCall's Magazine*.[13]

By 1925 it was estimated that for every domestic magazine sold in Canada eight were imported from the US. In total, about 50,000,000 copies of US magazines were sold in Canada annually.[14] Among the imports were the first issues of Benarr Macfadden's *True Detective*, launched in 1924, the precursor of a flood of sensational pulp magazines and tabloid newspapers that continues in our own day with the strong presence of the *Star* and the *National Enquirer* on supermarket newsstands. . . .

Government Protection for Canadian Magazines

Rationale and Contradictions

As an editorial in *Saturday Night* declared in 1924: 'The Government must get behind the product to the extent of giving publishers some degree of protection against the dumping process which is now going on and which over the space of ten years has increased the sale of United States periodicals in the Canadian market by upward of three hundred percent.'[15]

Mary Vipond states in her 1989 history of the mass media in Canada that there was nothing unusual about this in the world of business. Some Canadian industries had relied on tariff protection long before Confederation; the introduction of the Conservatives' national policy in 1879 'suited manufacturers perfectly, for while aiding them by reducing competition, it preserved the free-enterprise system. . . . Thus it is not surprising that the magazine publishers, also facing American competition rooted in economies of scale and prior establishment in the market, turned to the tariff as a remedy.'[16]

The publishers made three arguments, which Vipond summarizes as 'the puritanical, the economic, and the nationalist'. The first claimed that many US magazines were salacious and immoral, ostensibly unlike those produced by Canadian or British publishers. The economic argument was the same as that used by any other threatened industry: thousands of Canadians would be thrown out of work if the Americans' low-cost 'overflow' production was allowed to enter Canada unimpeded. To this argument was added what Vipond calls 'a unique twist . . . if Canada lacked its own magazines, it lacked a vital agency of national communication.'[17] She quotes Frederick Paul, the editor of *Saturday Night*, writing in 1926: 'Without the slightest notion of flag-waving or sloppy patriotism, it must be apparent that if we depend on these United States centers for our reading matter we might as well move our gov-

ernment to Washington, for under such conditions it will go there in the end.'[18]

The publishers' case, however, contained the seeds of its own rebuttal. In assigning a national role for their magazines—'a stronger cohesive agent than Parliament', in the words of Frederick Paul[19]—the publishers opened their argument to discussion of the character of a free press in a democratic society. An essential attribute of this press is freedom from government influence; the separation of press and state is an article of faith for journalists, as is a belief in the free flow of information. Asking the government to exert its influence on behalf of the magazine industry appeared, at least to some, to create the possibility of the government asking for something in return or, at the very least, of publishers and journalists being less critical towards a protective government. Suggesting that the government should exert this influence to interfere with the flow of publications across the border appeared to be even more dangerous, particularly to journalists who opposed censorship on principle.

A History of Half-Hearted Protection

These contradictions partly explained why successive Canadian governments hesitated to protect this particular industry, especially when the affected industry in the US was one of the most vocal and politically influential. From the 1920s until 1975, every economic crisis in the Canadian magazine industry brought forward the same arguments with the same internal contradictions and, as a consequence, the same half-hearted responses from the government in Ottawa.

The pattern was set in the 1920s when the Liberals, traditionally the party of low tariffs, rejected a request for protection from the newly formed Magazine Publishers Association. Two groups that supported this decision, for entirely different reasons, were the Consumers' League of Canada, whose members were concerned that a duty on US magazines would make them more expensive in Canada, and the American News Company, which since the 1880s had monopolized a large segment of the newsstand distribution business in both the US and Canada.[20] Having refused to impose a tariff, the Liberal government then, in another prototypal decision, slightly reduced postal rates for Canadian magazines, imposed a duty on a few US pulp magazines such as *Argosy* and *Real Romance*, and gave Canadian publishers some relief from customs duties on imported paper and printing materials.[21] This policy of combining a refusal to offer significant help, particularly if it threatened to annoy the United States, with minor concessions designed to alleviate the industry's most pressing problems became familiar to Canadian magazine publishers in the following decades as they followed a well-worn path to and from Ottawa.

The publishers glimpsed utopia briefly in 1930 when the unsympathetic Liberals were replaced by a Conservative government that imposed a tariff on US magazines based on their ratio of advertising to editorial matter. The freedom-of-the-press argument was made on that occasion by Mackenzie King, former and future prime minister, who stated from the opposition benches in Parliament, in defence of the rights of US magazines, that 'thought is cosmopolitan,'[22] presumably unaware of the pun. Between 1931 and 1935, the circulation of US periodicals in Canada decreased by 62 per cent while Canadian magazines, even in the face of depressed economic conditions, increased their circulation by almost the same proportion: 64 per cent. About fifty US periodicals began printing in Canada. As Mary Vipond wrote, 'The imposition of tariffs against imported magazines was an unprecedented act. . . . Yet, it did not prove to be the beginning of a whole new approach to fostering the Canadian media.'[23] In 1935, King and the Liberals, back in power again, signed a three-year Canada–US trade agreement that included removal of tariffs on magazines. Once again, the Liberals attempted

to sweeten this bitter pill for Canadian magazine publishers by adopting measures to cushion the effects of duties on imported paper, ink, and other publishing materials. Within three years of the removal of tariffs, American magazines tripled their total Canadian circulation.[24]

The next significant development occurred in 1943 when wartime paper shortages persuaded both *Time* and *Reader's Digest* to set up shop in Canada to obtain Canadian paper rations. After the war, they began to enlarge the distinctive editorial content of these Canadian editions and to aggressively sell advertising in them.

Competition from US periodicals and the initial effects of TV endangered the few established Canadian periodicals of general interest that had survived the Depression of the 1930s and the war years. *New World Illustrated*, a major periodical, disappeared in 1948, *National Home Monthly*, in 1950, and the *Canadian Home Journal*, in 1958. *Saturday Night* led a precarious existence. *Maclean's* survived only because its publisher, Maclean Hunter, owned a profitable stable of business magazines. Like Canadian newspapers, specialized magazines provided distinctive types of service information to their readers and consequently were immune to some extent from the kind of US competition that made life abnormally difficult for Canadian consumer magazines of general interest.

By 1954, US magazines were occupying 80 per cent of the Canadian market compared with 67 per cent in 1948. By 1955, the Canadian editions of *Time* and *Reader's Digest* were accounting for 37 per cent of the total advertising revenues of general-interest magazines in Canada; they had doubled their share of the advertising market since 1948.[25]

The last half of the 1950s saw another example of stop-and-go protectionism when a tax on advertising in Canadian editions of US periodicals, imposed by the Liberals in 1956, was removed by the Conservatives in 1958. By 1960, the state of Canada's magazine industry was so precarious that the Conservative government of Prime Minister John Diefenbaker appointed a Royal Commission on Publications under Senator Grattan O'Leary, a former Ottawa newspaper editor.

The O'Leary Commission: Freedom and Competition

Freedom of the press once again became a major issue as US magazines resisted any suggestion, during public hearings of the commission, that their right to do business in Canada be curtailed in any way. But from the outset, Grattan O'Leary indicated that he would resist an interpretation of press freedom that would allow unrestricted foreign competition in Canada. Freedom of the press is not an absolute freedom, he would often say; his favourite analogy was that freedom of expression did not give anyone the right to stand up in a crowded theatre and shout, 'Fire!'[26]

O'Leary's definition of press freedom prevailed in the commission's report. It stated as a principle that 'a nation's domestic advertising expenditures should be devoted to the support of its own media of communications,'[27] and it recommended that Canadian firms advertising in foreign magazines or Canadian editions of foreign magazines should not be allowed to deduct the cost of this advertising as a business expense for tax purposes. This would have the effect of doubling the cost of advertising placed in foreign publications or diverting it, as the Royal Commission hoped, to Canadian periodicals. O'Leary's controversial recommendations, juggled indecisively by the Diefenbaker government until it was defeated in 1963, and finally adopted with qualifications by the Liberals in 1965, stirred up what an inside observer later described as 'several nests of hornets of great ferocity'.[28] One was located in Washington where the US State Department warned that action against *Time* and *Reader's Digest* might jeopardize the future of US defence contracts offered to Canadian firms and congressional approval of the Canada–US Autopact.[29] Then

Finance Minister Walter Gordon recalled later that 'pressure was brought to bear on the prime minister not to do anything that would interfere with *Time* or upset its proprietor.'[30] . . .

Bill C-58 and the Renaissance of Canadian Magazine Publishing

Despite this opposition, the Pearson government in 1965 enacted legislation based on the O'Leary Report. Because of opposition from Washington, the legislation contained a grandfather clause that exempted *Time* and *Reader's Digest* from its provisions. The ineffectiveness of this measure was evident five years later to the Senate Committee on the Mass Media, which 'deeply regretted that *Time* and *Reader's Digest* were exempted from the O'Leary legislation' and said that this had been 'a bad decision'.[31] After five more years, the Liberal government of Prime Minister Pierre Trudeau introduced Bill C-58, which finally completed the legislation proposed by the O'Leary Commission almost 15 years earlier by including *Time* and *Reader's Digest* in its provisions. A few weeks after the legislation was passed in 1976, *Time* abandoned its Canadian edition, although the US edition with some Canadian advertising (not eligible as a business expense for tax purposes) is still available in Canada. *Reader's Digest* created a Canadian foundation to publish its Canadian edition, which remains eligible for tax deductibility, while ownership of its book- and record-distribution activities and other profitable enterprises remained in the US.

Bill C-58 coincided with, and was partly responsible for, the dawn of a renaissance period in Canadian magazine publishing that bore a closer resemblance to the creative optimism of the nineteenth century than to the depressed conditions and mentality of the first half of the twentieth century. Although there is disagreement about the precise effects of the legislation, most authorities would agree with Fraser Sutherland's assessment that 'there is no doubt that Bill C-58 had given an important psychological boost to many smaller magazines. . . . Certainly it was difficult to see that anyone lost from it.'[32] Although the Canadianized *Reader's Digest* remained the magazine with the largest circulation in Canada, and the American edition of *Time* continued to sell here in substantial if reduced numbers, other magazines signified a growing Canadian presence. The US-owned *TV Guide*, by then one of the most popular magazines, was taken over by Télémedia, a Montreal-based company. Maclean Hunter, one of the main beneficiaries of Bill C-58, was able in 1978 to fulfill its ambition to make *Maclean's* a weekly news magazine. Specialty magazines such as *Harrowsmith*, a periodical about country living that appealed strongly to affluent city dwellers and was successful almost from its first issue in 1976, demolished the notion that it was impossible for new Canadian magazines to achieve national renown and financial stability in their first few years. Publishing out of a village near Kingston, Ontario, *Harrowsmith* achieved both in its first few issues and continues to be successful under its current owner, Télémedia. Controlled-circulation magazines, paid for by advertisers and distributed without charge to selected groups of readers, multiplied so rapidly after 1975 that the whole concept of paying for a magazine was thrown into question for a time. Among the giveaways were dozens of city magazines that attempted to repeat the success of *Toronto Life*, one of the most prosperous city magazines in North America.

In the decade after 1975, the number of city and entertainment-oriented magazines published in Canada increased from 17 to 56.[33] From 1971 to 1986, the share of the national market occupied by Canadian publications increased from 30 per cent to 40 per cent.[34] Despite several sharp increases in postal rates, subscription sales jumped from 37 per cent to 60 per cent of the market in the same period.[35] In the 12 years following the adoption of Bill C-58, the annual revenues from circulation of Maclean Hunter Publications rose from about

$5 million to about $50 million.[36]

Not all of the new magazines prospered. The supernova of the new generation of Canadian periodicals was a glossy, controlled-circulation magazine called *Quest*, which appeared in 1972, reached 700,000 Canadian households by 1978, and went out of business in 1984. One of the most expensive failures was *Vista*, launched with a reported $10-million investment by automotive-parts manufacturer Frank Stronach in 1988, and killed two years later. This generally expansive period for the magazine industry also saw the demise, at the beginning of the 1980s, of such national weekly newspaper supplements as *Weekend* and *The Canadian*, among the most profitable Canadian magazines of the early 1970s. Despite this experience, the *Globe and Mail* entered the magazine field in 1984 with its monthly *Report on Business Magazine*, adding city magazines and others devoted to travel, fashion, and health to its stable by the end of the decade, all delivered to *Globe* subscribers at no extra cost. These ventures symbolized the expansionist spirit that still pervaded the Canadian magazine industry at the end of the 1980s after 15 years of unprecedented activity and prosperity, although the recession in the first half of the following decade curbed this trend. By 1994, for instance, the *Globe and Mail* had ceased publishing all its magazines except for the original *Report on Business*. Statistics Canada data indicates that total revenues of Canadian magazines hit a peak of $903 million in 1989–90 and subsequently declined to $846.4 million in 1991–2.[37] . . .

Competition by imported periodicals will always be a major factor, at least in English-speaking Canada. But it is noteworthy that, by 1987, only one of the 12 largest magazines sold in Canada (*National Geographic*) was US-owned, and that the circulation of *Maclean's* was about double that of *Time* in Canada.[38] Imported periodicals, primarily from the US, still accounted for 65 per cent of the consumer magazines sold in Canada, but it is also true that Canadians were reading more copies of more Canadian magazines than ever before. It is now difficult to imagine this trend being reversed, particularly in view of the protection afforded to Canadian cultural industries under the Canada–US Free Trade Agreement, the specific protection for the provisions of Bill C-58 under the agreement,[39] and similar protection included in the 1993 North American Free Trade Agreement (NAFTA).

. . .

Notes

1 Fraser Sutherland, *The Monthly Epic: A History of Canadian Magazines* (Toronto: Fitzhenry & Whiteside, 1989), l.

2 John Feather, *A History of British Publishing* (London: Routledge, 1988), 106.

3 Feather, *A History*, 107.

4 W.H. Kesterton, *A History of Journalism in Canada* (Toronto: McClelland & Stewart, 1967), 9.

5 Peter Desbarats, *Guide to Canadian News Media* (Toronto: Harcourt Brace Jovanovich, 1990), 11.

6 Desbarats, *Guide*, 10.

7 The great-grandfather of the author, elected to the Canadian News Hall of Fame in Toronto in 1987, an admitted example of posthumous or reverse nepotism. The author was on the selection committee.

8 Peter Desbarats, *The Canadian Illustrated News 1869–1883* (Toronto: McClelland & Stewart, 1970), 4.

9 Sutherland, *The Monthly Epic*, 81.

10 Desbarats, *Guide*, 12.

11 Sutherland, *The Monthly Epic*, 32.

12 John Tebbel, *The Media in America* (New York: Crowell, 1974), 279.

13 Sutherland, *The Monthly Epic*, 114.

14 Mary Vipond, *The Mass Media in Canada* (Toronto: James Lorimer, 1989), 24.

15 Quoted in Sutherland, *The Monthly Epic*, 114.

16 Vipond, *The Mass Media*, 25.

17 Ibid., 26.

18 Ibid., 27.

19 Ibid.

20 Ibid., 21, 27.

21 Sutherland, *The Monthly Epic*, 115.

22 Vipond, *The Mass Media*, 28.

23 Ibid., 29.

24 Sutherland, *The Monthly Epic*, 116.

25 Vipond, *The Mass Media*, 61.

26 Author's recollection.

27 Sutherland, *The Monthly Epic*, 186.

28 Tom Kent, *A Public Purpose* (Montreal/Kingston: McGill–Queen's University Press, 1988), 317.

29 Sutherland, *The Monthly Epic*, 187.

30 Walter Gordon, *A Political Memoir* (Toronto: McClelland & Stewart, 1977), 205.

31 Special Senate Committee on Mass Media, *Report*, vol. I, 164.

32 Sutherland, *The Monthly Epic*, 260.

33 Ibid., 262.

34 Ibid., 263.

35 Ibid.

36 Desbarats, *Guide*, 12.

37 'Circulation up, revenue down', *Masthead* 6, no. 10 (September 1993), 8.

38 *Canadian Magazine Publishing* (Cultural Industries and Agencies Branch, Government of Ontario, 23 May 1989).

39 Stan Sutter, 'Free Trade Presents No Direct Threat to Health of Canada's Business Press', *Marketing* 93, no. 21 (23 May 1988), 26–7.

'Mrs Chatelaine' vs 'Mrs Slob': Contestants, Correspondents, and the *Chatelaine* Community in Action, 1961–1969

Valerie J. Korinek

In 1960 the editors of *Chatelaine* magazine created a contest for Canadian homemakers called, appropriately enough, the Mrs Chatelaine contest. 'All homemakers living in Canada' were eligible.[1] Participants were required to send in photos of themselves, provide detailed personal information (height, weight, hair and eye colour, and age), and reveal their husband's occupation and income, as well as the number and ages of their children. Those were the easy questions. For the remaining eight questions, readers were requested to write essay-style answers about their housecleaning regimes and their monthly entertaining schedule, indicate any hobbies or projects and their recent achievements in this area, provide family and entertaining menu plans, draw the floor plan of their living room and furniture arrangement, list all their community activities, and finally, elaborate upon their philosophies of child-raising and homemaking. The prize for all this work: a pair of first-class tickets to Paris, a 10-day stay and $1,000 to cover expenses, a complete spring wardrobe, new luggage, and a rental car for use during the vacation. In later years the trip to Paris was cancelled and winners were given a similar collection of gifts, often including a movie camera, and the $1,000 cash prize.

The Mrs Chatelaine contest serves as an intriguing and unique case study of readers' relationships to products of popular culture. *Chatelaine* readers were inveterate letter writers and, as this contest attests, were as quick to criticize the publication as they were to praise it. Through the vast number of letters received by the magazine and published each month in the periodical, a letter-writing community was created. These letters were written to the editors, to the writers, and often, as this case study will illustrate, to other readers. The *Chatelaine* community was linked primarily by gender and nationality, while negotiating class, region, age, race, and ethnic difference to encompass a mass readership of women. Men also read the magazine but they were far less likely to participate in the community of letter-writers. Due to a number of factors, such as a limited number of cultural products for women, *Chatelaine's* position as the sole Canadian women's mass-market magazine, and the geographic vastness of the country (with the accompanying isolation and lack of alternatives), the magazine, its editors, writers, and readers created and participated in a cultural community of Canadian women. Finally, the correspondence relating to the Mrs Chatelaine contest permits an analysis of how readers received, incorporated, ignored, or challenged the 'preferred meanings' offered by the magazine. This correspondence indicates that while some readers found enjoyment in such 'preferred meanings', other readers were resistant, critical, or dismissive, and wrote to the magazine to challenge the sometimes narrow definitions of Canadian women.

The contest epitomizes the material for which women's magazines have been repeatedly criticized by writers and scholars, ranging from Betty Friedan to Susan Faludi.[2] Clearly, Maclean Hunter and the editors of *Chatelaine* created a contest that rewarded a middle-class, heterosexual, and ultimately, extremely conservative vision of Canadian women. The contest rules explicitly or implicitly excluded single women, working wives and mothers, older women,

Abridged from *Journal of the Canadian Historical Association* 7 (1996), 251–75. Reprinted by permission.

working-class women, and lesbians. However, despite the (in this case) extremely overt 'preferred meaning', the producers of this pop cultural material could not determine how their consumers, *Chatelaine*'s readers, would respond. While many readers revelled in completing their entries, an equally large number of critics actively ignored the 'preferred meaning' of the contest. These creative readers opted for alternate interpretations. 'Reading against the grain' and employing a very 'tongue-in-cheek' style of humour, these oppositional readers offered, instead, their own creation: the 'Mrs Slob 1961 Contest'. In letters to the editors, and in their communities, these self-identified 'slobs' were able to re-make a very traditional women's magazine contest into something that rewarded their way of life, accepted class, age, and marital difference, and rivalled the attentions given to the 'real' contestants.

The variety of responses to their contest that Maclean Hunter received is, as well, emblematic of the general dissonance in post-war society over the appropriate roles of women. Scholars have been quick to depict the Fifties, in particular, as a time of 'familism' or 'a search for stability' as home and family became a 'point of reference in an unstable world'.[3] However, this emphasis on home, family, and established gender roles masked considerable discontent and difference[4]—discontent on the part of some women who, by the 1960s, were increasingly quick to challenge the limitations of suburbia and the sexual status quo. In addition, recent attention to class, racial, and ethnic difference indicates that contemporary media accounts, as well as historical accounts, tended to ignore the newcomers and working-class women who had always worked outside the home.[5] Women's workforce participation expanded exponentially in the 1950s and 1960s, so that by the end of the decade women represented 35.5 per cent of the workforce, and the majority of women workers (over 56 per cent) were married.[6] Hence, both the contestants' and the anti-contestants' com-

ments deserve to be understood as part of an ongoing debate over the changing nature of women's roles.

However, they must also be understood within the context of the magazine. By the 1960s, as the summary that follows will indicate, *Chatelaine* was regularly publishing feminist editorials and articles. As well, there were frequent depictions of difference—of the working class, of immigrants, and of rural dwellers—in the periodical. All the images were not of middle-class, suburban families. Yet the conventions of the women's magazine genre dictated that the magazine must include traditional material as well—particularly departmental fare or 'service material'. According to *Chatelaine* promotional material, 'women read service magazines for ideas on how to improve their homes, their families, themselves.'[7] 'Service material' taught women how to consume and use the advertisers' products, and advertisers were key to the financial viability of the periodical.

Thus, the Mrs Chatelaine contest was influenced by both the temper of the times and the unique situation at the magazine. The contest appeared in the 1960s, at a time when women were returning to or entering the workforce in droves, and when women's roles were in a state of flux. Similarly, it appeared in a magazine undergoing considerable editorial revision. It was created to shore up the traditional material in the periodical and to serve as a celebration of traditional, middle-class femininity. Mrs Chatelaine celebrated the middle-class ideal of the stay-at-home wife and mother, who devoted herself to her family, church, and community. Clearly, she was intended to serve as a traditional role model for readers. However, it did not turn out that way, thus offering a compelling illustration of how readers respond to the most conventional women's magazine fare.

Before turning to the particulars of the contest and the contestants, it is necessary to sketch a brief overview of the periodical, its editors, and its readers. Doris Anderson assumed the editorship of *Chatelaine* in 1957; with her primarily female staff of associate editors, she was responsible for all the editorial material in the magazine. The business department, a predominantly male enclave, was responsible for advertising, circulation, and market research. The separation of editorial and business operations was standard at all consumer magazines but the corresponding gender division at *Chatelaine* provided the female editors with considerable autonomy. Anderson's personal commitment to featuring feminist issues, along with the more traditional components, in the magazine was aided by this organizational structure of female editorial autonomy. The male executives, while frequently uncomfortable with her formula, could not argue with the increased circulation nor with the resultant increase in advertisers.

Despite the changing editorial content *Chatelaine*'s format remained consistent. It was an oversized periodical (11″ x 14″) whose covers were dominated by images of young, white women, Canadian entertainers, or British royalty. An average issue was 112 pages in length, and a yearly subscription cost readers $1.50 Until 1967, when it was increased to $2.00. Since the 'Mrs Chatelaine' winner was almost always profiled in the May issue (the exception was 1961 when she appeared in April), a brief overview of the May 1965 issue will serve as an introduction to the magazine's contents.

Inside the front cover, and beside the regular advertisement for Miss Clairol hair colouring, 'Does She or Doesn't She', was Doris Anderson's editorial essay: 'Some women just aren't cut out to be mothers'. Anderson's editorial, usually devoted to feminist issues or ideas, was one of the key features that differentiated *Chatelaine* from the American women's magazines. The other entries in the 'News/Views' category were the 'What's New' columns which provided commentary on recent developments at the magazine, among Canadian women, in the shops, within the world of Canadian arts and entertainment, in healthcare, and in financial issues. In addition, Christina McCall (and later Adrienne Clarkson) contributed a regular books column, and the last page of the magazine (entitled 'The Last Word is Yours') was devoted to readers' letters. Within the formal layout of the magazine, readers had two sections devoted to their ideas and voices—the letters page and 'What's New with You'.

Of the seven feature articles in May 1965, five were examinations of social issues or sexism. They included Mollie Gillen's 'Canada's Seven Most Urgent Social Problems'; Kay Clefton's 'I am a Common-Law Wife'; 'What They Don't Tell You About Being a Beauty Queen'; and a two-part article by Florence Jones and Doreen Mowers, 'How Two Women Fought Race Prejudice: Teaching Freedom in Mississippi' and 'Growing Up Prejudiced in Ontario'. This was not the sort of material published in the *Ladies Home Journal* or *Good Housekeeping*. Although this issue had a larger component of social activist articles than most, the articles were typical *Chatelaine* fare of the late 1950s and throughout the 1960s. The other two articles, 'Meet Mrs Chatelaine' and 'Enter *Chatelaine*'s 8th Club Award Contest', offered more conventional articles which focused attention on homemaking, child-raising, and voluntary service in the community.

In addition to the features and news items, there were two fiction stories followed by the regular departmental material. The dominant section was Food and Homes, with Carol Taylor's 'Shopping with Chatelaine'; Elaine Collett's 'The Wonderful World of Summer Sausages' and 'Meals of the Month'; Una Abrahamson's regular column, 'Homemaker's Diary'; and a short feature on 'Sofabeds' by Alain Campaigne. Fashion editor Vivian Wilcox profiled 'Beach Sweaters', while craft editor Wanda Nelles tempted readers with 'Table Linen Heirlooms to Embroider'. Lois Wilson's gardening column was devoted to 'Fabulous Roses', while the 'Your Child' column urged parents to 'Give Him a Sense of His Own Worth'. This editorial content accounted for 50 per cent of the magazine. Numerous companies advertised in *Chatelaine*, including Nivea, Texmade, Aylmer, Kraft, Air Canada, Christie's, Arnel Knits, Yardley, Canadian General-Electric, Cat's Paw, Royal Doulton, and Canada Packers. Their advertisements offered compelling consumer fantasies on some of the magazine's most colourful pages.

In any given issue of *Chatelaine*, then, readers were exposed to a wide variety of material. While the profiles of Mrs Chatelaine or other material on Canadian homemakers, entertainers, or British royalty were clearly intended to offer portraits of bourgeois hegemony, other articles were counter-hegemonic. Of course, the readers themselves brought all their critical and analytical abilities to reading the magazine and, thus, while some readers enjoyed and were challenged by the newer material, others were openly critical of articles that strayed from conventional women's magazine topics.

. . .

Chatelaine's chief strength was that it attracted a mass audience of average Canadian women, and some men, from all regions of the country. The readers lived primarily in single-family homes, but they were more likely to live in a rural area than most Canadians. In terms of occupation, education, income level, and household income, they were average Canadians. Certainly, the socio-economic portrait illustrated convincingly that, in comparison with other periodicals and with the Canadian averages, the English-speaking *Chatelaine* community was most likely to come from the lower-middle class. In other words, in terms of advertising priorities, the readers represented women and families who had a small amount of discretionary spending and only a fair standard of living.

The demographic profile is very important because it illustrates one of the fundamental tensions at any mass-market magazine. *Chatelaine* readers were drawn primarily from the lower-middle class and, despite their vast numbers, in

terms of purchasing power (always the way class issues were defined at *Chatelaine*) these were not the 'better sort' of readers desired by the business department and advertisers. Because of this, their needs (and limited budgets) were seldom addressed in the beauty, fashion, and home decorating features. Those departmental features continually strove to attract more affluent readers to the magazine and to the pages of advertisements they supported. Only the food articles were primarily devoted to 'budget' menus and affordable entertaining. Yet the readers themselves were determined that the magazine reflect the reality of their lives. This was a consistent demand in the letters written to the editors, and in the particular responses to the Mrs Chatelaine contest. Unlike today's readers, who have a plethora of choices when it comes to consumer magazines, in the 1960s *Chatelaine* was the only Canadian women's periodical. Readers believed that the magazine's mandate was to provide a magazine of interest to *all* Canadian women.

Although it was not uncommon for readers to meet *Chatelaine* editors at women's groups or, in rarer cases, to tour the *Chatelaine* offices, the readers' messages were communicated loudest through their letters to the editor. . . .

The issue that generated the largest number of letters in the early 1960s concerned the reaction to the first Mrs Chatelaine winner in 1961. The April 1961 issue of *Chatelaine* introduced readers to the first Mrs Chatelaine—'Mrs Joyce Saxton, of Plenty, Saskatchewan, a mother of three—and a typical and, at the same time, a most exceptional homemaker!'[8] Whenever the magazine attempted to portray a 'typical' Canadian woman, it ventured into difficult terrain because readers expected 'typical' women to reflect themselves. When they did not—and that was a common occurrence in a magazine with such a diverse mass audience and a penchant for depicting the comfortable middle-class lifestyle to their lower-middle-class and working-class readers—controversy and a fury of letter-writing ensued. In future years, as the 'Mrs Slob' letters will illustrate, many interested women did not participate because the construction of the 'typical Canadian homemaker' did not mirror their images of themselves. Editor Doris Anderson remembers the Mrs Chatelaine contest as a yearly dose of realism, which gave the editors 'very good insight into where women were at with their lives'.[9] Yet the adjudicating committee, in contrast to the slobs' lament about the perfectionism of the winners or Anderson's vision of the contest's purpose, 'hated' the contest 'because it was a lot of hard work and they usually thought that Mrs Chatelaine didn't cook very well'.[10] Ultimately, the articles and letters concerning the Mrs Chatelaine contest will illustrate that the competition served multiple purposes— to celebrate Canadian homemaking, to act as a reader survey, and to foster interest and participation in the magazine—and multiple interpretations.

Internal memos from Maclean Hunter confirm that the contest exceeded expectations for participation and that those women who participated spent a vast amount of time compiling their entries. E.H. Gittings, assistant advertising sales manager for *Chatelaine*, was astonished by the contest's popularity:

> We received approximately 5,700 entries from our English edition and 400 entries from our French edition. Some of the entries were very elaborate indeed. They included such things as samples of pies, cookies, tape recordings of their voices, and in practically all cases, it was obvious that these readers had spent literally days preparing their entries. Mrs Saxton who won the contest last year, confessed after she had been selected that she had spent over 150 hours preparing her entry.[11]

On all accounts, both in number of entries received and in the amount of time contestants put into their entries, the contest was a success. J.L. Adams, *Chatelaine* manager for eastern Canada, wrote that the first winner, Mrs Joyce

Saxton, of Plenty, Saskatchewan, was a 'charming and delightful person', even though in the course of the day she had remarked that 'although she read *Chatelaine* every month from cover to cover, her favourite magazine was *Reader's Digest* because it didn't flop around when she was reading it in bed.'[12]

Saxton's views on marriage, child-raising, and the role of a homemaker were meticulously profiled in the article entitled 'Mrs Chatelaine—her home, her family, her everyday world'.[13] A farm wife and mother of three children, Saxton was an energetic housewife who that past year had 'preserved 140 quarts of fruit preserves . . . 60 jars of jellies, 260 packs of frozen fruit and vegetables; sews most of her children's clothes and some of her own'.[14] In addition to her household tasks, this former school teacher ran a community swim program in the summer, and was 'a member of or on the executive of nine clubs and community groups'.[15] Numerous black-and-white photos depicted Saxton cavorting with her children, organizing her pantry, watering houseplants, teaching swimming, and sharing a snack with her fellow church circle members. The article ended with her summation of her homemaking goals:

> I must find common ground with my husband so that family life may be mutually enjoyed; spend time with the children regardless of household tasks; plan my home for the family's comfort and convenience; serve nutritious and attractive meals; through some planning, try to get necessary household jobs out of the way by noon, so there is free time for extras; help to do my share in the community; keep up-to-date on current events.[16]

For the editors of *Chatelaine* Joyce Saxton embodied the middle-class virtues that *Chatelaine* advocated in their departmental features. Her emphasis on planning, nutrition, and effective time management was consistent with the prevalent themes of the food and home-planning features. The fashion and beauty department took centre stage in the remaining four-and-a-half-page photo essay. 'Mrs Chatelaine enjoys a whirl in Toronto before flying to Paris' allowed readers to follow Saxton's gruelling itinerary, her 'nights at the theatre; luncheons; shopping trips; rounds of meetings with celebrities; appointments with a stylist to find a new coiffure', and to study the 'series of beauty treatments and makeup lessons'.[17] As queen for a week she was fêted by *Chatelaine*'s staff and she hobnobbed with the likes of Pierre Berton, Gordon Sinclair, and the dancers of the Royal Ballet.

Although in future years the featured articles on the Mrs Chatelaine winners were not as lengthy, detailed, or lovingly sketched, it was clear that, with the exception of 1969, they all celebrated similar stories of middle-class feminine virtues. *Chatelaine* was never subtle about the contest's purposes, but as the years progressed the editorializing about the aims, ambitions, and effects of the contest was stated explicitly:

> Every year, when we read the many entries for the Mrs Chatelaine contest, we are impressed all over again with the happiness and sound family solidarity that exists across our country. In a way, the winner represents all of you, a symbol of all the love and care and effort that Canadian wives and mothers are pouring into their homes, the lives of their children, and their community. [. . .][18]

Ultimately, most readers who entered the contest tended to be consummate wives and mothers and very service-minded. However, that was not the case for all readers. For them, the Mrs Chatelaine contest highlighted actual or imagined inadequacies in their various roles as wives, mothers, and often workers. One woman, Mrs Beatrice Maitland of Chatham, New Brunswick, took matters into her own hands and decided to write to the magazine and nominate herself for the 'Mrs Slob 1961' contest. The following excerpt from her first letter to Anderson

includes her humorous yet trenchant critique of the contest's rules:

> Yesterday was the closing date for your Mrs Chatelaine contest, but I didn't enter. . . . I wish someone, sometime, would have a competition for 'Mrs Nothing!!' A person who isn't a perfect housekeeper, a faultless mother, a charming hostess, a loving wife, or a servant of the community. Besides being glamourous as a model, talented as a Broadway star and virtuous as a Saint. I have studied your questionnaire carefully but my replies are hopelessly inadequate. . . . To start with my appearance is absolutely fatal. . . . I am overweight, pear-shaped and bow legged. Consequently, not having much to work on I don't bother and cover it up with comfortable, warm old slacks. . . . Now, housework. Failure there too as I am a lousy housekeeper. . . . Entertaining? Practically never. [. . .] Meals? . . . We prefer plain meat and potato-vegetable meals with no frills. [. . .] You can't win. Make a fancy meal from a magazine and they look like they are being poisoned. . . . The decor is middle English European junk shop, especially when the children start doing their homework. Community activities? I have always belonged to and worked with other organizations . . . but I have become so sick and bored with meetings I quit. . . . My philosophy as a home-maker—I guess that is, be happy, don't worry. You do what you can with what you've got when you feel like it. Consequently I'm never sick and I've got no nerves or fears. That is poor me. . . . So if you want to run a contest for 'Mrs Slob 1961' I would be happy to apply and would probably win hands down. Thank you for your enjoyable magazine and my apologies for taking up your time.[19]

Maitland's self-deprecatory style of humour and her obvious send-up of the conventions of the contest made for a witty letter. However, there was a considerable edge to this piece since she challenged the presumption that all Canadian women aspired to or could afford the easy affluence of suburbia. As an RCAF wife with three kids, Maitland was clearly not part of the 'better sort' of reader the magazine's advertisers and publisher sought.

Anderson's response praised Maitland's 'wit' and 'good humour' and acknowledged that the 'Mrs Chatelaine contest sets up pretty formidable rules but, in our defense, the woman who won it last year was a fairly average homemaker in Western Canada who lived on a farm'.[20] Neither Anderson nor Maitland anticipated the response that would follow the publication of her letter in the February 1962 issue. Unlike most letters, which were usually edited down to a few key lines of commentary, Maitland's letter was published virtually in its entirety, with an accompanying headline and cartoon to draw further attention to her critique. According to Maitland's own description, having her letter published in Chatelaine was akin to having a 'best-seller':

When I wrote that letter to you, back in the fall, I never dreamed that such a furor would ensue. . . . My stars! It's as good as having a best-seller! Strangers have shook my hand and said, 'Welcome to the Club.' And it's buzzing all over our PMQ. I have also had a lot of letters all very much in agreement. Who would have thought there were so many slobs in the country?[21]

Who would have guessed so many slobs read *Chatelaine*? Despite the magazine's attempts to encourage household perfection and reward the ideal Canadian homemaker, the Mrs Slobs refused to re-create themselves in that mould. With Maitland's treatise as their rallying cry, they wrote to her and to the magazine professing support and encouragement to all the other Canadian slobs. Anderson's reply acknowledged that Maitland's letter and the ensuing letters in her support provided a wake-up call for the magazine: 'You certainly did stir up a furor. I for one found it extremely interesting to realize what a great load of guilt most of the housewives of this country carry around on their shoulders. It

makes me a little guilty that women's magazines probably contribute as much as any medium to this feeling. Thank you for reminding us.'[22]

The letters professing solidarity with Maitland came from all regions of the country. This brief sampling captures the spirit of the letters. Most continued Maitland's critique of the contest's middle-class bias and the rather limiting role prescribed for Canadian wives and mothers. Mrs F. Miller of New Westminster, British Columbia, wrote: 'I received my issue of *Chatelaine* about one half hour ago and turned immediately to "The last word is yours". I say Three Cheers for Mrs Beatrice Maitland.'[23] Mrs C. Cserick of Ottawa deduced that the magazine was to blame for its unattainable style of homemaking and its focus upon the suburban family: 'To be brutally frank I love *Chatelaine*. . . . But dear old *Chatelaine*, you write very little about us—don't you—we don't have a home of our own—2 bedrooms is all, but we do like to read, listen to good music, watch good TV shows, take in a really excellent movie, drink gallons of coffee at odd hours, love our husband and kids, care for them and do 100 menial jobs a day.'[24] Interestingly, none of the readers who sympathized and identified with Maitland decided that the magazine was not for them. They considered the magazine a general Canadian women's magazine, not one oriented to homemakers or urban, middle-class women. Many of these respondents remarked that, until Maitland's letter, they had thought they alone had difficulties coping with the demands of homemaking in the Sixties. . . .

The 'Mrs Slob' correspondence illustrates that the readers were adept at providing alternate interpretations of the magazine. They did not feel compelled to emulate the household perfectionism of the departmental material, nor did the contest encourage them to become super-volunteers, homemakers, and wives. Rather, the magazine was construed as out of step with the average Canadian homemaker. . . .

At issue was the notion of 'representation'. Of course, one housewife and her family could hardly be expected to represent the goals, ideals, styles, and dreams of all the readers, but many readers compared Mrs Chatelaine to themselves and often found her wanting or her perfection repellent. Great care was taken in the selection of the winner and the runners-up to avoid slighting one particular region or province. Thus the winners came from almost all parts of the country—only British Columbia and the Territories did not have a grand prize winner during the decade, although they did have runners-up each year. Mrs Saxton was followed by: Josephine Ouellet of Sillery, Quebec; Florence E. Holt of Regina, Saskatchewan; Ethelyn Mosher of Middleton, Nova Scotia; Leone Ross of Charlottetown, Prince Edward Island; Elsie Lee Fraser of Calgary, Alberta; Eva Hammond of St. Hilaire, Quebec; Diane McLeod of Toronto, Ontario; and in 1969, Bettie Hall of Montreal, Quebec.   All of them had at least three children and, with the exception of Bettie Hall, were very active in community, church, and cultural events in their respective communities. According to the supplementary information the editors provided each year, the contest continued to be extremely popular and many women entered repeatedly. For example, Mrs Henriette Van Der Bregen of Weyburn, Saskatchewan, was selected as provincial runner-up three years in a row. Another persistent runner-up was Ethelyn Mosher, crowned Mrs Chatelaine in 1964, who was a study in community involvement, maternal pride (she was the mother of four young children) and excellence in homemaking. . . .

For the winners, the 'Mrs Chatelaine' experience proved very enjoyable. One of the runners-up, Mrs Marjorie E. Hallman of Pictou, Nova Scotia, (Nova Scotia's runner-up for 1963), stated: '*Chatelaine* has been resource, teacher, companion, and friend. Also has reinforced my self-esteem when I made it as runner up in the "Mrs Chatelaine Contest".'[25] For each Marjorie Hallman, of course, there were plenty of sore losers and proud slobs who continued to share their views each year in the letters page of

the magazine.

Two years after the original Mrs Slob letter was published, readers' reaction to the perfection of Ethelyn Mosher in 1964, also undoubtedly influenced by Mrs Maitland's genre-defining letter, renewed the anti-contestants' correspondence. One reader, Marianne Fenton-Mart, nominated herself as 'Mrs Chatelaine' in her letter to the editors:

> I hereby appoint myself Chatelaine woman of the year. . . . I live in an ordinary bungalow. I have one child and two foster children. I bake all my own bread, cakes, pies, and cookies. I make good nourishing soups. I make all the clothes. I make my husband's shirts. I knit sweaters, make hats for myself. I do all my own washing and ironing. I take my boy to hockey, baseball, and lacrosse. In summer holidays we go camping. I do lots of gardening, make fruit into jams and jellies. Oh, I almost forgot. I teach my children and several neighbours children the violin. Will you ever publish this letter? Of course not, but I got it off my chest.[26]

Obviously a human dynamo around the home, Fenton-Marr either was a disconsolate loser in the contest or had never entered, believing that her chances of winning were not good because she did not appear to be actively involved in volunteer or community projects. Meanwhile, Mrs Houston of Bowmanville, Ontario, complained: 'How sweet, goody, goody and religious do you have to become to be able to measure up to your average Mrs Chatelaine winner? How original, they all are, with their Home and School, Scouts and Guides, Sunday schools, etc. . . . Well then, a big handshake to lousy housekeepers like me, who reads a book while she should be waxing floors.'[27] Fenton-Marr got a response, although not the one she was looking for, from Mrs John Barrett of Hearts Delight, Newfoundland: 'Re. the last word is yours [August] and here's happy reading to Mrs G. Houston of Bowmanville, Ontario, from one lousy housekeeper to another.

Long may she wave her book, and I don't care if Marianne Fenton-Marr drowns in her good nourishing soups and balls herself up in her hand knitted sweaters. Here's to our side.'[28] The perfectionists might have won the contest, but it certainly appeared that those who sided with the slobs took just as much pleasure, perhaps more, in ridiculing it and sanctimonious writers like Fenton-Marr. . . .

By the end of the decade, it was possible to chart subtle changes in entrants to the Mrs Chatelaine contest. In particular, women who worked outside the home started to infiltrate the list of regional runners-up. This was particularly true for the Atlantic-Canadian runners-up who were listed as teachers, nurses, and small-business owners. However, the grand-prize winner continued to conform to the full-time mother/part-time community volunteer model until 1969, when the unthinkable occurred. That year, the title of the profile said it all. 'I was a working mother when that term was a dirty word,' claimed Bettie Hall, the 1969 winner.[29] This mother of five sons was a 'genuine, all-her-life, full-time working mother' who had 'no regrets' and refused to make apologies for her choices.[30] Recently relocated from Tillsonburg, Ontario, to Chauteauguay, Quebec, this former assistant director of nursing and subsequent high-school teacher did not belong to any women's service clubs. In fact, she described women's clubs as 'so much wasted time and effort. So much tribal chatter.'[31] Hall's experience juggling work and home commitments was eased by a live-in nanny for 10 years, yet at this stage her boys were pulling their own weight in the household. The three teenagers were able to 'cook, wash and iron', while the younger two were responsible for their rooms and some family chores.

Reader reaction to Hall's comments and the article in general was, like virtually everything *Chatelaine* published, open to the varying interpretations of readers. Mrs M.H. Epp, Saskatoon, was critical of Hall's privileged position (although she did not frame her letter in class terms), her lifestyle, and her parenting skills, but in particular was angered by her offhand dismissal of all women's organizations:

I wish to protest your article on Mrs Chatelaine [May], not because she is a working mother, but because she is depicted as being so perfect. 'I insist on instant obedience.' How can she do that if she isn't home? How can she justify separating from her family for a year just for material gain? 'She reads voraciously.' When? 'She entertains formally.' Just how perfect can you get? No mother who chooses to stay at home and raise children properly should take this article seriously. Even more do I protest her attitude to women's groups. Who would staff Red Cross clinics, roll bandages, work in community kitchens . . . if it were not for unselfish women? [. . .][32]

In contrast, Mrs L. Mann of Heriot Bay, British Columbia, found Hall a 'most refreshing person' and enjoyed reading about 'a winner that seems so down to earth'.[33]

The Mrs Chatelaine case study, particularly the resource of the unpublished archival letters, permits a behind-the-scenes portrait of how the community of letter-writers responded to the published material. Despite the concerns of numerous critics who bemoaned the lack of mental stimulation provided in women's magazines or the hegemonic portraits of middle-class life, in the hands of readers this material underwent a startling transformation. The importance of readers' agency—to purchase the material, but more importantly to interpret and interact with the text—must not be underestimated. Some readers, like the entrants in the contests and particularly the winners, revelled in their existence as stay-at-home mothers who found pleasure and purpose in their husbands, kids, and community volunteer participation. They were, despite the magazine's overwhelmingly lower-middle-class and working-class readership, drawn from the middle- and upper-middle classes. The wives of successful farmers, professionals, or merchants, these were women who could afford to entertain and decorate their homes in style; they were creative and resourceful homemakers who were equally adept at canning vegetables, sewing drapes, and leading the family sing-song around the piano. They burned off the rest of their phenomenal energies directing and participating in community volunteer groups—particularly those in church, school, and women's organizations. If it all appeared a little too perfect, that was what it took to win the contest; and the prizes, even in the later years, made it worthwhile.

However, while these perfect homemakers and the perfectionist 'wannabes' concentrated on honing their entries, another group of equally devoted readers, the slobs, were crafting their letters of protest. They were not cowed by the prowess of the winners or the expectations of the magazine, but instead believed that the periodical, as Canada's only women's magazine, should reflect all Canadian women. The originality of Mrs Maitland's entry was never duplicated, but many members of the reading community wrote in the ensuing years to represent 'our side', as they referred to the non-participating 'slobs'. While the winners, their friends, and their communities celebrated their victories, the 'ordinary' readers, non-participants and (it seemed) the remainder of the *Chatelaine* community of readers, enjoyed the 'slobs' letters. Despite the effort and money Maclean Hunter and the sponsors poured into this showcase of Canadian homemaking, the slobs had more fun. They wrote to the magazine and to each other, loyally supported their side and forced the magazine to consider the issue of representation every year. The slobs represented the voices of the majority of *Chatelaine*'s readership who, as the demographic profile of readership makes clear, were average Canadians. Anderson's characterization of the contest as a 'dose of reality' for the editors was equally apt as a description of the process of discovery undertaken by the readers. In the face of

attempts to reconcile with those paragons of Canadian homemaking, many readers resisted and instead found solace in, and solidarity with, the slobs.

The concerns of the *Chatelaine* community illustrate part of the discontent and debate about the ideology of domesticity in post-war Canada. The magazine launched this contest honouring the ideal homemaker precisely at the time when vast numbers of Canadian women returned to or entered the workforce. The media representation of the stay-at-home mother as the ideal contrasted with the reality that many women were in the workforce. Ostensibly, *Chatelaine*'s editors supported this idea because it would counterbalance their more unconventional fare and attract what they hoped would be favourable attention to the periodical. As well, the valorization of middle-class feminine values tied in to the departmental features and the advertisements for household products. There was nothing exceptional in this; in fact, American magazines were full of similar material. But because *Chatelaine* had a heterogeneous, national audience of 'average' Canadians and not primarily an affluent urban or suburban audience, this material was received differently.

This contest illustrates the diversity and the participatory nature of the *Chatelaine* audience. It cautions against presuming that editors and producers of products of popular culture have all the power because they can determine the fare, whereas consumers' only choice is whether or not to purchase the product. Many *Chatelaine* readers were critical of the material and vocal in their criticisms. As well, by creating an alternative contest and, in later years, openly mocking the real winners, 'slobs' carved out their own oppositional niche within the magazine. The 'slob' letters demonstrate how published letters in the periodical instructed members of the community in the art of 'reading' *Chatelaine*. Clearly, those letters encouraged readers to reread the periodical, to read more critically and to read creatively; it encouraged them to remake the material in ways that would be meaningful to them. As conceived, the contest should have glorified and celebrated the ideal of the perfect homemaker, mother, and super-volunteer. Instead, readers demonstrated how out of step this 'ideal' was and forced *Chatelaine* to modify the contest. It is very doubtful that a working wife and mother would have won in 1969 had it not been for the 'slob' correspondence and the critical letters.

The Mrs Chatelaine contest serves as an example of the *Chatelaine* community in action. It illustrates that some readers were actively critical of the magazine's content and that they did not passively accept conventional (or, in this case, exceptional) portraits of middle-class women. While some readers derived enjoyment from participating in the contest and receiving accolades (and recognition) when they won, others derived pleasure from parodying, subverting, or criticizing the contest. This showcase of homemaking was ultimately a showcase of a lively community of readers and letter-writers who demanded that their ideas, concerns, and lifestyles be reflected in 'their' magazine. *Chatelaine*'s readers were not merely passive consumers or pawns of a cultural empire, but rather were active participants in a cultural community of Canadian women.

Notes

1 'Are *you* Mrs Chatelaine?' *Chatelaine* (December 1960), 15.

2 The legacy of Betty Friedan's *The Feminine Mystique* (New York, 1963) is the *a priori* assumption that all women's magazines foster women's second-class status and depict a narrow world bounded by the kitchen, the nursery, the bedroom, and the grocery store. Many academic and popular writers have followed in Friedan's wake, most recently Susan Faludi, *Backlash: The Undeclared War Against American Women* (New York, 1991). Academic works have shifted from this negative emphasis (with its attendant presumption that women are duped by women's magazines) to an acceptance of the cultural studies mode of analysis with its emphasis on issues of power, reader response and agency, and interpretation; but often these works suffer from ahistoricism, gender determinacy, or an over-reliance on the text and the creators at the expense of the readers' experiences. For the most recent academic contributions to this field, see Ros Ballaster, Margaret Beetham, Elizabeth Fraser, and Sandra Hebron, *Women's Worlds* (London, 1991); Ellen McCracken, *Decoding Women's Magazines: From Mademoiselle to Ms* (London, 1993); Helen Damon-Moore, *Magazines for the Millions: Gender and Commerce in the Ladies Home Journal and The Saturday Evening Post, 1880–1910* (Albany, 1994); and Joke Hermes, *Reading Women's Magazines: An Analysis of Everyday Media Use* (Cambridge, 1995).

3 Veronica Strong-Boag, '"Their Side of the Story": Women's Voices from Ontario Suburbs 1945–1960', in *A Diversity of Women: Ontario, 1945–1980*, Joy Parr, ed. (Toronto, 1995), 52, and Doug Owram, *Born at the Right Time: A History of the Baby Boom Generation* (Toronto, 1996), 12.

4 See, for example, Veronica Strong-Boag, 'Home Dreams: Women and the Suburban Experiment in Canada, 1945–1960', *Canadian Historical Review* (December 1991), 470–504; Joanne Meyerowitz, ed., *Not June Cleaver: Women and Gender in Postwar America, 1945–1960* (Philadelphia, 1994); and Wini Breines, *Young, White and Miserable: Growing Up Female in the Fifties* (Boston, 1992).

5 See Joan Sangster, 'Doing Two Jobs: The Wage-Earning Mother, 1945–1970', in Parr, ed., *A Diversity of Women*, 98–134; and *Earning Respect: The Lives of Working Women in Small Town Ontario, 1920–1960* (Toronto, 1995); and Franca Iacovetta, *Such Hardworking People: Italian Immigrants in Postwar Ontario* (Montreal/Kingston, 1992).

6 'The Labour Force', in *Canada Year Book 1969* (Ottawa, 1969), 765–6.

7 'Chatelaine Ad', *Canadian Advertising: Canadian Media Authority* 27 (September–October 1954),

114–15.

8 'Meet Mrs Chatelaine', *Chatelaine* (April 1961), 109.

9 Author's interview with Doris Anderson, 30 June 1994.

10 Ibid.

11 Archives of Ontario (AO), Maclean Hunter Records Series (MHRS) F-4-l-b, box 431, E.H. Gittings, Assistant Advertising Sales Manager for *Chatelaine*, to Mr F.D. Adams, 22 June 1961.

12 Ibid., J.L. Adams, Manager for Eastern Canada (*Chatelaine*), to L.M. Hodgkinson, 14 February 1961.

13 'Mrs Chatelaine—her home, her family, her every-day world', *Chatelaine* (April 1961), 110.

14 Ibid., 111.

15 Ibid.

16 Ibid.

17 Eveleen Dollery, 'Mrs Chatelaine enjoys a whirl in Toronto before flying to Paris', *Chatelaine* (April 1961), 112.

18 'Here's the winner of our contest Mrs Chatelaine 1964', *Chatelaine* (May 1964), 36.

19 AO, MHRS F-4-3-a, box 434, Mrs Beatrice Maitland, Chatham, NB, to Doris Anderson, 1 November 1961.

20 Ibid., Doris Anderson to Mrs Beatrice Maitland, 10 November 1961.

21 Ibid., Mrs Beatrice Maitland to Doris Anderson, 2 February 1962.

22 Ibid., Doris Anderson to Mrs Beatrice Maitland, 12 February 1962.

23 Ibid., Mrs F. Miller, New Westminster, BC, to Doris Anderson, 12 January 1962.

24 Ibid., Clara Cserick, 'Slob par excellence', Ottawa, to Doris Anderson, 27 January 1962.

25 Questionnaire dated 18 January 1994.

26 Marianne Fenton-Marr to Editors, 'The Last Word is Yours', *Chatelaine* (August 1964), 62.

27 Mrs G. Houston, Bowmanville, Ontario, to Editors, 'The Last Word is Yours', *Chatelaine* (August 1964), 62

28 Mrs John Barrett, Hearts Delight, Newfoundland, to Editors, 'The Last Word is Yours', *Chatelaine* (December 1964), 80.

29 'I was a working mother when that term was a dirty word', *Chatelaine* (May 1969), 34.

30 Ibid.

31 Ibid.

32 Mrs M.H. Epp, Saskatoon, Saskatchewan, to Editors, 'The Last Word is Yours', *Chatelaine* (August 1969), 68.

33 Mrs L. Mann, Herlot Bay, BC, to Editors, 'The Last Word is Yours', *Chatelaine* (August 1969), 68.

Section IV

Broadcast Media

Early radio was a technological wonder, the first mode of 'wireless' electronic communication. Guglielmo Marconi performed the first successful experiments with radio in the 1890s, the most notable of these involving shore-to-ship communication. In 1901, atop Signal Hill outside St John's, Newfoundland, he conducted the first trans-Atlantic radio broadcast. These messages were conveyed via Morse code, not by voice. The first voice transmissions, dubbed 'radio-telephony', were conducted by the Canadian inventor Reginald Fessenden, who, on Christmas Eve, 1906, broadcast a 'concert' of literary readings and music to ships at sea.

In the early 1900s, radio was a bidirectional medium: users could both send and receive messages. During World War I, governments in North America and Europe placed radio under military control, banning its use by ordinary citizens. The medium proved useful for naval communication, shell spotting, and transmitting orders. After the war, radio developed as a mass medium, an exemplar of 'one-to-many' communication. Radio-set manufacturers who were aiming to promote sales began broadcasting content on the airwaves. The first radio station licence in North America was issued to XWA in Montreal in 1919. By the early 1920s, radio was becoming a unidirectional medium, in which centrally transmitted messages were received by 'passive' listeners. Sales of radio sets grew, as did the number of broadcasters, which represented a range of social interests: newspapers took up broadcasting to cross-promote their print operations; labour and education groups offered public-service programming; church groups saved souls. The number of commercial radio stations increased. In 1925, the Canadian National Railway established the first radio network. By 1928 there were over 60 licensed radio stations in Canada.

As broadcasters on both sides of the border began to attract wider audiences, the federal government, which licensed broadcasters and assigned frequencies, sought a more active role in radio. In 1928, a Royal Commission was struck to study the issue, notably the mounting presence of US commercial radio in Canada. The commission recommended that Canada adopt the model of the British Broadcasting Corporation and nationalize private radio stations in order to create a national public broadcasting system. The public system established in 1932 proved less ambitious than the model recommended. This service, which in 1936 became the Canadian Broadcasting Corporation, relied on many private radio affiliates to form the national network. Other non-affiliated commercial radio stations continued to operate. Canada's radio system has been called a 'peculiar hybrid', owing to the mix of public and private broadcasters, popular and high-brow programming, and advertising and tax-based sources of revenue.

When television in the United States first gained popularity in the late 1940s, Ottawa again turned to a Royal Commission to chart its course. The Massey Commission, head-ed by Toronto businessman Vincent Massey, recommended that television in Canada fall under the control of the CBC and that its content reflect educational and civic-minded ideals. In 1952, CBC assumed control of television broadcasting, but, as with radio, the public network included a number of private station affiliates, owing to the country's geo-graphical expanse and the high cost of television production. Television broadcasting spread quickly, from just 2 stations in 1952 to 59 in 1960. That year, more than 90 per cent of Canadians lived within reach of a CBC signal. In 1961, 83 per cent of households had televisions, more than had indoor toilets, furnaces, or cars. CBC's network monopoly ended in 1961 when CTV, the country's first private network, took to the airwaves.

While successfully establishing a national transmission infrastructure, the govern-ment was unable to stem the flow of American programs into Canadian homes. By the 1960s, program content was predominantly American, as US border stations and Canadian stations showing US programs turned Ed Sullivan, June Cleaver, and Donna Reed into household names in Canada. Ottawa implemented the first Canadian content rules in 1960, requiring 55 per cent of airtime to be reserved for Canadian shows. But the lucrative prime-time slots continued to carry mostly American offerings. Since its for-mation in 1968, the Canadian Radio-television and Telecommunications Commission has made the promotion of Canadian programming one of its highest priorities. But the results here, at least on private television, are meagre. There are today two solitudes in Canadian English-language television. Between seven o'clock and eleven o'clock p.m., 91 per cent of private network programming is foreign, mostly American. On CBC, the cor-responding figure is 7 per cent.

New media require reliable sources of funding to operate. After World War I, many people asked the question: 'Who is to pay for radio?' The answer, Mary Vipond explains, turned out to be advertisers, after taxes and licence fees proved unpopular or unwork-able. But advertising remained controversial, especially 'direct' advertising, which inter-rupted programming in the form of spot advertising. Restrictions were placed on direct advertising during the 1920s. More amenable was 'indirect' advertising, in which a sin-gle advertiser sponsored an entire show with fewer program interruptions. Advertisers came slowly to radio, and large blocks of private radio aired without sponsors. When they did advertise, sponsors gravitated towards city stations, thereby widening the gap in program quality between urban and rural radio.

Radio waves carrying broadcasts cannot be purchased, only leased from the public through licensing arrangements. As such, state regulators require broadcasters to serve the public interest in various ways. During the early years of Canadian radio, Robert McChesney notes, the rationale and mechanisms for public control of radio were pro-moted by people like Graham Spry, head of the Canadian Radio League. Spry lobbied the Royal Commission struck in 1928 to determine the government's role in radio, and later mobilized public opinion behind its pro-public radio recommendations. The comparison with the United States is striking. While in Canada public radio began in 1932, south of the border commercial radio continued to dominate the airwaves.

Radio fostered communal identity among its listeners. This was seen with the Newfoundland radio program *The Barrelman*, presented by Joey Smallwood, who later entered politics and led the campaign to bring Newfoundland into confederation with Canada in 1949. Broadcast during the late 1930s, the program was a curious mix of island history, heroic exploits of man against nature, jokes and 'cuffers', and paeans to the scrappy mettle of the Newfoundland folk. Interspersed were ads for 'foreign' consumer goods brought from the mainland. As Jeff Webb documents, Smallwood encouraged listeners to write in, and their letters, when read on the air, served both as inexpensive program content and affirmation of the 'imagined community' of listeners. Radio broadcasting engendered new forms of social space and cultural expression. *The Barrelman*, melding ethnic nationalism and 'come-from-away' consumerism, underscored the contradictory impulses of a traditional society's embrace of modernity.

Canada's broadcasting system developed as an amalgam of American commercialism and British public service. Television public-affairs programming, David Hogarth argues, similarly inhabited a 'middle ground' between American showmanship and British edification. The Massey Commission, which laid the groundwork for the launch of television in Canada in 1952, championed high-brow ideals like 'information television' meant to foster 'citizenship training'. CBC public-affairs shows like *Tabloid* and *Close-Up*, however, would navigate between US-style entertainment and sensationalism, and the public-service ethos of documenting actuality. Shows like these are perhaps the historical forerunners of today's 'infotainment' programs.

Like radio, television turned to advertising to pay the bills. Enthusiasts promoted television as a new 'show window' for advertised goods, nestled in the nation's living rooms. As Paul Rutherford shows, advertising's growth was steady, if not buoyant; by 1971, television consumed 12 per cent of overall advertising spending. Television faced limitations not seen with newspaper and radio advertising. It relied mainly on national advertisers, capturing little of the local retail advertising available to newspapers and radio. Producing television ads proved expensive, as did buying the air time to run them, owing in part to government time limits on broadcast advertising. High costs contributed to the move away from single-sponsor, indirect advertising and towards 'spot' advertising, entailing 30- and 60-second commercials from multiple advertisers. The latter gave rise to complaints of intrusiveness and 'ad clutter', refrains of which are still heard today.

Specialty television has grown in popularity since its arrival in the early 1980s. Today, it accounts for about one-quarter of television viewing, up from 6 per cent in 1993. MuchMusic has been highly successful since its launch in 1984. Its formation reflected more than a desire to meet consumer demand for a Canadian version of MTV. Rather, as Ira Wagman details, political and economic considerations, encompassing the interests of the sound-recording industry and federal culture bureaucrats, were crucial. Department of Communications officials had already begun to put in place policies emphasizing market-based solutions for cultural industries, which included a newfound interest in the health of the sound-recording industry. Music television, it was hoped, would reverse sagging album sales and 'liberate' musicians from the restrictive playlists of radio programmers.

Questions for Critical Reading

1. What different options existed for funding radio in the 1920s? Why did advertising win out?
2. Why was advertising controversial among radio listeners? How was listener opposition overcome by the early 1930s?
3. Describe the salient features of American and British radio in the early 1930s. How did each impact on the development of radio in Canada?
4. What arguments in favour of a strong public radio system were presented by Graham Spry and the Canadian Radio League?
5. What were the key recommendations of the Aird Commission? Which of these were implemented, and why only after three years?
6. In what ways did the *The Barrelman* program promote both a North American consumerist ethos and a nationalist Newfoundlander perceptive?
7. What similarities and differences exist between Webb's article on *The Barrelman* and those by Charland on technological nationalism, McLuhan on radio, and Korinek on *Chatelaine* readers?
8. What was the Massey Commission's vision for Canadian television in the early 1950s?
9. Describe the key features of 'middle-ground' public-affairs programming as outlined by Hogarth.
10. Where would one situate a program like *Tabloid* on the continuum between pedagogy and pleasure, public and private, culture and commerce?
11. Why did sponsors shift from sponsorship advertising to spot advertising on television?
12. Why was television advertising so costly to produce and air in the 1950s and 1960s?
13. How did the creation of MuchMusic reflect a government policy shift away from 'Canadian identity' and towards 'cultural industries'?
14. Why was a national channel airing music videos so important to the Canadian sound-recording industry?

Further Readings

Hogarth, David. *Documentary Television in Canada: From National Public Service to Global Marketplace*. Montreal: McGill–Queen's University Press, 2002.
  • Focusing on Canadian documentary television beginning in the early 1950s, this book examines news magazines, docudramas, and science programs, among others.
Johnston, Russell. 'The Emergence of Broadcast Advertising in Canada, 1919–1932'. *Historical Journal of Film, Radio and Television* 17, 1 (1997), 29–47.
  • This article demonstrates how commercial radio became the dominant mode of radio transmission despite efforts of public radio advocates.
Nolan, Michael. 'An Infant Industry: Canadian Private Radio, 1919–36'. *Canadian Historical Review* 70, 4 (1989), 496–518.
  • This article represents a useful and informative corrective to the public radio/CBC bias of much broadcasting history.
Nolan, Michael. CTV: *The Network that Means Business*. Edmonton: University of Alberta Press, 2001.

- Based on archival research and interviews, this is the first scholarly history of CTV.

Raboy, Marc. *Missed Opportunities: The Story of Canada's Broadcasting Policy*. Montreal: McGill–Queen's University Press, 1990.

- A public policy–orientated history of Canadian broadcasting from the 1920s to the 1980s, this work provides a special focus on Quebec.

Vipond, M. 'The Beginnings of public Broadcasting in Canada: The CRBC, 1932–1936'. *Canadian Journal of Communication* 19 (1994), 151–71.

- The article offers a detailed, policy-oriented overview of early years of Canadian Radio Broadcasting Commission, Canada's first public radio broadcaster.

'Who is to Pay for Broadcasting?'

Mary Vipond

As radio broadcasting became more sophisticated in technology, programming, and audience, it also became increasingly costly. Rising expenses led the original broadcasters to seek more and more urgently for means to increase their revenues. Ultimately the solution to these twin problems was found in the interrelated phenomena of advertising-sponsored broadcasting and national networks, but the outcome was by no means a foregone conclusion from the perspective of the pioneers.

In the very early 1920s, one could open a station with little more than a licence ($50 per annum), some used parts, an ingenious engineer cum announcer (often seconded from other duties), and a stack of records. But that soon changed. In 1923 the minister of Marine and Fisheries estimated that it cost anywhere from $7,000 to $20,000 to set up a good broadcasting station and between $2,000 and $6,000 a year to maintain it.[1] A 1924 US survey showed that almost half of all stations had been installed for $3,000 or less and cost less than $1,000 per year to operate but that, at the other end of the scale, three American stations cost over $100,000 to build and more than $100,000 annually to operate.[2] Although the stations were not identified, clearly they were the flagship stations of the major manufacturers, those setting the standards by which all other broadcasters, American or Canadian, were judged.[3] By the end of the decade, one well-informed observer estimated, a 'total investment' of $54,100 was needed to construct a 500-watt station and $168,400 for one with 5000 watts power. . . . Because the amount of electrical interference was steadily growing and the tolerance of the public for static and fading diminishing, that much power had become a virtual necessity by that time. Clearly, establishing and operating a broadcasting station required a substantial investment by 1932; particularly in the context of the Depression, the ability of Canadian business interests to come up with that kind of financing was increasingly in doubt.[4]

Programming costs rose dramatically as the decade progressed as well. While records and amateur talent sufficed in the first two or three years of radio, listeners became more sophisticated and demanding as time went on. Government regulations required that most programs had to be live and audiences began to insist that they be 'high quality'. In the United States, one authority estimated that talent of high calibre could cost up to $1500 an hour by 1930.[5] Again, it was programming such as this that set the example for all of North America. Figures for two special series broadcast by CN stations in 1930 and 1931 give some idea of how expensive the best programming was. The orchestra, guest artists, and other miscellaneous costs for the 26 Toronto Symphony programs totalled over $27,000, while station rental (this was a network offering) came to almost $10,000 more. The much celebrated Romance of Canada historical drama series that same winter cost $12,500 for 18 programs, not including station rental.[6] Of course most programming was much less expensive, but broadcasts of this quality had to be offered if radio were to fulfill its potential.

. . .

As Canadian broadcasting developed over its

Abridged from *Listening In: The First Decade of Canadian Broadcasting, 1922–1932*, by Mary Vipond (Montreal and Kingston: McGill–Queen's University Press, 1992), 54–78. Reprinted by permission of McGill-Queen's University Press.

first 10 years, the cost of producing good programs on powerful stations grew considerably. Most stations claimed, most of the time, that they lost money; despite the profitability of the largest stations, the average profit for all the stations analyzed in 1931 was a measly $415.[7] Station-owners, whether individuals or corporations, of necessity became more and more preoccupied with the central question of early radio: 'Who is to pay for broadcasting?'[8]

Throughout the first decade of broadcasting, the issue of its financing received considerable attention in many countries, from those both within and outside the industry. Aside from certain schemes contemplated but never much tried, such as seeking patrons or voluntary listener contribution, four main alternatives were considered and attempted in various parts of the world. The first was the method that dominated in North America in the early 1920s, namely that stations were set up and carried as 'loss leaders' by those who stood to profit directly or indirectly from the growth of the radio industry in general.[9] The stations established by radio manufacturers, retailers, and, less directly, newspapers fell into this category. In many cases, these firms wrote the cost of the broadcasting station off as an advertising expense. Ultimately, of course, the real cost of the broadcasting done by these stations was borne by those who purchased the products of the owner. As H.S. Moore, manager of CFRB in Toronto, owned by the manufacturers of Rogers batteryless radios, told the Aird commission in 1929: 'We take a loss on the station. We never expect to make any profit on it; we did not build it to pay. The loss that we suffer is charged over to advertising which naturally in the long run gets into the cost of your product. . . .'[10] But even the largest manufacturers soon found the expense of operating a good station too great to be written off completely against other profits. Another source of financing was needed, if only as a supplement.

The second option was that adopted in Britain and a large majority of European countries, namely requiring the listeners to pay a substantial licence fee to the government, part of which was forwarded to the broadcaster(s) to help cover expenses. This method was also advocated in the early 1920s by some prominent American industry spokesmen, but it was a difficult measure to introduce in the United States once listeners had become accustomed to the 'free' service provided by the pioneer stations.[11] Another method with a somewhat similar effect also used in Britain in the early 1920s was the imposition of a special tax or royalty on each radio set produced, that cost of course being passed on to the radio consumer as well.[12] The licence-fee alternative was considered in Canada in the 1920s. From the beginning, annual licence fees were collected by the Radio Branch of the Department of Marine and Fisheries from receiver owners, and in 1923 an amendment was made to the Radiotelegraph Act enabling the branch to share this revenue with broadcasting stations in order to ensure continuing programming. As branch officials explained:

> There is the possibility that at some future date existing Canadian broadcasting stations will begin to drop out. This would not be a good thing for Canada, having regard to the many powerful stations to the south, and it is desirable that the Canadian stations should receive support. The only way, so far evolved, to achieve this end is the collection of a license fee by a central body such as the Federal Government, and to remit a portion of this fee to the different stations to assist in their upkeep. In this way the broadcast listeners in any area will be directly contributing to the support of the local stations which serve them.[13]

Despite the 1923 amendment, however, with the single exception of the money given to the Manitoba Telephone System's CKY Winnipeg, licence-fee receipts were never distributed to Canadian stations for use in financing broadcasting. Rather, the revenue collected went into the federal government's consolidated revenue fund and some of it was then allocated to the Radio Branch to be used primarily to investigate and solve technical problems such as electrical interference. As in the American case, the early establishment of broadcasting stations on a private-ownership basis militated against later adoption of the option of licence-fee financing. Canadian radio listeners were certain to object to the higher fees such a scheme would necessitate. More important, Canadian officials were extremely sensitive to the potential for complex and embarrassing political repercussions from a system that involved handing government-collected licence fees over to privately owned stations. It was one thing to distribute such moneys to a consortium of manufacturers, as in the case of the early British Broadcasting Company, or to a publicly owned entity such as the BBC or the Manitoba Telephone System, but private entrepreneurs were another matter. As deputy minister of Marine and Fisheries Alexander Johnston cautioned Jacques Cartier, general manager of CKAC Montreal, who wrote promptly after the passage of the 1923 amendment to inquire how his station might share in the largesse it augured: 'There is no question that the service given by CKAC reflects the greatest credit on its management, the bilingual feature being especially commendable. The station is, however, being primarily operated for the purpose of advertising *La Presse*, and the question at issue is whether the Government could, with propriety, subsidize a station operated for such purpose. This, of course, applies not only to *La Presse*, but to all stations of a similar character.'[14] On the whole, then, Radio Branch officials were inclined to leave well enough alone 'so long as commercial companies and private individuals [were] prepared to operate first class broadcasting stations at their own expense . . .'[15] This combination of concerns meant that, except in Manitoba, licence-fee receipts were not used to finance Canadian broadcasting stations before 1932.

A third option was direct government financing from general tax revenues, the practice in a few European nations. As in the previous case, however, it was extremely awkward for a government to subsidize any station other than one it owned, and the Canadian broadcasting system had initially been formed without government-owned stations. The stations set up and run by public corporations in the 1920s, the CNR stations and CKY, were operated to generate profits or at least to break even. If they did not always do so, any subsidies were granted reluctantly and were as small as possible. Moreover, it was politically difficult to request funds from general tax revenues for a service to which less than one household in three had access. The Aird commission in 1929 explicitly rejected the idea of financing the publicly owned system it advocated out of general revenues on these grounds, for example. Thus no private broadcasters were given direct government subsidies in Canada in the 1920s; indeed the option was never seriously considered.

The final alternative for financing broadcasting was, of course, advertising. In effect, as various scholars have pointed out, broadcasting paid for by advertising approximates a telephone model; that is, the broadcasting station may be likened to a giant pay-telephone booth with an extensive party line that can be rented for periods of time by anyone wishing to convey a message to the public.[16] The party originating the message pays for the use of the communications equipment; the listener pays nothing for the message. In truth, of course, as in all the options being discussed here, the consumer pays in the end—not necessarily the broadcast listeners only in this case, but all consumers of the product being advertised. To put it another way, the real transaction occurring in advertising-sponsored radio broadcasting is that the broadcaster sells the audience (the commodity) to the advertiser (who is really the consumer). The programming is merely a delivery vehicle; for efficiency it must appeal to the largest possible number.[17]

The gradual move toward advertising-financed broadcasting in North America in the 1920s was also a move toward the concept of radio broadcasting as a separate, self-sustaining, commercial enterprise. Indirectly, advertising was the basis of all private-enterprise broadcasting in Canada and the United States from the beginning. Most of the newspapers, retailers, and manufacturers opening stations in the earliest days did so at least in part for publicity, that is for the advertising value of the frequent repetition of the company name. Soon various other kinds of indirect advertising commenced. . . . Later in the 1920s it became common for a firm to advertise that it had paid for a program not only by regular reiteration of that information but also by its title (for example, 'The Eveready Hour') or by the nomenclature of the performers ('The Ipana Troubadours', for example, or 'The Lucky Strike Orchestra', or, the epitome of this genre, 'Paul Oliver and Olive Palmer', the singing celebrants of Palmolive Soap).[18] In both the United States and Canada throughout the 1920s, these forms of indirect advertising were generally accepted by both broadcasters and listeners on all stations at any time of day.

Direct advertising, that is the use of explicit messages promoting specific products in the context of a sponsored show, and especially the mention of prices, however, was much more controversial in the 1920s and much slower to gain acceptance than one might assume from today's perspective. So were 'spot' advertisements, those conveying a brief 100- or 150-word message but not implying sponsorship of the full program. Unusual in the very early period, spot ads were becoming increasingly common by 1932 and are of course the main type of advertisement on commercial radio or television today. The fiercely defended monopoly of the giant American Telephone and Telegraph Company over 'toll broadcasting' in the United States initially discouraged other stations from soliciting direct advertising.[19] Even after AT&T began issuing licences for this right in 1924, and then bowed out of broadcasting altogether in

1926, considerable reluctance to utilize direct ads remained. For at least the first half of the decade, virtually all leading spokesmen condemned direct advertising on radio as an unacceptable intrusion of the world of business into the privacy and sanctity of the home, or, as one American magazine colourfully put it, 'as a snake of commercialism in an Eden of entertainment'.[20] While such practices might be barely tolerated during business hours, they were quite unacceptable during the evening, which should be reserved for leisure activities. Even those involved in the advertising industry opposed overly direct and commercial advertising on radio, probably because they sensed a threat to the traditional advertising forums from which they still derived the bulk of their incomes and because they feared that negative listener reaction might hurt the credibility of the whole ad industry. The Montreal Publicity Association in 1924, for example, went on record as supporting the complete prohibition of direct advertising on the grounds that 'an evening's amusement— listening in—to delightful concerts is a sincere pleasure, but to have this pleasure marred by direct advertising is a pity.' To indirect advertising, on the other hand, the organization felt there could be 'no possible objection'.[21]

Similarly, in 1929 R.W. Ashcroft, one of Canada's leading advocates of commercial broadcasting, told the Aird commission that he thought all direct advertising should be banned, and as late as 1932 he claimed to find spot advertisements so objectionable that the station he managed, CKGW Toronto, deliberately charged a prohibitively high rate for them. Ashcroft admitted that he did, reluctantly, accept a few spot ads, from such reputable firms as Eatons, Simpsons, and the *Toronto Star*—but never would he advertise such a product as a corn plaster.[22] This 'moral' objection to direct advertising on radio, which was even shared at least rhetorically by such ardent devotees of private enterprise as US Secretary of Commerce Herbert Hoover, resulted in informal self-regulation by the better American stations that restrained its use until the latter 1920s; not until 1932 did the major networks allow prices to be mentioned in their advertisements. In Canada, more formal rules were in effect. Here, direct ads were restricted to daylight hours from 1923 until 1926 and then banned altogether until 1928, after which time stations were required to obtain individual dispensation to air them. Whether deliberately or not, these rules and attitudes tended to keep the potential of radio advertising in the hands of those who could afford to own a station or subsidize a full-length program.

Partly because of the early restrictions on ad use, but also because of lack of data about radio audiences and because they felt more comfortable with traditional media such as newspapers, magazines, and billboards, advertisers and advertising agencies alike were slow at first to turn to broadcasting.[23] Even in the United States it was not until 1928 that all the factors came together that made it practicable to conceive of the sale of advertising time as the principal means of permanent financial support for broadcasting.[24] Among those factors, increasingly sophisticated broadcasting technology and regularized, precisely timed program formats were crucial. Even more important, however, was the creation of national networks, both a cause and an effect of expanded use of radio by national advertisers. Indeed, advertising and networking were symbiotically linked; it was, for example, precisely the ability of AT&T to create networks by the use of its wirelines that made it attractive to major advertisers in the earliest days, while advertiser revenue was in turn necessary to pay the wireline expenses of networking.[25]

Growing levels of audience acceptance were also important to the increased use of advertising by broadcasters by the end of the 1920s. More and more, listeners seemed to accept that they must trade off intrusive ads for the free entertainment they were beginning to crave. By 1932 *Fortune* magazine in the United States reported that listeners seemed 'actually to like' advertis-

ing, and that sponsors were 'likely to lose more listeners by adding a symphony than adding a sales talk'.[26] Additionally, by making the importance of informed consumption more evident, the onset of the Depression helped destroy lingering prejudices against direct ads within both the business and regulatory communities. The firms first venturing into radio advertising tended to be those in flux: trying to expand their territories, introducing new brand-name products, facing harsher competition, and so on. They also were more likely to manufacture products either directly related to radio (for instance, batteries, tubes, receivers) or of the type that involved frequent small discretionary purchases (cigarettes, candy, toiletries, and the like).[27] In 1932, nevertheless, radio advertising still constituted only 5 per cent of total ad revenues in the United States. In that year, an American study showed that 36 per cent of airtime had commercial sponsorship.[28]

Although little hard information exists about the amount spent on advertising on Canadian stations in the first decade, it is highly unlikely that many of them were able to sell enough advertising time to break even, much less show a profit.[29] Little CFBO in Saint John, New Brunswick, for example, which was on the air for 572 hours between January and June 1929, had commercial sponsorship for only 88 of those hours. CKY Winnipeg earned the quite considerable sum of $10,696.35 from advertising as early as 1926; without additional revenue from its share of receiver-licence fees and from the rental paid by CNRW, however, it would have been almost $10,000 in the red for the year.[30] In the two months between 1 December 1931 and 31 January 1932, out of a total of six hours programming each day, CJCJ Calgary had sponsors for only ten minutes; for its more than seven hours of daily programming in the same period, CKCK Regina had sponsorship for only an average one hour and three minutes. On the other hand, CJOR Vancouver had six hours and ten minutes sponsored out of a total of fifteen, and

CKAC Montreal more than five-and-a-half hours sponsored out of a total broadcasting day of thirteen hours and forty-four minutes. On the average across Canada, 28 per cent of airtime was sponsored during those two months; in Alberta, however, that figure was only 18 per cent, and in Prince Edward Island only 16 per cent, whereas in Quebec 38 per cent of broadcasts were sponsored, and in Manitoba 41 per cent (demonstrating again CKY's commercial orientation).[31]

More than just the amount of sponsored air time is involved in determining the importance of advertising, however. A station's ultimate profitability depended as well on the rates it could charge for those ads. According to the testimony of Ernest Bushnell before the 1932 Special Committee of the House of Commons, CKNC in Toronto was able to cover its whole $177,000 operating expense in 1931 from ad revenues.[32] Similarly, by 1931 CKGW Toronto apparently had sufficient advertising revenue that it made a profit of almost $60,000; yet, as with the CKNC figure just quoted, depreciation was not taken into account.[33] Even the CNR station in Ottawa, despite various claims both then and since that CN stations were totally non-commercial, had enough ad revenue in 1930 to come close to breaking even; the station's expenses were $28,853.95 that year, its revenues $26,442.11.[34]

Advertising rates varied a great deal from year to year, hour to hour, and station to station. Indeed the lack of consistency in broadcasting ad rates illustrated the tentative nature of the venture. In 1932 Commander Edwards of the Radio Branch estimated that they ran from $25 to $225 per hour on Canadian stations, a very wide range depending upon the power of the station, estimated number of listeners, time of day, length of the advertising contract, and so on.[35] CKY Winnipeg, a mid-size urban station, for example, charged $100 per hour at night for one broadcast, reduced to $90 for a commitment to 13 broadcasts. The charge was only $70 per hour in the daytime. Short announcements were billed at $3 for less than 25 words, $6 for 26 to

50 words, and so on up to $15 for the maximum of over 150 words.[36] In Toronto in 1930, a spot announcement could be purchased on a small station for as little as $3 per minute, but an hour on CKGW in the evening cost $150.[37] Radio advertising rates were determined by the market.

Beginning as early as 1926, and increasingly common by 1932, broadcasting bureaus came into existence to act as brokers between radio stations and advertisers. The first such service was probably the one provided by Ernest Bushnell and Charles Shearer who in early 1927 began soliciting ads for CJYC Toronto.[38] As was to be the case later when more established advertising agencies began to take on broadcasting business, part of Bushnell and Shearer's job was to arrange the programs for the sponsors. They thus became booking agents and announcers as well. While Bushnell and his friend did not make much of a success of this particular job (although both went on to important radio careers), others followed them in the field, including such organizations as National Radio Advertising (Toronto), the British Columbia Broadcasting Bureau (Vancouver), and the Canadian Broadcast Bureau (Montreal). Rupert Caplan of the last organization (which in 1932 changed its name to the Canadian Broadcast Company) explained that his work consisted of 'building and presenting programs, supplying talent, writing continuity, and generally preparing Radio presentations for commercial or non commercial use'.[39] Most of these companies worked primarily in the local field, although some did arrange cross-Canada chain broadcasts as well. As of 1930, still only about 15 per cent of Canadian programs were handled by agencies. Normally, the agencies received 15 per cent commission, paid for by the radio station (paralleling the standard practice in the newspaper business).[40]

Before 1932 the viability of such bureaus was as marginal as that of many stations. The contrast between the situation of a station such as CFBO or CJCJ and that of CKNC and CKGW in

Toronto is important. The most powerful stations in the largest markets inevitably attracted the most advertising dollars. R.W. Ashcroft put it succinctly when he advised a group of advertisers: use the 'most powerful and most popular stations you can secure', he suggested, because otherwise you will be broadcasting 'mainly to the sun, and the moon, and the stars'. 'Just as lineage in a newspaper or magazine with 100,000 circulation is worth ten times that of a publication with 10,000 circulation,' he went on, 'so is an hour on a popular 5,000 watt station worth ten times the price of an hour on a 500-watter . . .'[41] The first comprehensive study of radio advertising in Canada, prepared for the Cockfield-Brown agency in Toronto in 1930, reached the same conclusion. While cautioning that radio coverage of the scattered prairie population was too expensive for most advertisers to contemplate, the author of the report pointed out that the Ontario and Quebec markets, within which resided 63 per cent of national purchasing power, could be 'cheaply and thoroughly covered by radio', and he recommended that the firm encourage its clients to consider this option.[42] Thus the reliance on advertisers to finance broadcasting encouraged a situation in which the most powerful stations and those located in the largest market areas had the largest revenues.

It was not, however, the sole reason for regional inequalities. Broadcasting in Canada from the beginning had operated on a commercial basis, which had encouraged concentration in areas of higher density and higher income. Access to skilled technicians and performers also gave urban centres an advantage. As the decade progressed and advertising became more important to station financing, the gap between the service provided by small stations and that provided by the big-city stations widened considerably—which in turn bolstered the advertising revenue of the latter even more. Dependence on third-party advertising revenue reinforced a tendency innate in the business from the start.

The 1932 House of Commons Special Committee on Broadcasting heard quite a bit about advertising as a means of paying for radio programming, both pro and con, from various parties with various interests. In the early 1920s everyone in the industry had wondered who would pay for broadcasting. By 1932 it was clear to all that if private broadcasting continued in Canada it would be primarily financed by commercial sponsorship. Even the Aird commission of 1929 had recommended that the fully publicly owned system it advocated should be partly funded by indirect advertising. In the context of a system in which stations had developed under private ownership, with listeners accustomed to 'free' radio shows and to the American model, no other alternative seemed feasible by the time the first decade of broadcasting ended, whatever the consequences for quality of programming or equity in distribution.

. . .

Notes

1 Canada, Parliament, House of Commons [HOC], *Debates*, 27 April 1923, 2285.
2 Hiram Jome, *Economics of the Radio Industry* (New York: Arno Press, 1971), 175–6.
3 See C.H. Sterling and J.M. Kittross, *Stay Tuned: A Concise History of American Broadcasting* (Belmont, CA: Wadsworth, 1978), 66.
4 E.A. Weir claimed that, of the 61 stations operating when the CRBC took over on 1 April 1933, only

12 fulfilled its technical standards. Weir, *The Struggle for National Broadcasting in Canada* (Toronto: McClelland and Stewart, 1965), 185.
5 'Radio Advertising', *Fortune* 1 (December 1930), 66.
6 National Archives of Canada [NAC], E. Austin Weir Papers, MG 30 D67, vol. 19, file 2, 'Cost of Toronto Symphony Programmes, 1930–', 'Cost of Dramatizations'.

7 See, for example, the claim that CFCF Montreal lost money every year from 1922 to 1928, NAC, Records of the Department of Communications, RG 97, vol. 149, file 6206-72, part 1, H.M. Short, Managing Director, Canadian Marconi, to A. Johnston, 28 September 1928; see also ibid., vol. 114, file BX-13, S.J. Ellis to Edwards, 23 March 1928. Other examples are cited in Michael Nolan, 'An Infant Industry: Canadian Private Radio, 1919–36', *Canadian Historical Review* 70 (1989), 503–4.

8 NAC, Records of the Marine Branch, RG 42, vol. 1076, file 7-3-1, C.P. Edwards, 'Radio. Administration: Legislation: Broadcasting: Regulations: Imperial Chain: New Development', 20 July 1923, 1.

9 Bill McNeil and M. Wolfe, *Signing On: The Birth of Radio in Canada* (Toronto: Doubleday, 1982), 17.

10 NAC, Records of Royal Commissions, RG 33, Series 14, vol. 1, file 227-9-9, 17 May 1929.

11 See Merlin Aylesworth, 'The National Magazine of the Air', in *The Radio Industry: The Story of its Development* (New York: Arno Press, 1974), 229.

12 Asa Briggs, *The Birth of Broadcasting: The History of Broadcasting in the United Kingdom*, vol 1 (London: Oxford University Press, 1961), 120.

13 NAC, Records of the Marine Branch, RG 42, vol. 1076, file 7-3-1, 'Radio, 1923–1924', 25 August 1924, 7. See also Alan N. Longstaffe, 'The Future of Radio in Canada', *Radio*, February 1923, 1.

14 NAC, Records of the Department of Communications, RG 97, vol. 151, file 6206-108, part 1, A. Johnston to J.N. Cartier, 14 November 1923. See also HOC, *Debates*, 27 April 1923, 2286.

15 NAC, Records of Royal Commissions, RG 33, series 14, vol. 5, 'Report for the British Broadcasting Committee on Radio Broadcasting Situation in Canada', 19 May 1923, 3. See also Records of the Marine Branch, RG 42, vol. 1076, file 7-3-1, 'Radio', 20 July 1923; RG 97, vol. 87, file 6040-1, part 1, C.P. Edwards to EJ. Haughton, 21 November 1924.

16 See W.P. Banning, *Commercial Broadcasting Pioneer: The WEAF Experiment, 1922–1926* (Cambridge, MA: Harvard University Press, 1946), 55–6, and Erik Barnouw, *A Tower in Babel: A History of Broadcasting in the United States*, vol. 1: to 1933 (New York: Oxford University Press, 1966), 106.

17. Dallas Smythe, *Dependency Road: Communications, Capitalism, Consciousness, and Canada* (Norwood, NJ: Ablex, 1981).

18 Roland Marchand, *Advertising the American Dream: Making Way for Modernity, 1920–1940* (Berkeley and Los Angeles: University of California Press, 1985), 94.

19 More specifically, other stations were prohibited from charging advertisers for airtime; non-telephone-company stations did, however, even before 1924, encourage sponsors to create and pay for programs, thus saving themselves the cost of program production. See Susan Smulyan, '"And Now a Word From Our Sponsors . . .": Commercialization of American Broadcast Radio, 1920–1934', Ph.D. dissertation, Yale University (1985), 80.

20 'Radio Advertising', 66. See also Fourth National Radio Conference, *Proceedings*, 18, in J. Kittross, ed., *Documents in American Telecommunications Policy*, vol. 1 (New York: Arno Press, 1977), and Sydney W. Head with C.H. Sterling, *Broadcasting in America: A Survey of Television, Radio, and New Technologies*, 4th edn (Boston: Houghton Mifflin, 1982), 136.

21 NAC, Records of the Department of Communications, RG 97, vol. 87, file 6040-1, part 1, C.N. Valiquet to Edwards, 15 August 1924.

22 NAC, Records of the Marine Branch, RG 42, vol. 1077, file 227-9-3, R.W. Ashcroft to Aird commission (personal communication), 17 May 1929, 3; HOC, Special Committee on the Operations of the Commission under the Canadian Radio Broadcasting Act, 1932, 332, 339.

23 See Banning, *Commercial Broadcasting Pioneer*, 152–5. Advertising agencies also apparently feared alienating newspaper customers by moving too enthusiastically to the new medium. See Marchand, *Advertising the American Dream*, 92. The earliest American large-scale radio-audience surveys were conducted in 1929; there was no similar Canadian survey until after 1932.

24 J.W. Spalding, '1928: Radio Becomes a Mass Advertising Medium', *Journal of Broadcasting*, 8, 1 (1963–4), 32*ff*.

25 D.J. Czitrom, *Media and the American Mind: From Morse to McLuhan* (Chapel Hill, NC: University of North Carolina Press, 1982), 76.

26 Quoted in Marchand, *Advertising the American Dream*, 110.

27 Smulyan, '"And Now a Word From Our Sponsors . . ."', 96; T. Eoyang, *An Economic Study of the Radio Industry in the United States of America* (New York: Arno Press, 1974), 176.

28 Sterling and Kittross, *Stay Tuned*, 112, 114, 516.

29 'The Future of Broadcasting Stations', *Radio News of Canada*, June/July 1927, 28.

30 NAC, Records of Royal Commissions, RG 33 series 14, vol. 2, file 227-11-6, C.A. Munro to J.B.M. Baxter, 30 May 1929; *Winnipeg Tribune*, 10 February 1927, 8.

31 HOC, Special Committee 1932, 35–7.

32 Ibid., 166.

33 NAC, T.J. Allard Papers, MG 30 D67, vol. 27, file 9, 'G and W Case', 10 October 1946.

34 Ibid., vol. 19, file 3, 'Total Actual Cost of Operation, Year 1930'. The other owned CN stations, however, CNRA and CJYCV, had only modest commercial revenues.

35 HOC, Special Committee 1932, 9.

36 NAC, Records of the Department of Transport, RG 12, vol. 864, file 6206-162-3, leaflet 'Manitoba Telephone System Radio Service', 1 March 1932.

37 Cockfield-Brown Ltd, 'Radio as an Advertising Medium' [1930–1], Appendix A, 2 (copy in author's possession, thanks to John Twomey).

38 NAC, T.J. Allard Papers, MG 30 D304, vol. 8, file 8-4, E.L. Bushnell, 'Draft Reminiscences', 3–10.

39 NAC, Records of the Marine Branch, RG 42, vol. 494, file 209-32-111, part 3, Caplan to assistant deputy minister of Marine, 10 May 1932.

40 Cockfield-Brown, 'Radio as an Advertising Medium', Appendix A, 4.

41 NAC, Richard B. Bennett Papers, MG 26K, M-1314, R.W. Ashcroft, 'The Fifth Estate', October 1929, 389145–6.

42 Cockfield-Brown, 'Radio as an Advertising Medium', 4.

Graham Spry and Public Broadcasting

Robert W. McChesney

Public broadcasting systems are in retreat across the planet. With the rise of multi-channel television systems and the Internet, many argue that public broadcasting is no longer necessary, that the spectrum scarcity that justified public broadcasting in the past is no longer justified. In addition, with the plethora of channels, there will be the possibility of fare to suit every conceivable taste; hence, there is not justification for public intervention in the marketplace, which is the proper steward of communication. I believe these arguments are wrong-headed. Many of those who struggled for public broadcasting in its formative years did so not on technical grounds of spectrum scarcity as much as a profound critique of the limitations of the market for regulating a democratic media system. By that measure, the justification and need for public broadcasting is as substantial today as it ever has been. In this article I chronicle the activities and arguments of Graham Spry and the other public broadcasting organizers in Canada in the 1930s, and their relationship with like-minded US reformers who were engaged in a similar struggle at the same time. In my view, this experience sheds necessary historical light on the current dilemma concerning public broadcasting, and points the way toward a superior resolution to the current crisis.

The Rise of Public Broadcasting

The starting point for any understanding of the current predicament of public broadcasting is debunking the notion that broadcasting was assumed to be a commercial enterprise from day one. In fact, when radio broadcasting emerged in the 1920s, almost every nation considered its usage a political issue with distinct social implications. If we look at the relevant history of the rise of broadcasting, we can see how divorced from the actual record is the assumption that broadcasting is automatically, organically, and necessarily a profit-driven, commercial enterprise.

When radio broadcasting emerged in the years immediately following the First World War, it presented a distinct problem for the nations of the world. How was this revolutionary technology to be employed? Who would control radio broadcasting? Who would subsidize it? What was its fundamental purpose to be? The problem of broadcasting was especially pressing in North America and western Europe, where the overwhelming majority of radio receivers were to be found until the 1940s and later. It was clear that national governments would play the central role in determining the manner in which broadcasting would be developed, if only because the radio spectrum was a limited resource which defied private appropriation. Beyond that, however, the matter was far from settled. In all the relevant countries, different interests made claims upon the new technology. They ranged from educators, labour, religious groups, political parties, amateur radio enthusiasts, listeners' groups, and journalists to radio manufacturers, telephone and telegraph companies, naval and military interests, advertisers, electric utilities, and the commercial entertainment industry. Each group claimed, in various ways and to varying degrees, to be the rightful steward of the nation's radio broadcasting service.

So strong was this social role that the outcome was different in every nation. Most strik-

From *Canadian Journal of Communication* 24 (1999), 25–47. Reprinted by permission.

ingly, the United States and Great Britain—two nations which had so much in common culturally, economically, and politically—developed systems of broadcasting that were, in principle, diametrically opposed.[1] The British established the British Broadcasting Corporation (BBC) in the 1920s to serve as a non-profit and non-commercial broadcasting monopoly. Under Lord John Reith, the BBC established the principles of what would become the paragon of public service broadcasting, although many other nations, like Weimar Germany and the Netherlands, also created successful and quite different versions of public service broadcasting. The United States, on the other hand, adopted a system dominated by two networks, NBC and CBS, which were supported exclusively by commercial advertising. The hallmark of this system was its emphasis upon maximizing profit by any means necessary, which meant popular entertainment programming, usually provided by advertising agencies. These two systems, the British and the American, thereafter became the archetypes employed in virtually all discussions of broadcasting policy in democratic nations.

It was also during the 1920s and 1930s that vibrant political debates look place in all of these nations over how best to deploy broadcasting. The decisions made then would effectively direct the course of radio and television into the 1980s and 1990s. In Britain, for example, advertisers worked diligently in the early 1930s to have the BBC accept advertising. They were unable to generate even minimal public enthusiasm for commercial broadcasting. With the approval of the Ullswater Committee Report in 1936, the primacy of non-profit and non-commercial broadcasting was established as non-negotiable for a generation. In the United States, after commercial broadcasting became established in the late 1920s, there arose a feisty movement to eliminate or markedly reduce for-profit, advertising-supported broadcasting and replace it with a non-profit system operated on public service principles.[2] With the passage of the *Communications Act*

of 1934 and the creation of the Federal Communications Commission, however, this US broadcast reform movement disintegrated, and the profit-motivated basis of US broadcasting was politically inviolate forever after.

If the 1920s and 1930s, specifically the years from 1926 to 1935, form a critical juncture in the formation of national broadcasting systems, it was a critical juncture with a distinct international edge quite unlike anything that had preceded it. Broadcasting was an international phenomenon that respected no political boundaries. Messages from one national broadcasting system often were audible in all surrounding nations. Broadcasting required international regulation to prevent neighbouring nations from utilizing the same wavelengths and thereby jamming each other's signals. Finally, short-wave broadcasting, which emerged full force in the 1930s, was suitable only for international broadcasting; technologically, it was ill-suited for domestic purposes except in enormous nations such as the Soviet Union. In short, the national debates over broadcasting occurred in an international context. It is not surprising, therefore, that US commercial interests worked with their British counterparts in their efforts to commercialize the British airwaves. Similarly, advocates of public broadcasting worked as closely as possible with the BBC in their efforts to promote non-commercial broadcasting in the United States. During this formative period, the protagonists in the struggles for national systems of broadcasting recognized that they were being fought on a global playing field.

Radio broadcasting emerged in Canada in the 1920s much as it did in the United States (see Vipond, 1992). For most of the 1920s, nobody had a clue how to make any money at it. Broadcasting was taken up by various private groups, but it was not an engine of profit-making. In the United States at mid-decade, almost one-third of the stations were run by non-profit groups, and those stations operated by for-profit groups were intended to shed favourable publicity on the owner's primary enterprise, not generate profit. Indeed, the hallmark of both Canadian and US broadcasting was its chaotic nature, which prevented long-term planning. (Indeed it was this chaos that influenced the British to formally adopt the BBC in the early 1920s, long before other nations had formalized their broadcast systems.[3]) By 1928, however, US capitalists began to sense the extraordinary commercial potential of broadcasting. With the support of the newly established Federal Radio Commission, the US airwaves were effectively turned over to NBC and CBS and their advertisers (see McChesney, 1993). This transformation was staggering—both in scope and the speed with which it took place. As Barnouw (1966) has noted, between 1928 and 1933 US commercial broadcasting sprang from non-existence to full maturity. But this stunning event did not pass unnoticed. As mentioned above, the emergence of commercial broadcasting in the United States was met by a vociferous opposition that argued that commercial broadcasting was inimical to the communication requirements of a democratic society.

By the late 1920s the Canadian public wanted to see broadcasting put on a more stable basis, in order to ensure receiving broadcasts over expensive receiving sets (see O'Brien, 1964). The sudden rise of US commercial broadcasting forced the hand of Canada, which either had to determine a distinct policy or see its radio broadcasting collapse into the orbit of NBC and CBS, both of which had already established affiliations with powerful stations in Montreal and Toronto.[4] In December 1928 the Canadian government appointed a royal commission to make a thorough study of broadcasting and report to the House of Commons on the best system for Canada to adopt. The Aird Commission, named after its chairperson, held extensive public hearings across Canada. In addition, the commissioners spent four months in 1929 travelling in the United States, Britain, and other countries to examine other broadcasting systems. In New York, NBC executives candidly expressed their

plans to incorporate Canada into their network (O'Brien, 1964). But the Aird Commission was most impressed by the non-profit and non-commercial systems in Europe, and eventually it recommended that Canada adopt a cross between the BBC and the German public service system, which (unlike the British) gave the provinces greater control over broadcasting. Commercial advertising would be severely restricted, perhaps even eliminated; the broadcasting service would be supported by licence fees, as in Britain (Royal Commission on Radio Broadcasting, 1929). The nationalist sentiment was unmistakable; as one Canadian newspaper put it, 'The question to be decided by Canada is largely whether the Canadian people are to have Canadian independence in radio broadcasting or to become dependent upon sources in the United States' (cited in O'Brien, 1964, p. 64). . . .

The Aird Commission's report did not settle matters for Canada, for its recommendations did not have the force of law. First, the Supreme Court of Canada had to rule that the national government and not the provincial governments had the right to regulate broadcasting ('Provincial Control', 1931). Second, the Supreme Court decision had to be upheld by the British Privy Council in London (Codel, 1932b). Once this was accomplished, in February 1932, the Canadian House of Commons could then act on the Aird Commission's recommendations. In the intervening three years, however, conditions had changed dramatically in Canada. The extraordinary growth of commercial broadcasting in the United States had made a profound impression on Canadian advertisers and important elements of the business community. In particular, the Canadian Pacific Railroad had developed a plan to provide for a private, national, advertising-supported broadcasting service for Canada, to be supervised by the railroad. It began a campaign to coordinate the efforts of Canada's private broadcasters and advertisers to gain public support for the measure. Those elements supporting commercial broadcasting in

Canada were allied with the US commercial broadcasters and their Canadian subsidiaries. To some, it seemed that the momentum of the Aird Commission's report, with its call for non-profit, non-commercial broadcasting, had been lost amidst all the judicial haggling. Fears mounted that Canada might emulate the United States and adopt full-blown commercial broadcasting (see Raboy, 1990, ch. 1).

It was in this context that the Canadian Radio League was founded in 1930 by Graham Spry and Alan Plaunt, two young Canadians determined that Canada adopt the system recommended in the Aird Report. The purpose of the Radio League was to mobilize support for public service broadcasting and to counter the campaign to bring commercial broadcasting to Canada.[5] The Canadian Radio League emphasized how commercialism would undermine the democratic potential of broadcasting for Canada. 'Democracy is by definition that system of Government responsible and controlled by public opinion. Radio broadcasting is palpably the most potent and significant agent for the formation of public opinion,' Spry argued. 'It is no more a business than the public school system' (Canada, House of Commons, 1932, pp. 546–7). Spry detested the effect of advertising upon radio broadcasting: 'To trust this weapon to advertising agents and interested corporations seems the uttermost folly' (Spry to Alexander, 1931).

Most importantly, Spry and the Radio League emphasized the threat to Canadian culture and political autonomy posed by a commercial broadcasting system. Spry argued that such a system was suitable only for those Canadians 'who believe that Canada has no spirit of her own, no character and soul to express and cultivate' (Canada, House of Commons, 1932, p. 546). The Radio League declared that US commercial interests were working surreptitiously to undermine the consensus for public service broadcasting in Canada, and that the US broadcasters were spreading lies and misinformation about both the Radio League and the BBC. 'I have

really come to feel', Spry wrote to one Canadian editor, 'that this is a struggle to control our own public opinion, and to keep it free from an American radio monopoly behind which stands General Electric, J.P. Morgan, . . . Westinghouse, the motion picture and theatrical group, etc., in a word "Capitaleesm" with a vengeance' (Spry to Ferguson, 1931). In all of its communications, the Radio League emphasized what it regarded as the asinine character of US commercial broadcasting: 'At present, the advertisers pay the piper and call the tune,' Spry declared. 'And what a tune. The tune of North America is that of the peddler boosting his wares' (Spry, [1931a]).

The Canadian Radio League was able to use this fear of US commercial domination as a trump card in the Canadian deliberations over broadcasting. 'The fact that the Radio Corporation of America and its associates are primarily American in their outlook colours our feelings,' Spry wrote to one US reformer. 'We fear the monopoly not only as a monopoly, but as a foreign monopoly' (Spry to Perry, 1931). Elements of the Canadian business community that might have opposed government broadcasting shared this concern that the United States might dominate a private Canadian system. There was the very real concern that well-heeled US advertisers could afford to purchase extensive radio advertising in Canada over a commercial system, and thus gain a competitive advantage over their smaller Canadian rivals. There was also the concern that if Canada permitted commercialism to continue, capitalists might use the few Canadian frequencies to broadcast commercial programming into the heavily populated US market, thereby turning their backs on Canada. 'Indeed,' Spry wrote to an American reformer, 'if the fear of the United States did not exist, it would be necessary, like Voltaire's God, to invent it' (Spry to Alexander, 1931). Still, the evidence suggests that Spry's enthusiasm for public service broadcasting was as much or more the consequence of his democratic socialism than it was the result of his Canadian nationalism. His primary concern, arguably, was that a commercial broadcasting system disenfranchised the public and empowered big business, regardless of nationality.

In this light, it did not take very long for Spry and the Canadian Radio League to establish close relations with broadcast reformers in the United States. There, the leading reformers were journalists and civil libertarians, or were associated with various educational, labour, and religious groups. In fact, the reformers were a cross-section of US society much like that enjoyed by the Canadian Radio League, though without the Radio League's business support. The US reformers also lacked the Canadian Radio League's political savvy, and they could never agree upon one specific reform proposal and then coordinate their efforts to work for its passage. . . . In the summer of 1931 Spry made an extended trip to the United States to meet with US reformers (Spry to Murray, 1931). He was especially interested in getting any information on the US broadcasting industry's activities in Canada. In Columbus, Ohio, he spoke about the Canadian situation to an enthusiastic audience at the annual convention of the Institute for Education by Radio (Spry, 1931c). 'Whatever the objective of commercial broadcasters in our country may be with reference to Canada,' one US activist informed Spry afterward, 'I can assure you that the educators have no desire to interfere in any way with Canadian affairs. On the contrary, they are ready to co-operate in every possible way' (Perry to Spry, 1931). For the next two years Spry and leading US reformers stayed in constant contact. As Spry wrote to one American, 'If Canada establishes a non-advertising system . . . your whole position in the United States will be enormously strengthened' (Spry to Morgan, 1932a). Spry repeatedly emphasized the existence of the US broadcast reform movement as discrediting the notion that commercial broadcasting was popularly embraced by listeners. . . .

The marriage of the Canadian Radio League and the US broadcast reformers was abetted by their mutual hatred for the US commercial broadcasting industry. Spry was convinced that NBC and CBS were working behind the scenes with the Canadian Pacific Railway to get a private system authorized by Parliament. Spry believed there was tremendous incentive for the US broadcasters to support a private system; once it was in place, NBC and CBS would affiliate with private broadcasters in all the other major Canadian markets besides Toronto and Montreal (Spry to Morgan, 1932a). . . .

That belief notwithstanding, the actual evidence of US commercial broadcasters' involvement in the Canadian radio debates is thin and patchy. Spry was quick to concede that the Americans used 'quiet methods' and that much of their work was to dispatch eloquent speakers to Toronto and Montreal 'to praise the American system and damn the British' (Spry to Ferguson, 1931). . . . But circumstantial evidence does suggest considerable involvement by US commercial interests. For example, the leader of the fight for commercial broadcasting in Canada, R.W. Ashcroft, was an advertising professional who had served as NBC's representative in Canada (Canada, House of Commons, 1932; Spry to Mac, 1931). The NBC and CBS affiliates in Toronto and Montreal sometimes carried programming highly critical of the BBC and all forms of broadcasting other than commercial.[6] By then, the threat posed by the US reformers, whether real or perceived, had become an obsession among the US commercial broadcasters, and they were determined to win at any cost. Hence the broadcast reformers, American and Canadian, were of no mind to grant the US commercial broadcasters the benefit of the doubt. . . .

If the US commercial system served as one reference point for the Canadian debates, the BBC served as the other. By the early 1930s the BBC was widely admired the world over, in a manner that had eluded NBC and CBS. The BBC was held up by the Canadian Radio League as the ideal to which Canadian broadcasting should aspire.

When Canadian Prime Minister R.B. Bennett went to London in 1930, Spry used all his contacts to ensure that Bennett visited the BBC headquarters; he was convinced that if the conservative Bennett saw the BBC operation, he would forever oppose the move to commercial broadcasting in Canada (Spry to Herridge, 1930). . . . There was also an element of imperial rivalry between Britain and the United States with regard to the path of Canadian broadcasting. The explicit goal of the dominant US communication firms since the First World War had been to reduce, if not actually eliminate, the presence of the British in the Western Hemisphere. In this contest, the Canadian sympathies tended toward the British, a fact which the Radio League played upon (Spry, 1976a).

In order for the proponents of commercial broadcasting in Canada to succeed, they needed to deflate the exalted image of the BBC. This they did, with relish. As Canadian reformer Brooke Claxton wrote to Gladstone Murray of the BBC, 'The private companies get out the wildest kind of propaganda about the BBC' (Claxton to Murray, 1932). The attack on the BBC reached its height in 1931 when John Gibbon, the publicity director of the Canadian Pacific Railway, the group leading the fight for a commercial system, published a scathing critique of the BBC in the *Canadian Forum* (Gibbon, 1931). Gibbon wrote that the weak performance of the BBC, combined with the popularity of US commercial programs, made it absurd for Canada to proceed with the recommendations of the Aird Commission. Instead, he argued, only an advertising-supported system would give Canadians the type of programming they wanted.

The Canadian Radio League immediately sent a copy of Gibbon's article to the BBC, which was so irate it threatened to take the matter to the British House of Commons. Eventually, the Canadian Pacific Railway apologized to the BBC for the factual errors contained in the article, and Gibbon was severely reprimanded by his employer.[7] In addition, the *Canadian Forum* permitted Spry to write a response to Gibbon, in which he decisively countered the attacks on both the Radio League and the BBC (Spry, 1931b). In sum, this attempt to soil the BBC and the notion of public service broadcasting backfired.

In the spring of 1932 the Canadian House of Commons held extensive and widely publicized hearings on the recommendations of the Aird Commission. The US broadcasting trade publication *Broadcasting* anticipated vindication for commercialism: 'Most of Canada's citizens are accustomed to broadcasting by the American Plan and many will accept no substitute' ('Watch Canada', 1932, p. 16). But Sir John Aird testified to the contrary: 'The broadcasting medium in Canada should be protected from being reduced to the level of commercial exploitation as it has been reduced in a neighboring country' (cited in *Education by Radio*, 1932, p. 98). Graham Spry coordinated the testimony of those endorsing the Aird Commission's report. 'The choice before the committee is clear,' he testified. 'It is a choice between commercial interests and the people's interest. It is a choice between the state and the United States' (Canada, House of Commons, 1932, p. 46). Spry also emphasized that unless Canada established a national public broadcasting system, it would be unable to claim its fair percentage of the world's radio frequencies at a forthcoming international radio conference to be held in Madrid (Canada, House of Commons, 1932).

The United States loomed large in these Canadian debates. The House of Commons requested that NBC president Merlin Aylesworth testify in Ottawa regarding NBC's plans for Canada. Aylesworth declined. Privately, he wrote RCA president David Sarnoff saying that to testify would be a 'great mistake' on his part: 'it would draw the fire up there and down here' (Aylesworth to Sarnoff, 1932). US reformers showed no such hesitation. US radio inventor Lee De Forest submitted a statement on broadcasting to the Canadian House of Commons. De Forest's hatred of radio advertising was so intense he spent a year in the early 1930s attempting to invent a device that would automatically mute radio advertisements and then return the volume to audible levels when the programming returned (Kittredge, [1930]). . . . After lambasting US radio for its 'moronic fare', De Forest called upon 'you in Canada to lead radio in North America out of the morass in which it has pitiably sunk' (Canada, House of Commons, 1932, p. 491).

Most damning was the testimony of US educator Joy Elmer Morgan, the only American to travel to Ottawa to testify in person. Morgan emphasized that commercial broadcasting had relegated public affairs and education to the margins and that the existence of the US broadcast reform movement was 'inescapable evidence of dissatisfaction' with the status quo. Morgan emphasized the importance of the Canadian hearings: 'The important thing is not that a few people shall make money out of radio broadcasting, but rather that this new tool shall be used to beautify and to enrich human life. Now is the time to take a long look ahead to avoid mistakes which it would take decades or even centuries to correct' (Canada, House of Commons, 1932, p. 470).

Not surprisingly, Graham Spry was ecstatic about the effect of Morgan's testimony. 'Until your appearance', he wrote Morgan, 'the committee had regarded the American situation as largely satisfactory and . . . that educational broadcasts were eminently possible through commercial stations. . . . Your evidence gave an entirely new complexion to the situation and we are entirely grateful to you for your assistance' (Spry to Morgan, 1932b). The recommendations of the Aird Commission carried the day. At the completion of the hearings, the Canadian Parliament approved the complete nationalization of broadcasting with the elimination of direct advertising (Codel, 1932a).

The formal approval of nationalization elated the US reformers. On one hand, those Americans living near the Canadian border—a not inconsiderable number—would now be able to hear quality non-commercial programming. . . . Defenders of US commercial broadcasting envisioned this same scenario, though they viewed it with alarm, not elation. 'The existence and development of this Government owned system will be a challenge to American radio station owners,' one US senator who favoured commercialism stated. 'They must prove themselves more satisfactory to the people than the Canadian system, or the Government system will inevitably be established in the United States' (Senator C.C. Dill, Democrat of Washington, cited in 'Dill Sees US Radio in Danger', 1932).

In addition, the Canadian Radio League was seen by US reformers as providing the model for how the reform effort should be organized in the United States (Evans to Woehlke, 1933). Morgan wrote to the Canadian Radio League: 'We in the United States who are working for radio reform have been greatly encouraged by your success' (Morgan to Plaunt, 1932). The inability of the US reformers to coalesce had been a major weakness for the Americans, especially when confronted by a powerful adversary like the commercial broadcasting lobby, which had immense power on Capitol Hill. Unfortunately, however, the Canadian model never became more than that for the US reformers.

The nationalization of Canadian radio also led to a major tactical reversal for the US reform movement in the fall of 1932. Rather than lobby for specific measures—for example, reserving 15 or 25 per cent of the frequencies for non-profit broadcasting—the US reformers began to lobby for Congress to authorize a full-blown investigation of broadcasting, much like the Aird Commission, which would then recommend a wholly new manner of organizing US broadcasting ('A Congressional Investigation', 1932). The reformers considered it axiomatic that any neutral audit of broadcasting, conducted by people with no material link to commercial broadcasting, could only recommend non-profit broadcasting, as in Canada. However, they never had a chance to see this belief tested. The commercial broadcasting lobby flexed its muscles to undercut the momentum for reform on Capitol Hill and all but eliminate congressional hearings on broadcast legislation. With the passage of the *Communications Act* of 1934, broadcast structure was no longer a legitimate political issue, and the commercial basis of the industry became politically sacrosanct.

The activities of the Canadian and US broadcast reformers of the early 1930s are of interest not only because of their clear historical importance in understanding the development of each nation's broadcasting system. In the work and writings of Spry, Morgan, John Dewey, and many others from the era like Charles Siepmann and James Rorty, we have the contours of a sophisticated critique of commercial broadcasting, a critique which in certain respects is every bit as valid today as it was then. It is a political critique which places the fight for public service broadcasting necessarily in the broader context of the fight for a more social democratic, even democratic socialist, society. These activists also recognized, from the very beginning, that theirs was a political struggle with clear global dimensions. The work of this first generation of public broadcasting activists is a continual reminder that control over broadcasting (and communication) must always be the duty of the citizenry in a democratic society; it should never ever be entrusted to the tender mercies of corporate and commercial interests. To the extent that the aims of these activists were thwarted, or have subsequently been thwarted, it was never the result of an informed public debate on broadcasting issues. To the contrary, it was the result of powerful commercial forces getting their way, often by circumventing or undermining the possibility of such a debate.

. . .

Notes

1 For the best treatment of the development of broadcasting in Britain, see Briggs (1961). Two books that chronicle the development of broadcasting in the United States in the 1920s are Rosen (1980) and Smulyan (1994). The classic work is Barnouw (1966).

2 I discuss this period in detail in McChesney (1993).

3 For a discussion on this point, see Coase (1950).

4 By 1928 NBC was working with Canadian General Electric to establish a network of affiliates in Canada (see Sheen to McClelland, 1928).

5 The most comprehensive account of the Canadian Radio League can be found in O'Brien (1964). For Spry's account, see Spry (1971). See also Prang (1965).

6 I discuss this in McChesney (1993), ch. 7.

7 O'Brien (1964), pp. 202–13.

References

A congressional investigation of radio (1932, December 8). *Education by Radio,* p. 105.

Aylesworth, Merlin H., to Sarnoff, David. (1932, April 30). National Broadcasting Company Papers, State Historical Society of Wisconsin, Madison, WI, container 14, file 1.

Barnouw, Erik. (1966). *A tower in Babel: A history of broadcasting in the United States to 1933.* New York: Oxford University Press.

Briggs, Asa. (1961). *The birth of broadcasting: The history of broadcasting in the United Kingdom* (Vol. 1). London: Oxford University Press.

Browne, Donald R. (1985). Radio Normandie and the IBC challenge Io the BBC Monopoly. *Historical Journal of Film, Radio and Television,* 5(1), 3–18.

Canada, House of Commons. (1932). *Special Committee on Radio Broadcasting: Minutes and proceedings of evidence.* Ottawa: F.A. Aclund.

Canada pays a compliment to our BBC system. (1929, October 4). *Public Opinion.*

Carson, Gerald. (1960). *The roguish world of Dr Brinkley.* New York: Holt, Rinehart & Winston.

Chomsky, Noam (1997, October) What makes mainstream media mainstream. *Z Magazine,* pp. 17–23.

Claxton, Brooke, to Murray, Gladstone. (1932, January 26). Brooke Claxton Papers, National Archives of Canada [NAC]. Ottawa, MG 32 B5, vol. 5.

Coase, R.H. (1950). *British broadcasting: A study in monopoly.* London: Longman, Green.

Codel, Martin. (1932a, May 15). Canadian broadcasting to be nationalized. *Broadcasting,* p. 7.

———. (1932b, February 16). *Canadian control of radio upheld.* Clipping located in Martin Codel Papers, State Historical Society of Wisconsin, Madison, WI, vol. 61.

Dill sees US radio in danger. (1932, May 14). *Broadcasters' News Bulletin. Education by Radio,* (1932, October 13), p. 98.

Evans, S. Howard, to Woehlke, Walter V. (1933, January 4). Payne Fund Papers, Western Reserve Historical Society, Cleveland, OH, container 60, file 1168.

Fowler, Gene, & Crawford, Bill. (1987). *Border radio.* Austin, TX: Texas Monthly Press.

Gibbon, John Murray. (1931, March). Radio as a fine art. *Canadian Forum,* 11, 212–14.

Herman, Edward S., & McChesney, Robert W. (1997). *The global media: The new missionaries of corporate capitalism.* London & Washington: Cassell.

Kittredge, Arthur. [1930, October]. *De Forest devises radio ad quietus.* Clipping located in Marlin Codel Papers. State Historical Society of Wisconsin, Madison, WI, vol. 60.

McChesney, Robert W. (1993). *Telecommunications, mass media, and democracy: The battle for the control of US broadcasting, 1928–1935.* New York: Oxford University Press.

Morgan, Joy Elmer, to Plaunt, Alan. (1932, June 9). Joy Elmer Morgan Papers, National Education Association, Washington, DC. 1932 correspondence, FCB 2, drawer 3.

Multinational Monitor. (1996, October). p 13.

O'Brien, John Egli. (1964). *A history of the Canadian Radio League: 1930–1936.* Unpublished doctoral dissertation, University of Southern California, Los Angeles.

Parkes, Christopher. (1997, June 28–9). Murdoch rails against regulators. *Financial Times,* p 2.

Perry, Armstrong, to Spry, Graham. (1931, April 24). Payne Fund Papers. Western Reserve Historical Society, Cleveland, OH, container 58, file 1122.

Prang, Margaret. (1965, March). The origins of public broadcasting in Canada. *The Canadian Historical Review,* 46(1). 1–31.

Propaganda pipelines. (1931, September 24). *Education by Radio,* p. 110.

Provincial control of radio denied. (1931, July 11). *Editor & Publisher,* p. 14.

Raboy, Marc. (1990). *Missed opportunities: The story of Canada's broadcasting policy.* Montreal: McGill–Queen's University Press.

Resler, Ansel Harlan. (1958). The impact of John R. Brinkly on broadcasting in the United States. Unpublished doctoral dissertation, Northwestern University, Evanston, IL.

Rosen, Philip T. (1980). *The modern Stentors: Radio broadcasters and the federal government, 1920–1934.* Westport. CT: Greenwood Press.

Royal Commission on Radio Broadcasting (1929). *Report.* Ottawa: F.A. Aclund.

Sheen, H.L., to McClelland, George F. (1928, March 22). National Broadcasting Company Papers, State Historical Society of Wisconsin, Madison, WI, container 2, file 86.

Smulyan, Susan. (1994). *Selling radio: The commercialization of American broadcasting, 1920–1934.* Washington, DC: Smithsonian Institution Press.

Sparks, Colin. (1995). The future of public broadcasting in Britain. *Critical Studies in Mass Communication,* 12, 328–9.

Spry, Graham. [1931a, March]. *A Canadian radio broadcasting company.* Graham Spry Papers, NAC, Ottawa, MG 30, D297, vol. 97, file 11.

———. (1931b, April). The Canadian broadcasting issue. *Canadian Forum,* 11, 246–9.

———. (1931c). The Canadian radio situation. In Josephine H. MacLatchy (Ed.), *Education on the air:*

Second yearbook of the Institute for Education by Radio (pp. 47–60). Columbus: Ohio State University.

———. (1935) Radio broadcasting and aspects of Canadian–American relations. In W.W. McLaren (Ed). *Proceedings of the Conference on Canadian-American Affairs* (pp. 106–27). Conference held at St Lawrence University, Canton, NY, 17–22 June 1935.

———. (1960–1, Winter). The costs of Canadian broadcasting. *Queen's Quarterly*, 67(4), 503–13.

———. (1961a, Autumn). The Canadian Broadcasting Corporation. 1936–1961. *Canadian Communications*, 2(1), 1–13.

———. (1961b, Summer). The decline and fall of Canadian broadcasting. *Queen's Quarterly*, 68(2). 213–25.

———. (1965, June). The origins of public broadcasting in Canada: A comment. *The Canadian Historical Review*, 46(2), 134–41.

———. (1971). Public policy and private pressures: The Canadian Radio League 1930–36 and countervailing power. In Norman Penlinglon (Ed.), *On Canada: Essays in honour of Frank H. Underhill* (pp. 24–36). Toronto: University of Toronto Press.

———. (1976a, July 27). *Empire broadcast*. Graham Spry papers, NAC, Ottawa, MG 30, D297, vol. 84, file 84-13.

———. (1976b, July 21). *Visit to Washington and Federal Radio Commission 1931* [dictation]. Graham Spry Papers, NAC, Ottawa, MG 30, D297, vol. 84, file 84-13.

———, to Alexander, Gross W. (1931, May 12). Payne Fund Papers, Western Reserve Historical Society, Cleveland, OH, container 59, file 1136.

———, to Ferguson, George. (1931, March 2). Graham Spry Papers, NAC, Ottawa, MG 30, D297, vol. 94, file 11.

———, to Herridge, W.D. (1930, October 15). Graham Spry Papers, NAC, Ottawa, MG 30, D297, vol. 94, file 6.

———, to Mac. (1931, March 2). Graham Spry Papers, NAC, Ottawa, MG 30, D297, vol. 94, file 11.

———, to Morgan, Joy Elmer. (1932a, April 7). Joy Elmer Morgan Papers, National Education Association. Washington, DC, 1932 correspondence, FCB 2, drawer 3.

———, to Morgan, Joy Elmer. (1932b, May 2). Payne Fund Papers, Western Reserve Historical Society, Cleveland, OH, container 42, file 822.

———, to Murray, Gladstone. (1931, May 28). Graham Spry Papers, NAC, Ottawa, MG 30, D297, vol. 95, file 4.

———, to Perry, Armstrong. (1931, May 12). Payne Fund Papers, Western Reserve Historical Society, Cleveland, OH, container 45, file 873.

———, to Roberts, Henry. (1931, February 17). Graham Spry Papers, NAC, Ottawa, MG 30, D297, vol. 94, file 10.

The New Republic. (1933, January 11). p. 227.

Vipond, Mary. (1992). *Listening in: The first decade of Canadian broadcasting, 1922–1932*. Montreal: McGill–Queen's University Press.

Watch Canada. (1932, March 1). *Broadcasting*, p. 16.

Weed, Joseph J. (1938, December 22). Canada's radio system. *Printers' Ink*, pp. 24–6.

Weinraub, Bernard. (1997, October 10). Disney hires Kissinger. *The New York Times*.

Constructing Community and Consumers: Joseph R. Smallwood's *Barrelman* Radio Program

Jeff A. Webb

This essay examines one radio program in the late 1930s which sought to reconstruct listeners into members of an 'imagined community' and into consumers. In July 1937, the journalist and author Joseph R. Smallwood began a *Daily News* column entitled 'From the Masthead' by 'The Barrelman'.[1] In September, Smallwood convinced the privately owned St John's radio station VNOF to begin broadcasting his column, marking the launch of an important cultural phenomenon in pre-Confederation Newfoundland. As Smallwood later described the program:

> It was a peculiar blend of Newfoundland history, geography, and economic information, with stories of courage, endurance, hardship, inventiveness, resourcefulness, physical strength and prowess, skill and courage in seamanship, and a hundred other aspects and distinctions of our Newfoundland story—all of them 'making Newfoundland better known to Newfoundlanders' and intended to inspire them with faith in their country and in themselves, and to destroy what I continually denounced as our inferiority complex.[2]

Although it was a commercial program, it continued to be broadcast on the state-owned Broadcasting Corporation of Newfoundland, which was formed in 1939, and it lasted well after Smallwood left in 1943. The program has received considerable attention. Smallwood's biographers have pointed to the role it played in making him a public figure.[3] It helped launch a political career that included his dominating the broadcasts of the National Convention, leading the Confederate party, and serving as premier of the province between 1949 and 1972. . . .

This essay argues that the program strove to create a nationalist Newfoundland culture that was not non-ideological. While the program validated some cultural elements, clearly Smallwood was selective in his borrowing from that culture. He chose the program's content with a political agenda of fostering a rebirth of the Newfoundland spirit and creating a greater self-reliance among the Newfoundland people. As a commercial program, it had another discourse imbedded in it—that of incorporating people into a North American consumer lifestyle. The program's form was determined by the needs of commercial programming. *The Barrelman* created an audience for commercial programming and both effectively and unobtrusively advertised products. As such, the program worked to incorporate Newfoundland into North American consumer culture at the same time that it fostered nationalism. Because Smallwood's nationalism was decentred from the state, a nationalist popular culture was possible while commercialism undercut the political independence of that nationalism. Smallwood constructed a program that consisted in part of items submitted by listeners and as such assumed the form of a dialogue with Newfoundlanders. This enhanced the polemical potential of Smallwood's message since it had the illusion of coming from the Newfoundland community rather than from Smallwood himself.

Every radio program is produced within a particular social and economic context, and the late 1930s was a difficult time for Newfoundland.

Abridged from 'Constructing Community and Consumers: Joseph R. Smallwood's Barrelman Radio Programme', in *Journal of the Canadian Historical Association* 8 (1998), 165–86. Reprinted by permission.

After struggling towards greater independence and self-government, Newfoundland faced the risk of insolvency during the Depression, an indignity avoided only by suspending responsible government.

The British-appointed Commission Government ensured that the bondholders received their interest, but the poverty and the frustrations of the Depression continued. The lack of any mechanism for people to participate in public life encouraged Newfoundlanders to engage in cultural discourse as a surrogate for political discourse.[4] Two such people were the writer-broadcaster Joseph Smallwood and *The Barrelman's* sponsor, Francis M. O'Leary. More than any other person, Smallwood promoted a nationalistic Newfoundland culture. He was born to lower-middle-class parents in 1900, and as a boy in St John's he developed a love of reading and boundless ambition. He dabbled in many things as a young man, most notably in journalism in Newfoundland, New York, and London, and trade unionism and politics at home. Smallwood engaged in socialist politics in the 1920s, but he had also worked for the Liberal party in Newfoundland and had distanced himself from radical politics in such things as his 1927 radio broadcast 'Why I Oppose Communism'.[5] Smallwood was a liberal who argued for a fairer deal for workers within capitalism, not radical change.[6] He also accepted the idea prevalent in the 1930s that the working class needed to develop greater self-sufficiency. Smallwood was intensely nationalistic, and had several nationalist cultural projects to his credit, which included writing *The New Newfoundland* (1931) and editing the two-volume *Book of Newfoundland* (1937).[7] As with many people of his generation, Smallwood had political ambitions that were blocked by the suspension of democracy. For a man with ambition that outstripped his resources and standing in the community, a career in broadcasting allowed Smallwood the profile and influence that only a life in elected politics could otherwise have given him. While democratic government was suspended, Smallwood used broadcasting to engage in political discourse with the public.

During the second month that the program was on the air, the 'commission agent', F.M. O'Leary, agreed to sponsor the program. O'Leary likely hoped to counter his business competitor Gerald S. Doyle's advertising when he first agreed to sponsor *The Barrelman*.[8] O'Leary and Doyle were both in the business of distributing consumer goods manufactured outside Newfoundland. Rural Newfoundlanders had traditionally earned the necessities of life by bartering the products of their labour to a local merchant with whom they had a social as well as economic relationship. Commission agents circumvented these economic and social bonds by retailing directly to 'consumers'. Both O'Leary and Doyle collected and promoted their own versions of folk culture through print and broadcast while advertising their merchandise. An advertising strategy aimed at simulating a sense of community while promoting the purchase of goods from an 'outsider' may have been effective. There is little doubt, however, that O'Leary's nationalism was genuine. In addition to his sponsorship of many cultural projects, he was a member of several nationalist organizations during the 1940s, such as the Newfoundland National Association, the Newfoundland Patriotic Association, and the Responsible Government League, of which he was the president.[9] While both O'Leary and Smallwood were nationalists, O'Leary was conservative in political and social outlook, yet he agreed with the Barrelman's emphasis on encouraging the working class to be more independent and self-reliant. . . .

As with any commercial radio program, Smallwood's primary task was to construct a listening audience that would consume the advertising content. *The Barrelman* program began each evening, Monday to Saturday at 6:45 p.m., with Smallwood striking a ship's bell six times, followed by the announcement, 'F.M. O'Leary Ltd . . . presenting *The Barrelman* in a program of making Newfoundland better known to

Newfoundlanders.' The 15-minute program consisted of brief entertaining stories interspersed with advertisements. The format was particularly effective as the advertising content fit more unobtrusively between the bits of 'information' or 'entertainment' than in a music or drama program, where the entertainment might have to stop in midstream for the sponsor's message. Advertising is also most effective when it has 'the same qualities as the ostensibly non-advertising content: it must catch and hold audience attention and present its message in an entertaining way; that is, it must tell an effective story of some kind.'[10] The shift back and forth between entertainment and advertising in *The Barrelman* was unobtrusive, with both appearing to be information of interest to the listener. After reading each item, Smallwood struck a ship's bell once and went on to the next item. The listener would not know whether the following text would be another item about Newfoundland or an advertisement. To ease the transition from 'cultural content' to 'advertising content', Smallwood would sometimes introduce the advertisements in the same manner that he introduced his non-advertising copy. On some occasions, one cannot make a sharp distinction between the advertising copy and the text meant to hold listeners' attention between advertisements.[11]

Commercial broadcasters in the 1930s had both to create an audience and to demonstrate to their sponsor that the audience existed. The primary technique used to measure audiences was to encourage listeners to write to the station. Smallwood asked listeners to write to O'Leary to show that the expense of the program was justified, explicitly outlining the symbiotic relationship between himself and his listeners.[12] To gauge his audience's size, he asked listeners to let him know how many radio receivers were in their home towns, and encouraged people to write the station by offering free samples of his sponsor's products. The Barrelman also used the device of giving promotional products to those who sent in a proof of purchase.[13]

Correspondence from listeners not only demonstrated the existence of the audience but also gave Smallwood raw material to be broadcast. He encouraged listeners to write in with stories, providing him with a potentially unlimited source of programming at next to no cost. Listeners responded with bits of oral tradition, accounts of things they had witnessed and people they knew, and occasionally poems of their own composition. Listeners not only submitted material but also began asking the Barrelman questions. After one woman asked the value of an old postage stamp in her possession, Smallwood found himself giving out information on stamps and coins.[14] Since listeners had been submitting questions to him, Smallwood suggested that they ask him questions about Newfoundland. He promised a pound of Lyon's tea to any listener who submitted a question that he was unable to answer.[15] Most questions concerned trivia, but some listeners needed practical information. Smallwood wrote the script of both the questions and the answers, and sometimes gave tea to people whose questions he could have answered with a little research.

Advertising generated the money to pay Smallwood's salary and it also had its own political message. Advertising, Michael Schudson suggests, served the hegemonic function of selling capitalism, and converting workers into consumers.[16] Stuart Ewen concurs in seeing business leaders, whom he calls 'captains of consciousness', serving a hegemonic function through advertising: 'business hoped to create an "individual" who could locate his needs and frustrations in terms of the consumption of goods rather than the quality and content of his life (work).'[17] Despite inequities in wealth, modern capitalism offered everyone with money the opportunity to purchase modern happiness. As Smallwood told the listeners, 'One of the few things in this world in which there is no class distinction, and within reach of the rich and poor alike, is a comfortable shave.'[18] Rich and poor alike, he said, both used Gillette razors.

Such messages helped to sublimate class divisions as they incorporated Newfoundlanders into North American consumer capitalism. Not that Newfoundlanders had been living lives isolated from international capital; they were as much participants in it as other North Americans. But the social relations involved in purchasing international brands rather than local products had to be 'sold' to people habituated to bartering the product of their labour for the necessities of life. Furthermore, in the crisis of the Depression all people had to be constantly reconstructed as consumers if capitalism were to survive.

The advertising material was not the only thing that the program produced. It also provided information and entertainment to keep the attention of the listeners. On occasion, Smallwood took on a role appropriate to a news or public affairs program. A person wrote asking Smallwood to broadcast the details of a missing schooner. 'Will anybody who knows anything about her present position please send word?' Smallwood asked.[19] On another program he relayed a message to a woman in Conception Bay that her husband had arrived safely in St John's.[20] . . .

In his quest to entertain, Smallwood did not mind telling jokes, and he made no claims about their veracity.[21] More common on *The Barrelman* program than jokes were tall tales.[22] Rural Newfoundlanders called tall tales 'cuffers', although Smallwood did not use this word in his program.[23] Cuffers were told among men who knew each other—in the intimate situations in which men gathered to socialize at their places of work. An ethnographic account of the cuffer suggests that for a person to successfully cuffer, he (for it is described as an exclusively male phenomenon) must have a certain level of prestige among his peers.[24] This perspective raises interesting questions about the Barrelman. He was a stranger participating in a familiar activity through the new technology of radio, and when he solicited contributions he was allowing listeners to cuffer along with him in a new kind of social space. Smallwood provided an interesting anecdote that illustrates how the program fit into existing social structures:

> There's at least one other place in Newfoundland where there's only one radio, and where a crowd listens in every night and that['s] Lumsden, on the Strait Shore, Fogo District. The radio is owned by Mr Howell, the merchant of the place. He has the radio in his house, and leading from the house out to the shop . . . he had a wire which connects with an additional loud-speaker in the shop, and every night at quarter to seven, Mr Howell tells me, there are thirty or forty men on hand to hear the broadcast.[25]

This is a clear case of access to a radio being used to reinforce paternalistic social relations between a merchant and fishermen. One will also note how this radio broadcast fit into the traditional pattern of men gathering in a public place to share stories. Howell provided radio reception to the men of the community, but kept them separate from his family. They became dependent on the generosity of the merchant for access to the radio.

A program that included a large number of tall tales posed a potential problem. If he told tall tales, how could he ensure that listeners would believe him when he described the merits of a product? Smallwood tried to keep his credibility intact by insisting that he only reported the facts to the best of his knowledge:

> I can't help it if you refuse to believe the story I'm going to tell now. I'm told, as a matter of fact, that I'm beginning to get a frightful reputation as a liar. It seems that some listeners at least have found it hard to believe some of the stories I've told in these broadcasts. I can only say that on no occasion have I uttered a single word on these broadcasts that I didn't believe to be true. More than that: I've made every honest endeavor to check up on my information, and when even I

was in doubt at all I indicated the fact quite plainly.[26]

Some listeners complained that tall tales spoiled the programming.[27] Few such complaints were received, however, and Smallwood later lowered his stated standards of veracity when dealing with tall tales. He defended the stories and came to his own defence simultaneously:

> Now some people call them lies—why tell lies in these broadcasts they ask. I'm afraid I can't agree with that description of these tall tales—they're not lies. A lie is something that is meant to deceive you . . . if a man tells you something that he knows you won't believe, and he is not trying to deceive you, how can you call it a lie?[28]

Smallwood did not encourage tales that stretched the bounds of credibility. At one point he joked that he had brought in a couple of 'Chicago gangsters' to 'bump off' anyone who sent in a particular tall tale.[29] He maintained that he did not like tall tales, but could not 'escape the conclusion that tall stories are liked by a great many people—there wouldn't be so many coming in if people weren't interest[ed] in them.'[30] Smallwood insisted that while he was responsible for the ultimate selection of material, he had to tell a tall tale from time to time 'to meet popular demand'.[31] He broadcast tall tales, so his condemnation of them cannot be taken all that seriously, but he did not encourage the public perception of his program as fiction.

While Smallwood maintained that his program tried to 'make Newfoundland better known to Newfoundlanders', it served more to sell Newfoundland to Newfoundlanders. Smallwood's selection of material was not an impartial reflection of Newfoundland culture and society: instead, it reinforced his vision of what the ideal Newfoundlander should be. The Amulree Report had argued that Newfoundlanders had become too dependent on the government and were no longer self-suffi-

cient. Smallwood denied this was the case in each of his broadcasts, although one might conclude that he protested too much. One of the main themes of *The Barrelman* was how tough and resilient Newfoundlanders were in the face of harsh conditions. . . . The Barrelman argued that Newfoundlanders were able to endure and thrive despite the harsh environment. Each day he recounted stories of shipwrecks, storms, and sealing disasters, all of which provided ample examples of heroism and strength.

Much of the entertainment of the program seemed to be aimed at men, while the advertising had to be directed at women to be effective. Stories of the sea and hardship were well suited to reinforce characteristics associated with masculinity: courage, strength, endurance, and stoicism. These were all characteristics that would make a man an effective 'breadwinner', and such stories might appeal to a man (who might have been assumed to be 'in charge' of the radio). The potential problem was that women were often in charge of purchasing the consumer goods that were being advertised. After one correspondent in St John's wrote Smallwood to complain that he had been ignoring women, he made a point of telling stories that showed the courage and strength of Newfoundland women.[32] Smallwood hired a female announcer to read some of the advertising copy, perhaps thinking that listeners would be more convinced by the 'Palmolive Girl' extolling the virtues of the various products than his own male voice. His decision to bring in a female announcer may also have been a strategy to retain the credibility of the text of the advertisements while allowing himself free reign to engage in hyperbole when describing the attributes of Newfoundlanders.

. . .

Newfoundland's past passionately interested Smallwood and both oral tradition and written historical anecdotes were cheap and easy to collect. Much of Smallwood's program material came from various Newfoundland publications, such as D.W. Prowse's *A History of Newfoundland* (1895) and from unpublished historical records.[33] This provided a mine of anecdotes from the past which allowed him to set up a contrast between the rough conditions of Newfoundland's past and the relatively progressive society of his day. . . . He reported that one listener had written him arguing that Newfoundlanders were not as good as they had been in the past. Smallwood challenged listeners to send in stories of Newfoundlanders that proved the correspondent wrong:

> No doubt you've often heard me make the claim—that the stock, the breed, that's in the Newfoundland people is too good, too sound, to wear out in one or two generations. . . . This listener disagrees violently with that view. . . . However, to prove which of us is right, my correspondent or I, I'm willing to let the listeners decide.[34]

Many listeners responded to Smallwood's appeal by submitting stories of elderly Newfoundlanders who were still performing prodigious feats of work. In Smallwood's view this proved that

> Things may be in the doldrums—there may not be the same opportunities in Newfoundland that there were forty or fifty years ago—everything in Newfoundland and in the world may be topsy-turvey: but the fact stands out sharply that so far as industriousness and energy, and willingness to work, are concerned, the Newfoundlander is just as good a man as ever he was—and the Newfoundland woman too.[35]

In the tradition of the greatest Newfoundland boomers Smallwood accepted that Newfoundland had 'vast undeveloped resources'.[36] The bulk of the blame for Newfoundland's lack of development, in Smallwood's view, lay with the British authorities who were responsible for 'three whole centuries of misrule, of injustice, of suppression

and oppression' before the granting of self-government. The irony that Newfoundland had lost self-government in 1934 must have been apparent to listeners, many of whom would have recognized that once more Newfoundlanders were subject to the rule or misrule of officials an ocean away. As with many Newfoundland nationalists, Smallwood walked a fine line between criticism of the imperial government and loyalty to Britain. A listener asked Smallwood to say something positive about the British, to which he responded that there was a distinction between the English people and the English government.[37] This expressed well the ambivalence many people in the colonies felt towards Britain. The British officials could not live up to the romantic expectations held by Newfoundlanders raised on stories of the Empire.

In keeping with his view that the qualities of the people were more important than the form of government, Smallwood implied that the British government and the Commission could not solve Newfoundland's problems. He argued that what was needed was a cultural change among Newfoundlanders:

> It's only a case of harnessing that spirit to the undeveloped wealth, and prosperity is bound to be the result. I must resist the temptation to preach in this program, but this much I'll allow myself to say . . . that if Newfoundland is to become a great country, if we're to have a real and enduring prosperity, if this country is to be made fit to live in—it's the people themselves who must do it. It's their country, nobody else's. It's my conviction that the people of Newfoundland don't begin to realize what a precious and what a powerful thing is this spirit of courage and determination and never say 'die'. Once that spirit is fully aroused, we're going to have a wonderful little country. It's a long time coming, yes—but that's because it's not thoroughly aroused.[38]

Smallwood told his fellow Newfoundlanders that the Commission was not going to be the author of prosperity for the island, that the people had to remake their economy and society. To this end Smallwood bolstered nationalism whenever he could. . . .

Despite Smallwood's nationalistic view of Newfoundland, not all the program was unabashed boosterism. Smallwood admitted that among the many letters that came to him were occasional tales of 'sadness and misfortune to remind us that many of our fellow countrymen are finding it anything but easy to make their way in the world'. He rarely related these stories, and when he did he resisted the notion that the unemployed were to blame for the absence of work. Smallwood drew attention to 'the ordinary, everyday courage of our people who, in spite of what a few may say, are just as anxious and just as eager today to earn an honest living, and to toil hard to earn it, as ever the people were in bygone days.'[39] During one broadcast, Smallwood related a man's difficult walk to St John's in search of work, and appealed for someone in the audience to give the man a job.[40]

The political discourse of the program could also be used in a more direct way than fostering self-sufficiency among the public. A couple of listeners tried to engage in public criticism of the Commission government through *The Barrelman* program. Walter Pike of Bristol's Hope, for example, wrote to complain about the low level of the relief payments.[41] A listener in St John's criticized the Commission itself. . . . Such examples show the need for a forum in which to discuss the public affairs of the country, and the position that Smallwood found himself in as a broadcaster. . . . These incidents also underline a difference between broadcasting and newspapers. Smallwood had a lot of experience with the partisan press and was not shy when it came to the rougher aspects of political rhetoric. Hiscock noted that Smallwood was much more explicitly political and critical of the Commission in his Masthead column than in *The Barrelman* program.[42] This was probably the result of two factors. First, despite Smallwood's passion for poli-

tics, O'Leary's need to remain entertaining and the desire not to offend listeners or the government ensured that Smallwood would not publicly criticize the Commission on the government-owned station. More fundamentally, radio, as a medium that brought messages into the home for the whole family, was thought to be a technology that should take care to not offend. The press, on the other hand, had long engaged in unrestrained rhetoric. The press was clearly in the public sphere and did not need to maintain a genteel decorum. Those who objected to partisan fighting would not buy a newspaper allied to a political rival, while radio came into people's homes.

. . .

In 1939, Smallwood found himself working on 'public' radio when the Commission bought the privately owned VNOF and created a state-owned broadcaster, the Broadcasting Corporation of Newfoundland.[43] The BCN continued to allow commercial programming, so O'Leary and Smallwood had no problem with the transition to the new owner. Smallwood praised the Commission's support for Newfoundland culture, and hoped that the new station would bring Newfoundlanders closer together:

> It's going to provide a new medium to enable all the people of Newfoundland to get together, not just once in a while, but every day and every night throughout the year. From now on we're all going to be neighbors—all one big Newfoundland family—with the north bound together with the south, the east knit closely with the west. [. . .]

Smallwood had high hopes that radio broadcasting could overcome the difficulties of communication among a thinly spread population. When the Department of Education started a series of educational broadcasts, Smallwood expressed his belief in the role broadcasting could take in Newfoundland:

[. . .] I admit that perhaps the prime purpose of broadcasting should be that of providing entertainment: but what thoughtful Newfoundlander will fail to see that these two fine broadcast stations should also be used, at least in part, for the spread of information, the dissemination of knowledge, the formulation of a sound public opinion, and anything else that helps to form the type of enlightened, well-balanced character that will enable our Newfoundland people to overcome and vanquish the present difficulties which beset them.[44]

He could have been describing the goals he had for his own program. Smallwood also hoped that the new public broadcasting station would provide a venue for Newfoundland culture, and thus foster nationalism:

I certainly hope that plays, sketches, poems and other forms of literature with the 'stamp of Newfoundland' on them will begin to be written for frequent presentation on this powerful new transmitter that'll soon be covering the whole Island of Newfoundland. In that way more perhaps, can be done for Newfoundland patriotism than any other medium.[45]

. . .

The Barrelman had expanded into a formidable cultural operation. In June 1938, O'Leary launched a free monthly magazine under the same name as the radio show. *The Barrelman* newspaper published a selection of the items that had been broadcast, and a brief summary of local and international news. The magazine extended the Barrelman's influence well beyond the listening audience. By April 1939, the 24-page paper boasted a circulation of 21,000 copies to all 1,328 communities in Newfoundland.[46] At the same time that *The Barrelman* newspaper marked the expansion of the program into homes that did not own radios, Smallwood, in a less-than-astute business move, sold all his rights to the trade name 'Barrelman'

to O'Leary for one dollar. In exchange O'Leary hired Smallwood for one year at $35 per week for the radio show and $50 per month as editor of the newspaper.[47] . . .

Although radio broadcasting is a monologue in which one agent produces a message and many people receive it, *The Barrelman* cultivated the appearance of a democratic medium in which the culture was produced by the community. On one occasion, a listener caught Smallwood in a minor factual error and suggested that Smallwood get his facts right before he 'presumes to educate the people of Newfoundland'.[48] In his defence, Smallwood claimed his program was democratic:

If he thinks that I'm setting myself up to educate the people of Newfoundland, he's making a mistake, because I'm not. It's the other way about— the people of Newfoundland are educating me. Whose program is this, anyway? Is there anybody so badly-informed that he thinks it's my program? Does anybody really think that all the material and information I've been giving every night for nearly three years past came out of my head? Of course it didn't. It came from my listeners, from the people of Newfoundland.[49]

Despite his efforts to create the illusion that the program was a forum for the expression of the Newfoundland people, Smallwood set the terms of discourse, and the program remained committed to his political agenda. In the new public space that *The Barrelman* created, Smallwood promoted his view of an independent and self-reliant people. In a rhetorical device that was likely intended to make his message more persuasive, he presented it as coming from the Newfoundland people, rather than coming from himself.

. . .

As an episode in the creation of nationalism, *The Barrelman* program is revealing. At one level Smallwood fostered nationalism and independence, while encouraging Newfoundlanders to want a North American consumer lifestyle at another level. This desire for material goods may have encouraged some people to vote to join Canada. This argument must be approached with caution, however, in light of the fact that the Avalon Peninsula, the area with the highest level of radio ownership and the most reliable radio reception, voted overwhelmingly against Confederation. The prospect of Smallwood, the quintessential Newfoundland nationalist, leading a movement to make the island a part of another country might seem unlikely. This seems to be a contradiction, however, only if one holds the state to be the centre of the nation. Smallwood's Newfoundland nationalism was not based on 'traditional' political institutions such as responsible government, nor upon symbols, but on his perceptions of the qualities of the people. Newfoundland had the unpleasant distinction of being a nation that had voluntarily relinquished democracy. Since nationalism almost always crystallizes around the state, Smallwood had to construct a popular nationalism without a democratic state.

Notes

1 On the newspaper column and its relationship to the broadcast, see Philip D. Hiscock, 'The *Barrelman* Radio Program, 1937–1943: The Mediation and Use of Folklore in Newfoundland', Ph.D. thesis, Memorial University of Newfoundland, 1994.

2 Joseph R. Smallwood, *I Chose Canada: The Memoirs of the Honourable Joseph R. Smallwood* (Toronto, 1973), 206.

3 Richard Gwyn, *Smallwood: The Unlikely Revolutionary* (Toronto, 1968 and 1972), 53–6; Harold Horwood, *Joey: The Life and Times of Joey Smallwood* (Toronto, 1989), 63–7.

4 For examples of people expressing their patriotism in cultural forms see Hiscock, 'The *Barrelman* Program', 263–7.

5 Centre for Newfoundland Studies [CNS(A)], Coll. 075, 7.02.001, J.R. Smallwood, 'Why I Oppose Communism'.

6 Jim Overton, 'Economic Crisis and the End of Democracy: Politics in Newfoundland During the Great Depression', *Labour/Le Travail* 26 (Fall 1990), 99–100.

7 J.R. Smallwood, *The New Newfoundland* (New York, 1931), and J.R. Smallwood, ed., *The Book of Newfoundland* (St John's, 1937).

8 Peter Narváez, 'Joseph R. Smallwood, "The Barrelman": The Broadcaster as Folklorist', in *Media Sense: The Folklore-Popular Culture Continuum*. Peter Narváez and Martin Laba, eds

(Bowling Green, 1987), 48–50.

9 Jeff A. Webb, 'The Responsible Government League and the Confederation Campaigns of 1948', *Newfoundland Studies* 6, 2 (Fall 1989): 203–20.

10 Dallas W. Smythe, *Dependency Road: Communications, Capitalism, Consciousness, and Canada* (Norwood, 1981), 15.

11 CNS(A), Coll. 028, 1.01.002, October 1937, p. 72.

12 CNS(A), Coll. 028, 1.01.004, 17 January 1938.

13 CNS(A), Coll. 028, 1.01.010, 4 July 1938, p. 702.

14 CNS(A), Coll. 028, 1.01.005, February 1938, p.341; 2.02.003, Kay Lebis to Smallwood, 19 February 1935.

15 CNS(A), Coll. 028, 1.01.009, June 1938, pp. 611–12.

16 Michael Schudson, *Advertising, The Uneasy Persuasion: Its Dubious Impact on American Society* (New York, 1984), 218.

17 Stuart Ewen, *Captains of Consciousness: Advertising and the Social Roots of the Consumer Culture* (New York, 1976), 42–3. See also Jackson Lears, *Fables of Abundance: A Cultural History of Advertising in America* (New York, 1994).

18 CNS(A), Coll. 028, 17 March 1938, 1.01.006.

19 CNS(A), Coll. 028, 1.01.002, November 1937, p. 126.

20 CNS(A), Coll. 028, 1.01.006, March 1938, p. 440.

21 For example see CNS(A), Coll. 028, 1.01.001, October 1937, p. 55. For a discussion of verisimil-

itude in the program, see Hiscock. '*The Barrelman* Radio Program', 194–259.

22 Narváez, 'The Broadcaster as Folklorist', 56.

23 A 'cuffer' is a tale or yarn, a friendly chat, an exchange of reminiscences or a gathering for this purpose. See G.M. Story, W.J. Kirwin, and J.D.A. Widdowson, *Dictionary of Newfoundland English* (Toronto, 1982), 128.

24 James Faris, *Cat Harbour: A Newfoundland Fishing Settlement* (St John's, 1972): 141–51.

25 CNS(A), Coll. 028, 1.01.008, 28 May 1938, p. 589.

26 CNS(A), Coll. 028, 1.01 .(X)2, November 1937, p. 87.

27 For examples see CNS(A), Coll. 028, 2.02.003, Samuel Brace to Smallwood, 7 February 1938 and 2.02.005, Ethel Wheeler to Smallwood, 16 March 1937.

28 CNS(A), Coll. 028, 1.01.005, February 1938, p. 297.

29 CNS(A), Coll. 028, 1.01.006, March 1938, pp. 402–3.

30 Ibid.

31 CNS(A), Coll. 028. 1.01.005, February 1938, p. 297.

32 CNS(A), Coll. 028, 1.01.002, November 1937, p. 105

33 D.W. Prowse, *A History of Newfoundland* (London, 1895).

34 CNS(A), Coll. 028, 1.01.005, 8 February 1938, p. 315.

35 Ibid., p. 320.

36 CNS(A), Coll. 028, 1.01.018, 11 April 1939.

37 Ibid., 20 April 1939.

38 CNS(A), Coll. 028, 1.01.005, February 1939, pp. 320–1.

39 CNS(A), Coll. 028, 1.01.011, 8 September 1938, pp. 825–6.

40 CNS(A), Coll. 028, 1.01.006, March 1938, pp. 440–1.

41 CNS(A), Coll. 028, 2.02,008, Walter Pike to Smallwood, 23 June 1938.

42 Hiscock, '*The Barrelman* Radio Program', 60.

43 Jeff A. Webb, 'The Origins of Public Broadcasting: The Commission of Government and the Creation of the Broadcasting Corporation of Newfoundland', *Acadiensis* 24, 2 (Autumn 1994): 88–106.

44 CNS(A), Coll. 028, 1.01.024, 2 November 1939.

45 CNS(A), Coll. 028, 1.01.017, 2 March 1939.

46 CNS(A), Coll. 028, 1.01.009, 28 June 1938, pp. 682–3.

47 CNS(A), Leo Moakler Collection, box 6, file 10, Contracts between F.M O'Leary Ltd and J.R. Smallwood, 29 June 1938 and 30 June 1938.

48 CNS(A), Coll. 028, 1.01.025, 20 December 1939.

49 Ibid.

Public-Service Broadcasting as a Modern Project: A Case Study of Early Public-Affairs Television in Canada

David Hogarth

Introduction

In the early 1950s, Canadian broadcasters developed a set of strategies to engage the public in a way British and American television had not. Canadian television would stake out what one broadcaster at the time called a 'middle ground' between UK (information) and US (entertainment) TV, featuring public-affairs programs that Canadians would actually choose to watch in a more or less competitive North American broadcast market (Moore, 1952). It is these middle-ground information-entertainment public-affairs programs that I want to examine in this paper, along with the perpetual struggles over representation that surrounded them in the 1950s. It is my contention that these shows and the controversies they generated should make us rethink conventional theories concerning public-service broadcasting as a quintessential disciplinary machine dedicated to the containment of meaning and pleasure within orderly boundaries. In this paper, I thus question the idea of a 'modern era', at least as it applies to the world of Canadian public-affairs broadcasting.

My argument rests in large part on a distinction between public-service theory and practice. I offer a study in counterpoint, beginning with a detailed look at public-affairs television as it was conceived by Canadian policy makers and educators in the early 1950s, followed by a review of production and critical discourses surrounding the programs in the early years of Canadian television. In my conclusion, I consider what this study might tell us about the nature of periodization in contemporary television research.

Public-Affairs Television in Theory: The Modern Project

Canadian policymakers tended to view television as a pedagogic service with public-affairs programming as its cornerstone. Canada's Massey Commission, for instance—which presided over the introduction of Canadian television service in 1952—argued that television should inform Canadians about various aspects of their lives while helping to instill in them a certain 'discriminatory sense'. Specifically, the Massey Commissioners hoped information programming would encourage Canadians to concern themselves with real as opposed to synthetic situations, and pay attention to the particularities of place as opposed to the homogeneous world of fantasy. Information television would thus serve as a countervailing force against the twin dangers of propaganda and mass culture, serving as a sort of grounded citizenship-training course in the early Cold War era. As the genre most explicitly concerned with the nitty-gritty of Canadian public life, public-affairs broadcasting was regarded as a cornerstone of liberal-humanist culture (Canada, *Report of the Royal Commission on national development in the arts, letters and sciences*, 1951, pp. 37–8, 50–1).

Policymakers and educators also had definite ideas about how public-affairs programs should be produced and watched. The *Massey Report* called for the maintenance of proper boundaries between information and entertainment programs and was particularly critical of broadcasters who lacked specialized knowledge and cultivated 'certain base forms of popular appeal' (*Report*, p. 297). The emergence in radio of sub-

From *Canadian Journal of Communication* 26 (2001), 351–65. Reprinted by permission.

jective modes of address and opportunities for audience involvement was also frowned upon. Overall, the Commission urged the 'maintenance of good taste' in public-affairs television (p. 304).

In a similar spirit, policymakers and educators recommended the regulation of images and stories in public-affairs programming. Images in public-affairs television, according to the *Massey Report*, should be employed with restraint and purpose: programs should 'teach not by pictorial or dramatic effect but by coherent and logical presentation of fact' (p. 311). Narrative structures should adhere to a rigorous cumulative expository structure, along the lines of the National Film Board's documentary films. Canada's information-television aesthetic should thus be governed by well-established (mostly literary and cinematic) principles of representation in public-service broadcasting.

Finally, the Commission and many of its academic interveners recommended close supervision of the way the programs were watched. Policymakers and educators argued that viewing information-television programs at home should ideally be rather like watching documentaries at the cinema or local community centre, the audiovisual information venues of the previous decade. Home viewers were to be focused, engaged, and, as much as possible, collectively involved with the new public-affairs TV shows. They should give programs their undivided attention and then discuss them with their families or neighbours (Johnson, 1952).

Educators hoped children might watch information programs after school and be tested on them the next day (*CBC Times*, 1954a), though even here, according to the CBC's assistant director of children's TV broadcasts, the new younger public-affairs audience should be discouraged from 'long periods [of viewing] . . . they should not lie on the floor . . . [and] there will be a need for constant vigilance by the men and women with taste and judgment' (Rainsberry, 1957). For both children and adults, programs should be scheduled at precise but varying times, this pre- sumably to discourage casual viewing habits associated with American audiences. Canadian viewers, it was hoped, would come to appreciate the rigour of the new schedule, just as the idealized comprehensive listeners of radio shows such as the CBC's *Wednesday Night* had learned to appreciate eclectic information-drama-music fare, effortlessly making the switch from genre to genre, often for hours on end—and much better for it, according to critic Mavis Gallant (1949).

By these accounts, Canadian television would have to dedicate itself to the production of difficult programs for disciplined audiences. In the post-war era, policymakers and educators tended to regard television as a functional apparatus with which representations of Canada could be systematically produced and consensually understood within more or less orderly networks of signification. From this vantage point, Canadian television would be a modern project: one whose meanings and pleasures would be regulated in accordance with well-established hierarchies of knowledge and representation, for the good of the Canadian public.

Public-Affairs Television in Practice: 'Middle Ground' Programming at the CBC

But what about Canadian television in practice? Did Canadian television, in the defining program genre of its public-service age, even loosely adhere to the pedagogic protocols set forth in early policy documents? There are reasons to be skeptical. Modes of production, textual organization, distribution, and reception differed in fundamental respects from the plans laid out in the *Massey Report*. As we shall see, public-affairs television is a fairly weak model of paternalist public broadcasting and modern representation.

The New Public-Affairs Audience
First, and perhaps most basically, Canadian public-service television seemed fundamentally incapable of regulating its audience. Research at the CBC in the late 1940s and early 1950s, for

instance, suggested that dispersed home viewers would be hard to organize into disciplined community circles. According to one 1953 report, broadcasters would have to address themselves to 'one person at a time' and 'learn to compete with bridge, poker and gossip and many other factors not encountered in stage or screen' (Jackson, 1953). Television's modes of reception were seen to be largely uncontrollable compared with previous modes of mass communication.

CBC documents of the time further indicate a widespread sense that getting Canadians to watch Canadian television at all, let alone in the 'correct' ways mandated by educators and policy makers, would be a challenge in the early days of Canadian television. Canadian TV would, after all, need not only to attract new viewers but to win over many more from its American competition, especially in major metropolitan markets such as Montreal and Toronto, which were already receiving US television over the border. As *Food for Thought*'s Alan Sangster lamented just three months after the service went on the air: 'What [Canadian audiences] now demand and all they will accept from TV is straightforward entertainment. As a result of years of exposure to American commercial TV, their viewing habits may already be set' (Sangster, 1953b). Even children would have to be won over to the public-affairs program because, as the producers of *Junior Magazine* noted in 1953, 'Whereas the young viewer may have to pay attention to lessons in school, in the living room he [sic] has only to change channels' (*CBC Times*, 1953b).

In short, CBC research indicated that Canadian television viewers were hardly the pedagogically available citizens forecast in policy documents and educational briefs. Public-affairs producers had ceased to regard viewers as an ideal public-service audience—as comprehensive viewers, for instance, ready and able to take up serious or popular positions in turn as required by the text; or as a segmented body, the lower orders of which might eventually be led on to better things. Public-affairs viewers instead

quickly came to be seen as a sort of brute common denominator, the needs and desires of which should be more or less accepted—that is, accommodated, or at least addressed by, the programs themselves. All in all, new spaces of watching were seen to render Canadian television's pleasures quite unamenable to pedagogic control.

The New Public-Affairs Text

Second, and related, Canadian public-affairs programs seemed incapable of maintaining established public-service hierarchies of knowledge and representation in the texts themselves. True, documentary programs, particularly those supplied by the National Film Board, could be doggedly instructional and 'wordy', as one producer himself put it in an internal memo (Hallman, 1955, p. 2). But, overall, programs produced by the Corporation were determinedly televisual and quite at odds with the textual models laid out in pedagogical charters.

The most important model for documentary programming, and the one most at odds with educational-disciplinary theory, was the television magazine. The documentary form as such took shape in the earliest production workshops of Canadian television, most notably in April 1952, when American producer Gilbert Seldes was invited to Toronto to give a 10-day course on factual programs based on his experiences in American commercial television. Documentaries, Seldes had noted in his book *Writing for Television*, were cheaper than fiction and variety shows with their 'orchestras, ballets and multiple sets', and might even become profitable if their material was 'tractable enough to be worked into popular television' (1952, p. 183). Seldes went on to suggest a number of concrete steps by which the new Canadian genre could become as popular as an 'entertainment rag'. First and foremost, programs should be organized as magazines, made up of distinct but complementary segments that would be constantly 'billboarded' during the show. Public-affairs stories could borrow some tricks from variety programs and quiz shows. 'Under the "Big D for Documentary"', noted Seldes, 'are other d's—for demonstration, dramatization and discussion' (p. 190). A lighter touch for lineups was also advised. 'You will discover after a few months in the business', Seldes warned his students, 'that documentary seems to deal exclusively with unpleasant subjects such as Communism, crimes, syphilis and the like' (p. 192). Genuinely 'middle ground' programming should instead draw upon all the stories and storytelling tools at producers' disposal.

While the CBC's supervisor of public affairs Eugene Hallman noted that documentaries would always be more than a 'commercial enterprise' on Canadian television, he agreed with Seldes that the television magazine could adequately meet 'cultural objectives' of public-service broadcasters. Magazines in fact served a number of purposes for the Corporation. Hallman pointed out that the shows would allow the Corporation to deal with a large number of topics in a short amount of time, 'preventing capture of the airwaves by any one special interest'. Their general-interest format promised to attract a 'wide range of viewers', boosting the popular legitimacy of the Corporation as it struggled to make a case for public broadcasting. And if nothing else, magazines were a 'television original' that would prevent the 'documentary from fall[ing] into [the NFB's] hands by default' (1955, p. 2).

There were thus sound (and sometimes selfish) institutional reasons for adopting the magazine show as the cornerstone of public-affairs television in Canada. But whatever their public-service origins and aims, the programs did have the effect of radically undermining established traditions of knowledge and representation at the CBC, and it is these cultural effects to which I now turn. First, distinctions between pulp and the pedagogy were almost impossible to maintain in magazine programming, given the way the shows were produced and scheduled. In 1953, for instance, the CBC's first English news magazine, *Tabloid*, received stories from six different information and entertainment departments, concerning farm topics, sports, public affairs, and highbrow cultural matters (*CBC Times*, 1953b). *Tabloid* was expressly designed to be eclectic and popular, and in its later stages was developed in consultation with the CBC's new Audience Research Department—partly at the insistence of CBC affiliates, which complained existing network public-affairs programs lacked commercial potential. The program was then given a good deal of showbiz publicity in newspapers and trade magazines and inserted into the CBC's prime-time schedule, between the nightly newscast and the nightly entertainment lineup. It's clear that *Tabloid* was produced, promoted, and scheduled in ways increasingly indistinct from entertainment television.

The (uncertain) mix of information and entertainment was even more evident in the lineups of the shows themselves. CBC *Newsmagazine*, for instance, covered 'everything from bums to beauties, crime to politics' in its first year on the air. 'You meet so many interesting people,' reported Rassky (1953). The current-affairs show *Close-Up* featured stories on beatniks, unwed mothers, mixed marriages, communism, and homosexuality in its first two seasons. Other programs mixed styles to get the message across. *Scope*, for instance, used 'drama, dance, documentary and even rock and roll' to explore social and cultural issues (*CBC Times*, 1954d).

Clearly the traditional precedence accorded to information over entertainment and traditional distinctions between fact and fiction were not always maintained in early program planning and production. Many critics accused the service of 'rank sensationalism', noting that 'taste and good judgment' had fallen by the wayside in the quest for ratings and shock value (Lepkin, 1956b). As one bemused observer put it in 1956, the CBC seemed 'determined to cover everything in every way' (Poulton, 1956), leaving established public-service hierarchies of knowledge and representation in question if not in ruins.

The New Public-Affairs Personality

Public-affairs programs further upset the boundaries and hierarchies of public-service representation by allowing increasingly subjective modes of address and opportunities for audience involvement. To be sure, personalized journalism evolved more slowly than surely at the CBC. As late as 1939, for instance, public-affairs announcers in radio were recruited exclusively from 'positions of authority' (including only 'educated men possessed of clear Canadian voices with a masculine quality' [Seldes, 1952, p. 190]). Hosts were also limited to recording in the studio (partly by technological constraints, partly by union restrictions) and prohibited from identifying themselves by name. The same traditions carried on into television in its very earliest days, with *Newsmagazine* starting out in 1952 as 'little more than a TV counterpart of a newsreel or film . . . impersonal and briefly factual', as one producer later put it (*CBC Times*, 1957). Public-affairs broadcasting thus seemed to effectively preclude all opportunities for subjective address and audience identification in its programs.

But producers also drew on a different public-affairs tradition, personified by the more subjective reports of Matthew Halton and his wartime radio colleagues. In these reports, Halton and others spoke not just as institutional representatives, but as personal witnesses to the events they were covering, in a way mere news announcers could not. In the earliest days of television, public-affairs producers recognized the importance of a documentary subject of this sort giving something of a 'personal stamp to the program [and] becoming a personality with whom the audience can identify' (Hallman, 1955, p. 3). Personalized journalism was hard to resist given the hectic production schedules and threadbare economies of the new information medium, which allowed for brief encounters between reporters and events but often not much more. But it was also endorsed by the increasingly market-conscious public-service culture at the time. The success of personality-driven shows in the United States was well known and often envied in Canada, and audiences north of the border were deemed to be 'ready for adult companionship and interesting people with stimulating and provocative ideas and information' (Gillis, 1958). By the mid-1950s, then, television had effectively re-located the voice of public affairs in the person of the personality-host.

Personalized journalism was, certainly, more than just a market strategy at the CBC. Program authorities pointed out that on-air personalities served a pedagogical purpose by helping to guide viewers through the chaotic new world of television public affairs. Public-affairs personalities were seen to help shows make sense. Hosts and commentators, the *CBC Times* pointed out, gave the programs a 'distinctiveness and a unity which the printed magazine achieves through a distinctive writing style' (1957). Some hosts were authoritative, *Close-Up*'s Frank Willis appearing to one journalist as the 'great mover . . . who summons the people, who brings them before our eyes and who makes them important . . . all with a colossal assurance' (Brehl, 1957). Others were more personable, but they still worked to make a fantastic world of 'scattered times and places' cohere in a meaningful way, as one 1954 critic put it with respect to *Tabloid*'s Dick Macdougal (Garner, 1954). In a sense, then, personalized journalism was a pedagogic device, required by the exigencies of television.

But hosts were also seen to allow for more affective and unpredictable types of audience involvement, clearly at odds with the civic detachment recommended in early policy reports. Even as they were promoted as instructors, program personalities were encouraged to speak directly to viewers to encourage affective rather than purely cognitive modes of identification. *Tabloid* featured wisecracking reporters and claimed its viewers took up the 'cudgel for individual members of the cast . . . [sending] letters saying I like you but I don't like the others' (Brehl, 1957). *Junior Magazine* was even more aggressive in its 1955 season, requiring its hosts to sing a verse of 'Getting to Know You' at the beginning of each show (Lepkin, 1956b). In short, viewers were encouraged to regard reporters as something more than teachers and public affairs as something more than information in the early days of documentary television.

Affective involvement was also carefully cultivated by repositioning reporters as a visible presence in the studio and in the field. Producer Ross Maclean adopted a general policy of dispatching reporters on location to develop in each reporter 'that TV standby, the familiar friend' (*CBC Times*, 1955b). Reporter Percy Saltzman, one of the new breed, reminded one reviewer of a 'small boy trying to get into every picture of the *Tabloid* show' (Garner, 1954). More and more, announcers and journalists emerged as the full-fledged personality-subjects of public-affairs discourse, the 'happy chums, sincere helpers, and affable fellows of television', as Gilbert Seldes had put it (1952, p. 190). Producers thus worked to make stories not just meaningful, but dramatic, with protagonists attached. . . .

Finally, producers worked to encourage audience identification by producing more intimate and involving forms of documentary imagery. Overall, it was felt, the pictures of public-affairs television should make viewers feel they were not just *learning about* a story, but *experiencing it* through the eyes of the reporter. A *Newsmagazine* feature on art schools, for instance, had camera operators dangling out of windows, lying at dirt level, and pushing cameras around on toy wagons to give the impression of 'going in there with Harry [Rassky]' (*CBC Times*, 1955b). By methods such as these, viewers were encouraged to enter the psychic process of identification by delegating their look to reporters and hosts of the day.

All of this was conceived with something more than an educational intent, and was clearly at odds with the Corporation's rather austere instructional mandate. Harry Rassky summed up the new direction of public-affairs television with a story about a viewer catching up with him on the street and giving him a hug for having captured the (then-notorious) Boyd Gang of Toronto. 'Somehow the fact that I was the one who brought the story vividly into her living room was confused with the actual arrest,' he explained (1953). Apocryphal or not, such stories indicate the degree to which producers expected, and sometimes encouraged, emotionally involved (and sometimes cognitively confused) pleasures of public affairs. Information television was clearly designed to attract fans, not just citizens.

Documentary Images and Documentary Stories
Documentary television veered even further away from modern disciplinary theory in the ways it used sounds, images, and story structures to get its message across. Of course, formal experimentation, like personalization, was tentative at the CBC, and public-affairs programs could be highly conventional stylistically. Qualified personnel were in short supply, which obviously curtailed the development of a public-affairs television aesthetic. Moreover, experimentation, such as it was, had to be conducted within the confines of a rigid organizational structure. All camera and sound work, for instance, was supplied by a centralized and aesthetically rigid CBC film unit and engineering department. Innovators were also kept in line by ratings pressures. The experimental arts and documentary series *Scope*, for instance, was dropped by four affiliates and carried by others only under protest in the 1955 season (CBC National Program Office minutes, 1955, p. 3).

Producers themselves frequently viewed public-affairs shows as no-nonsense instructional devices with little room for stylistic play. Most had gotten their start in radio and struggled to imagine programs visually, let alone experimentally. Rules concerning how sounds and images were to be used and stories told were certainly restrictive by today's standards. In technical journals such as *Radio*, for instance, film editors were advised that dissolves, fades, and rapid transitions would lend acceptable vitality to the shows, while jump-cuts were to be avoided because they might make the interview subject's head spin around, causing the viewer to become disoriented (Wright, 1954a). Close-ups and broad, simple designs were recommended because of the limited resolution of TV screens, so as to not unduly tax the eyes of the viewer (Wright, 1954b). Graphics should be 'pleasing to the eye', remarked *Tabloid*'s Jack Kruper in 1953, 'but they must never obtrude themselves on the observer . . . They must never detract or compete with the story.'

With respect to sound, producers were advised to seek out appropriate ambient noises in lieu of the more remote non-synch narrations of Canadian documentary films. Excessive multi-track recording was discouraged due to receiver limitations, as were sounds that could not be immediately identified and clearly matched with the stripped-down images on the screen (Normandin, 1956). Music, for its part, should help guide the viewer through the narrative structure of the show, serving as a bridge between story items, between stories and commercials, between opening and closing segments and the body of the show, and between the constantly juxtaposed live studio and (usually) recorded location sites of television actuality (*CBC Times*, 1955a). Constant collaboration was recommended to ensure that these various levels of signification worked together to produce coherent meanings in public-affairs television.

By some accounts, images, sounds, and graphics worked just this way. Critic Marion Lepkin, for instance, praised the documentary program *Explorations* for 'really using the medium . . . [with] cartoons, lectures and film clips and dramatic skits and graphs . . . in short everything but the kitchen sink, but all of a piece, with not a rag or a tatter anywhere' (1956a). At the same time, critics and producers themselves

worried that this new razzmatazz world of multiplying signifiers and diegetic fields might not always make sense. Some degree of confusion was to be expected according to Gilbert Seldes: the best that producers could hope for was a sort of low-key engagement, a fine line between audience stimulation and techno-fatigue or even schizoid dissociation (1952, p. 189). Many critics called for more semiotic and narrative regulation at the CBC. Miriam Waddington of *Canadian Forum* complained in 1956 that images and sounds were straying from a linear, educational path, with 'words pulling one way and pictures another' (1956). The CBC's own technical officer had complained two years earlier that editing in the programs was often 'deplorable . . . inject[ing] synthetic action into shows by a series of unmotivated cuts' (Wright, 1954a). Similarly, the Corporation's National Program Office noted that graphics 'often competed with stories' and that scripts were often devoid of any logic other than building a bridge between program items and commercials (CBC National Program Office Minutes, 1953, pp. 7–8).

Many observers in fact believed that public-affairs television was in a state of crisis in its earliest years. It was not just that television was now teaching by dramatic and pictorial effect. Or that stories were veering away from traditional expository structures. Or even that established literary principles of representation had been superseded by an unruly televisual aesthetic. For many, public-affairs television simply no longer represented Canada in a meaningful and informative way. The new programs 'might be sensational', noted one critic, but they 'hardly helped viewers make sense of their world' (Lepkin, 1956a).

An Example: Women's Television Magazines
Inane language, sensational editing, excessive graphic embellishment, the unleashing of audiovisual signs in an attempt to please or excite the viewer—all represented for many critics Canadian public-affairs television's dangerous slide into generic disorder in the early 1950s.

Canadians had witnessed their public broadcaster's 'final embrace of US commercial values', as one 1953 critic put it (Sangster, 1953a). Women's TV magazines represented, for many, the worst of these excesses.

The shows themselves were introduced to Canadian television in 1954 partly because of complaints from critics about soap operas, partly because of demands from advertisers for consumer-oriented programs. As daytime magazines such as NBC's *Today Show* took off in the United States, CBC programmers came to believe that the Canadian housewife would soon learn to 'plan her day around her set and the information it provided' (Gillis, 1958).

Critics of all stripes agreed that women's shows brought entirely new subjects and styles to Canadian information television. Programs such as *Living* introduced informal film features on fashion, gardening, and home decoration, as well as social and political affairs. *Place aux dames* and *Pour Elle*, on the French network, mixed women's reports with songs and variety sketches. On the English network, *Open House* and later *Take 30* covered everything from cooking to sexuality to international affairs in a personable and direct way. More than other programs, the daytime shows mixed filmed reports with live pictures, and toward the end of the decade used lighter and more mobile video cameras to give their programs a more intimate and immediate feel. Female producers such as *Graphic*'s Jo Kerwin also introduced more subjective approaches to public affairs, offering 'thought-sync' programs in which audiovisual tracks conveyed not just information about the outside world but the inner feelings of program subjects.

For some observers, the programs were a welcome addition to the documentary form. Ohio University, for instance, somewhat patronizingly awarded its 'special interest' award to *Open House*, citing the show's 'mood-evoking use of intimate camera and restrained commentary' (*CBC Times*, 1961). Such praise was not

unknown, but in Canada the shows were the subject of much derision in the quality press. Critics complained of their frenetic pace: 'Eight minutes of this, 10 minutes of that . . . Is women's attention really so short?' asked one reviewer in 1953 (Sangster, 1953a). Others noted the shows' flagrant commercialism and their self-promotional inserts to keep viewers glued to the set (Sangster, 1953a). Still others condemned the programs' 'unrestrained imagery' and their 'melodramatic' story structures (Korwin, 1956).

Critics worried that the new programs degraded Canada's patriarchal public space and the various competencies it demanded of its citizens. 'By the time these programs are finished,' commented one 1953 reviewer, 'everyone with a TV set is reduced to a mass of quivering sentimental jelly' (Singer, 1953). New rules of representation thus seemed to call into question the most basic (mostly gendered) distinctions on which public-service broadcasting had been founded in Canada: distinctions between pedagogy and pleasure; between culture and commerce; and, of course, between public and private affairs.

. . .

Conclusion

So what does all this tell us about public-service broadcasting as a modern project in Canada? One might argue, 'Not much.' One might dismiss the middle-ground experiment as mere neo-paternalism, for instance: as plain old public-service broadcasting with a showbiz veneer, born out of a desperation to keep American commercial television at bay. And one might argue, as have many researchers, that pleasure always remained instrumental to Canadian television's pedagogic framework (see, for example, Collins, 1990). Indeed, one might conclude that despite its allowance for new modes of address and new opportunities for audience identification, Canadian television remained firmly dedicated to the task of using sounds and images to make sense of all aspects of Canadian life for all Canadians in more or less predictable ways. In fact, such a view probably fairly sums up the hopes of the original architects of Canada's public-service television service.

But clearly the middle-ground experiment was never so neat and easily contained as that. The Canadian service, for instance, never managed to systematically contain meanings and pleasures within fixed liberal–patriarchal boundaries. Nor did it manage to consistently and effectively police television's semiotic systems, to harness its images, sounds, and graphics to the logic of the written word. Nor, finally, did it seem able to maintain a strictly modernist set of distinctions between pedagogy and pleasure, between the sensational and the sublime, between ostensibly public and private modes of representation. In short, Canadian television, in its defining genre, and even in its golden age, fell well short of its high modernist ideals.

Of course, public-service broadcasting in Canada may have been exceptional in this regard. 'Middle ground' television may have been a natural site for the 'queering' of semiotic protocols and the epistemological and moral boundaries of modernist television. My point, however, is simply that the monolithic periodization that has come to dominate European and American media histories, based on a clear-cut, relatively contained 'modern era' of television, does not really apply in the Canadian case. Here—and perhaps elsewhere?—the relationship between television and modernity was never so straightforward.

References

Ang, Ien. (1991). *Desperately seeking the audience.* London & New York: Routledge.

———. (1996). *Living room wars.* London: Routledge.

Baudrillard, Jean. (1986). *The ecstasy of communication.* Montreal: Semio(Texte).

Blumer, J. (1992). *Television and the public interest.* London: Sage.

Brehl, B. (1957, June 22). McLean gets plum job. *Toronto Daily Star.*

Canada. Royal Commission on National Development in the Arts, Letters and Sciences. (1951). *Report of the Royal Commission on national development in the arts, letters and sciences, 1949–51.* Ottawa: E. Cloutier, Printer to the King.

CBC National Program Office Minutes. (1953, November 17–18). CBC National Archives Papers RG 41/Volume 893/Series A-V-2/PG81-1/Pt. 1; Public Affairs Program Reports.

———. (1955, March 2–4). CBC National Archives Papers RG 41/Volume 895/Series A-V-2/PG8-3/Pt. 1; Public Affairs Program Reports.

CBC Times. (1953a, February 26–March 3), p. 7.

———. (1953b, September 9–15), p. 3.

———. (1954a, March 14–20), p. 13.

———. (1954b, October 14–20), p. 4.

———. (1954c, October 17–23), p. 4.

———. (1954d, December 19–25), p. 3.

———. (1955a, March 11–17), p. 1.

———. (1955b, August 23–9), p. 5.

———. (1957, July 21–7), p. 5.

———. (1958, August 29–September 5), p. 6.

———. (1961, May 13–19), p. 31.

———. (1965, September 18–24), p. 10.

Collins, Richard. (1990). *Culture, communications and national identity.* Toronto: University of Toronto Press.

———. (1998). *From satellite to single market.* London: Routledge.

Gallant, Mavis. (1949, October 8). Culture on the air. *The Standard*, p. 16.

Garner, H. (1954, January 19). Ad lib, news and tabloid. *Saturday Night*, p. 13.

Gillis, Hugh. (1958, April). Talks and public affairs. *Radio*, p. 9.

Hallman, Eugene. (1955, December 6). *Life magazine on the air.* CBC internal memo by Supervising Producer, Talks and Public Affairs. CBC National Archives Papers RG 41/Series A-V-2/Volume

895/PG8-3/Pt. 1: Public Affairs Program Reports.

Jackson, Felix. (1953, December 6–12). Television and its rivals in the living room. *CBC Times*, p. 11.

Johnson, Edward. (1952, July–August). Television for Canada. *Radio*, p. 12.

Kerwin, Jo. (1956, August 24). CBC internal memo. CBC National Archives Papers RG 41/Volume 895/Series A-V-2/PG1-1/Pt. 1; Programming— General Correspondence.

Kruper, J. (1953, August 16–22). *CBC Times*, p. 5.

Lepkin, Marion. (1956a, August 4). Speaking of television. *Winnipeg Free Press*.

———. (1956b, August 11). Speaking of television. *Winnipeg Free Press*.

———. (1956c, August 16). Speaking of television. *Winnipeg Free Press*.

Litt, Paul. (1992). *The muses, the masses and the Massey Commission*. Toronto: University of Toronto Press.

Low, Harold. (1956, June 17). CBC at large. *Ottawa Journal*.

Merter, Jonathan. (1955, October 8). Close-up on Canada. *Winnipeg Free Press*.

Moore, Mavor. (1952, May 24). What we'll do with TV. *Saturday Night*, pp. 4–6.

Morse, Margaret. (1986). The television news personality and credibility. In Tania Modleski (Ed.), *Studies in entertainment* (pp. 55–79). Bloomington: Indiana University Press.

Normandin, Pierre. (1956, December). Le bruitage. *Radio*, p. 10.

Poulton, R. (1956, September 8). Tabloids razzmatazz. *Toronto Telegram*.

Rainsberry, Fred. (1957, March 17–23). Is television bad for children? *CBC Times*, p. 3.

Rassky, Harry. (1953, August 22–9). *CBC Times*, p. 5.

Sangster, Allan. (1953a, January). *Canadian Forum*, p. 231.

———. (1953b, February). On the air. *Canadian Forum*, p. 254.

Seldes, Gilbert. (1952). *Writing for television*. New York: Doubleday.

Singer, Steven. (1953, November 21). Women's work is never done. *Saturday Night*, p. 10.

Spigel, L. (1996). High culture in low places. In C. Nelson & D. Goankar (Eds), *Disciplinarity and dissent in cultural studies* (pp. 313–46). New York: Routledge.

Waddington, Miriam. (1956, July). Radio and TV. *Canadian Forum*, p. 234.

Wright, Harold. (1954a, January). For better cutting in television. *Radio*, pp. 16–17.

———. (1954b, March). Technical aspects of TV production. *Radio*, p. 16.

'And Now a Word from Our Sponsor'

Paul Rutherford

. . .

The official response of the advertising industry to the arrival of Canadian television in 1952 might best be summed up as cautious. On 5 July 1952, the *Financial Post* carried a lengthy story about the conclusions of *Television as an Advertising Medium for Canadian Advertisers*, a report authored by a joint working committee of the Association of Canadian Advertisers and the Canadian Association of Advertising Agencies. The big warning: television 'is not a magic device which works well for all who use it'. Some manufacturers might be better advised to avoid television altogether. Even those who could benefit from the new exposure ought not to take their ad money away from proved media. The fundamental problem was cost. The CBC intended at this time to charge sponsors $1,600 for a one-hour show in Toronto and $500 in Montreal, a price that included not just station time but a minimal production crew as well. One of the ways the industry estimated costs was on the basis of cost-per-thousand households, or cpm (later rate-per-thousand individuals). Judged this way, the 'guestimate' was that Toronto's TV cpm amounted to $27, falling perhaps to $13 a year later, whereas the radio cpm at that moment was a mere $0.50! Being a pioneer on TV did indeed seem to be a risky and expensive business. This report might be cited as a further proof of the conservative and cautious side of the Canadian character; but, in fact, it was an example of the natural tendency of an established industry to avoid upsetting a profitable status quo.

The official response wasn't the final word, though. There were already some Canadian industries that had experimented with advertising on American stations: John Labatt apparently paid $3,864.40 to WXYZ-TV Detroit for ads during a three-week period in December 1951. . . . By October 1952, one month after Toronto went on the air, there were quite a lot of big-name companies who'd taken the plunge and bought time on CBLT-TV: Canadian Westinghouse, Ford of Canada, Campbell's Soup, and B.A. Oil, all were sponsors; Bulova Watch, Consumers Gas, Imperial Tobacco, and Salada Tea were spot advertisers. The most aggressive agency was MacLaren, which soon boasted television accounts for Imperial Oil (*NHL Hockey*), Canadian General Electric (*Showtime*), Buick (*Milton Berle*), General Motors (*General Motors Theatre*), Chevrolet (*Dinah Shore*), and Pontiac (*Dave Garroway*) plus flash and spot advertising for Bulova Watch and Buckingham cigarettes.[1]

These advertisers, many of them branches of American companies, were simply jumping on a bandwagon. The mystique of television had already taken hold of advertisers and agencies down south. Tales were making the rounds of companies that had leapt into television early and reaped huge benefits, such as Hazel Bishop lipsticks whose sales shot from $50,000 a year in 1950 to $4.5 million in 1952.[2]

The fact is that more and more advertisers believed the television commercial was a surrogate for the actual salesman. Back in March 1949, after surveying what was happening in the United States, an enthusiastic Joseph Compton told Canadian businessmen what was 'inevitable': television 'will become a show window

Adapted from Chapter 9 of *When Television was Young: Primetime Canada 1952–1967*, by Paul Rutherford (Toronto: University of Toronto Press, 1990), 309–35. Reprinted by permission of the publisher.

for a variety of goods and services' because it offered advertisers the extraordinary advantage of displaying their wares in customers' homes. 'Eventually it may prove to have no equal in the merchandising field.' By the middle of the 1950s, Oliver Tryeze, president of the TV Bureau of Advertising in New York, was telling Canadians that TV could replicate 'the personalized approach', bringing back 'face-to-face selling aimed at the young housewife' who was so important to mass sales. A bit later A.M. Lawrence, ad manager for Nestlé Canada, which had just completed a successful television campaign, argued that TV was 'the closest possible thing to personal sell', especially for the instant products his company marketed.[3]

By this time, of course, advertising on television had taken off, following in the wake of the rapid expansion of TV services and of the boom in sales of TV sets across the country (see Figure

1). Television's share of advertising revenue may not appear to be all that impressive, though. Yes, television soon surpassed magazines, and by the early 1960s eased in front of radio as well. But this explosive rate of growth didn't continue during the next decade. In 1961 TV secured 9.6 per cent of all advertising revenues, radio 8.8 per cent, and daily newspapers 30.8 per cent; 10 years later, TV's total was only 12.2 per cent, radio's 11.1 per cent, and the dailies' 29.0 per cent, although all had experienced substantial dollar increases since advertising expenditures in general had multiplied by 75 per cent. Television in Canada did not match the record in the United States where, even in 1961, TV's share was 14.3 per cent of advertising revenues. Canadian television was especially weak as a medium of local advertising, which includes classifieds, retail and supermarket ads, real estate promotions, and the like, the most lucrative

Figure 1 Media and Advertising Revenues

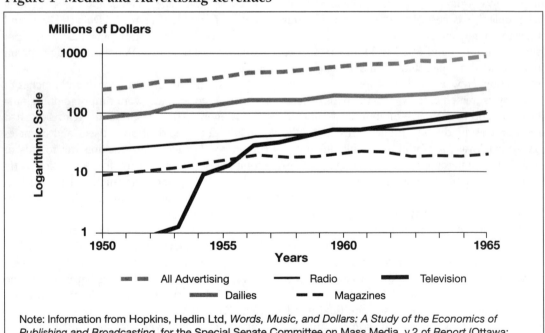

Note: Information from Hopkins, Hedlin Ltd, *Words, Music, and Dollars: A Study of the Economics of Publishing and Broadcasting*, for the Special Senate Committee on Mass Media, v.2 of *Report* (Ottawa: Queen's Printer 1970) 121, 192, and 191, plus O.J. Firestone, *Broadcast Advertising in Canada: Past and Future Growth* (Ottawa: University of Ottawa Press 1966).

source of funds for newspapers and increasingly radio as well. By far the biggest chunk of television revenue, on average four-fifths each year by the mid-1960s, was generated by national ads.[4]

Two important constraints, time and money, had shaped television's career as an advertising medium. Print media could simply expand their size to incorporate an increased volume of ads. Television couldn't. The actual amount of ad time allowed in an hour or half-hour of programming was regulated by government agencies, initially the CBC's board of governors and later the Board of Broadcast Governors. In 1964, for example, the BBG reduced the maximum number of ad minutes from 16 to 12 per hour (and 16 commercial units); the regulation was slightly more restrictive for non-Canadian sponsored shows where ad time was limited to 4 minutes and 15 seconds in a half-hour program. The CBC was even stricter with itself. Its network news and public-affairs shows simply were not available to advertisers. Its 1968 rules allowed only 4 minutes of commercial time on other types of programming in each half-hour period, although that was supplemented by some further time during network breaks. The one way of accommodating more advertising was to reduce the actual length of the commercial. Right from the beginning, advertisers had been offered 10- and 20-second 'flashes', 30- or 60-second spots, and a few 2-minute periods to showcase a variety of products. During the 1960s there was an increasing tendency to move away from the 60-second standard to 30-second commercials: on Thursday evening, 24 February 1966, for instance, CFTM-Montreal (the independent francophone station) aired eighty-three ads, thirty-eight running 60 seconds, twenty-six 30 seconds, and the final nineteen for periods ranging from 10 to 120 seconds. Even so, there was generally more demand for primetime spots on popular programs, notably American imports, than the networks could fill, a situation that naturally raised the value of this scarce resource.[5]

Advertisers were forever grumbling about costs, especially when they compared their plight with what was common below the border. The initial investment came in the making of the commercial itself. The early days of live and, therefore, reasonably cheap commercials soon gave way to much more costly filmed and videotaped commercials. Sut Jhally has argued convincingly that these commercials should be seen as 'capital goods': they aren't meant to be consumed but rather to manufacture sales; they are made for repeated showings over a short period of time, unlike the programs themselves; and they are tax-deductible, much like machinery purchased for factories. That explains why so much time and money was devoted to ensuring their quality—traditionally more care and expense has always been lavished on capital than on consumer goods. In 1966 Janice Tyrwhitt estimated that a top-flight commercial could involve 100 people, take 20 hours to complete, and cost more than $50,000. An average figure, according to Keats, Peat, and Marwick, was around $20,000. The overall cost of the commercial minutes could easily be much higher than the cost of the program that carried the advertisers' messages.[6]

At first, roughly in the mid- and late-1950s, most commercial dollars (85 per cent, according to one estimate) were spent in New York. It was a lot cheaper for a multinational to import an existing, tested commercial that had proved its worth in the United States. Even if a new commercial had to be made, New York seemed a logical choice: the facilities and personnel there were the best in the world, an important consideration if the advertiser wished to employ animation or sophisticated camera techniques. Besides, the temptation to go down and enjoy the pleasures of New York's night-life was considered a marvellous perk for the ad managers of Canadian companies, or so comments in *Marketing* suggest. A 1968 survey by the Institute of Canadian Advertising found that roughly a quarter of the commercial messages aired on anglophone television were imports.[7]

By contrast, 61 per cent of the commercials were produced in Canada, and another 10 per cent modified in Canada, a slightly more impressive level than was true for the actual programs. The private film industry had made a determined bid to win more and more of the business away from New York, even persuading Ottawa to slap a special duty on imported productions. In 1962 Dean Walker estimated that the cost of buying a $10,000 American-made commercial for Canadian use was, what with taxes and the exchange rate, around $16,855. Much was also made of the advantages of using Canadian talent, which, presumably, had a better grasp of the national character. Some messages had to be tailored to the Canadian market, which might require a certain amount of adaptation (translation into French, a new soundtrack, an additional cut). Restrictions on commercial language were much tighter in Canada than in the United States: such expressions as 'bad breath', 'rich and creamy', '99 per cent fat-free', and 'natural' were on the list of no-no's generated by government agencies and the CBC. But I suspect that advertisers cut loose from New York more because local filmmakers had improved their facilities, especially in the area of videotape production where costs were once estimated at 50 per cent to 100 per cent higher in New York than in Toronto. The centre of production became Toronto: three-quarters of the 2,822 Canadian-made or -modified commercials in 1970 were produced in Ontario, and fully 740 of these were in French (either original or adapted).[8]

But the costs of making a commercial were modest compared to the expense of buying time. In 1956 an advertisers' brief to the Fowler Commission claimed that the cost-per-thousand homes in the United States ran from $2.50 to $3.00, whereas in English Canada the cpm ranged from $5.00 to $8.50 and in French Canada from $7.00 to $15.00. One C.O. Hurly of Chrysler Canada decided that advertisers had 'spoiled' broadcasting in their zeal to reach the home, thus creating a kind of 'monster'. While

the cpm soon improved because television coverage increased so rapidly, the dollar value of time also grew. In 1959, according to a report in *Marketing*, Ford Canada alone signed an agreement for $2.5 million with the CBC to sponsor what became *Startime*, two French-language shows, local news and sports, a co-sponsored Hollywood western, and *The Tennessee Ernie Ford Show*. Between 1964 and 1969, for example, the cost of a 60-second, primetime spot on CFTO rose from $335 to $500, on CBLT from $325 to $450, on CFCF from $300 to $475, and on the booming CFTM from $340 to a whopping $700. Rates, admittedly, were much lower in smaller markets, such as Winnipeg, where a CBWT spot went for $230 in 1968, or Vancouver, where CHAN charged $265. There at least local advertisers could afford to buy air time on a regular basis. Elsewhere the big advertisers dominated primetime.[9]

It was the increasing cost of air time that weaned advertisers from the notion of exclusive sponsorship. The assumption had been that a sponsor benefited directly from the association with a quality or a popular program. For years General Motors sponsored CBC teleplays because of the supposed prestige attached to this genre of programming. O'Keefe sponsored *En haute de la pente douce*, a téléroman about upper-middle-class life in Quebec City, because it hoped 'to upgrade the social image of its beer'. But the extra payment seemed less and less worthwhile, especially when advertisers discovered their messages might reach a broader audience, at a cheaper cost, through a careful selection of spot advertisements on a number of different programs. This 'magazine' concept of advertising attracted television managers because it freed their programming from direct sponsor involvement and enabled them actually to produce more value from commercial time by selling to a wider range of clients. The CBC did stay with the technique of sponsorship, although most of its so-called sponsored shows had two or more advertisers. CTV didn't allow for any sponsorship, selling only spots, or what it called 'participation', to advertisers. The most famous of the commercial broadcasts, *NHL Hockey*, managed by MacLaren, which produced the package and bought time on Radio-Canada, the CBC English network, and CTV, was actually supported by Imperial Oil, Ford of Canada, and Molson's Brewery. The definition of the terms 'sponsorship' and 'participation' was, under these circumstances, blurred by the reality of a number of different commercial messages.[10]

That had already begun to cause some upset among advertisers and agencies. Late in 1963 *Marketing* carried a number of comments on the new peril of ad clutter on primetime TV, or 'overloading the burro' in the colourful phrase of writer Jeff Holmes. The fear was that the stacking up of multiple spots and sometimes network or station promotions could only irritate the viewer and undo the impact of any one message. But given the fact that primetime was a finite 'resource', there wasn't too much that advertisers could do but whine about the problem—and try to exact lower rates.[11]

Even the biggest advertisers often supplemented their television time with space-buying in the print media and time purchases on radio. An enthusiastic believer in the 'visual appeal of television', ad manager J. Edgar of Texaco nonetheless admitted that his firm bought radio time 'to obtain greater reach and frequency' and to back up the television campaign. When Jerry Goodis's agency mounted its television campaign to push Shirriff Instant Potatoes in 1963, which was 'an extended parody on the over-popular television taste-test', it employed 'straight-face newspaper ads' to announce the tests and later the 'awful truth'—that the instant potatoes tasted good, but not 'like the real thing'. A survey of the habits of heavy spenders in 1971 found that while the drugs and cosmetics industry devoted 73 per cent of its $49.1 million budget to television commercials, food and food products only expended 44.1 per cent (of $60.3 million), the automotive sector 37.9 per cent (of $42.9 million), and financial and insurance services 34.4

per cent (of $19.4 million). It just didn't seem wise to most advertisers to put all their eggs in one basket, especially when they had to pay so much for the privilege.[12]

Nonetheless, the power of television to work miracles in a highly competitive marketplace appeared so great—to introduce new products, to create a brand image, to incite a buying enthusiasm, to counter rival claims—that most of the major companies in the business of selling consumer goods put more and more of their dollars into video. 'The return from investment in television advertising, although not quantifiable, is believed to be the highest for many products,' intoned the Hopkins, Hedlin report to the Davey Committee on the mass media. The suggestion that some noble agency lead the crusade against ad clutter by pulling its clients off a station was greeted with the comment that its rivals would be right 'there five minutes later buying up the time—whether we'd agreed on a boycott or not.' Could companies afford not to invest? (Some did, of course: during the mid-1960s Goodis, Goldberg, Soren kept Westinghouse out of television for roughly four years, apart from a few special commercials, because its $650,000 budget seemed too slight 'to make a notable splash on TV'.) Before long television in Canada had jumped ahead of all the other media as the chief vehicle of national advertising. In 1963, for example, TV received $55.1 million from national advertisers, radio $24.9 million, and dailies $51.1 million. The gap increased in later years until, by 1972, almost half of all dollars spent by national advertisers in the three media went to television. The result was that a larger and larger percentage of the business done by advertising agencies was made up of television accounts (see Figure 2, p. 212). The age-old hegemony of the daily newspaper as the grand spokesman of commerce had finally given way. The dominance of television in the field of national advertising signified that it had now become the most important instrument of the 'ideology' of advertising in Canada.[13]

Figure 2 Advertising Agencies: Distribution of Billings by Media

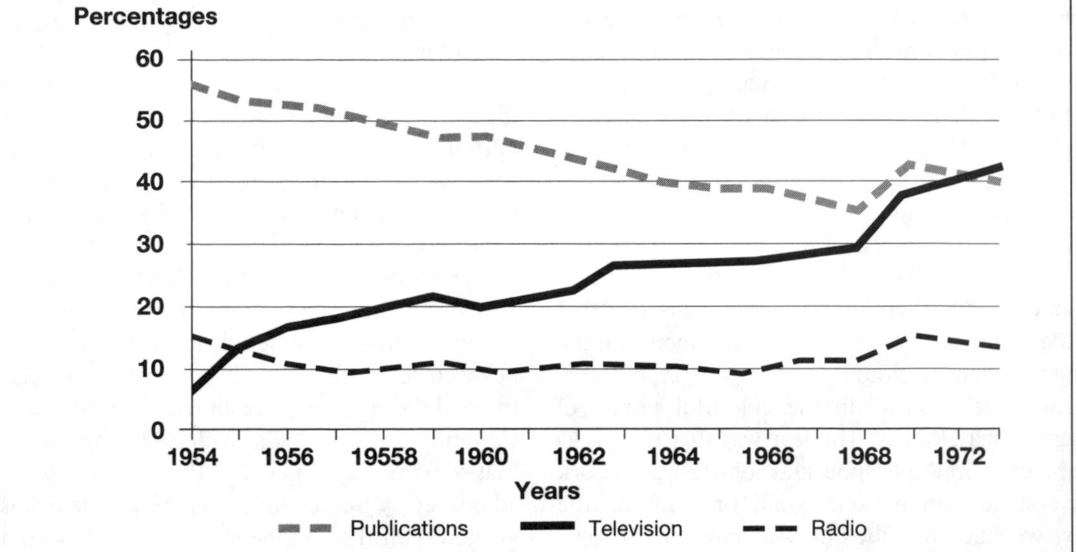

Percentages

Note: The Nature of the statistics altered slightly after 1968, following which the chart tracks changes every two years. Data Taken from *The Canada Year Book*.

Notes

1 *Financial Post*, 5 July 1952, 3; and 11 October 1952, 2; MacLaren advertisement in 'Canadian Retail Sales Index, 1953–1954', published by *Canadian Broadcaster*.

2 Erik Barnouw, *The Sponsor: Notes on a Modern Potentate* (New York: OUP 1978), 46.

3 Compton, 'The Advertiser Looks at Video', *Canadian Business*, March 1949, 50; Tryeze quoted in *Marketing*, 27 January 1956, 4; Lawrence quoted in *Marketing*, 1 November 1957, 4.

4 Statistics on the media shares, 1961 and 1971, from Kates, Peat, Marwick & Co., *Foreign Ownership and the Advertising Industry* [hereafter KPM & Co.], for Ontario, Legislative Assembly, Select Committee on Economic and Cultural Nationalism, June 1973, 50; O.J. Firestone, *Broadcast Advertising in Canada: Past and Future Growth* (Ottawa: University of Ottawa Press 1966), 32 and 153; Hopkins, Hedlin Limited, *Report*, vol. 2: *Words, Music, and Dollars: A Study of the*

Economics of Publishing and Broadcasting [hereafter Hopkins, Hedlin], for the Special Senate Committee on Mass Media (Ottawa: Queen's Printer 1970), 277.

5 Firestone, *Broadcast Advertising in Canada*, 68–70; Grant, 'The Regulation of Program Content in Canadian Television', *Canadian Public Administration*, 11 (1968), 345–6: Canadian shows were allowed an extra minute; Hopkins, Hedlin, 277; CFTM ad breakdown from Elliott Research, *National and Local Advertisers using CFTM-TV-Montreal, 19 February–4 March 1966*.

6 Jhally, *The Codes of Advertising: Fetishism and the Political Economy of Meaning in the Consumer Society* (New York: Routledge 1988), 111; Tyrwhitt, 'What Do You Mean You Don't Like Television Commercials,' 21; and KPM & Co., 128.

7 Franklin Russell, 'How TV Commercials Conversion Saves Money for Cdn Advertisers', *Marketing*, 31 March 1961, 18; on the advantages

of going down to New York, see, for example, Franklin Russell, 'Why Buy Our TV Commercials in the US?' *Marketing*, 17 March 1961, 44; ICA survey noted in KPM & Co., 118.

8 Walker, 'In Sight', *Marketing*, 3 August 1962, 11; regarding prohibitions see KPM & Co., 124; on videotape, see Walker, 'In Sight,' *Marketing*, 26 July 1963, 20. See also Walker's 'When 60 Seconds Can Cost $15,000.00', *Industrial Canada*, February 1962, 19–24.

9 Firestone, *Broadcast Advertising in Canada*, 117, n. 86; Hurly quoted in *Marketing*, 28 June 1957, 8; *Marketing*, 18 September 1959, 2; Hopkins, Hedlin, 280: the equivalent rate for radio station CFRB in Toronto was $150 (275).

10 The O'Keefe story in *Marketing*, 23 October 1959, 6; on MacLaren and hockey, see Hopkins, Hedlin, 148.

11 See the issue of 29 November, 1963, 20–1 and 34–5.

12 Edgar's views noted in *Marketing*, 30 November 1962, 64; Goodis, *Have I Ever Lied to You Before?* 99 and 101; KPM & Co., 48.

13 Hopkins, Hedlin, 121; *Marketing*, 29 November 1963, 35; Goodis, *Have I Ever Lied to You Before?* 68: when Foster took over the account, it brought Westinghouse back to TV; statistics on national advertising from Hopkins, Hedlin, 127, and calculated from data in KPM & Co., 47.

Rock the Nation: MuchMusic, Cultural Policy, and the Development of English-Canadian Music Video Programming, 1979–1984

Ira Wagman

MuchMusic, English Canada's national music video service, made its debut on 1 September 1984, with six hours of original programming. Most of the videos offered on the first day consisted of heavy-rotation singles from Van Halen, the Cars, Elvis Costello, and Frankie Goes to Hollywood. However, the station also featured works by Canadian artists, including the world premiere of the Spoons' 'Tell No Lies' (Fraser, 1984, p. E7). Originally available exclusively to pay-television subscribers, the station has become part of many basic cable packages in English Canada and has expanded, adding an additional English-language music service (MuchMoreMusic); two French-language services (MusiquePlus and MusiMax); and international operations in Argentina (MuchaMusica), Finland (Jyrki), and the United States (MuchMusic USA). MuchMusic has also achieved a position of considerable influence as a promotional 'gatekeeper' (Hirsch, 1972), facilitating or frustrating the exposure of new musicians and contributing to 'the embedding of music within complex layers of discourse *about* music, surrounding it with performer gossip, concert news and other information' (Straw, 1996, p. 109). It has even incorporated a public-service philosophy into some of its program content, seen through its coverage of federal elections. Together, these elements make MuchMusic arguably one of Canada's most successful media properties both domestically and abroad. . . .

MuchMusic's strategic location, at the intersection of various communications media and industries, makes it a rich object of study. In his discussion of the Canadian film industry, Ted Magder argued that 'the history of cultural policy

with respect to the cultural industries—and in particular its feature film policy—must be understood within the context of imperialism, but also within the context of domestic social relations and political conflicts' (1993, p. 18). I believe this perspective can be extended to an analysis of MuchMusic. Like radio, MuchMusic draws upon the productive output of another player within the cultural sector, the sound-recording industry. Firms within Canada's music- and video-production sector, (the branch plants of multinational media conglomerates, industry lobby groups, cultural bureaucrats, and the federal broadcast regulator) have all interacted in ways that have shaped the operations and successes (or failures) of the music video channel.

Beginning with the station's slogan, 'The Nation's Music Station', we can pose a number of questions: When and why was it decided that Canada needed a national music video service? Who decided this was necessary? How did MuchMusic earn the right to fulfill this need? The answers to these questions can be found by examining the interrelationships between the Canadian sound-recording industry and Canadian cultural policy between 1979 and 1984. An analysis of this time period will reveal important clues not only as to major shifts in Canadian cultural policy, but also with regard to the curious position of the English-Canadian sound-recording industry within Canada's media ecosystem.

With the 1982 release of the *Report of the Federal Cultural Policy Review Committee*, co-chaired by Louis Applebaum and Jacques Hébert, government policy toward the cultural realm began to emphasize the marketing and

From *Canadian Journal of Communication* 26 (2001), 503–18. Reprinted by permission.

distribution of Canadian cultural products both domestically and in the international marketplace. Included within that discussion was the sound-recording industry, a sector that had been largely ignored within cultural policy discourse. To provide justification for additional support of the sound-recording industry, the authors of the Applebaum-Hébert report utilized a combination of imagery and rhetoric that closely aligned the sound-recording industry with other cultural industry sectors that had garnered government support.

The inclusion of sound recording within the context of a larger governmental emphasis on the marketing and distribution of cultural products was welcome news to an industry suffering through a period of decreased sales and fractured relationships with radio, its key promotional channel. With the tremendous success of American broadcaster MTV in promoting new musical talent, the English-Canadian sound-recording industry saw a music video channel as a lifeline, one not dissimilar to the Canadian content regulations enacted in 1970. The prospects, then, for a national music video service represented the solution both for Canadian cultural policymakers and for the Canadian sound-recording industry. The successful applicant for the music video service would not only have to satisfy these demands, but would also have to demonstrate solid financial footing for a broadcast regulator still reeling from the disastrous results stemming from Canada's first experience with pay television. It is within this context that the application for MuchMusic put forward by Toronto-based broadcaster CHUM Limited emerged as the most viable candidate for the national music video service.

Sound Recording, Canadian Cultural Policy, and the Music Video

On 4 May 1983, the CRTC called for applications for new specialty television licences that would be available to subscribers on a discre-tionary basis. The request for proposals marked the second phase of pay television and came three months after the initial round of pay-television licences went on the air. Within a year, the broadcast lives of the C Channel, TVEC (available in Quebec), and Super Channel were cut short, leaving only First Choice to survive due to a last-minute bailout by the CRTC (Raboy, 1990, p. 276). The reasons for the failure of these pay-television services are many, but the combination of unimaginative program content (mainly Hollywood feature films on First Choice and Super Channel) and a lack of subscriber demand are often cited as important factors.

To avoid repeating the embarrassing situation from the first experience with pay television, the CRTC's call for specialty program services stressed that prospective entrants to the broadcasting landscape would not jeopardize the operations of existing broadcasters. In its 'definition and nature of specialty programming services', the CRTC outlined its interest in narrowcast television programming 'designed to reflect the particular interests and needs of different age, language, cultural, geographic, or other groups' (CRTC, 1983, p. 4444). These services might comprise such theme programming as news, sports, health and medical awareness, multicultural, and children's content. However, receiving special mention in the CRTC's discussion was a music video program format 'which could include productions of recording artists in concert, video adaptations of studio recording sessions or experimental music video recordings' (CRTC, 1983, p. 4445).

The decision to accept applications for the specialty television license, including a national music video service, needs to be understood in the context of a number of developments occurring at the time within the broadcasting and sound-recording industries at the level of Canadian cultural policy. The 1982 report of the Federal Cultural Policy Review Committee, co-chaired by Louis Applebaum and Jacques

Hébert, would provide the rationale for future policy initiatives, particularly those directed at the Canadian sound-recording industry and, not coincidentally, at the development of the national music video service.

Mike Gasher maintains the Applebaum-Hébert report represented a significant shift in the philosophy used for state intervention in the cultural realm and in the role played by the private sector within Canadian cultural production. He explains that '[i]n a radical departure from its predecessors, Applebaum-Hébert insisted cultural production was an end in itself, rather than a tool of nationalism,' and that the role of government within the cultural realm was to 'remove obstacles and enlarge opportunities, without seeking to direct' (1997, p. 24; see also Federal Cultural Policy Review Committee, 1982, p. 75). Gasher explains that rather than aping the anti-commercial and anti-American tone of the earlier Aird, Massey-Lévesque, and Fowler Commission reports, Applebaum-Hébert lamented the dominance of American cultural products in the Canadian marketplace not because of any pernicious American influence, but because Canadian cultural works were correspondingly under-represented. The authors of the report seemed more interested in reclaiming Canada's place in the international marketplace than in trying to rewrite the rules of media capitalism (1997, p. 25). . . .

Another significant element of the Applebaum-Hébert report was its expression of concern over the effectiveness of Canadian content regulations, the CRTC's primary mode of implementing policy initiatives. While recognizing the importance of Canadian-produced programs, the report claimed that the CRTC's actual power to enforce content restrictions was mitigated by the threats to the economic viability of broadcasters (Raboy, 1990, p. 283). As a result, the commissioners suggested, '[S]ome other solution must be found to ensure that cultural values and goals are not completely expunged from private broadcasting' (Federal Cultural

Policy Review Committee, 1982, p. 287). When the new policy strategy was issued by the Department of Communications in 1983, many of its initiatives were adaptations of proposals made by Applebaum-Hébert, with a central emphasis on increasing the private sector's capacity to produce high-quality programs that could be marketed on an international scale (Raboy, 1996, p. 187).

Concerns about the effectiveness of Canadian content regulations were also an important element of the report's analysis of the state of the Canadian sound-recording industry. As was the case with Canadian television, Applebaum-Hébert acknowledged that Canadian content regulations for radio broadcasters, the key promotional channel for recorded music, were not sufficient in providing Canadian listeners with a diversity of locally produced musical talent. This caused the report's authors to explain that 'if quality Canadian recordings are to be available in sufficient quantity and variety for AM and FM stations to play, and Canadians to enjoy, federal policy must also concern itself with production, distribution, and, marketing issues' (Federal Cultural Policy Review Committee, 1982, p. 239).

The fact that the sound-recording industry received attention in the pages of the Applebaum-Hébert report represents an important development. In his 1983 study of Canada's cultural industries, Paul Audley pointed to the government's relative lack of attention to the sound-recording industry by explaining 'from an economic perspective, the industry is relatively small and categorized as part of the 'miscellaneous' manufacturing industry group, while as a cultural activity its significance has been largely overlooked by government' (1983, p. 141). The Applebaum-Hébert report had earlier presaged these sentiments, stating that current support programs consisted of a small fund established by the CBC to assist the recording of some musical genres, a Canada Council program supporting the production of more 'serious music', a grant to the Canadian Independent Record Producers Association (CIRPA) to devise a catalogue for retail outlets, and support for conventions from the Department of Industry, Trade, and Commerce. Not surprisingly, the committee concluded, '[A]s helpful as those measures are, they constitute only the bare beginnings of a federal policy for Canadian sound recording' (Federal Cultural Policy Review Committee, 1982, p. 236). The report recommended federal assistance to Canadian-owned record companies to strengthen distribution and contribute to marketing costs—all to bring Canadian artists to the public in a manner more effective than Canadian content regulations.

Before giving its recommendations, the committee needed to provide the justification for increased support to the Canadian sound-recording industry. One of the subtle tactics used by the authors of the Applebaum-Hébert report was to re-establish the importance of sound recording, and in particular popular music, within Canadian cultural policy discourse. The chapter on sound recording begins by aligning the underserved sector with one already recognized as worthy of policy support, and by then implying its equivalent value, stating that '[s]ound recording, like broadcasting, with which it is closely involved, has become a pervasive feature on the social and cultural landscape' (Federal Cultural Policy Review Committee, 1982, p. 236). Later on the authors assert that sound recording is 'one of the seminal cultural influences of our times . . . yet paradoxically, the sound-recording industry has not usually been included among other cultural industries when major support policies were being considered by the federal government' (Federal Cultural Policy Review Committee, 1982, p. 236). With its cultural importance, and its conspicuous absence within policy established, the authors of the Applebaum-Hébert report could now set about bolstering the image of the Canadian musical experience:

What we hear on record can depend on personal taste or merely on circumstance. The content may consist of any number of types and styles of music; it may even consist of the spoken word. Sound recordings can appeal to mass audiences, young or old, or be interesting to only small segments of the population. But whatever their content, they share the convenience of being relatively inexpensive, and highly portable, and therefore accessible to many; a sound recording is a movable concert hall, stage or classroom, available for enjoying in the place and at the time of the listener's choosing, able to leap time and space to bring the individual into intimate touch with the artist. (Federal Cultural Policy Review Committee, 1982, p. 235)

A few elements of this passage warrant brief discussion. First, we can see the attempt at distancing music's 'popular' (and, within the context of traditional nationalist policy discourse, American) connotations with the language of access and consumer choice, echoing the sentiments of the commissioners. What follows is the transposition of a more refined 'cultural' perspective onto the musical experience itself, through the analogy of the sound recording as concert hall, stage, or classroom. . . .

The effect here is important. If the sound-recording industry had been ignored within cultural policy, the members of the Federal Cultural Policy Review Committee needed to provide the rationale for government support. Reformulating the experience of Canadian music at the level of policy in a way that incorporated a 'character building, space-binding, and artful' musical experience represented an attempt at accomplishing this goal.

This change in position was welcome news to Canada's sound-recording industry, which, like that in the United States, had been going through an uncharacteristic period of decline. Since the advent of rock music in the 1950s, the American sound-recording industry had enjoyed unbroken success for more than 25 years. Over this period, sales grew consistently at a rate of 20 per cent per year, finally peaking in 1977 and 1978 (Banks, 1996, p. 31). Historical sales data on the Canadian sound-recording industry has been more difficult to ascertain. Statistics Canada's 1977 survey of the recording industry represents the first comprehensive work in this sector. However, using data concerning the volume and value of record imports and exports and the value of Canadian manufacturing activity, Paul Audley was able to show a trend in record and tape sales beginning in 1970. This trend corroborates growth trends occurring in the United States (Audley, 1983, p. 143). The back cover of the 20 May 1978 issue of *Billboard* magazine announced that Fleetwood Mac's album *Rumours* had become the first to sell a million copies in Canada. However, sales figures for both the American and Canadian sound-recording industries experienced periods of sharp decline, recovery, and decline between 1981 and 1983.

One important reason for this difficult period was the changing relationship between record companies and radio stations across North America. Some have suggested that conservatism within the radio industry during the 1970s created its own constraints on innovation and diversity (see Lopes, 1992, pp. 67–9). A 1980 *Billboard* article entitled 'In Canada: Programming Hurting New Product Sales' suggested that, as was the case with American radio, Canadian radio station playlists became markedly conservative as program directors chose to exploit established performers over the untested newer artists promoted by record companies (20 December, p. 43).

An already popular mode of exposing audiences to new acts in the United Kingdom, the music video emerged on the North American scene as the possible antidote to the conservatism of radio and the diminishing promotional influence of the medium felt at the time.[1] Music videos were appearing on some American and Canadian television programs and becoming popular fare at local discotheques and videotheques. Meanwhile a new station, MTV, had begun broadcasting on 21 August 1981. By 1984 its audience had grown to 22 million, with advertising revenue reaching US $1 million per week (Kaplan, 1987, pp. 1–3). In addition, it appeared that music video was beginning to represent an important promotional tool leading to increased music sales.

A Nielsen study of the day found that 63 per cent of survey respondents reported purchasing an album after viewing a video clip featuring the artist's music (Banks, 1996, p. 36). MTV's ability to deliver national exposure of new acts was dramatically different than the uneven reach of FM radio, even if radio appealed to a larger aggregate audience (Straw, 1993, p. 8). This was particularly true for new artists who had produced videos for consumption on European television. When MTV began broadcasting, the limited number of music videos produced by American acts meant that British performers such as Duran Duran, the Eurythmics, and the Human League received heavy airplay.

The prospects for a music video channel to reinvigorate the Canadian sound-recording industry and to liberate Canadian artists from the restrictive practices of radio programmers stirred considerable excitement, particularly among industry-association lobby groups. In his testimony before the CRTC during the licence hearings for the specialty broadcast service, CIRPA president Earl Rosen was unequivocal, restating all earlier written submission that 'the future of the music industry will be determined by the licensing decision of the CRTC.' . . .

> [W]ithout a Canadian music video channel to give us access to our most important audience, no record company, either independent or major, can afford to invest heavily in music videos. Without videos, we are precluded from international markets. The failure to establish a Canadian music video service would be the same as condemning the record industry to manufac-

ture only 78s after the introduction of 33 LPs. (CRTC, 1984a, p. 3222)

In contrast to Rosen's enthusiasm, Canadian Recording Industry Association (CRIA) president Brian Robertson's presentation before the CRTC was measured. Robertson did not question the importance of music videos as a promotional tool, but rather expressed concern that since the licence was to be granted on a discretionary basis, the music video channel would not meet its desired goals to reach a broad Canadian audience. Robertson also reminded the commission of the cost of music video production and further aligned the futures of the speciality service and the sound-recording industry by explaining that 'when a video music applicant relies so heavily on another industry to supply the majority of his programming at little or no cost, then it is only realistic to recognize the problems and needs of the supplier' (CRTC, 1984a, p. 117). However CRIA's plea for understanding was somewhat undermined by one of its own witnesses. After explaining that there were probably fewer than a hundred high-quality Canadian music videos in circulation, A&M Canada vice-president of promotion Larry Chappell maintained that their promotional potential might offset the costs of development:

I might add that I do not think we are really looking for compensation right now. Our main objective is to reach as many people as possible with the music channel, and at that point—at this present time, I think we are ready to absorb our costs of the production, as long as the end product will reach a quantity of people. (CRTC, 1984a, p. 129)

On the subject of a domestically owned and operated video service, however, Robertson and Rosen were in agreement:

Finally Mr Chairman, on the question of importation of foreign music video programming serv-

ices, we recommend that no consideration be given to importing in whole, or in part, music video program services that originate outside of Canada. (Robertson, in CRTC, 1984a, p. 120)

If the emergence of music video and the transformation of the broadcasting industry supplied the industrial motivation for a Canadian music video channel, the developments from the Applebaum-Hébert report provided the policy rationale for the support of the domestic sound-recording industry and broadcasting landscape. With the prospects of a national music video channel, the interests of the various sectors began to intersect; the position of the sound-recording industry within Canadian cultural policy began to solidify; and the need for a national music video station emerged. The successful applicant for the music video channel would not only have to satisfy the demands of a fiscally sensitive federal regulator and a market-driven, 'private sector–friendly' cultural policy orientation, but also those of a recovering domestic sound-recording industry seeking to capitalize on its new-found importance within policy discourse.

Fighting for the Right to Rock: MuchMusic and the CRTC

Of the 41 candidates for the specialty television licence, five were vying for the specialty music video service. In addition to the application put forward by the CHUM/Citytv contingent were submitted the following: the Music Channel, by Rogers Radio Broadcasting Limited and Molson Limited; Canadian Music TV (CMTV), led by Montreal real estate developer Gilles Chartrand; and two applications by concert promoter Donald Tarlton in conjunction with Astral Communications and Michael Sheridan, a Torontonian with little broadcasting experience (Miller, 1984b, p. 1). Early in the licensing process, it became apparent that only the CHUM/Citytv, Rogers/Molson, and Chartrand applications would have a legitimate chance of winning the broadcasting licence.

One of the most convincing aspects of the MuchMusic application was its assertion of superior marketing savvy and commitment to Canadian music. In Canada, the period between 1981 and 1984 saw only a few random segments of music video programming broadcast over local stations and national networks. The most active user of music video programming was Citytv, an independent UHF/cable station based in the Toronto area and owned by CHUM. In 1979, the station premiered its music news and information program, entitled *The New Music*. The program was the creation of John Martin, a former producer in the current affairs department at the CBC. By mixing coverage of musical trends, performer spotlights, and promotional videos and clips from performances within the Toronto area, *The New Music* treated popular music as a serious journalistic subject. This can be seen in its coverage of such events as Bob Marley's funeral and the riot that erupted during Alice Cooper's failure to appear for a Toronto concert in 1980 (Fay, 1997, p. 15).

An important feature of *The New Music* was a series of televised concerts featuring new Canadian (and some American) talent, which were simulcast on local radio stations. These *New Music Specials* began in 1978 (a year before *The New Music* began airing regularly) and continued until 1983. The series represented the most consistent effort to showcase new artists on Canadian television during this period. The program featured concerts with Bruce Cockburn, Bob McBride, Murray McLachlan, the Downchild Blues Band, Carole Pope, the Madcats, the Good Brothers, Lene Lovich, Streetheart, Canadian Brass, Goddo, the Minglewood Band, Lisa dalBello, and Max Webster. After successfully airing in Toronto, *The New Music* achieved additional status as the authoritative source for Canadian and international music information through syndication in 15 markets across Canada (Flohil & Harry, 1983, p. 16). . . .

As part of its presentation before the CRTC, the Citytv application maintained that MuchMusic would offer a number of programs on a range of subjects, thus allowing Canadian performers of different musical genres the opportunity to have their videos shown on the channel. Since the Canadian recording industry had not yet produced an extensive range of music videos, the new service would be established in such a way as to stimulate activity in the Canadian production sector.

If the CHUM/Citytv application had the blessing of members of the sound-recording industry, the company's fiscal approach also seemed to satisfy the nervous broadcast regulator. The failure of the C Channel, as we have seen, had made the CRTC wary of issuing broadcasting licences. The limited potential of pay television at this time, witnessed not only by C Channel's failures but also by the tenuous positions of First Choice and Super Channel, forced applicants to prove they had the financial power to absorb start-up costs and to remain in the Canadian broadcasting landscape over the long term.

In its presentation to the CRTC, the CHUM/Citytv contingent emphasized the financial health of the new station by stating unequivocally that it would break even within five years of receiving the broadcasting licence. Station representatives also highlighted the fact that its existing facilities and its library of music video programming placed the prospective channel in a better position for broadcast than the other applicants. Although using the Citytv studios and staff to perform many of the functions involved in running the new-music station would result in losses of $9 million after five years, the application stated that half of this figure could be recovered by the CHUM radio group through tax rebates (Miller, 1984a, p. B4). By comparison, the CHUM/Citytv contingent argued, another organization would not be able to capitalize on these synergies, resulting in debts of up to $15 million (Miller, 1984b, p. F1). Here the company was placed at an advantage over all of the other candidates. . . .

In its decision to award the broadcasting licence, the CRTC began by restating the importance of music video as a medium allowing for the 'increased exposure of new as well as established artists and the emergence of new talent and musical styles'. It then turned its direction inward, focusing on the fact that Canadian record companies and artists had experienced tremendous difficulty reaping the promotional benefits of the music video in the absence of a Canadian music video service. In line with the new initiatives stated throughout the Applebaum-Hébert report and integrated into the Communications department policy objectives (see Raboy, 1990, pp. 286–8), the CRTC decision maintained that

[t]he establishment of a Canadian specialty music network should, therefore, assure a marked increase in the production of Canadian music videos and the exposure of Canadian talent, and should stimulate both the independent Canadian production and the Canadian recording industries to experiment and respond to the demands of the growing audience for music video programming. (CRTC, 1984b)

As a result, the commission awarded the broadcast licence to MuchMusic. One of the conditions of MuchMusic's licence application was that a minimum of 10 per cent of all the music video clips broadcast on a daily basis be Canadian. This requirement would increase to 20 per cent in the beginning of the third year of operation (CRTC, 1984b). To help increase the number of Canadian content–oriented videos on the broadcaster, the CRTC attached as a condition of the broadcast licence a requirement whereby the broadcaster would have to contribute 2.4 per cent of its gross revenues (to a maximum of $100,000 per year) toward a video-production fund administered by an independent advisory board composed of representatives from MuchMusic, CIRPA, and other members of the Canadian music industry. This fund, called VideoFact, was established in 1984. By 1991, more than 450 videos had been made with $2.8 million of VideoFact support, including 127 in 1990 alone (Miller, 1992, p. 895). . . .

Conclusion

Since acquiring its television licence, MuchMusic has established itself as a significant force within the Canadian sound-recording industry. By isolating the period surrounding MuchMusic's debut, one can clearly see that while changes occurring in the American music industry (such as the entry of MTV) influenced the development of Canadian music video programming, a number of crucial events occurring in Canada also played a determining role in MuchMusic's evolution. These were directly related to Canada's own experience with pay television (one marked by failure and embarrassment) and to changing attitudes of policy makers toward the cultural industries, particularly the Canadian sound-recording industry. The shifting policy strategy for the sound-recording industry modelled itself after similar strategic initiatives carried out earlier by the film and television industries. Beginning in the late 1960s, Canada had begun to alter its relationship to its cultural production—to one that considered Canadian films, programs, and artistic works not simply as important artifacts of 'Canadian identity', but as something produced by the 'cultural industries'. While the unchanging goal of cultural production remained one of articulating a Canadian identity, this shift in perspective by the state represented the belief that the best form of autonomy was to be attained through economic independence to be won by the development of the cultural industries (Dowler, 1996).

By 1980–1, the 'social' elements of the Canadian cultural system were almost completely marginalized by the Department of Communication's position, which held that the role of cultural policy was for the development of cultural industries (Dorland, 1996, p. 351). This transformation would have major ramifications, affecting the ways government was to conceive of and administer to the cultural sector in the years that followed. As a result of the particular orientation expressed by the Applebaum-Hébert report, the CHUM/Citytv application was now the only serious contender for the national music video licence, as it possessed the marketing prowess, commitment to Canadian music promotion, and solid fiscal footing needed to placate the various interested parties that stood to benefit from MuchMusic's influential national reach.

Note

1 For a 'pre-history' of music video, including discussions of early musical films and musical television programs, see Banks (1996, pp. 23–62) and Denisoff (1988, pp. 7–57) for the United States, Fryer (1997) for the United Kingdom, and Rutherford (1990) for Canada.

References

Acland, Charles. (1997). Popular film in Canada: Revisiting the absent audience. In David Taras & Beverly Rasperich (Eds), *A passion for identity: An introduction to Canadian studies* (pp. 281–96). Toronto: ITP Nelson.

Audley, Paul. (1983). *Canada's cultural industries.* Toronto: James Lorimer & Company.

Aufderheide, Pat. (1986). The look of sound. In Todd Gitlin (Ed.), *Watching television* (pp. 111–35). New York: Pantheon Books.

Banks, Jack. (1996). *Monopoly television.* Boulder: Westview Press.

Baxter, R.L., De Riemer, C., Landini, A., Leslie, L., & Singeltary, M.W. (1985) A content analysis of music videos. *Journal of Broadcasting and Electronic Media, 29*: 333–40.

Brown, Jane, & Kenneth Campbell. (1986). Race and gender in music videos: The same beat but a different drummer. *Journal of Communications. 36*(1), 94–106.

Canadian Radio-television and Telecommunications Commission (CRTC). (1983, May 4). Public Notice 1983–93. Call for new specialty programming services. *The Canada Gazette* (Part 1, pp. 4444–9). Ottawa: Minister of Supply and Services.

———. (1984a). CRTC *public hearing on specialty programming services: Transcript of proceedings* January 24 and February 6, 1984, Hull, PQ.

———. (1984b). *Decision 84-338: Applications for a network licence to distribute a Canadian music specialty programming service.* Ottawa: Minister of Supply and Services.

———. (1984c). *Public Notice 84-94: Recognition for Canadian programs.* Ottawa: Minister of Supply and Services.

Denisoff, R. Serge. (1988). *Inside MTV.* New York: Transaction.

Dorland, Michael. (1996). Cultural industries and the Canadian experience: Reflections on the emergence of a field. In Michael Dorland (Ed.), *The cultural industries in Canada* (pp. 347–65). Toronto: James Lorimer & Company.

Dowler, Kevin. (1996). The cultural industries policy apparatus. In Michael Dorland (Ed.) *The Cultural industries in Canada* (pp. 328–46). Toronto: James Lorimer & Company.

Fay, Lee. (1997, Summer). I'm with the band. *Ryerson Review of Journalism,* 13–17.

Federal Cultural Policy Review Committee. (1982). *Report.* Ottawa: Minister of Supply and Services.

Flohil, Richard, & Harry, Isobel. (1983, November). The video explosion: L'ère de la vidéomanie. *Le compositeur canadien / The Canadian Composer, 185,* 14–21.

Fraser, Matthew. (1984, September 1). Glitzy bash launches MuchMusic. *Globe and Mail,* p. E7.

Freedman, Adele (1981, February 21). Don't look now, Chuck, but you're famous. *Globe and Mail,* p. E1.

Fryer, Paul. (1997). Everybody's on *Top of the Pops*: Pop music on British television. *Popular Music and Society, 21*(2), 51–71.

Gasher, Mike. (1997). From sacred cows to white elephants: Cultural policy under siege. *Canadian Issues / Thèmes canadiens, 19,* 13–30.

Goodwin, Andrew. (1992). *Dancing in the distraction factory:* MTV, *music television and popular culture.* Minneapolis: University of Minnesota Press.

———. (1993). Fatal distractions: MTV meets postmodern theory. In Simon Frith, Andrew Goodwin, & Lawrence Grossberg (Eds), *Sound and vision. The music video reader* (pp. 45–66). London: Routledge.

Gow, Joe. (1990). The relationship between violent and sexual images and the popularity of music videos. *Popular Music and Society, 14*(4), 1–9.

Hardin, Herschel. (1985). *Closed circuits: The sellout of Canadian television.* Vancouver & Toronto: Douglas & McIntyre.

Hayes, David. (1983, November/December). Videos now a fact of life. *The Music Scene, 334,* 8–9.

Hirsch, Paul. (1972). Processing fads and fashions: An organization-set analysis of cultural industry systems. *American Journal of Sociology, 77*(4), 639–59.

In Canada: Programming hurting new product sales. (1980, December 20). *Billboard,* 43.

Kaplan, E. Ann. (1987). *Rocking around the clock.* London: Routledge.

Lopes, Paul. (1992). Innovation and diversity in the popular music industry, 1969–1990. *American Sociological Review, 57,* 56–71.

Magder, Ted. (1993). *Canada's Hollywood: The Canadian state and feature films.* Toronto: University of Toronto Press.

Miller, Jack. (1984a, January 31). CHUM's video pitch music to CRTC ears. *Toronto Star,* pp. B1, B4.

———. (1984b, June 7). Who will give Canada musical pay-TV? *Toronto Star,* p. F1.

Miller, Mark. (1992). Music video & MuchMusic. In *The encyclopedia of music in Canada* (pp. 895, 914–15). Toronto: University of Toronto Press.

MuchMusic. (2000). *MuchVote 2000.* MuchMusic Web site. URL: http://www.muchmusic.com/events/elections2000 [20 November 2000].

Pegley, Karen. (1999). *An analysis of the construction of national, racial, and gendered identities on MuchMusic (Canada) and* MTV *(United States).* Ph.D. dissertation, York University, Toronto.

Prozzak. (2000). *The official underage election.* Prozzak Web site. URL: http://prozzak.com/vote. [20 November 2000].

Raboy, Marc. (1990). *Missed opportunities.* Montreal: McGill–Queen's University Press.

———. (1996). Public broadcasting. In Michael Dorland (Ed.), *The cultural industries in Canada* (pp. 178–202). Toronto: James Lorimer & Company.

Rutherford, Paul. (1990). *When television was young: Primetime Canada 1952–1967.* Toronto: University of Toronto Press.

Straw, Will. (1993). Popular music and postmodernism in the 1980s. In Simon Frith, Andrew Goodwin, & Lawrence Grossberg (Eds), *Sound and vision: The music video reader* (pp. 3–21). London: Routledge.

———. (1994). The English-Canadian recording industry since 1970. In Tony Bennett, Simon Frith, Lawrence Grossberg, John Shepherd, & Graeme Turner (Eds), *Rock and popular music: Politics, policies, and institutions* (pp. 52–65). London: Routledge.

———. (1996). Sound recording. In Michael Dorland (Ed.), *The cultural industries in Canada* (pp. 95–117). Toronto: James Lorimer & Company.

———. (2000). In and around Canadian music. *Journal of Canadian Studies / Revue d'études canadiennes, 35*(3), 173–183.

Cultural Industries: Film and Sound Recording

The Canadian film production and sound-recording industries share certain similarities. Both industries are dominated by large foreign multinationals. Both are content-producing sectors dependent on others to promote and distribute their goods. Both depend in part on television for their livelihood—documentary and feature filmmakers depend on income from television broadcast rights, while recording artists depend on MuchMusic to bolster music sales. Both are heavily subsidized by the federal government. Telefilm Canada and the Canadian Television Fund, housed in the Canadian Heritage Department, provide over $100 million annually to Canadian film and television producers. The Canadian Music Fund, also administered by Canadian Heritage, will funnel $28 million to the music industry between 2001 and 2004. Film producers and music artists similarly benefit from Canadian content quotas on television and radio. And each group faces similar disconcerting financial news: less than 3 per cent of Canadian box-office receipts are derived from Canadian films, and Canadian music artists account for just 12 per cent of industry sales in Canada.

Canada has a rich history of documentary filmmaking, much of it produced by the National Film Board. John Grierson, a transplanted Scotsman, helped found the Board in 1939 and led the organization until 1945. A documentary filmmaker and social theorist, Grierson was an unabashed 'propagandist' for democracy and the Allied cause. As Gary Evans notes, the documentary-as-propaganda constituted purposeful education, instilling in people regimens of thought and feeling designed to buttress visions of the Good Society. In this way, the documentary 'raised the intellectual level of mass society'. Wartime propaganda preoccupied the Board, which produced dozens of short documentaries to mobilize public opinion behind the war effort. Among these were standards like 'The War for Men's Minds', 'Inside Fighting Russia', and the Academy Award–winning 'Churchill's Island'.

Canada's record in feature film production pales in comparison to its history of documentary filmmaking. Ted Magder describes the historical underdevelopment of feature filmmaking in Canada, an account steeped in American dominance of the production and distribution sectors. Canadian filmmakers have had to struggle to overcome attitudes of indifference and disdain towards feature-length films: the Canadian government acquiesced to Hollywood pressures by refusing to impose film quotas, as had been done in other countries; the NFB dismissed feature films as diversionist pap and avoided the enterprise; the Massey Commission saw little need for the state to involve itself in the perceived puerility of feature-length cinema. When, in the 1960s, Ottawa did take action by setting up the Canadian Film Development Corporation, which subsidized film production, it left alone the oligopolistic structure of theatrical exhibition in Canada, which all but excluded Canadian films.

Like the domestic film industry, the Canadian sound recording industry exists within a network of multinational corporations. Prior to the 1970s, Will Straw shows, the indigenous recording industry dealt mainly with manufacturing (record pressing) and distribution. By the 1970s, multinational companies had taken control of the distribution sector in Canada. There were also fewer American independent labels with which to contract for Canadian re-issues. In response to these changes, the Canadian industry shifted to talent management and recording functions, typified by new labels like True North, Anthem Records, and Attic Records. None of these integrated vertically into record pressing or distribution. The music industry was characterized by a working relationship between small Canadian recording companies and large, foreign-owned distributors.

In 1970, the CRTC imposed Canadian content requirements on Canadian radio stations, mandating that 30 per cent (now 35 per cent) of musical selections be Canadian. While performers like Bruce Cockburn praised the content rules for helping Canadian musicians, others disagreed. Gordon Lightfoot and Anne Murray balked at having their commercial success attributed to government policies. They and others were also unhappy with their assigned roles as musical ambassadors for Canadian nationalism. As Robert Wright argues, there is some irony in the fact that musicians like Joni Mitchell, Neil Young, and Lightfoot drew upon traditions of American folk and protest music when writing 'nationalist' songs critical of the Vietnam War and American race relations.

Questions for Critical Reading

1. Describe John Grierson's 'propaganda crusade'. In what ways was he 'totalitarian for the good'? How have views of propaganda changed since 1945?
2. What role did the National Film Board play during World War II?
3. How does one account for the strong US presence in Canada's feature film industry before the 1960s? How did the Canadian government react to this situation?
4. What was the purpose of the Canadian Film Development Corporation? How effective was it?
5. How did the recording industry in Canada change between the 1960s and the 1980s? What effect did this have on music artists?
6. What aspects of the history of the Canadian recording industry do Quality Records and Attic Records characterize?
7. What role did Canadian nationalism play in the development of independent recording labels during the 1970s?
8. What impact did American folk and rock music have on Canadian popular music during the late 1960s and early 1970s?
9. How did Canadian nationalism influence musical styles and lyrics?
10. Why were Canadian content rules on radio a bittersweet offering for certain Canadian musicians?

Further Readings

Armitage, Kay, et al., eds. *Gendering the Nation: Canadian Women's Cinema*. Toronto: University of Toronto Press, 1999.

- Among the essays in this collection is a very good article by Armitage on Nell Shipman, a pioneer Canadian woman filmmaker of the 1910s, who was later shut out of the feature film industry by the vertically integrated Hollywood system.

Evans, Gary. *In the National Interest: A Chronicle of the National Film Board of Canada*. Toronto: University of Toronto Press, 1991.

- This is a history of the NFB from 1945, when it fended off anti-communist attacks, until the cost-cutting era of the 1980s.

Gasher, Mike. *Hollywood North: The Feature Film Industry in British Columbia*. Vancouver: University of British Columbia Press, 2002.

- One chapter of this work has historical material on the emergence in the 1970s of the BC feature film industry.

Jennings, Nicholas. *Before the Gold Rush: Flashbacks to the Dawn of the Canadian Sound*. Toronto: Viking, 1997.

- This is a pop-historical account of the Toronto music scene of the 1960s, with an emphasis on Yorkville and performers like Gordon Lightfoot and Joni Mitchell.

Magder, Ted. *Canada's Hollywood: The Canadian State and Feature Films*. Toronto: University of Toronto Press, 1993.

- This is a solid political-economic analysis of why Canada's feature film industry remains underdeveloped.

Morris, Peter. *Embattled Shadows: A History of Canadian Cinema, 1895–1939*. Montreal: McGill–Queen's University Press, 1978.

- This book offers a descriptive and analytical overview of filmmaking in Canada and of the cultural impact of cinema-going in Canada before World War II .

Pendakur, Manjunath. *Canadian Dreams and American Control: The Political Economy of the Canadian Film Industry*. Detroit: Wayne State University Press, 1990.

- With much historical content, this book examines the American dominance of the feature film industry in Canada from a Marxist perspective.

John Grierson and the National Film Board: The Politics of Wartime Propaganda

Gary Evans

Introduction

He was short, wiry, and sandy-haired, a firebrand of a personality whose wide blue eyes could rivet the person being addressed, while a staccato of phrases ranging from Calvin to Spinoza, from Marx to Gobineau, from Goya to Charlie Chaplin, from the greatest English poetry to the most vulgar epithets, peppered the mind like a machine-gun burst. Never at a loss for words or images, he hammered, cajoled, coaxed, demolished, then resuscitated those he chose to work for and with him. He believed he made it clear to his political masters he belonged to no man or party. From 1939 to 1945 Canada was in a world at war again and he was its propaganda maestro. No one ever called him by his first name; he was always Grierson.

Prime organizer of the documentary film movement and one of the single most important figures in documentary film in this century, John Grierson came to Canada to proselytize for the film movement he had begun; upon the outbreak of war, he found himself called upon to rally a depression-exhausted Canada to answer the fascist challenge to civilization. Grierson, who had made documentary portray peacetime with the same verve and excitement as he would later portray wartime, was given the task of boosting national morale. The organization he had just helped to create, the National Film Board of Canada, was to become the national film propaganda agency.

The impact of Canada's film propaganda would be far-reaching and permanent because Grierson turned it into a crusade which to him had near-religious overtones. Grierson, propagandist, educator, mastermind, and high priest of totalitarian information, was planning to build a brave new world based on the changes he could see coming as a result of the new age and techniques of mass communications. The crusade was to change Canada's ideas about film, about propaganda, and perhaps even about the way it perceived itself as a nation. Wartime film propaganda forced Canadians to see themselves as individuals and as groups thrust on to the world stage. Every citizen was an actor in the great drama of world war. New world relationships like geopolitics and internationalism replaced old self-images of friendly tourist guides in a country of romantic natural wonders. On every level Grierson was making Canadians understand their roles as raw-material suppliers, as food producers and munitions makers, and as essential military components in the fight to save the democratic ideals which fascism wanted to crush. When he moved laterally into print propaganda, he intensified campaigns to urge Canadians to enlist, buy victory bonds, sacrifice, salvage, produce munitions and aircraft, co-operate with management, understand inflation, eat nutritionally, avoid loose talk, prepare for electrification, and perform a whole host of other communal activities whose purpose was to unite the nation.

Film propaganda was as bewildering as it was new, for it made a world war thousands of miles away urgent, immediate, and personal. The visual images which millions saw each week at Canadian theatres and in non-theatrical screenings brought them close to the crisis, imposed on

Abridged from the introduction to *John Grierson and the National Film Board: The Politics of Wartime Propaganda*, by Gary Evans (University of Toronto Press, 1984), 3–15.

them a kind of collective responsibility to act selflessly, and pointed to the great rewards to accrue in the post-war world of peace. War was the context of most films, with a constant messianic promise of peace.

Why does wartime film propaganda deserve so much attention? Because in the pre-television age, the cinema was the common national entertainment medium. During the world crisis, theatre-owners voluntarily donated screen time and paid rental fees to screen official propaganda. These films reached millions on a regular basis both in Canada and in the United States. Until television, film was the most pervasive audio-visual means of reaching mass audiences, especially the young and less literate. Non-theatrical film circuits were expanded and millions more saw official propaganda films regularly. With such an available audience, the official propaganda film could and probably did make a substantial impact upon the population over six years of war. It is not possible to assess that impact exactly, but one may safely assume that regular exposure most certainly left an impression on national audiences. For Grierson, it was an opportunity to reach the population in a way that the British documentary movement never had. He was engaged in a totalitarian war for the population's minds, something which he fearlessly enunciated in a 1943 propaganda film called *The War For Men's Minds*.

This remarkable Scotsman's public career in Canada is the focal point of this book. He transplanted the documentary movement to Canada from Britain with characteristic energy, drive, and devotion. The crisis of war gave Grierson the freedom to reshape the propaganda film. It differed substantially from its First World War antecedents, and from the documentary films of 1930s Britain. Casually monitored by his busy superiors, he not only dominated the war propaganda machinery but also created an environment to protect the young filmmakers. Shielded by what he called a 'ring of steel', they produced their propaganda almost unhampered by the political powers whose attention seemed fixed elsewhere. Grierson's brilliant British lieutenant, Stuart Legg, became the intellectual force behind the two theatrical series *Canada Carries On* and *The World in Action*, and set standards for the next generation of Canadian filmmakers. . . .

Grierson believed that the ideas he promoted were far more important to the future of film and communications than were the strengths and weaknesses of his personal character. When I first met Grierson in 1970 at McGill University, he pointed me constantly away from the biographical and always toward the idea, the material realities and the politics of his era. It was one way of demonstrating the Hegelian, Marxist, and Machiavellian influences on him. Also, he was trying to demonstrate that what documentary had done for the world was far more important than what he as a catalyst had done for documentary. We first met after I had spent weeks preparing for our encounter by reading everything I could about the documentary movement. Characteristically, he dismissed me brusquely and told me to go read everything I could find about Goebbels. Not only was he testing the hopeful author's threshold of endurance, he was also saying that what Goebbels did for the Nazis, Grierson and his movement were trying to do for democracy. After reading and digesting hundreds more pages of material, I slowly realized that the Second World War was at least on one level a chess game between the Goebbels and Grierson teams, a game whose winner would determine the alignment of loyalties and nations (perhaps) for centuries to come. The Canadian wartime propaganda film was part of the nascent communications revolution. It also was part of a crusade which tried to rationalize modern man's activities and consciousness.

The Italian Marxist Antonio Gramsci was also thinking and writing about communications issues as he pined away in an Italian prison in the 1930s.[1] His major ideas on ideological hegemony and class struggle may be convenient reference points to analyze the conflict which was unfolding between fascism and democracy, and on a lesser level between Goebbels and Grierson. Though it is unlikely that Grierson had even heard of Gramsci, he was partly engaged in the process Gramsci was writing about, albeit from a different perspective. Gramsci was seeking to establish an organic unity between the intellectuals and the lower strata in an effort to lead the simple people to a higher conception of life. One of the most important ideas to filter down from the 1930s and from Gramsci himself was the realization that the state now had the tools to use media to control and manipulate the population. This meant that the state could become more repressive than it had ever been: not only could it dominate its population by direct physical coercion, but it could also mystify power relations and public issues and events while wielding its power. The state used bureaucracy and technology as its source of cultural, intellectual, and ideological domination, thereby obscuring class and power relations. Grierson saw fascism abuse the power of the state and realized that the same abuses could happen in liberal democracy. He seized upon the documentary idea as being the vehicle for the democratic state to avoid abuse of power and to propagate new conceptions. War let him mobilize film to give the story of a great historical event. This would secure the present. To secure the future he wanted films to portray everyday things, the values and ideals that make life worth living. In this context he talked about educating people who shared the same manias. Grierson believed that the documentary idea, in shunning repression and mystification, could play the role of honest broker between the power of the state and the people, a kind of friendly medium in the service of two-way communication between the governors and the governed. Unlike Gramsci, Grierson and the documentary movement refused to consider the option of revolution in their attempt to communicate a higher conception of life. His documentary film of the 1930s and later the Canadian war propaganda film promised to change mass con-

sciousness within the existing structures while providing the working class with a unified rather than fragmented consciousness. The Canadian war propaganda film would never tire of repeating its arguments and would work incessantly to raise the intellectual level of mass society.

The methodology or technique which documentary film employed was 'direct address'; that is, the viewer was aware of himself as the subject to whom the film was addressed. A narrator communicated with the viewer almost always as a voice of authority whose non-stop narration was unashamedly propositional, representing the point of view the film was trying to affirm.[2] This direct, authoritarian approach was not necessarily 'preachy' but in true classical style used synchronization of narration and visuals to interrelate elements whose internal structure was otherwise unspecified. Thus a library stock shot of a Chinese woman footbound and crawling toward the camera as a crowd of refugees streamed past her became analytically precise as the voice of authority insisted that 'with such proof of their own towering strength, the people of the earch march forward in their new age—march in the certainty that the gates of hell cannot prevail against them.' This sequence, predicting a brave new 'people's' post-war world, was the conclusion of the film Grierson thought was one of the Film Board's best, *The War for Men's Minds*. Theatrical wartime film propaganda continued the tradition of 'classical' expository cinema in which narrated sequences set in place a block of argumentation which the image track illustrated redundantly. It was one form of 'the creative interpretation of actuality', Grierson's universal definition for documentary.

The approach to film was materialist, dealing with material and geopolitical factors which were affecting a world at war. But materialist factors or no, Grierson shunned Marxist dogma. Tom Daly, then an apprentice, explained how he understood the Grierson outlook: 'It was more an organic view of the world. It was not a political matter, but a human matter of correspondence. Grierson believed that democracy began with the manias people shared with each other. The manias created conviction and with conviction, a point of understanding begins.'

Documentary had not been associated with left labour causes; this meant of course that there were no political reservations about the expanded use of documentary at the beginning of the war. Prime Minister King knew what he wanted: not to have propaganda as that term was understood, but rather 'an interpretation of information using different media for the purpose'. He did not want public information to have two sides. His government was not seeking to mislead anyone, least of all to advertise itself. But the war effort had to be made better known. He nodded to Grierson.

That nod was interpreted by Grierson as a signal to undertake an evangelical mission. The mission soon extended further than film. In 1943 he would find himself in the unprecedented position of managing the government's information apparatus at the Wartime Information Board as well as continuing as film commissioner of the National Film Board. He became known as 'the propaganda maestro' as he orchestrated numerous national campaigns, in the belief he was advertising the country, not the government.

'Propaganda' is one of those Pavlovian words which more often than not sets people frothing, not salivating, at the mouth. Most liberal democracies have been very slow to use the medium of film propaganda to reach the masses other than in times of national crisis. This is probably because, in peacetime, liberal democratic governments have generally not been keen to elicit overtly positive and common responses from their citizens. While such governments this century have come to provide more and more social welfare for their citizens, there is still a strong incoherent belief that government ought to diminish its presence in the daily life of a society. Many people possess a deeply entrenched aversion to systematic government communica-

tion because of the fear that 'they' might manipulate 'us'.

From the First World War there grew a belief that propaganda was what the enemy started; that is, he was spreading ideas, facts, or allegations to further his cause and to damage the opposing side's cause. Hence the opposing side was obliged to do its part to offset this by spreading its own information from its own point of view. Propaganda from the other side came to be recognized as something one did not like and which was easily recognized for its mendacity. One's own side (the side of God) spread the truth in order to offset the enemy's lies. Of course, one's own propaganda was good and it furthered one's cause. From 1945, liberal democracies have ceased using the words 'information' and 'propaganda' interchangeably, preferring to use only 'information' in official titles. Today, most will accept the assertion that it is the others who use propaganda and one's own side which uses information. Propaganda continues to be 'what you don't like', and the sophisticated world of advertising (goods and politics) works from the premise that contemporary society should not recognize information components as ideas, facts, or allegations for one's own cause but as values which everyone shares by common consent. These values are not controversial and do not try to convince. They only affirm. Most of us believe that advocacy of what we believe in is education and advocacy of what we do not believe in is propaganda.[3] Contemporary advertisers would be hard pressed to deny that they are engaged in promoting mass suggestion—and that is precisely what propaganda tries to achieve. This book hopes to show how Canadian government film propaganda during the Second World War was unashamedly propositional. Its purpose was to further national goals and institutions. The propaganda was educational, inspirational, and evocative. Grierson, who saw no distinction between propaganda and education, used film and print to promote a strange blend of mass suggestion and education. To him, education promoted a point of view while suppressing difficulties and objections. Traditionally in a liberal democracy education faces those difficulties and objections. But curiously, in times of national crisis, the population seems willing to accept the Grierson approach. Wartime Canada seemed eager to accept the unifying element of mass suggestion, which by virtue of its communal appeal helped ease the individual's fear of having to cope with the world crisis alone. Perhaps this is why in wartime Canada the propaganda film was welcomed so widely and developed in a *laissez-faire* atmosphere with practically no official opposition. There is no record of official complaint that the National Film Board avoided totally the divisive issue of conscription or that it covered up and failed to illuminate the disastrous Dieppe raid. Grierson was there to inspire, not question, and to promote hope over cynicism or despair.

. . .

Grierson's idea of propaganda as education would have special application to Canada in the Second World War. The element of chance also played happily into Grierson's hands as the 1930s drew to a close. He was planning to seek other sponsors on the international level when the Canadian government approached him to suggest a new cosmetic for the faded national image. He was brought to Canada to help clear up the impasse left by the moribund Canadian Government Motion Picture Bureau. He created a new agency, the National Film Board of Canada. The outbreak of the Second World War gave him an opportunity to use North America's commercial theatres as outlets for his inspirational propaganda campaign. Coincidentally, he could act as an agent to help the British in their hour of need: fire the enthusiasm of the Canadian population and then coax gently from isolationist America positive thoughts about the global conflict and Britain's will to survive it.

As well, Canadian wartime propaganda extended to non-theatrical film. The National Film Board widened a pre-war system of non-theatrical distribution to reach every corner of working Canada. Films made for various government departments were often circulated through this network. Field officers took the pulse of the country by reporting on audience reaction to films and they could recommend to the central office in Ottawa what audiences thought the country needed. Grierson would try occasionally to channel this advice to the prime minister's office. As he described it later with more optimism than fact, 'the great development of the war was the decentralization of responsibility to the furthest corners of the state.'

From late 1939, he and his associates produced monthly issues for commercial theatres and information 'shorts' for non-theatrical audiences. As self-proclaimed propagandist and educator, Grierson continued his mission and encouraged a blend of non-partisan progressivism and idealism, promising a better world to come after the war. He orchestrated a system whereby the state was to act as a diffuser of information over all aspects of society. Through all these channels he intended to build national consensus and national will. It was a process he would call 'being totalitarian for the good'. The phrase itself smacks of extremism and might have contributed to the failure of Grierson's crusade. Perhaps, too, a certain political recklessness in combination with his fierce individual style of operating may have been a factor. Some could attribute failure to the crusade's simplistic underpinnings. There is some reason to believe also that the entire edifice may have been built upon sand. Zeal and enthusiasm characterize a crusade; the propagandists might have been taken in by their own idealism.

Mackenzie King's government was satisfied with the film propaganda and paid Grierson scant attention. Yet most political personalities, even while caught up with their own particular responsibilities, viewed the Scotsman as an outsider and a dreamer. The prime minister, perhaps the person most sensitive of all to political breezes, was never comfortable with the free-wheeling Grierson. His attention lay elsewhere until Grierson drew political heat because of his dabbling with international themes, the prime minister's own jealously guarded area of expertise. King grew nervous because the films started to preach internationalism, understanding the Soviet Union, and a brave new post-war world no longer based on traditional concepts of balance-of-power politics. Until then, the lucky Scotsman survived the war years relatively unscathed, standing, as he put it, 'one inch to the left of the Party in power'. It was, in fact, one inch too far. Just as he was preparing to leave Canada for a fling at internationalizing his propaganda crusade, he slipped and the prime minister let him fall from public grace. Grierson watched in despair as the hungry Opposition pounced on the Film Board's 'political' and 'controversial' propaganda. The government dissociated itself from the internationalist propaganda line and messianic rhetoric of its film agency. Almost overnight Canada forgot Grierson and his crusade. A slimmed-down National Film Board remained for his successor, Ross McLean,

to administrate. Wartime film propaganda had affirmed the importance of the individual in a democratic society and had appealed to collective action to ensure victory on behalf of society as a whole. Victory itself had become the Promised Land. Victory achieved, and the Cold War developing, there was no place for propaganda about 'tomorrow'. Fascist aggression may have been crushed, but there would be no enjoyment of peace, no fulfillment of the years of promises, no swords beaten into ploughshares.

In so far as the government was concerned, the propagandists had been brought in to fill the vacuum created by the onrush of events. Once the crisis had passed, there was no need to preach about a better world to come. One is left wondering if, despite its measured success, the propaganda crusade had played itself out by the end of the war. To the surprise of few, fundamental political power relationships among international ruling elites remained unchanged as the media turned millions of minds toward the Cold War. John Grierson and his propaganda missionaries stayed outsiders, who by definition were contenders not expected to win.

Notes

1 Antonio Gramsci, *The Modern Prince and Other Writings* (New York, 1957).
2 See Bill Nichols, 'Documentary Theory and Practice', *Screen*, 17:4 (Winter 1976–7), 34–48,

3 These fundamental attitudes toward propaganda were discussed in 1923 by an early American 'public relations' man, Edward L. Bernays. See *Crystallizing Public Opinion* (New York, 1923) and *Propaganda* (New York, 1928).

A 'Featureless' Film Policy: Culture and the Canadian State

Ted Magder

As a burgeoning field of inquiry, the study of what is commonly known as the 'culture industry' has explored the increasing concentration and internationalization of capital, new forms of production and consumption, and new forms of state practice in the era of international cultural flows. With a few noteworthy exceptions, however, most of the discussion in Canada has taken place within the discourse of liberal analysis, with the fundamental question being: Should the policy apparatuses of the state be enlisted to defend the so-called 'national culture' and reduce dependency on the inflow of foreign—mostly American—products? Thus, the issues associated with the internationalization of cultural production have been posed as 'problems' for the Canadian state. From the standpoint of liberal nationalism, the question has been: Can the state develop policy mechanisms that will offset the processes of cultural homogenization and develop both a viable domestic sector of cultural production and a vigorous cultural expressiveness? Clearly, in this way attention is drawn to the nature of the advanced capitalist state, but what is all too often lacking is an in-depth and sophisticated analysis of the state's role within the social formation.

This article is an intervention into the discussion of the Canadian state and its cultural policy, but from a different perspective. Rather than bemoaning the ambiguity of the state's actions in relation to cultural dependency, the article attempts an explanation of cultural policy as a manifestation of the specific historical and developmental characteristics of Canadian society. Of course, the state does have a real interest in the establishment of a cultural policy. The claim that communications and cultural production are key sectors because of their role in establishing a popular sense of national identity—the experience of sovereignty—is not mere rhetoric. But saying this in no way implies the existence of an autonomous, self-generating or coherent policy process. In other words, state policy is not to be idealized as the practice of a neutral, techno-rational institution, nor should the policy process be situated above the contradictory dynamics of capitalist democracy.

What we want to disclose are the ways in which the substance of cultural policy has shifted over time in conjunction with changes in the social totality, even to the extent that there has been a change in the definition of 'culture' itself. From a societal perspective, it is ultimately a question of understanding how state activities in the cultural sector affect the reproduction of hegemony—the unstable equilibrium of economic, political, and ideological dominance at large. The feature-film sector is taken as the focus of analysis for three basic reasons: first, it is representative of the cultural industries, the most highly capitalized sector of cultural production in the contemporary period; second, it is the clearest example of foreign domination—measured in terms of production and consumption—in the whole field of culture in Canada; and third, it has recently been subject to a major policy initiative of 'Canadianization'. What is depicted here is the changing nature of the state's role in cultural production, as well as the factors that have shaped the process of change.

. . .

From *Studies in Political Economy* 16 (1985), 81–109.

Monopolization, Branch Plants, and the NFB

The early history of the feature-film industry in Canada is marked by three general trends: first, the consolidation of a production, distribution, and exhibition network that established the predominance of American films and capital in the Canadian market; second, the general complicity of the state in this process, through its explicit acceptance of the private-accumulation dynamics of feature-film production; and third, the establishment of a tradition of state-sponsored film organizations, producing non-commercial, non-fiction, educational films consistent with the state's perception of the limited role popular culture should play in the formation of national identity.

By the end of World War I, the American film industry had developed a mature, export-oriented, oligopolistic structure. As of 1925, its films had captured 95 per cent of the British market, 70 per cent of the French market, and 68 per cent of the Italian market.[1] The key to success lay in the vertical integration of the three distinct spheres of the industry. To reach its audience, a film must first be produced, then sold (or rented) to a distributor, who then markets the film by renting it to exhibitors (theatres). Vertical integration of these functions, which often involves illegal cartel-like arrangements that prohibit screen access to unintegrated producers, is crucial for commercial success because only secure access to the distribution and exhibition networks can justify and offset the high costs of production.[2]

In Canada, the sparse population and great distances between urban centres could not sustain the scale of investment necessary to induce the same rapid shift in film production from a locally based, almost vaudevillian venture to a highly capitalized and centralized industry. . . . Therefore, in an effort to secure a constant product line, Canadian exhibitors began to forge links with various American production/distri-bution organizations. The most effective alliance was that of N.L. Nathanson, a Canadian exhibitor, and Adolph Zukor, the founder of Paramount Pictures, who together founded Famous Players. By the late 1920s they had theatres in every major Canadian city and controlled the supply of films from Paramount, MGM, Pathe, and British International. Independent exhibitors and producers found it increasingly difficult to secure either financial backing or market access in the face of this emergent monopoly.

During the same period, a number of European states began to question the financial and cultural consequences of the American-based network. At the Imperial Conference of 1926, the British settled on a quota system designed to guarantee British films a certain percentage of screen time in theatres supplied primarily by US distributors. Prime Minister Mackenzie King managed to have the definition of 'British' extended to include films of Canadian origin. But if the action was intended to encourage private *Canadian* production, it did not. The main consequence of King's initiative was the production of 'quota quickies' made by new American subsidiaries in Canada, which managed to fulfill only the bare requirements of the regulation.[3] . . .

Far from representing any plot on the part of American capital, this strategy of branch-plant film production fit very neatly into the Canadian state's overall 'branch-plant export strategy of import substitution industrialization.'[4] The 1920s and early 1930s were characterized by a broad alliance between US and Canadian capital and the Canadian state—an alliance designed to exploit the economic advantages of preferential tariffs within the British imperial market. As in the manufacturing sector, the state was prepared to use imported American technology and capital in film production to improve the nation's overall economic stature. The policy as a whole proved to be short-sighted and ineffectual: 'When the British changed their quota law in

1938 (mainly because of the way Canada had allowed Hollywood to circumvent the intent of the original laws) the Canadian companies involved closed their doors and disappeared."[5] No other state assistance to domestic commercial-film production was forthcoming, and several attempts by independent Canadian exhibitors and producers to break the industry's monopolistic practices through the Combines Investigation Act all met with failure.[6]

During this period, as well, the state pioneered the first government-sponsored film-production agency—the Canadian Government Motion Pictures Bureau, established in 1918. In general, the Motion Pictures Bureau produced non-commercial educational films whose impact on the private sector remained marginal.[7] The assumption that feature films fell within the range of commodity production—and therefore outside the range of direct state intervention—was not challenged. By the mid-1930s, the bureau had run aground; it had become underfunded and disorganized. As a replacement, the National Film Board of Canada (NFB) was established in 1939, a Crown corporation with a mandate

> to initiate and promote the production and distribution of films in the national interest and in particular . . . to produce and distribute and to promote the production and distribution of films designed to interpret Canada to Canadians and to other nations. . . .[8]

There is no doubt that interpreted broadly, the NFB's mandate could have challenged the entrenched interests of the American-based monopoly network, because it did make the promotion of Canadian-based cultural products a policy objective. In fact, a number of nations had come to see the importance of facilitating the development of cultural industries, not least because of the widely held hypothesis that 'mass culture' was a powerfully persuasive instrument of social change and social control. In particular, the US State Department had clearly articulated

a strategy of cultural exports as ideological support for the export of American capital, and the 'American way of life'.[9] A number of US state-assistance programs were designed to facilitate the 'free flow' of American films abroad. In Canada, however, the state's perception of the role of the NFB was far removed from any plan to promote domestic cultural industries.

John Grierson, whose personal influence as director of the NFB cannot be underestimated, maintained that the traditional Hollywood feature film was 'lazy, weak, reactionary, vicarious, sentimental and essentially defeatist. . . .'[10] In fact, there is a strongly elitist tone in much of the Canadian literature of this period—a literature which eschews mass culture as untutored and base; certainly Grierson himself would not have tolerated an approach that pegged the production of Canadian culture to the imperatives of the 'mass' market. Arguments over the cultural and political implications of dependent capitalist development found little if any concrete articulation within the state. Moreover, those cultural concerns that were articulated embodied a highly critical, negative appraisal of mass culture as being an improper basis for social and national identity. These themes will emerge even more clearly when we examine the immediate postwar period.

As wartime propaganda, in the form of newsreels and documentaries, NFB films played alongside feature productions, but their service was defined strictly as government information and public education. Interestingly, the NFB's concentration on documentary and non-fictional forms did not prevent it from establishing a network of organizational support, including trade unions and local church, education, and leisure groups. It is fair to say that in this era before television, there was the possibility of reasonably strong popular support for an alternative to the commercial cinema. As well, the success of NFB wartime films throughout the allied countries probably led the major American production and distribution companies to believe that the

NFB could become a commercial threat in the post-war period. The peculiar ferocity of the attack on the NFB during the early Cold War period was no doubt informed by the assumption that the NFB could have become a vocal and critical dissenter, particularly in the wake of a few films which praised the Soviet wartime efforts and the Chinese Revolution. If these attacks seem hysterical in retrospect, it is because the NFB—even given its popular support—never seriously challenged the commercial film network and its private, market-based practices; the full-scale production and distribution of feature films by a state agency was ruled out from the start.

The Canadian Cooperation Project and the Massey-Levesque Report

In 1947, the outflow of capital from film rentals was over $17 million, and a number of private organizations and state officials began to consider the possibility of a protective duty, similar to those being implemented in most advanced capitalist states. Reflecting certain immediate postwar feelings of nationalist and social-democratic sentiment, the Co-operative Commonwealth Federation (CCF) proposed a protective tariff and a revenue fund to promote domestic, commercial film production.[11] Typically, the CCF's proposal represented only a minor threat to the industry's status quo (the distribution/exhibition network would not be affected and the tax was similar to those imposed in most European countries); nonetheless, the Motion Picture Export Association of America (MPEAA), the organizational arm of the major Hollywood production and distribution companies, vehemently denounced the proposal.

In its place, the MPEAA suggested what came to be known as the Canadian Cooperation Project. The Hollywood majors offered to produce a few films in Canada, to release some NFB films in the US, and to insert Canadian sequences into regular Hollywood features (the ubiquitous Mountie) to promote tourism. In exchange, the film distribution companies would not be taxed at a discriminatory rate. The Canadian government agreed to the proposal and the withholding tax on capital outflows remained at 10 per cent, even after the general rate was raised to 15 per cent.[12] . . . The arrangement clearly had very little to do with promoting a domestic, self-generating production sector. In fact, it is much more accurate to situate the Canadian Cooperation Project within the context of the Canadian state's post-war macro-economic policy of dependent accumulation—a policy that made the building of branch plants the 'government's explicit goal'.[13] As it turned out, even the establishment of a branch-plant film industry was not forthcoming, as the MPEAA fulfilled only the barest requirement of the project. The agreement quietly ended in 1958.

Meanwhile, one year after the signing of the Canadian Cooperation Project, the government initiated its first full-scale review of cultural policy—the Royal Commission on National Development in the Arts, Letters and Sciences (the Massey-Levesque Report), which reported its findings in 1951. The mandate of the commission articulated the fundamental premise of the state's intervention into the sphere of culture and communications: 'It is in the national interest to give encouragement to institutions which express national feeling, promote common understanding and add to the variety and richness of Canadian life, rural as well as urban.'[14] Such institutions would be able to overcome the geographic and ethnic barriers within the country, and they would help stem the tide of the 'American invasion' which Massey-Levesque characterized as 'formidable'.[15] Like the Aird Royal Commission on Radio Broadcasting in 1929, Massey-Levesque articulated the need to establish some form of national communications infrastructure that would promote specifically 'Canadian' interests. However, any intervention into the free flow of cultural products and individual choice would, of course, be tempered by the limitations inherent in the capitalist-democratic state. The commission framed its central problematic around this very point: 'How can government aid be given to projects in the field of arts and letters without stifling efforts which must spring from the desires of the people themselves?'[16] The answer was that the state would first accept the premise that the cultural demands of the people are realized through the private marketplace and commodity production, and then directly assist only those cultural practices that would properly articulate Massey-Levesque's own notion of national cultural development.

In this respect, the commission's proposal for state-sponsored cultural development was founded upon an idealist conception of culture. 'Culture', as the 'education which enriches the mind', was explicitly separated from day-to-day material or popular experiences.[17] . . . With such a definition of culture behind it, Massey-Levesque made the classic distinction between 'high' culture, which was most valued in terms of its metaphysical and educational content, and 'low' culture, which was, at best, mere entertainment and, at worst, the debilitating instrument of the emerging mass society. . . .

The problem of dealing with 'low' culture from this perspective is illustrated in the commission's treatment of the film medium. Massey-Levesque argued that the entertainment provided by the commercial cinema was 'not only the most potent but also the most alien influence shaping our Canadian life. . . . Hollywood refashions us in its own image.'[18] Conversely, the NFB clearly fulfilled the educational function of culture, and Massey-Levesque strongly applauded its documentary productions as promoting Canadianism. But in its attempt to reduce the influence of American films, the commission could not overcome its self-imposed dichotomy between education and entertainment, nor its tacit acceptance of the marketplace as a natural phenomenon. The commission recommended increased funding of the NFB and improved rural distribution; it also expressed the hope that a few private producers in Canada would take it upon themselves to make documentaries. However, the commission relegated the production of commercial films to the prevailing market forces. Interestingly, the commission never mentioned either the Canadian Cooperation Project or the monopoly structure of the industry—the economics of the cultural industries were completely divorced from the realm of metaphysical concerns within which Massey-Levesque seemed to move. In the end, Massey-Levesque became caught in its own analytic framework. Its definition of real culture as a practice standing above production in the mass market made it impossible to recommend either protective and discriminatory measures against the entrenched film network, or the promotion of a Canadian-based cultural industry. Implicitly, the commission recognized (but could not overcome) the fundamental contradiction of the liberal-nationalist's strategy, that is, how the development of Canadian 'mass' culture could avoid the processes of homogenization and internationalization inherent in the production processes of the cultural industries.

The Canadian Film Development Corporation, the Capital Cost Allowance, and Canadian Commercial Film Production

By the 1960s, a number of factors that called into question the Massey-Levesque approach to cultural policy had emerged. Frustrated by the lack of opportunities to produce and exhibit feature films, and buoyed by their own increasing expertise and success, the growing number of filmmakers and workers within the Canadian Broadcasting Corporation (CBC) and NFB began to pressure the state for some form of assistance along the lines of the National Film Finance Corporation in Britain. The rise of Québécois nationalism lent vitality and legitimacy to the lobby, through its explicit argument that the state—in this case the provincial government—

had a crucial role to play in the formation of a broad-based popular culture. This argument began to find its parallel in English Canada, where a growing uneasiness with dependent development evolved into a vocal economic and cultural nationalism. The emergence of nationalism in English Canada coalesced with the formation of the Waffle movement with the New Democratic Party (NDP) in 1969, and the formation of the Committee for an Independent Canada in 1970.[19]

Together, these movements challenged the prevailing assumptions about the nature of culture and its relationship to the economy. It was precisely in the area of popular culture that state support was needed if Canada was to develop a distinct, national identity. . . . The crucial difference between this new position and Massey-Levesque was the argument that culture (as opposed to entertainment) was inextricably linked to the economy via the cultural industries; thus a restructuring of the economy towards increased Canadian ownership was the necessary first step in any strategy of cultural development. Sovereignty had come to be defined both in terms of an increase in domestic accumulation and the development of all spheres of cultural production to reflect specifically Canadian norms and values.

What is of immediate interest to us here is how the demand for the development of a feature-film industry was played out within the state. Efforts in the 1960s to curtail the special status of *Time* and *Reader's Digest*, and to impose more stringent Canadian-content regulations for both television and radio, as well as the work of the Royal Commission on Bilingualism and Biculturalism, attest to the increasing salience of cultural concerns within the state. Yet it would be a serious error to conclude that the state had (or would) completely internalize the nationalists' demands. Although the movement did garner a lot of public attention, it never managed to articulate its demands as the dominant political strategy. . . .

In an article published before final reading of the Canadian Film Development Corporation (CFDC) bill in 1966, Judy LaMarsh, then secretary of state, explained the rationale behind the government's intentions:

It seems to me that the establishment of a Canadian feature film industry can be argued from at least three general points of view. First, it is recognized that the film industry provides work for thousands of people, and brings additional revenue to the state. The image of Canada projected on world scenes will contribute importantly to the promotion of tourism. This economic factor, a strong one in other countries, is equally valid for Canada. The second reason is social. A nation cannot permit itself the luxury of being exclusively a consumer in the field of culture; it must encourage the creative spirit and ingenuity of its people. The last reason is of a political-cultural order, the promotion of Canadian culture in other countries.[20]

The aim of the policy was to promote the development of a cultural industry, to create employment, to increase domestic capital accumulation, and lastly to create specifically 'Canadian' products, *without disturbing the monopolistic control of the film marketplace*. While LaMarsh admitted that 'distribution . . . [was] the keystone to financial success,' the government was not prepared to institute measures to regulate the distribution or exhibition aspects of the industry.[21] Canadian productions would have to break into the monopolized market through their own creative effort. . . .

The CFDC began operation in 1969 with a mandate 'to foster and promote the development of a feature film industry' through the use of investments, loans, awards and advice.[22] In its first annual report, the CFDC articulated the industrial and export-oriented intentions of the nascent feature-film policy when it centred its main objective around the support of producers, not directors:

Can financial support for Canadian feature film producers in the private sector enable them to launch themselves upon the world market or are other measures required? . . . The main task of the government's special agency in film feature production—the CFDC—is to find the answers to this question.[23]

At the same time, the consolidation of the Canadian market under the Hollywood majors continued apace. By 1974, Canada had become the number-one foreign market for US distributors, which earned $54.4 million in Canada, compared with $36.5 million in the United Kingdom, and 35.0 million in France.[24] The arrangement between US distributors and the two largest Canadian theatre chains, Famous Players and Odeon, guaranteed screen-time for US-backed films in Canada and produced a situation in which Canadian films typically occupy less than 5 per cent of annual screen-time. The structure of the industry thus continued to discriminate systematically against independent Canadian distributors, exhibitors, and producers.

In response to this situation, support for some form of quota legislation that would make compulsory the showing of Canadian films as a certain percentage of total screen-time grew amongst filmworkers and their supporters. In 1973, the major unions in the film-production sector (ACTRA, the Director's Guild, NABET, the Canadian Society of Cinematographers, and the NFB union) formed the Council of Canadian Film Makers (CCFM) and undertook a major lobbying effort in favour of quota legislation and a box-office tax that would redirect capital into the Canadian production sector.[25] In the meantime, the number of major English-language productions dropped from 13 in 1972 to 4 in 1974, and the CCFM estimated that unemployment within the Canadian film industry was running around 80 per cent. By 1974, the CFDC concurred with the filmworkers' evaluation. Its annual report stated that the CFDC was 'interested in quotas' as a way of overcoming the 'acute'

distribution problems.

In other countries (except the United States), protective quotas and a box-office levy were standard devices to facilitate domestic production, but in Canada the proposals challenged the fundamental character of the supposedly 'non-antagonistic' Canada–US relationship and the entrenched interests of the MPEAA and its allies. Opposition to any proposals for quota or levy legislation was strong both outside and within the state. In particular, events point to the intractability of the Department of Finance and the Treasury Board, which together considered cutting off funds to the CFDC in 1975. When Secretary of State John Roberts proposed the relatively aggressive notion of a 10 per cent levy on the American distributors' annual gross revenue from non-Canadian films exhibited in Canada, with a rebate being conditional on their distributing Canadian films in domestic and foreign markets, the measure was strongly opposed by the major Canadian theatre owners, the MPEAA, and the Department of Finance. Exhibitors in Ontario termed the proposed levy a 'rip-off' and could find 'no justifiable reason for any form of taxation that would have as its objective the transference of revenue from one sector of the industry to another.'[26] Yet the most significant pressure undoubtedly came from the MPEAA through its president, Jack Valenti, and its Canadian branch, the Canadian Motion Pictures Distributors Association (CMPDA). The MPEAA held out the threat of restricting the distribution of Canadian films even further, and intimated as well that the US government might consider the introduction of tax legislation withdrawing the right of American advertisers to deduct the cost of advertising in Canadian periodicals or broadcast outlets, if the levy legislation was introduced. In its brief to the Department of Finance, the CMPDA declared that

the US is likely to regard any significant discriminatory taxation of the industry by this country as being capable of being regarded in the international community as a precedent. There would appear to us, therefore, to be real risk of a serious US reaction that would not necessarily be limited to the taxation of film royalties, indeed the whole field of taxation.[27]

The Department of Finance supported the CMPDA position. It was clearly upset that the CFDC would not, as originally intended, become self-financing; moreover, the Canadian cultural sector had just won an important discriminatory amendment with respect to the Income Tax Act, one that prohibited the deduction of advertising expenses by Canadian firms in non-Canadian media. At its initiative, the proposal was shelved.

This episode highlights the fact that within the state apparatus, the protectionist bias of the CFDC and its supporters in the Secretary of State had been effectively marginalized by the still-dominant continentalist bias of more powerful departments such as Finance. This interdepartmental conflict again illustrates the extent to which competing interests within society do in fact materialize within the bureaucratic structure of the state itself. As Mahon has argued, 'it would appear that the Department of Finance indeed constitutes the "seat of power" of the hegemonic class.'[28] It was the dominant faction within the film industry that found a commonality of interests and expression within this most powerful government department.

By 1975, then, it had become clear that the state's objective would be to promote a commercially viable, profit-making industry geared to international markets through distribution by the US majors. Secretary of State officials introduced two basic policy changes: an amendment to tax legislation to encourage greater funding from the private sector; and the formalization of a negotiated agreement for voluntary exhibition quotas. Negotiated through the CMPDA, and intended to remove pressure for stricter legislation, the voluntary quota agreement of August 1975 called for Famous Players and Odeon 'to guarantee a minimum four weeks per theatre per

year to Canadian films, and to invest a minimum of $1.7 million in their production.'[29] Interestingly, since the agreement stipulated only theatres, and not screens, 'multiple theatres—those containing several screens under one roof as is now common in urban centres—[could] comply with the requirements by devoting only a tiny proportion of their total screen time to Canadian films.'[30] By 1976, 41 per cent of Famous Players theatres and 27 per cent of Odeon theatres had met the quota standard.[31] In sum, the voluntary agreement did very little to change the status quo within the industry.

. . .

Final Considerations

While it can be said that the advanced capitalist state does have a specific institutional interest in the establishment of a comprehensive cultural and communications network, this article has pointed to the need to understand the historical socio-economic factors within which state policy takes shape. It is abundantly clear that in the period before the formation of the CFDC, state policy facilitated the dominance of an American-based production, distribution, and exhibition network that monopolized the commercial market for feature films in Canada. The weak enforcement of antitrust laws, the intent of the 'quota quickies', the Canadian Cooperation Project, and the limited scope accorded the NFB all complemented the overall strategy of dependent development which the state endorsed. The benefits of this 'featureless' film policy accrued to that fraction of Canadian capital already integrated into the US film network (i.e. Canadian-owned exhibition companies), and more generally to those fractions of Canadian capital and Canadian labour that benefited from the dominant ideology that Canadian prosperity would best be secured through an alliance with the expanding US empire. The strategy of dependent development neither required nor encouraged the entrenchment of a strong, collective, *nation-*

alist identity; therefore, rhetoric aside, the state never aggressively set about the task of creating one. Indeed, the project of cultural development was explicitly divorced from considerations of the sphere of economic relations. As embodied in Massey-Levesque, cultural development would not challenge the existing commercial ventures because it concentrated on education and the metaphysics of 'elite' culture.

The establishment of the CFDC and the new film policy indicate a shift in the orientation of the state's cultural policy. The economics of culture and the culture of economics have become explicit objects of concern. As the nationalists maintained, the massive importation of popular culture had to be dealt with. What we have examined is the specific and limited manner in which the twin thrusts of cultural autonomy and nationalism have been mediated within the state apparatus. The great irony of the present period is that in equating culture and sovereignty with economic control, the nationalist movement has produced industrial/cultural policy that undermines the very goals of the cultural nationalists. The new film policy illustrates the constant concern for accumulation within the Canadian state and, more explicitly, the hegemonic power of internationally aligned capital in the articulation of public policy.

. . .

Notes

1 Thomas Guback, *The International Film Industry* (Bloomington 1969), 9. Cf. idem, 'Film as International Business', in *Communication and Class Struggle: Vol. I*, ed. A. Mattelart and S. Siegelaub (New York 1979); and United Nations Educational, Scientific and Cultural Organization (UNESCO), *Statistics on Film and Cinema 1955–1977* (Paris 1981).

2 In the US, the vertical integration of theatres was broken up by the application in 1948 of the Sherman and Clayton antitrust acts. A few attempts at the provincial level in Canada to apply similar antitrust laws in the 1930s met with failure through a combination of American pressure and lack of federal government support. See Kirwan Cox, 'Hollywood's Empire Canada', in *Self-Portrait*, ed. P. Veronneau and P. Handling (Ottawa 1980).

3 See Cox, 'Hollywood's Empire Canada', 29–30.

4 Glen Williams, *Not For Export: Towards a Political Economy of Canada's Arrested Development* (Toronto 1983), 80. Cf. chap. 5.

5 Peter Morris, *Embattled Shadows: A History of Canadian Cinema 1895–1936* (Montreal 1978), 182.

6 See n. 2 above.

7 See Morris, *Embattled Shadows*, 60, 127–74.

8 See section 9 of the National Film Act of 1939. See Piers Handling, 'The NFB in Canada 1939–1959', in Veronneau and Handling, *Self Portrait* (see n. 2 above); and David Jones, *Movies and Memoranda: An Interpretative History of the NFB* (Ottawa 1981).

9 See Herbert Schiller, 'Genesis of the Free Flow of Information Principles', in Mattelart and Siegelaub, *Communication and Class Struggle* (See n. 1 above.)

10 See Peter Morris, ed., *National Film Board of Canada: The War Years* (Ottawa 1965), 5.

11 See Susan Crean, *Who's Afraid of Canadian Culture?* (Toronto 1976), 77–8.

12 Cox, 'Hollywood's Empire Canada', 33.

13 See David A. Wolfe, 'Economic Growth and Foreign Investment: A Perspective on Canadian Economic Policy 1945–1957', *Journal of Canadian Studies* 13:1 (Spring 1978), 8.

14 *Report of the Royal Commission on National Development in the Arts, Letters and Sciences* (Massey-Levesque Report), (Ottawa 1951), xvii.

15 *Report of the Royal Commission on National Development*, 18.

16 Ibid., 13.

17 Ibid., 7.

18 Ibid., 58–9.

19 For a discussion of the nationalist movement in

English Canada, see M. Janine Brodie and Jane Jenson, *Crisis, Challenge and Change: Party Politics and Class in Canada* (Toronto 1980), 280–6; and Philip Resnick, *The Land of Cain: Class and Nationalism in English Canada 1945–1975* (Vancouver 1977), esp. chap. 5 and appendices I and II.

20 Judy LaMarsh, 'Close-up on Bill C-204', *Take One* 1:1 (1966), 4–5. LaMarsh was also one of the original members of the Committee for an Independent Canada.

21 Ibid., 5.

22 Useful overviews of the CFDC and the new film policy include: M.W. Bucovetsky, et al., *Tax Incentives for Film Production: The Canadian Experience* (Toronto 1982); Daniel Lyon and Michael Trebilcock, *Public Strategy and Motion Pictures* (Toronto 1982); and Manjunath Pendakur, 'Film Policies in Canada: In Whose Interests?' *Media, Culture, Society* 3 (1981).

23 Canadian Film Development Corporation (CFDC), *Annual Report 1968–1969* (Ottawa 1969), 7.

24 See Table 2 in Manjunath Pendakur, 'Cultural Dependency in Canada's Film Industry', *Journal of Communications* 31: 1 (Winter 1981), 50.

25 See Peter Pearson, in Canada, House of Commons, *Minutes of Proceedings and Evidence of the Standing Committee on Broadcasting, Films and Assistance to the Arts*, Issue no. 10 (25 April 1974); and Canadian Council of Film Makers, 'Policy Statement on Feature Films', *Cinema Canada* (February–March 1974). ACTRA stands for Alliance of Canadian Cinema, Television and Radio Artists; NABET stands for National Association of Broadcast Employees and Technicians.

26 See Lyon and Tebilcock, *Public Strategy and Motion Pictures*, 90. (See n. 22 above.)

27 Pendakur, 'Film Policies in Canada', 160. (See n. 22 above.)

28 Rianne Mahon, 'Canadian Public Policy: The Unequal Structure of Representation', in *The Canadian State: Political Economy and Political Power*, ed. Leo Panitch (Toronto 1977), 177.

29 Sandra Gathercole, 'As the Grapefruit Grows: A Short Critical History of Canadian Film Policy', *Cinema Canada* (March 1983), 30.

30 Lyon and Trebilcock, *Public Strategy and Motion Pictures*, 94.

31 CFDC, *Annual Report 1976–77*, 9.

The English-Canadian Recording Industry since 1970
Will Straw

When it is spoken of at all, the sound-recording industry in Canada is discussed almost invariably in terms of those relationships (of subordination and interdependence) in which it finds itself *vis-à-vis* the international industry of multimedia conglomerates. There are good and clear reasons for this, rooted in the persistent Canadian impulse to link questions of institutional organization to those of a transformative public policy. In the still-embryonic scholarly literature dealing with the Canadian recording industry, however, one finds a tendency to gloss over basic questions having to do with the nature of recording companies, the processes by which they take shape out of music-related practices, and their relationships to a larger musical culture. The model of a 'record company' is normally accepted as given, and the implicit assumption within both journalistic and scholarly accounts is that Canadian record companies are simply firms which attempt, with less success, to do what multinational companies operating within Canada regularly achieve on a grander scale. This chapter attempts, in a very preliminary fashion, to raise certain questions concerning the status and historical emergence of recording companies within Canada, pointing towards a larger, more comprehensive history wherein the character of national musical industries might be delineated in finer detail.

In the study of national music industries, it is worth recalling that such industries normally rest upon informally organized cultures of music-related activity. This is a banal observation, but it serves to highlight differences between the recording industry and other cultural industries,

such as those involved in broadcasting or the production of films. The television and film industries support forms of cultural activity which are unlikely to exist on a significant scale in their absence (outside the circumscribed spaces of experimental film and video) and they have come, over time, to be principal providers of the training on which a career within them depends. In contrast, music-related activities are perpetuated within and between a wide range of institutional and social spaces, by people who are themselves likely to invest in the training and resources which they require. These activities are, at the same time, likely to unfold within artistic communities which resist definition, constituted as they are in the overlap between the education system, sites of entrepreneurial activity (such as bars or recording studios) and the more elusive spaces of urban bohemia.

It is in relation to these differences that divergences in the governmental treatment of individual cultural industries, in Canada as elsewhere, have taken shape. While the condition of most spheres of cultural activity has been designated a 'problem' at various points in recent Canadian history, the nature of the public responsibility which this problem is seen to incur has varied considerably from one sphere to another. The continued underdevelopment and dependency of the film and television production industries in Canada are commonly posited as failures *vis-à-vis* a national collectivity which suffers (knowingly or not) from a weakened national imagery. These industries are to be nourished or summoned into being so that they may displace the popular appeal of others located elsewhere. In

Abridged from *Rock and Popular Music: Politics, Policies, Institutions*, ed. Tony Bennett et. al. (London and New York: Routledge, 1993), 52–65. Reprinted by permission of Taylor & Francis Books Ltd.

contrast, the condition of the music industries is more typically diagnosed in terms of its failures towards communities of producers and creators whose cultural presence within Canada, however fragmented, is persistent and recognized. For a quarter-century at least, critical discourse within Canada has asserted the richness of popular musical activity within Canada, and it is in relation to this richness that the achievements of public cultural policy are normally judged. While calls for public support or protection of a domestic film industry in English Canada often involve a rhetoric of scarcity, calling for an industry which would itself bring forth and sustain creative activity, arguments for the defence or expansion of the recording industry commonly begin by acknowledging the high level of activity which already exists.

This activity includes the operations of corporate entities involved in a variety of ways in the production, distribution, and sale of recordings. Studies of the recording industry frequently take the existence of record companies as a point of departure, overlooking those processes through which what are commonly known as record 'labels' (i.e. companies engaged in signing artists and producing master tapes) emerge from variable combinations of other activities in which music or recordings are involved. In the Canadian case, as later sections of this chapter will seek to demonstrate, the sorts of activities out of which domestically owned record labels have typically grown have changed substantially over time, and their relationships, both to an indigenous musical culture and to an international recording industry, have likewise been transformed.

. . .

The remainder of this chapter represents an attempt to map the broad outlines of a history of the English-Canadian recording industry since 1970. If the early 1970s constitute a turning point in the development of a domestic recording industry in Canada, this is in part because of the introduction of 'Canadian Content' regulations for broadcasters. This protectionist measure, whose success is widely acknowledged, was not, nevertheless, the only cause of important changes in the Canadian recording industries during the 1970s. Throughout this period, in addition, the organizational form of Canadian recording firms, and the nature of their links to the transnational music industries, would undergo major transformations. By tracing some of these shifts, across a number of individual cases, I hope to account for the distinctiveness of recent developments and to establish frameworks of analysis within which a larger, more comprehensive history of Canadian recording might be undertaken.

Pre-1970 Organizational Forms

From the 1950s through to the end of the 1960s, the Canadian music-recording industry was a relatively underdeveloped and fragmented one. It resists historical reconstruction, in part because its low levels of corporate and geographical concentration have blocked the recognition of overall tendencies or the isolation of forms of corporate structure which might be called typical. Compared with those firms which emerged in the 1970s, most Canadian-owned recording companies during this period were not 'record labels' in the sense of being engaged exclusively or even predominantly in the signing of performers and recording of master tapes. More often, they were record-pressing or distribution concerns which had moved into artists-and-repertory activity or the custom duplication of Canadian-made masters so as to maximize the revenue potential of existing operations. Profits from the pressing of foreign masters were drawn upon to underwrite the production of new recordings by Canadian-based performers; these recordings themselves might, in certain cases, be licensed to other firms for release in foreign territories.

To a certain extent, this fragmentation echoed the low level of corporate concentration within the US recording industry during this period.[1] Inasmuch as the Canadian record industry has derived a large portion of its revenues from the licensing of masters originating in the US, the viability of small firms in Canada has depended in part on the existence of large numbers of US companies whose product is available and attractive to them. Until the early 1970s, when major multinational firms established so-called 'branch' distribution networks across Canada, significant numbers of such companies existed within the US. Masters from Capitol Records, for example, were pressed and distributed in Canada by the Musicana and Regal labels until the establishment of a Canadian subsidiary for Capitol in 1955 (Moogk 1980). Phonodisc (established in 1955) was, throughout the 1960s, the manufacturer and distributor of Motown Records, and Quality (established in 1950) pressed recordings licensed from MGM and a number of other US-based labels. The last two companies were among the most active in creating and distributing Canadian-based record labels, and were associated with significant Canadian successes through the 1960s, such as The Beaumarks' 'Clap Your Hands' (1960), Ronn Metcalfe's 'Twisting at the Woodchopper's Ball' (1961) and The Guess Who's 'Shakin' All Over' (1965).

By the 1970s, however, the viability of Canadian record labels based in the manufacturing or distribution sectors of the music industries had begun to wane. This was in large measure the result of a long-term process by which major, transnational firms consolidated their own 'branch' distribution activities across Canada—a development which mirrored similar patterns in the US, but whose effects on the Canadian situation were more complex.[2] The emergence within Canada of a distribution oligopoly dominated by foreign-owned firms precipitated the decline of large, Canadian-owned manufacturing and distribution firms throughout the 1970s, but not simply because the latter were no longer able to compete within their domestic market. Equally importantly, perhaps,

the same process within the US had reduced the number of independent, unaffiliated labels whose product was available to Canadian firms for licensing. As smaller US companies (such as MGM or ABC Records) were absorbed within large media conglomerates throughout the late 1960s and early 1970s, their capacity to enter into separate agreements with foreign firms was diminished. As a result, the ability of Canadian firms indirectly to subsidize the production of Canadian recordings from the manufacturing and distribution of foreign repertory declined.

The effects of these changes are perhaps best observed using the example of Quality Records, known throughout much of its history as 'Canada's oldest and largest independent' (*Billboard* 1977).[3] Quality's success had rested upon the foundation of its manufacturing operations which, as recently as 1980, were estimated to be responsible for 20 per cent of all records pressed within Canada (*Billboard* 1980). As suggested, Quality was a significant issuer of Canadian recordings, supporting these in part through its licensing of successful US product lines. During the 1970s, however, it was forced to drop several of these lines as a result of moves toward concentration within the US and European record industries. In 1973, Quality lost the rights to MGM Records and its subsidiaries when PolyGram bought these labels and their distribution moved to Polydor within Canada. In 1977, the rights to a successful independent label, Casablanca, likewise shifted from Quality to Polydor. During this decade, Quality attempted, in a variety of increasingly desperate ways, to stabilize its revenue base, most notably by seeking to sign those US labels which remained independent, but the number and profile of these were declining steadily. It also attempted, on two unsuccessful occasions, to set up its own US subsidiary, over-extending its resources in the process. In 1979, Quality succeeded in acquiring the rights to Motown Records in Canada, but the international shift of such rights to MCA in 1986 terminated this arrangement and provoked the company's collapse. Its manufacturing operations were sold to a growing CD pressing operation, Cinram, and Quality itself continued to exist primarily as a marketer of compilation albums promoted through television advertisements.

The virtual disappearance of Quality Records may stand as emblematic of a more general decline in levels of vertical integration within the Canadian recording industry. Canadian-owned companies involved in artist-and-repertory activities have in large measure confined themselves to such activities since the early 1970s, and pressing plants have been less likely to engage in the signing and recording of artists. As a 1988 report by the Canadian Independent Record Production Association pointed out, even foreign-owned labels which once owned manufacturing or retail operations in Canada had moved, over the preceding decade, to divest themselves of many of these interests, concentrating their activities within the distribution sector (CIRPA 1988). While record distribution has emerged, over the last twenty years, as the activity through which oligopolistic control is most effectively ensured, particularities of the Canadian situation have magnified its importance. The geographical expanse of Canada and the existence of two distinct linguistic communities have encouraged the development of distribution operations which are either regional in scope (such as those operating within Quebec), or directed towards dispersed, international markets (such as those for dance music recordings.) Most Canadian-owned distributors have confined themselves to such markets, leaving pan-national distribution as the province of multinational firms operating in Canada.

New Forms of Independence

In the wake of the developments described above, a different organizational model emerged within the English-Canadian recording industry during the 1970s. This model was one in which a particular construction of small-scale entrepreneurial 'independence' took shape, reinforced regularly in journalistic profiles of record company heads which stressed their upstart, nationalistic impulses, and by the formation in 1975 of the Canadian Independent Record Production Association. Less readily acknowledged is the extent to which the emergence of this new class of record companies was inseparable, historically, from the consolidation by multinational firms of a branch distribution system within Canada. The development of a domestic recording industry over the last two decades has depended in large measure on the institution of new forms of affiliation between small, Canadian-owned recording firms and large, foreign-owned distributors. In many cases, this development has followed patterns which one can observe elsewhere and which, in larger countries like the US, typically involve independent labels whose distinctiveness lies in their generic specializations rather than their national location. Nevertheless, it has had distinctive effects on the music industries in Canada, and on the ways in which their problems and successes are diagnosed.

The principal English-Canadian record companies which formed or became prominent in the 1970s were not based in the manufacturing or distribution sectors of the recording industry, and in virtually all cases they have not involved themselves in those sectors. Typically, these firms emerged out of 'talent'-related activities, such as artist management or concert booking. In many cases, as well, their roots were in small-scale music-related enterprises of the late 1960s, such as folk music clubs or freeform FM radio stations. The initial success of these firms was usually dependent upon a core performer or small roster of acts with whom label owners were involved in managerial or other capacities. These artists were, for the most part, working within musical styles long enshrined as those in which Canadians have proved successful—in particular, the singer-songwriter and hard-rock traditions. The normal longevity of these styles, and of performer careers within them, has partially ensured a certain level of stability for these firms, most of which have survived until the present day. (In addition, it has contributed to the sense that the recent history of popular music in Canada is best explored in auteurist terms, as the unfolding of a number of distinct careers—those of Gordon Lightfoot, Murray McLaughlin, the group Rush, and so on.)

Arguably, the first company to form along these lines was Aquarius, which was founded in Montreal in 1968 by individuals active in the local recording and concert-booking industries. Its most prominent artists, for many years, were the hard-rock band April Wine, who achieved a certain measure of success outside Canada. In 1970, True North records was co-founded in Toronto by a talent manager and the owner of the Riverboat, a prominent local coffee house. It has been associated with the recording careers of Bruce Cockburn and Murray McLaughlin, and, more broadly, with the contemporary folk styles for which those artists are known. Anthem Records, also from Toronto, began in 1977 as a production company for the hard-rock group Rush, who are its owners, and expanded with regular signings over the next decade. Stoney Plain, a country-oriented label based in Edmonton, Alberta, was formed in 1976 by a specialist public radio disc jockey, and has combined the release of new recordings by Canadian country music performers with the distribution of 'roots' music recordings licensed from other countries. The most successful independent label in English Canada, Attic Records, has been owned since its beginnings by the manager of singer Gordon Lightfoot, though his managerial and record company activities were from the very beginning kept distinct, and Lightfoot's own recordings were released by a major multinational.

The specific details of these companies' histories are less important for our purposes than is the new mode of entrepreneurship which they represented. Inasmuch as their original assets were, in most cases, a contractual or informal connection to performers of recognized potential—or to a local musical scene—these labels conceived themselves as production houses rather than as vertically integrated recording firms involved in distribution or record pressing. (Integration has instead followed 'horizontal' lines, to include publishing, tour management, and international licensing activities.) From their inception, these companies sought distribution through one of the multinational companies operating within Canada: London Records (Aquarius, Attic and Stoney Plain), CBS (True North), PolyGram (Anthem). In most cases, these affiliations would change over the next ten to fifteen years, but the underlying relationship of these firms to major distributors would not, nor would their relatively low investment in fixed assets, which gave them the flexibility necessary to change affiliations when it proved advantageous to do so.

Nevertheless, firms such as these have confronted tensions between their dual roles within the Canadian recording industry overall. On the one hand, as independently owned firms engaged in the signing of artists and production of records, they are normally compelled to operate in the international recording market, selling licences for their recordings in foreign territories and, on occasion, purchasing foreign masters for release in Canada. At the same time, as a result of their affiliation with major distributors, these firms have come increasingly to serve as the means by which multinational companies may establish a connection to a national musical culture without investing funds or allocating resources on their own. In a recent example, True North Records, which had been dormant for five years, was reactivated on the request of its distributor, Sony Music Canada, which suggested to its owner that he look around to see if any artists in Canada looked potentially successful (*The Record* 1991).

In understanding this tension, a second case study may prove useful. The success of Attic Records of Toronto, over a 20-year period, is normally attributed to a strategy of diversification which it has followed since its founding (e.g. *Billboard* 1977). This diversification is evident, not only in the number and range of performers whose recordings it has released, but also in the diversity of markets in which it has been involved. While many of the Canadian labels discussed above have been active primarily in the production of recordings by high-profile singer-songwriters or heavy-metal groups— that is, in musical genres where performer careers are marked by higher than usual levels of stability and longevity—Attic has involved itself in markets as different as those for disco singles and albums of Irish traditional music. In doing so, it has succeeded in establishing a catalogue of steady-selling albums, while deriving significant revenues, in isolated cases, from the more turbulent markets for dance and pop musics.

In the mid-1970s, while its own records were distributed by London Records within Canada, Attic undertook to license a number of its performers within foreign territories. Patsy Gallant, for example, who had a hit record with 'From New York to LA' in 1977, was licensed to EMI in the UK and Private Stock in the US, and the terms of these licences normally involved publishing rights which Attic itself controlled. By the end of the 1970s, in fact, participation in the international trade shows was central to the strategies of a number of Canadian independent labels, whose own national market offered limited revenue potential. In this respect, Attic participates actively in those processes through which relatively decentralized networks between independent recording firms in dozens of countries are established and exploited. In 1991, for example, it entered into an agreement with the South Korean company Han Yang Records under whose terms the latter would release albums by a number of Canadian performers (such as The Nylons or Lee Aaron). In the same year, it acquired the rights to the Canadian release of masters from the US-based Scotti Bros label.

The histories of these independent firms have been marked by regular changes of affiliation, as they seek more advantageous guarantees of promotional support or cash advances from multinational distributors. In 1979, Attic switched its major label affiliation to CBS of Canada, distributing its records through that company's Epic, Portrait, and Associated Labels marketing system, and continuing its own promotion at the level of individual radio stations. In 1982, Attic changed distributors once again, signing a two-year affiliation with Quality Records in return for a significant investment of money to be used in the signing of new acts. After five months, this arrangement—one of the few in recent years which linked a Canadian independent to a large, domestically owned distributor—was concluded by mutual consent, and Attic switched again, first to PolyGram and subsequently to A&M (which was itself bought by PolyGram in 1989). A&M's responsibility in the promotion of Attic recordings is reportedly defined in one line of the affiliation agreement between them, which specifies that A&M will treat recordings by Attic artists no differently from those of its own artists of equal stature.[4]

Changes of affiliation have not interfered to a significant degree with Attic's capacity to build up a roster of performers and back catalogue of recordings over time, though they might affect the manner in which this back catalogue is marketed.[5] Somewhat paradoxically, recent changes in the sales patterns of popular music recordings may well alter the role of those independent Canadian recording companies which emerged in the early 1970s. While traditionally, as argued, their functional role within the international industry has been one of discovering and developing emergent performer careers, their current value is derived increasingly from the back catalogues which they have accumulated. In 1990 and 1991, one could argue that Attic's role *vis-à-vis* its multinational distributor was partly that of a specialized subsidiary, incurring a large part of the risk posed by musical forms, such as rap, wherein Canadian sales and performer careers were often uncertain. By 1992, Attic had withdrawn to a significant extent from these markets, as broadcast media programming policies and rising costs of promotion reduced or eliminated their profitability.[6] The expense incurred in launching new performers, the continued growth of the CD market, and growing dominance of the retail sector in Canada by large chains of catalogue-oriented stores have led many Canadian labels to concentrate on the marketing of their accumulated inventories of older recordings.

The recording firms discussed in this section offer important models in a number of respects. Their relationship with multinational distributors has served to guarantee a certain stability, while the restriction of their activities to those typically seen as creative has ensured their owners an observable prominence within the Canadian entertainment industries. At the same time, these firms are among those most active in lobbying for continued government subsidies for the recording industry, and for the maintenance or tightening of Canadian Content rules for radio broadcasters. Paradoxically, the dependence of these firms on distribution by major multinational companies has guaranteed a trans-Canadian presence for the recordings which they produce, inasmuch as there exists no Canadian-owned distributors operating on a similar scale.

At the time of their emergence, most of the companies described in this section were associated with musical currents and artists which have subsequently been canonized within histories of English-Canadian popular music. The values present at their founding have continued to be those which shape the terms of music criticism in Canada, and through whose prism questions of public policy towards the music industries are typically framed. The valorization of artistic careers undertaken by the 'independent' record companies which emerged in the 1970s has helped to give English-Canadian popular music a place within ongoing debates over the substance of a national cultural identity.[7] Those book-length treatments of recent Canadian popular music which do exist have tended to rely implicitly on literary models which stress the continuities within distinctive artistic visions (e.g. Adria 1990), and their irrepressibility within a national condition of economic and cultural dependence. The furor over the failure of Bryan Adams' recent album to qualify as Canadian Content for broadcasting purposes—because its co-writer, producer and place of recording were not Canadian—offers evidence of the extent to which concern over the condition of the Canadian music industries has focused almost exclusively on the fate of individual performers.[8]

In a manner one might not have predicted, however, the role of independent record companies in Canada in producing a canon of perennially popular artists and recordings may work in the future to restrict their activities. It appears more and more likely that these firms will serve, within an internationalized industry, as repositories for a particular corpus of older Canadian recordings—most of which date from the 1970s and early 1980s—and that their capacity to engage in the active discovery and development of newer performers will diminish.[9] In this respect, such companies may become the latest in a long line of custodians of Canadian resources who witness the erosion of their value over time while innovation and change occur elsewhere.[10]

Notes

1 The decline in the overall level of corporate concentration within the US recording industry during the years 1958–72 is discussed in Belinfante and Johnson (1983).

2 The move to 'branch' distribution, through which major firms handled the distribution of recordings from their own and subsidiary labels—rather than relying on independent distributors—is discussed by Frith (1981: 139–40).

3 My description of record label histories, in this and later sections, is based on information gathered from *Billboard*, the US music industry trade magazine, and *RPM* and *The Record*, trade magazines published in Canada.

4 Personal conversation with Al Mair, president of Attic Records, February 1992.

5 In 1992, for example, Attic announced plans to release a compilation of greatest hits by The Nylons through PolyTel, the division of PolyGram which produces recordings for television marketing. Personal conversation with Al Mair, president of Attic Records, February 1992.

6 Al Mair, personal conversation.

7 I have argued elsewhere (Straw 1991) that attempts to define a specifically English-Canadian musical tradition have resulted in regrettable oversights and blindspots.

8 In January 1992, during a worldwide tour, Adams called a press conference for the repeal of Canadian Content regulations on the grounds that if he, an obviously successful Canadian artist, could not qualify, these regulations were not effective as forms of support for Canadian music.

9 Increasingly, the activity of Canadian labels born in the late 1960s and early 1970s involves the reissuing of materials issued during the 1970s. Ownership of this material (rather than the ability to sign new artists) seems the principal reason for major label interest in them.

10 The early 1990s have seen more and more Canadian performers sign directly with the US head offices of multinational firms, bypassing both independent companies and the Canadian subsidiaries of these multinationals. For one account, see *Billboard* (1991).

References

Adria, Marco (1990) *Music of our Times: Eight Canadian Singer-Songwriters*, Toronto: James Lorimer & Company.

Audley, Paul (1983) *Canada's Cultural Industries*, Toronto: James Lorimer & Company.

Belinfante, Alexander and Johnson, Richard L. (1983) 'An economic analysis of the US recorded music industry', in William S. Hendon and James L. Shanahan (eds), *Economics of Cultural Decisions*, Cambridge, Massachusetts: ABT Associates.

Berland, Jody (1991) 'Free trade and Canadian music: level playing field or scorched earth', *Cultural Studies* 5 (3), October: 317–25.

——— and Straw, Will (1991) 'Getting down to business: cultural politics and policies in Canada', in Benjamin Singer (ed.), *Communications in Canadian Society*, Scarborough: Nelson Canada.

Billboard (1977) 'Labels strive for product balance', *Billboard* 29 October: C-5.

——— (1980) 'Indie labels push for tax incentives', *Billboard* 26 January: C4.

——— (1991) 'Many Canadian acts still outside the int'l spotlight', *Billboard* 23 March: 72.

CIRPA (1988) *Investor's Guide: An Overview of the Sound Recording Industry*, Toronto: The Canadian Independent Record Production Association.

FACTOR (1991) Untitled pamphlet, Toronto: The Fund to Assist Canadian Talent on Record.

Frith, Simon (1981) *Sound Effects*, New York: Pantheon.

Labbé, Gabriel (1977) *Les Pionniers du disque folklorique québécois 1920–1950*, Montreal: L'Aurore.

Laroche, Karyna and Straw, Will (1989) 'Radio and sound recording policy in Canada', *Australian–Canadian Studies* 7 (1–2): 163–6.

Moogk, Edward B. (1975) *Roll Back the Years: History of Canadian Recorded Sound and its Legacy*, Ottawa: National Library of Canada.

—— (1980) 'Capital Records—EMI of Canada Limited', in *The Encyclopedia of Music in Canada*, Toronto: University of Toronto Press.

The Record (1991) 'Hoskins reactivates True North label', *The Record* 4 March: 16.

Straw, Will (1991) 'Systems of articulation, logics of change: communities and scenes in popular music', *Cultural Studies* 5 (3), October: 368–88.

Tremblay, Danielle (1991) 'L'industrie du disque au Québec', *Moebius* 48, Spring: 101–23.

Wright, Robert (1991) '"Gimme shelter": observations on cultural protectionism and the recording industry in Canada', *Cultural Studies* 5 (3), October: 306–16.

'Dream, Comfort, Memory, Despair': Canadian Popular Musicians and the Dilemma of Nationalism, 1968–1972

Robert A. Wright

Canadian popular music came of age during Richard Nixon's presidency. Direct government involvement in the so-called cultural industries—a reasoned and consistent effort to protect Canada from absorption into the mass culture of the United States—became the policy of federal governments beginning in the mid-1950s. Slowly that policy and the environment it had fostered yielded internationally recognized theatre, scholarship, television programming, and journalism. Yet as late as 1970 *Rolling Stone* magazine observed that, with respect to popular music, Canada was 'notorious for virtual non-support of its own talent'.[1] It is today axiomatic that the exodus of Canadian performers to the United States after the Second World War was a great national loss; critics still cite the careers of Guy Lombardo, Percy Faith, the Diamonds, and especially Paul Anka as evidence of Canada's prolonged indifference toward popular music. Only in the late-1960s did it become acceptable, or profitable, for a young Toronto folk singer to write a 'Canadian Railroad Trilogy' or for a Winnipeg rock band to make a hit single out of 'Running Back to Saskatoon'. Canadians recall with great pride how a soft-spoken teacher from Nova Scotia began a career of superstardom with a song written in a Prince Edward Island farmhouse, and how 'Four Strong Winds' blew across *their* prairies.[2] They remember that two of the anthems of the 'Sixties generation' in North America—'Woodstock' and 'Ohio'—were written by introspective folk singers raised in small Canadian towns.

The aim of this paper is to explore the dynamics of national self-consciousness in English-Canadian popular music during this 'golden age', 1968–72. Of special concern is the tension that grew out of the connection of Canadians to the American musical mainstream on the one hand and the mounting pressure Canadian musicians and songwriters faced from the cultural nationalists of the centennial era on the other. Much of the music written by Canadians in this period seemed to celebrate life in the Dominion and, as is so often the case in periods of intense Canadian nationalism, it criticized the United States. Not far beneath this facile exterior, however, lurked a haunting anxiety about what it meant to be nationalistic. The commercial imperative of the English-language pop music industry was, and remains, a profoundly homogenizing force: even among Canadian musicians who did not relocate to New York or Los Angeles, there was an implicit recognition that success meant cracking the American market.[3] Canadian musicians travelled widely in the United States and recognized that there were a good many Americans unhappy with the social and political status quo; they recognized as well that Canada was not without problems of its own. Underscoring this dilemma, above all, was the pervasive influence upon their music of what were quintessentially American musical styles and lyrical themes. The emergence of mature, politically sensitive, and broadly accessible Canadian popular music in this era, it may be argued, had less to do with homage to Canadian geographical and historical landmarks than with the extent to which it had

From *Journal of Canadian Studies* 22, 4 (Winter 1987–8). Reprinted by permission of Journal of Canadian Studies.

co-opted and preserved an earlier American folk-protest tradition.

In the mid-1950s, when most learned Canadians believed the only music worthy of study was 'high brow', essayist Leslie Bell made the courageous observation that 'the endless "pop" tunes that are born and buried each month play a vital part in Canada's life and, despite their frequent lack of musical worth, offer a valuable index to her habits, customs and ways of thinking.' Although less than impressed by the continental phenomenon by then known as the 'Hit Parade', mainly because it tended to have an homogenizing effect on youth in all North American urban centres, Bell revered the preservation of rural Canadian folk traditions in which one could find 'a truly independent national taste'. Don Messer in Prince Edward Island, 'singing cowboys' like Wilf Carter and Hank Snow, square dances on the prairies, and the traditionally isolated folk traditions of Quebec and Newfoundland—these were the list bastions of musical distinctiveness in Canada. But even these, Bell despaired, were 'losing ground against the onslaught of American radio'.[4]

For the most part, of course, 'American radio' was also homogenizing whatever American regional traditions had persisted into the age of the electric guitar. The Jeremiahs of the rock-and-roll age in the United States were themselves busy lashing out against pop music's 'lack of musical worth' as well as against Elvis Presley's lasciviousness. Canadian and American suspicions of this new music differed, however, on at least one level. For reflective Canadians there was something additionally troubling about the fact that the sound, the styles, and the records themselves were American. Here was further evidence in this era of continental integration of Canada's incapacity to resist the mass culture of the United States. A recently published survey-history of post-war Canada has made the sardonic but not altogether misguided point that some Canadians breathed a sigh of relief when

Paul Anka's 'Diana' proved that 'they could do it too'.[5] In such differing responses the first stirrings of the ambivalence that would later permeate the Canadian popular music industry can be seen; however, as the authors of this volume are quick to add, in Canada 'no one cared very much.' Voices like Leslie Bell's cried in the wilderness.

The year 1967 was Canada's centennial and, just as Confederation had been consolidated in part out of disgust for the 'noisy' republic to the south, Canadians expressed their celebration of this anniversary in terms of the relief they felt at not being part of the United States. Canadians recoiled when ghettos in Newark and Detroit exploded into violence that summer, when the Tet Offensive of February 1968 revealed the futility of the Vietnam War, and when Robert F. Kennedy and Martin Luther King, Jr were gunned down the following spring. Lyndon B. Johnson's popularity as president slipped to an all-time low just as, on a wave of jubilant nationalism, Pierre Trudeau was elected prime minister—even the youth of America looked to Trudeau's Canada to harbour draft evaders and lead the crusade to liberalize marijuana laws. . . .

'Cultural nationalism' in the late 1960s was the beginning of the end of Canadian indifference toward popular music. Along with the Liberal government's crackdown on foreign ownership in Canada came the imposition by the Canadian Radio-Television Commission of a quota system for radio broadcasting. Commencing in January 1970, the CRTC ruled, 30 per cent of the radio programming in Canada must be 'Canadian', that is, it must be written, performed, or produced in Canada. This opened the recording industry to Canadian talent as nothing had done previously, and a great scramble to build record companies and to sign artists followed. Many who came to be identified with the nationalism of this era—Bruce Cockburn and Murray McLaughlin, for example—owe the relative ease with which they broke into the industry to this regulation. The Juno Awards, named after CRTC president Pierre Juneau and based upon strict Canadian-content criteria, were also founded in 1970.

Paradoxically, however, the CRTC ruling was problematic for Canadian performers. Perhaps unexpectedly, it fostered a keen and what would become an enduring awareness in the Canadian pop music industry of the limitations of nationalism. Canadian musicians did not want their success to appear to be due solely to the meddling of the government. Musicians of every stripe attempted to dispel the perception that they had a nationalist axe to grind or, worse, that their work was officially sanctioned. It was widely known, for example, that prior to 1970 Anne Murray had identified very closely with her maritime Canadian roots; as Jon Ruddy of *Maclean's* pointed out, only this could explain why she had 'languished' for several years in the chorus of CBC's 'Singalong Jubilee'.[6] Gene McClellan's 'Snowbird' (1970) made her the favoured child of Canadian pop music critics, for unlike Joni Mitchell and Neil Young, they said, she had not forgotten the way back to Canada from the United States. Laudatory articles like John Macfarlane's 'What If Anne Murray Were an American?' abounded.[7] Less than two years later, however, when Murray had moved to an exclusive Toronto suburb and had begun to savour enormous success in the American market, she reflected: 'I don't like being used by journalists. You know, as some kind of a national symbol. I'm an entertainer. I just want to share some joy with other people. That's all.'[8]

Gordon Lightfoot's cool attitude toward Canadian content rules was no secret in the burgeoning Canadian record industry. In 1971, he told Robert Markle:

Well, the CRTC did absolutely nothing for me, I didn't want it, I didn't need it, absolutely nothing . . . and I don't like it. They can ruin you, man. Canadian content is fine if you're not doing well. But I'm in the music business and I have a huge American audience. I'm going to do Carnegie Hall

for the second time. I like to record down there, but I like to live up here. I really dig [Canada], but I'm not going to bring out any flags.[9]

Nevertheless, the fact remained that Lightfoot was a pioneer in the Canadian popular music industry and a hero to cultural protectionists precisely because he wrote nationalistically and did not take up residence in the United States. In a calmer moment that same year he admitted: 'I guess there was a Canadian flavour, a Canadian feeling to my music. And the "Canadian Railroad Trilogy" exemplified it.'[10]

One of the few Canadian artists to admit openly that he had benefited from the CRTC regulation (and that he had received a Canada Council grant) was Bruce Cockburn. Nonetheless, he felt compelled, like the others, to put as much distance as possible between his music and overt political nationalism. His first album was the inaugural release of Bernie Finkelstein's True North Records, a production company established to promote Canadian talent under the CRTC umbrella. It earned such dubious compliments as Toronto music pundit Peter Goddard's observation that 'radio's new appetite for Canadian music has created for Bruce Cockburn an audience that it took Gordon Lightfoot years to gather.'[11] In 1971 Cockburn told journalist Ritchie York:

I'm a Canadian, true, but in a sense it's more or less by default. Canada is the country I dislike the least at the moment. But I'm not really into nationalism—I prefer to think of myself as being a member of the World. . . . The Canadian music scene is not yet as rotten as the US scene. But it's showing signs of catching up.[12]

It is apparent in retrospect that Canadian musicians were attempting to distance themselves not only from the protective shield of government regulations but also from the intensely nationalist music media in Canada. Critics like William Westfall of *Canadian Forum* and Jack

Batten and John Ruddy, both of *Maclean's*, had been adamant in 1968 and 1969 about the need to check 'derivativeness' in Canadian pop music. They argued that everything about Canadian music, from rock festivals to programming at CHUM in Toronto, was a shallow, predictable imitation of American sources.[13] Typical of this hostility was a November 1969 article by Ruddy entitled 'How To Become An American Without Really Trying'. Its subtitle read, 'Your First Move? Get With The "Canadian" Music Scene: It's as Yankee as Dylan and Drive-ins'.

Having lobbied for the introduction of government legislation to protect Canadian music, the critics were at first euphoric about the CRTC decision. They did not fancy themselves 'protectionists' but they had come to realize that subtle persuasion and even threats of regulation were having no impact on Canadian broadcasters.[14] The tone of pop music criticism in Canada changed almost instantly. One month after the CRTC ruling went into effect, Courtney Tower produced an article for *Maclean's* entitled 'The Heartening Surge of a New Canadian Nationalism', in which she wrote:

> Canadian pop songs, contrary to the notions of most adults, don't deal exclusively with sex, drugs and the hassles of adolescent love. Many recent lyrics are, in the words of Ian Tyson of Ian and Sylvia, 'getting into the patriotism bag'. Increasingly, composer-performers such as Tyson, Gordon Lightfoot, Neil Young (of Crosby, Stills, Nash, and Young) and Robbie Robertson (of The Band) are producing songs that celebrate a fresh awareness of Canada.[15]

Under this kind of pressure, it is little wonder that by 1970–1 many Canadian musicians felt constrained rather than liberated by such pervasive cultural nationalism.

Whether coincidentally or not, the government had intervened in Canadian music at the moment when Canadian songwriters had begun to respond lyrically to the political crises arising in the United States. No sooner had Pierre Juneau been made the Canadian recording industry's man of the year for 1970 than a song by a Canadian band made *Billboard's* Number One position for the first time. The song was the Guess Who's 'American Woman', which featured the refrain

> American woman, stay away from me
> American woman, let me be
> I don't need your war machines
> I don't need your ghetto scenes.[16]

Life in this instance appeared to copy art.

In the 1950s and even the early 1960s Canadians knew that they had no chance of breaking into the Top 40 in the American-controlled music industry with songs that challenged the status quo. Any doubt about the importance of conformity and the necessity of avoiding controversy, especially in the form of criticizing the capitalistic ethos that ruled the pop music business, was erased in 1963 when the American television network ABC blacklisted pioneer folksinger Pete Seeger from its national music show.[17] 'Protest' singers who could fill university coffee houses night after night had trouble getting recording contracts and, in any case, they were simply not welcome on the tightly controlled playlists of AM radio stations. Canadians, like aspiring American and British performers, quickly learned the lesson that kept rock-and-roll free of disruptive folk influences: Top 40 pop stars did not bite the hand that fed them. As critic John Orman suggests, rock-and-roll served to 'maintain the status quo by diverting people from serious political thought'.[18] How, then, did Canadians come to be writing hit songs like 'American Woman' less than a decade later?

Even though protest musicians had faced extraordinary pressures from the recording industry, their music was sufficiently powerful and popular to chip away at the hegemony of repetitive, conformist pop music. Led by Pete Seeger and Woody Guthrie, a handful of left-leaning American folk singers persevered coura-geously through the barren years of McCarthyism and emerged in the late 1950s as heroes to a gen-eration of North American youth that rejected the strait jacket of post-war conformity in all of its manifestations. American music critics agree that the origins of the politically inspired music of the Vietnam generation in the United States lay squarely in the Seeger/Guthrie tradition.[19] Much in the Canadian folk movement of the 1960s can also be traced to this source. Resurgent interest in the protest songs of the 1950s prompted the release of several recordings beginning in 1958—*Pete Seeger* (1958), *Ballads of Sacco and Vanzetti* (1960), *Dustbound Ballads* (1964)—to which Canadians had relatively easy access. Asked in 1971 what his formative musical influences had been, Gordon Lightfoot recalled listening to 'folk music, things by Pete Seeger and Bob Gibson', after studying music in California in the late 1950s.[20]

Like most of the American folk and pop singers of the 1960s, however, Canadians were heirs to the Guthrie/Seeger tradition through a crucial conduit, Bob Dylan. From an adolescence of Top 40 rock-and-roll, according to Jerome L. Rodnitzky, Dylan 'picked up the mantle of Woody Guthrie and carried protest songs to new heights of popularity and power.'[21] More than this, adds John Orman, Dylan 'liberated the lyrics of rock music'.[22] Dylan's influence on American folk, rock, and pop music in the mid-1960s was nothing less than revolutionary, for, in contrast to Seeger's experience, his favoured place in the recording industry gave him access to an enormous audience. In Canada, where there had been no indigenous tradition of polit-ically motivated folk music, his influence was in general terms nothing less than formative. Neil Young recalls trading in his Gretsch guitar for a twelve-string acoustic in the summer of 1965 under the sway of Dylan and others who had turned to folk,[23] and virtually all other Canadian 'folkies' spoke of similar experiences. . . .

Since the 1960s, scholars and lay critics of popular music have debated the difference between 'folk' and 'rock' music. This distinction is crucial to understanding the development of Canadian popular music in the centennial era. For Rodnitzky, a Guthrie/Seeger purist, Dylan's significance as a 'folk' singer was on the wane by 1963 precisely because he had electrified folk music and forced its accommodation to the com-mercial standards of AM radio. When folk music became 'folk-rock', he argues, 'mood replaced message' and eventually the explicit social or political meaning of the folk tradition was lost to a feeling of 'general alienation and a hazy, non-conformist aura'. The 'assimilation' of protest music into rock was all the more 'sad' because it had been 'gradual and practically unnoticed'.[24] Orman is not as pessimistic about the superfi-ciality of rock music in the mid- and late-1960s, seeing in much of the politically inspired music of performers like the Jefferson Airplane, Jimi Hendrix, and Janis Joplin the social awareness of the earlier folk movement.[25] In any case, both Rodnitzky and Orman would agree with Carl Beltz that, by the 'troubled period' of 1969–71, music in America became 'disillusioned, direc-tionless [and] plagued by uncertainty about its own identity'.[26]

The superficial integration of protest themes in rock music is nowhere clearer than in the Guess Who's 'American Woman'. Ritchie York may have been correct when he wrote in 1971 that the Guess Who had done more for Canadian music than anything in history.[27] But the truth was, as *Rolling Stone* continually reminded its readers, they had done so at the expense of orig-inality.[28] Burton Cummings, the lead singer and primary songwriter of the Winnipeg band, rec-ognized that there was nothing 'intrinsically Canadian' in its music: 'We weren't influenced by anything except a rehash of North Dakota AM radio.'[29] 'American Woman' was not a considered political statement in the Seeger/Dylan folk style; it was conceived spontaneously during a jam session, a product of Cummings's 'Bubblegum instinct for the quick, ordinary, foolishly memorable phrase'.[30] Any doubt about the superficiality of the song was put to rest in the summer of 1970 when the Guess Who accepted an invitation to play at the White House, agreeing to omit 'American Woman' from the performance. Bassist Jim Kale later explained: 'We're not American, so we don't get involved in American politics. . . . We're anti-war, of course, but the Vietnam War isn't Richard Nixon's war. He didn't start it. He simply inherited it.'[31] Kale added, 'Neil Young told me we shouldn't play [the White House] at all.'

Jerome Rodnitzky has dissected the protest music of Woody Guthrie and concluded that he was 'essentially a piece of rural Americana reacting to the Depression'. The social issues in his music were clear and simple, and the protest it expressed was always explicit. That rurality and directness were the hallmark of this folk music seems indisputable, he argues, since the predominantly urban Sixties generation found it 'corny, simplistic and irrelevant'.[32] This helps to explain why folk artists like Phil Ochs, who refused to follow Dylan's shift toward amplified, commercial music and 'hazy' lyrics, could not maintain popularity through the 1960s. The youth of an increasingly complex and urban United States gravitated toward commercial musical forms because commerciality characterized the world in which they lived.

By and large, this characterization of the folk/rock dichotomy has held sway in popular music criticism, though most scholars are less likely than Rodnitzky to see the two camps as wholly separate. Myrna Kostash recently applied the same typology to the Canadian context:

Folk music, by definition, is rooted in particularity, in locales and events and personalities which are historically specific and are *named*, and the singer-songwriter was valued precisely for the individuality and personality s/he brought to the corpus of the tradition. . . . But rock music was part of a continental culture produced by and distributed from the commercial and political centres of North America (that is, the United States) which, because of their metropolitan and corporate character, were deemed to be of universal significance and value.[33]

Admittedly very much a product herself of the Sixties generation in Canada, about which she is both critical and reminiscent, Kostash is vigilant in her differentiation of Canadian 'folk singers'— Ian and Sylvia, Gordon Lightfoot, Buffy Sainte-Marie, Humphrey and the Dumptrucks—from pop and rock music. The evidence suggests, however, that any hard definition of the distinction between folk and pop music obscures more than it illuminates about Canadian music in the late 1960s and early 1970s.

Rurality, directness, and simplicity were, indeed, the cornerstones of Canadian folk music; but these qualities were also evident in much of the pop and rock music written by Canadians who had crossed over from folk in the late 1960s. Even *Rolling Stone* observed in 1968 that a common feature of Canadian rock bands was that they 'have their country roots showing'.[34] Canadian musicians seem not to have abandoned the folk themes they had co-opted from Woody Guthrie and Bob Dylan, even when Guthrie had become anachronistic and Dylan had strapped on an electric guitar. For musicians like Gordon Lightfoot, Bruce Cockburn, Neil Young, and Joni Mitchell, folk was a medium perfectly suited to express what they, as Canadians, were seeing in the world around them. Bruce Cockburn attempted to articulate this experience in 1972:

I think a lot of the songs that are being written are distinctively, if not obviously, Canadian. Playing something close to American music but not of it. I think it has something to do with the space that isn't in American music. Buffalo Springfield had it.

Space may be a misleading word because it is so vague in relation to music, but maybe it has to do with Canadians being more involved with the space around them rather than trying to fill it up as Americans do. I mean physical space and how it makes you feel about yourself. Media clutter may follow. All of it a kind of greed. The more Canadians fill up their space the more they will be like Americans. Perhaps because our urban landscapes are not yet deadly, and because they seem accidental to the whole expanse of the land.[35]

Myrna Kostash is suspicious of the 'back to the land' movement that characterized the Sixties counterculture, calling it 'essentially nostalgic' and even 'American'.[36] But, in truth, Canadian musicians have betrayed a deeply rooted reverence for rural life and for natural ecology, and very often these values were identified as 'Canadian' and juxtaposed with urban America. This attitude was not mere romanticism; it was based on experience. Gordon Lightfoot, for example, was raised in Orillia, Ontario, and identified himself throughout the 1960s with rural simplicity in songs like 'Early Mornin' Rain' and 'Pussywillows, Cat-Tails'. In 1968 he wrote a personal musical memoir describing his increasing alienation as he travelled from Toronto via Albany to New York City. 'Cold Hands from New York' documented the myriad social problems of large urban centres in the United States—greed, poverty, fear, street violence; it also featured one of the first references in Canadian music to the Vietnam War:

> There were men who lived in style
> And others who had died
> Where no one knew them
> 'Cause they couldn't win.[37]

Like many young Canadians, Lightfoot had gone to New York 'to find what I'd been missin'' and found it instead 'unreal'.

Bruce Cockburn's music was rooted in a profound love of wilderness. Though raised in an Ottawa suburb, Cockburn's childhood fondness for his grandfather's farm and his far-reaching tours of rural Canada as a young man solidified his affinity for nature. 'I prefer the country to the city', he remarked in 1972, 'because I feel better there and I like myself better there.'[38] Cockburn abandoned an early career in rock music and some dabbling in jazz for introspective folk music, making a name for himself by performing the soundtrack to the acclaimed Canadian film *Going Down the Road* and by writing songs like 'Going to the Country'. Like Lightfoot, Cockburn's experiences of urban America had been troubling. During a year at Boston's Berklee School of Music, he claimed to have developed an intense distrust of America and a 'sensitivity to the atmospheric tension so that he could tell, even in his sleep, when his bus had crossed the border to the States.'[39]

The Canadian musicians who had moved to the United States and 'forgotten the way home' expressed similar sentiments. Neil Young was raised in Omemee, a rural village in Ontario, and as a high school student aspired to attend the agricultural college at Guelph and become a farmer.[40] He left Canada to pursue a career in music because he was 'fed up with the Canadian scene' in the late 1960s, but by all accounts he was never comfortable with life in America. Young's second solo album, *Everybody Knows this is Nowhere* (1969), was 'about the need for and the impossibility of escape from Los Angeles.'[41] Escape, for Young, meant Canada. In 1970, at the height of his 'rock' success with the supergroup Crosby, Stills, Nash, and Young, he retreated to Omemee to contemplate his recent divorce. There he wrote one of his most sensitive country-folk songs, 'Helpless':

> There is a town in North Ontario
> There's dream, comfort, memory, despair
> And in my mind I still need a place to go
> All my changes were there
>
> Blue blue windows behind the stars
> Yellow moon on the rise
> Big birds flying across the sky
> throwing shadows on our eyes.[42]

Though not identified as explicitly with rural life *per se*, Joni Mitchell's concern for environmental issues in songs like 'Big Yellow Taxi' (1970) established her reputation as a singer of unusual 'innocence'.[43] It was rumoured in late 1969 that Mitchell had become sufficiently alienated by the American music industry that she was retiring to her home town, Saskatoon, to paint and write poetry.[44] Earlier that year she described her attitude toward life in the United States: 'It's good to be exposed to politics and what's going down here, but it does damage to me. Too much of it can cripple me. And if I really let myself think about it—the violence, the sickness, of it all—I think I'd flip out.'[45]

This reverence for 'space' and the need to be able to escape from the 'crippling' effects of life in violent, urban America did not, however, find expression as simplistic anti-Americanism in the music of these Canadians. For all that they disliked and feared in the United States of the turbulent 1960s, they recognized that there were many Americans who shared their estrangement. They also knew that Canada was no Utopia, that it was naive to look to life in Canada, or to any rural myth, as a panacea for the ills of the United States. These conflicting impulses produced a remarkable ambivalence in the protest music Canadians wrote: they were able to judge life in America from the vantage point of the outsider and the insider simultaneously, blending toughness and sympathy in a way that was unique to the American music scene.

In 1968, the same year that he wrote 'Cold Hands From New York', Gordon Lightfoot produced what was, in retrospect, the best song about the Detroit race riots of 1967. 'Black Day in July' was a song of explicit social criticism in the tradition of Pete Seeger, expressing Lightfoot's sympathy for American blacks driven out of desperation to violence. With his usual flair for history, he recognized that the origins of the trouble lay in the distant past:

> Black day in July: and the soul of Motor City is
> bared across the land
> And the book of law and order is taken in the
> hands
> Of the sons of the fathers who were carried to
> this land.

Though explicit lyrically, this song betrays none of the self-righteousness of 'American Woman'. Lightfoot indicted those who believed they could remain aloof to the crisis, adding the verse:

> Black day in July: The printing press is turning
> and the news is quickly flashed
> And you read your morning paper and you sip
> your cup of tea
> And you wonder just in passing, is it him or is it
> me?[46]

'Black Day in July' was, predictably, ignored by AM radio in the United States but 'underground' FM stations gave it wide coverage and American music critics cited it as an important contribution to the American protest tradition.[47]

The best known protest song of Bruce Cockburn's early career was, ironically enough, produced in a pop, rather than folk, style. 'It's Going Down Slow' (1971) opened with a graphically anti-Vietnam verse set to a bouncy piano rhythm:

> Go tell the Sergeant Major to get that thing
> repaired
> They're losing their pawns in Asia
> There's slaughter in every square
> Oh, it's going down slow.[48]

. . . The most poignant example of a Canadian's capacity to write with ambivalence about American society in the Vietnam era is to be found in Joni Mitchell's 'The Fiddle and the Drum' (1969). Though not a 'hit' by any means, this song expressed the pathos and the confusion felt by those who believed they were seeing the 'good' in the United States turn inexplicably to aggression. Typically, Mitchell's poetic lyrics spoke volumes:

And so once again, my dear Johnny, my dear friend
And so, once again, you are fighting us all.
And when I ask you why, you raise your sticks and
  cry
And I fall.
Oh, my friend, how did you come to trade the fid-
  dle for the drum?[49] [. . .]

Of all the protest songs of the Vietnam era, no doubt Neil Young's 'Ohio' was, and remains, the best known. On 4 May 1970, Ohio National Guardsmen killed four students at Kent State University during a rally to protest Nixon's deci-sion to invade Cambodia. Though remarkably passive in interviews, Young must have been enraged. Although he had no history of writing protest music, by 21 May Crosby, Stills, Nash, and Young were in the studio recording 'Ohio':

Tin soldiers and Nixon's coming
We're finally on our own
This summer I hear the drumming
Four dead in Ohio.

Gotta get down to it, soldiers are cutting us down
Should have been done long ago
What if you knew her and found her dead on the
  ground?
How can you run when you know?[50]

Although it was banned on many radio stations, 'Ohio' had instant appeal among American youth and stirred Vice President Spiro Agnew to a speech denouncing rock music.[51] Asked about the genesis of the song a month after its release, David Crosby chided, 'Neil surprised everybody. It wasn't like he set out to write a protest song. It's just what came out of having Huntley-

Brinkley for breakfast.'[52] Young himself was just as vague: 'I don't know; I never wrote anything like this before . . . but there it is. . . .'[53]

In the end, it was the natural affinity of Canadians for the American folk tradition and their uniquely ambivalent perception of American society, not anti-Americanism, that accounted for their remarkable ascendance as heroes of the Sixties generation. Canadians did not simply offer a foreigner's critique of American society—this kind of parochialism would only have alienated them from their American audience. Rather, they had preserved in their music the explicitness, sen-sitivity, and vitality of a protest tradition that was, in its essence, American.

In the half-decade after Canada's centennial year, Canadian popular musicians were at odds with the concept of 'cultural nationalism'. Some left the country—'fled' was the term most often used in the Canadian music press—and were, there-fore, spared much of the sentimental praise that accrued to those who stayed. For the likes of Anne Murray, Gordon Lightfoot, and Bruce Cockburn, the pressure to be 'Canadian' was unceasing and often stultifying. More than most Canadians listening to their music perhaps, these artists had become, by virtue of the music busi-ness itself, 'members of the world'. However grateful they may have been for protective legis-lation that allowed them a greater opportunity of success in the music business, they were frus-trated by the tensions inherent in being national symbols as well as artists; and however proud they may have been to be Canadian, intimate contact with the United States and the world at large had sharpened their awareness of the limi-tations of nationalism. . . .

Notes

1   Juan Rodriguez, 'Jesse Winchester's Trip to Canada', *Rolling Stone*, 19 March 1970.

2   Myrna Kostash reminisces about Ian Tyson's 'Four Strong Winds' in *Long Way From Home: The Story*

of the Sixties Generation in Canada (Toronto: James Lorimer, 1980), 138.

3   Bruce Cockburn's utter refusal to accommodate his music to the commercial standards of the United

States–dominated recording industry was exceptional.

4 Leslie Bell, 'Popular Music', in Ernest MacMillan, ed., *Music in Canada* (Toronto: University of Toronto Press, 1955).

5 Robert Bothwell, Ian Drummond, and John English, *Canada Since 1945: Power, Politics and Provincialism* (Toronto: University of Toronto Press, 1981), 174.

6 Jon Ruddy, 'The Pit and the Star', *Maclean's*, November 1970, 43.

7 John Macfarlane, 'What If Anne Murray Were an American?' *Maclean's*, May 1971.

8 Anne Murray, quoted in Bill Howell, 'Upper Canada Romantic', *Maclean's* May 1972. 'Snowbird' reached the Number Eight position on the *Billboard* chart in 1970.

9 Gordon Lighffoot, quoted in Robert Markle, 'Early Morning Afterthoughts', *Maclean's*, December 1971.

10 Gordon Lightfoot, quoted in Richie York, *Axes, Chops and Hot Licks* (Edmonton: Hurtig, 1971), 81.

11 Peter Goddard, 'A Maple Leaf on Every Turntable Means Made-In-Canada Pop Stars', *Maclean's*, November 1970.

12 Bruce Cockburn, quoted in York, *Axes, Chops and Hot Licks*, 56.

13 See, for example, Jack Batten, 'Canada's Rock Scene: Going, Going . . .', *Maclean's*, February 1968; William Westfall, 'Pop Counter-revolution?' *Canadian Forum*, August 1969; and Jon Ruddy, 'How to Become a Rock Star Without Really Trying', *Maclean's*, November 1969.

14 Ritchie York was especially critical of Canadian broadcasters. See *Axes, Chops and Hot Licks*, 11. Ironically, in the foreword to this book Pierre Juneau included broadcasters among those who had helped the Canadian music industry.

15 Courtney Tower, 'The Heartening Surge of a New Canadian Nationalism', *Maclean's*, February 1970.

16 The Guess Who, 'American Woman' (Cirrus Music, 1970).

17 Jerome L. Rodnitzky, *Minstrels of the Dawn: The Folk-Protest Singer as a Cultural Hero* (Chicago:

Nelson-Hall, 1976), 14; see also Tony Palmer, *All You Need is Love: The Story of Popular Music* (New York, London: Penguin, 1977), 206–7.

18 John Orman, *The Politics of Rock Music* (Chicago: Nelson-Hall, 1984), xi.

19 Rodnitzky, Orman, and Palmer subscribe to this view, as does Carl Belz, *The Story of Rock* (New York: Oxford, 1972).

20 Gordon Lightfoot, quoted in York, *Axes, Chops and Hot Licks*, 80.

21 Rodnitzky, 20; see also Palmer, 208.

22 Orman, 51.

23 Scott Young, *Neil and Me* (Toronto: McClelland and Stewart, 1984), 59.

24 Rodnitzky, 20–1, 137.

25 Orman, ch. 1.

26 Belz, ch. 5.

27 York, *Axes, Chops and Hot Licks*, 13.

28 See, for example, Nancy Edmunds's review of *Wheatfield Soul*, *Rolling Stone*, 14 June 1969; Lester Bangs's review of *Canned Heat*, *Rolling Stone*, 7 February 1970; and Craig Modderno, 'Guess Who: Good Business Partners', *Rolling Stone*, 7 January 1971.

29 Burton Cummings, quoted in York, *Axes, Chops and Hot Licks*, 24. 'Signs', by Canada's Five Man Electrical Band, was another pop song to appeal to protest lyrics in vogue at this time. It reached Number Three on the *Billboard* chart in 1970.

30 Jack Batten, 'The Guess Who', *Maclean's*, June 1971. Batten was critical of musicians who casually politicized their lyrics after seeing an arena full of Guess Who fans shaking their fists during 'American Woman'.

31 Jim Kale, quoted in Modderno.

32 Rodnitzky, ch. 8.

33 Kostash, *Long Way From Home*, 137–8.

34 n.a., Review of Buffalo Springfield, *Last Time Around*, *Rolling Stone*, 24 August 1968.

35 Bruce Cockburn, quoted in Kostash, 'Pure, Uncluttered Spaces', 21.

36 Kostash, *Long Way From Home*, 140.

37 Gordon Lightfoot, 'Cold Hands From New York' (Warner Brothers, 1968).

38 Bruce Cockburn, quoted in Kostash, 'Pure,

Uncluttered Spaces', 21.

39 Bruce Cockburn, quoted in Ibid., 22.

40 Young, *Neil and Me*, 42.

41 n.a., *Rolling Stone*, 9 August 1969.

42 Neil Young, 'Helpless' (Broken Arrow-Cotillion Publishing, 1970).

43 n.a., 'Joni Mitchell', *Rolling Stone*, 17 May 1969. 'Big Yellow Taxi' made *Billboard*'s chart twice: in 1970 the studio version reached Number 67, and in 1974 the live performance climbed to Number 24.

44 n.a., 'Joni Mitchell Hangs It Up', *Rolling Stone*, December 13, 1969.

45 n.a., 'Joni Mitchell'.

46 Gordon Lightfoot, 'Black Day in July' (Warner Brothers, 1968).

47 Lightfoot did not get his first 'pop' hit—'If You Could Read My Mind'—until 1970, and of the 14 AM hits he subsequently wrote, none had a political theme.

48 Bruce Cockburn, 'It's Going Down Slow' (Golden Mountain Music Corporation, 1970).

49 Joni Mitchell, 'The Fiddle and the Drum' (Siquomb Publishing Corporation, 1969).

50 Neil Young, 'Ohio' (Broken Arrow-Cotillion Publishing, 1970).

51 Young, *Neil and Me*, 110.

52 David Crosby, quoted in n.a., 'Tin Soldiers and Nixon's Coming', *Rolling Stone*, 25 June 1970.

53 Neil Young, quoted in Ibid.

Report of the Royal Commission on Radio Broadcasting (Aird Commission)

The Royal Commission on Radio Broadcasting

SIR JOHN AIRD,
President, Canadian Bank of Commerce (Chairman),
Toronto, Ontario.

CHARLES A. BOWMAN, Esq.,
Editor, 'Citizen',
Ottawa, Ontario.

AUGUSTIN FRIGON, D.Sc.,
Director, 'Ecole Polytechnique', Montreal, Quebec;
Director-General, Technical Education, Province of Quebec,
Montreal, Quebec.

Secretary:
DONALD MANSON, Esq.,
Chief Inspector of Radio,
Department of Marine,
Ottawa, Ontario.

TERMS OF REFERENCE

'To examine into the broadcasting situation in the Dominion of Canada and to make recommendations to the Government as to the future administration, management, control and financing thereof.'

The Honourable P.J.A. CARDIN, Minister of Marine and Fisheries,
Ottawa, Ontario.

Sir,—We have the honour to submit the following report on the subject of Radio Broadcasting, in accordance with the requirements of Order in Council P.C. 2108:

Object of Commission

The Royal Commission on Radio Broadcasting was appointed by the Government to inquire into the existing situation in Canada and to examine the different methods adopted in other countries.

Document 10: Report of the Royal Commission on Radio Broadcasting, September 1929, from *Documents in Canadian Broadcasting*, ed. Roger Bird (Ottawa: Carleton University Press, 1989), 44–54. Reprinted by permission of McGill–Queen's University Press.

The purpose of the inquiry was to determine how radio broadcasting in Canada could be most effectively carried on in the interests of Canadian listeners and in the national interests of Canada.

According to the terms of reference of the Order in Council appointing the Commission, it was required:—

'to examine into the broadcasting situation in the Dominion of Canada and to make recommendations to the Government as to the future administration, management, control and financing thereof.'

Methods in Other Countries

Before setting out to hold meetings in Canada, we considered it wise to visit some of the countries abroad where broadcasting is well organized or is in process of organization, so that we would be in a position, if necessary, to discuss with the provincial authorities in Canada and others, the relative merits of the different methods employed. We found broadcasting especially well organized in Great Britain under the British Broadcasting Corporation, and in Germany where the radio service is also under a form of public ownership, control, and operation. In France the situation has been studied by a government commission. No definite statement, however, can be made at the present time as to the recommendations of the Commission. Everywhere in Europe we found inquiries being conducted under government auspices for the purpose of organizing broadcasting on a nation-wide basis in the public interest. In addition to London, Berlin, Paris, and Lille, we visited The Hague, Brussels, Geneva, Dublin, and Belfast. A visit was also made to New York, where methods followed by the National Broadcasting Company were observed. We have also received information from 'Union Internationale de Radiophonie' at Geneva, and other sources concerning broadcasting in countries which were not visited. A statement of methods followed in other countries is shown in Appendix I.

Situation in Canada

We have held public sessions in twenty-five (25) Canadian cities, including the capitals of the nine provinces. One hundred and sixty-four persons submitted verbal statements at these sessions; in addition we have received 124 written statements (see Appendix II).

Conferences were held with the authorities of the nine provinces, who gave every assistance to the Commission and promised their co-operation in the organization of broadcasting. Written statements giving this assurance have been received from them (see Appendix III). Resolutions have also been received from numerous representative bodies, the large majority favouring the placing of broadcasting on a basis of public service.

In our survey of conditions in Canada, we have heard the present radio situation discussed from many angles with considerable diversity of opinion. There has, however, been unanimity on one fundamental question—Canadian radio listeners want Canadian broadcasting. This service is at present provided by stations owned by private enterprise and with the exception of two owned by the Government of the province of Manitoba, are operated by the licensees for purposes of gain or for publicity in connection with the licensees' business. We believe that private enterprise is to be commended for its effort to provide entertainment for the benefit of the public with no direct return of revenue. This lack of revenue has, however, tended more and more to force too much advertising upon the listener. It also would appear to result in the crowding of stations into urban centres and the consequent duplication of services in such places, leaving other large populated areas ineffectively served.

The potentialities of broadcasting as an instrument of education have been impressed upon us; education in the broad sense, not only as it is conducted in the schools and colleges, but in providing entertainment and of informing the public on questions of national interest. Many persons appearing before us have expressed the view that they would like to have an exchange of programs with the different parts of the country.

At present the majority of programs heard are from sources outside of Canada. It has been emphasized to us that the continued reception of these has a tendency to mould the minds of the young people in the home to ideals and opinions that are not Canadian. In a country of the vast geographical dimensions of Canada, broadcasting will undoubtedly become a great force in fostering a national spirit and interpreting national citizenship.

At the conclusion of our inquiries, it is our task, the importance of which we are deeply conscious, to suggest the means as to how broadcasting can be carried on in the interests of Canadian listeners and in the national interest of Canada. The Order in Council appointing us to undertake this work contains the suggestion that the desired end might be achieved in several ways provided funds are available, viz:—

(a) the establishment of one or more groups of stations operated by private enterprise in receipt of a subsidy from the Government;

(b) the establishment and operation of stations by a Government-owned and financed company;

(c) the establishment and operation of stations by Provincial Governments.

We have examined and considered the facts and circumstances as they have come before us. As our foremost duty, we have concentrated our attention on the broader consideration of the interests of the listening public and of the nation. From what we have learned in our investigations and studies, we are impelled to the conclusion that these interests can be adequately served only by some form of public ownership, operation and control behind which is the national power and prestige of the whole public of the Dominion of Canada.

Proposed Organization

The system which we propose does not fall within the exact category of any of those suggested in the Order in Council, but is one which might be regarded as a modification of (b), i.e. 'the establishment and operation of stations by a Government-owned and financed company'. As a fundamental principle, we believe that any broadcasting organization must be operated on a basis of public service. The stations providing a service of this kind should be owned and operated by on[e] national company. Such a company should be vested with the full powers and authority of any private enterprise, its status and duties corresponding to those of a public utility. It is desirable, however, that provincial authorities should be in a position to exercise full control over the programs of the station or stations in their respective areas. Any recommendation which we offer is primarily made with this object in view. As to what extent the provinces should participate in effecting this control, of course, is a matter which could be decided between themselves and the Dominion Government authorities.

In order satisfactorily to meet these requirements which we have outlined, we recommend the following organization:—

(1) A national company which will own and operate all radio broadcasting stations located in the Dominion of Canada, the company to be called the Canadian Radio Broadcasting Company (C.R.B.C.);

(2) A Provincial Radio Broadcasting Director for each province, who will have full control of the programs broadcast by the station or stations located within the boundaries of the province for which he is responsible. Some provinces might consider it desirable to place the control of broadcasting under a provincial commission. This is a matter to be determined by the provinces concerned;

(3) A Provincial Advisory Council on radio broadcasting for each province to act in an advisory capacity through the provincial authority.

Personnel

The Company. — It is important that the board or governing body of the company should be fully representative of the Dominion and provincial interests so that the closest co-operation among different parts of the country may be maintained. In order that this may be accomplished we would recommend that the governing body or board of the company should be composed of twelve members, three more particularly representing the Dominion and one representing each of the provinces; the mode of appointment of the provincial directors to be decided upon by agreement between the Dominion and provincial authorities.

Provincial Control. — The representative of the province on the Board of the National Company would be the Provincial Director. In the event of any province appointing a provincial commission, the Provincial Director should be the chairman of such commission.

Provincial Advisory Councils. — We would suggest that each council should be composed of members representative of the responsible bodies interested in radio broad-casting.

Broadcasting Stations

Stations under Proposed Organization. — It is to be hoped that the system will eventually cover effectively and consistently that vast northern territory of Canada which at present has comparatively few inhabitants at remote and scattered points but which may come to be as densely populated as some European countries in the same latitude. The Company's immediate objective should be, however, to provide good reception over the entire settled region of the country during daylight or dark under normal conditions on a five-tube receiving set.* How this requirement can best be met will be a question with which the experts entrusted with the responsibility will have to deal. However, from our own observations and from information we have received, we believe it has been fairly well established in practice that high-power stations are needed to reach consistently with good results the maximum number of people. We would like, therefore, to recommend as a matter for consideration, the establishment of seven (7) stations, each having an aerial input of say 50,000 watts; one station to be suitably located in each province, except in New Brunswick, Nova Scotia, and Prince Edward Island, where one station could be centrally located to serve these three provinces. The proposed high-power stations could form the nucleus of the system and as each unit were brought into operation it could be ascertained what local areas, if any, were ineffectively served and stations of smaller power could accordingly be established to serve these places.

We would also suggest that the high-power stations might be so designed as to permit, in time, an increase of power to an economic maximum and of being so modelled as ultimately to provide for two programs being broadcast simultaneously on different wavelengths.

It is well, perhaps, to point out here the necessity of locating broadcasting stations at suitable distances from centres of population to obviate blanketing of reception from outside points. The need for this has been amply demonstrated to us.

We think it is important that, to provide the fullest scope for the proposed system and in the interests of the whole country, all facilities necessary for chain broadcasting be made available in order to permit simultaneous broadcasting by the entire group of stations from coast to coast or by such grouping in different regions as may be considered desirable from time to time.

We are of opinion that the question of the development of broadcasting far beyond its present state, which may include television, is one of great importance and should be closely kept pace with so that the service in Canada would continue equal to that in any other country.

Provisional Broadcasting Service. — While we believe that the proposed organization should be adopted and establishment of the high-power stations proceeded with as soon

---

* Receiving sets employing less than five tubes are, in general, tending to go out of use.

as possible, it seems necessary that provisional service be furnished. To do this, we recommend that one existing station in each area be taken over from private enterprise and continued in operation by the Canadian Radio Broadcasting Company until such time as the larger stations in the proposed scheme are placed in operation. The existing stations carrying on the provisional service could then be closed.

The stations selected for the provisional service should be so chosen from those at present in existence as to provide maximum possible coverage. All remaining stations located or giving a duplication of service in the same area should be closed down. We understand that under the provisions of the Radiotelegraph Act, the licences now in effect may be allowed to expire at the end of the fiscal year or they may be terminated at any time at the pleasure of the licensing authority without legal obligation to pay compensation. We would recommend, nevertheless, that reasonable compensation be allowed such of the broadcasting stations at present in active operation for apparatus as may be decided by the Minister of Marine and Fisheries, the licensing authority.

The apparatus for which compensation is paid should, we think, become the property of the Canadian Radio Broadcasting Company. The more modern and efficient sets of such apparatus could then become available for re-erection as might be deemed necessary by the company.

Finance

Cost of Establishing Stations in Proposed Organization. — The stations forming the system in the proposed organization should be well and fully equipped. The cost of installing the seven high-power units would probably approximate $3,000,000. There would, however, be considerable salvage value in the plants taken over. Assuming that four smaller stations, three 5,000 watt and one 500 watt, would be needed to furnish a supplementary service in local areas not effectively reached by the high-power units, an additional amount of possibly $225,000 would have to be spent in re-erecting apparatus taken over from present station owners. These expenses would represent a capital expenditure of $3,225,000.

In addition to this, compensation would have to be paid to owners of existing stations which we think should be met out of an appropriation made by Parliament.

Cost of Operation. — The service provided would necessarily have to be of a high order. A total annual expenditure for operation of the entire organization proposed, including supplementary stations, would seem to require a minimum of approximately $2,500,000. In addition, the question of interest on capital and sinking fund would have to be considered.

Revenue. — Various methods have been suggested to us as to how revenue might be raised fully to meet the cost of a broadcasting system. If the general public as a whole were listeners, there might be no just reason why the full cost of carrying on a broadcasting service could not be met out of an appropriation made by Parliament from public funds. It is conceivable that that time will come, but under existing conditions, we would not feel justified in suggesting that the general public should be required to pay for the whole of the service which only those possessing radio receiving sets can enjoy. On the other hand, however, radio broadcasting is becoming more and more a public service and in view of its educative value, on broad lines and its importance as a medium for promoting national unity, it appears to us reasonable that a proportion of the expenses of the system should be met out of public funds.

Three sources from which revenue could be derived are suggested, viz: —

(1) Licence fees;

(2) Rental of time on broadcasting stations for programs employing indirect advertising;

(3) Subsidy from the Dominion Government.

Licence fees. — A fee of $1 is at present charged for a receiving licence. Fifty per cent of all licence fees collected in Manitoba is paid over to the Government of that province towards the maintenance of the provincial-owned broadcasting stations at Winnipeg and Brandon. With this exception, no contribution to the cost of broadcast programs in Canada is made from fees collected, which revert to the revenue fund of the Dominion Government.

It should be pointed out, however, that the Marine Department, through its Radio Branch, maintains a service to broadcast listeners in suppressing extraneous noises interfering with radio reception, at an expenditure in proportion to the amount of revenue received from licence fees.

The information we have received seems to indicate that listeners would not be averse to an increase in the licence fee, if an improved Canadian broadcasting service could be provided. In Great Britain the fee is ten shillings (10/) per annum. In Germany and Japan, an amount approximating six dollars ($6) a year is collected. In Australia, the annual fee is twenty-four shillings (24/). We are of opinion, however, that while the present fee should be increased, the amount should not be so high as to prove burdensome for those of limited means. A fee of three dollars ($3) per year would seem reasonable and would at the same time yield a fair amount of revenue. We recommend that the fee be fixed at this amount.

On the basis of the number of licences now in effect, approximately 300,000, a gross revenue of $900,000 per annum would be available from this source. The number of licences may be expected to increase from year to year. We think that radio dealers should be required to collect the licence fee whenever a receiving set is sold.

Rental of Time for Programs Employing Indirect Advertising. — The ideal program should probably have advertising, both direct and indirect, entirely eliminated. Direct advertising is used to considerable extent by broadcasting stations at the present time as a means of raising revenue to meet the expense of operation. In our survey of the situation in Canada, we have heard much criticism of this class of advertising. We think it should be entirely eliminated in any national scheme. Direct advertising is defined as extolling the merits of some particular article of merchandise or commercial service. Manufacturers and others interested in advertising have expressed the opinion that they should be allowed to continue advertising through the medium of broadcasting to meet the competition coming from the United States. We think that this can be satisfactorily met by allowing indirect advertising which properly handled has no very objectionable features, at the same time resulting in the collection of much revenue. An example of indirect advertising would be an announcement before and after a program that it was being given by a specified firm. Programs of this kind are often referred to as sponsored programs. Until such time as broadcasting can be put on a self-supporting basis, we would recommend that the stations' time be made available for programs employing a limited amount of indirect advertising at so much per hour per station.

It is rather difficult to estimate what revenue would be collected for rental of time, but we think that an amount of approximately $700,000 annually could be expected at the beginning.

Subsidy from the Dominion Government. — As compared with many of the European countries where the responsibility of broadcasting has been assumed by the Government, Canada has a comparatively small population, scattered over a vast tract of country. The large territory requires a greater number of stations while the relatively small population makes it obviously impossible to finance the entire scheme from licence fees, if the same are to be kept at a moderate figure. Revenue from programs employing indirect advertising will, we believe, supplement the deficiency in licence fees to a considerable extent. The most desirable means of meeting the additional expenditure required would seem to be by a subsidy from the Dominion Government. We would recommend that the proposed company be subsidized to the amount of $1,000,000 a year for a period of say five years renewable, subject to review, for a further period of five years after expiry of the first.

We believe that broadcasting should be considered of such importance in promoting the unity of the nation that a subsidy by the Dominion Government should be regarded as an essential aid to the general advantage of Canada rather than as an expedient to meet any deficit in the cost of maintenance or the service.

Programs

General. — The question of programs, we have no doubt, will be in capable hands if and when they come within the control of the representative bodies which we have suggested. The general composition of programs will need careful study.

Chain Broadcasting. — Chain broadcasting has been stressed as an important feature. We think that an interchange of programs among different parts of the country should be provided as often as may seem desirable, with coast to coast broadcasts of events or features of national interest, from time to time.

Programs from Other Countries. — The possibility of taking programs from Great Britain has already been demonstrated. While the primary purpose of the service would be to give Canadian programs through Canadian Stations, we think that every avenue should be vigorously explored to give Canadian listeners the best programs available from sources at home and abroad.

Programs employing Indirect Advertising. — Time should be made available on the various stations singly or for chain broadcasting for firms desiring to put on programs employing indirect advertising. We think that it is important that all such programs should be carefully checked to see that no direct advertising or any objectionable feature would be put on the air. We are strongly against any form of broadcasting employing direct advertising.

Education. — Certain specific hours should be made available for educational work both in connection with the schools and the general public as well as the so-called 'adult education', under Provincial auspices.

Religion. — The representative bodies which we have suggested to advise upon the question of programs would be called upon to deal with the matter of religious services, and it would be for them to decide whatever course might be deemed expedient in this respect. We would emphasize, however, the importance of applying some regulation which would prohibit statements of a controversial nature and debar a speaker making an attack upon the leaders or doctrine of another religion.

Politics. — While we are of opinion that broadcasting of political matters should not be altogether banned, nevertheless, we consider that it should be very carefully restricted under arrangements mutually agreed upon by all political parties concerned.

Wavelengths. — We are aware that the question of wavelengths is not one with which we are called upon to deal. But in our survey of the situation in Canada, the inadequacy of wavelengths at present available for broadcasting in this country, namely six 'exclusive' and eleven 'shared' channels, has been persistently pointed out to us. This has been emphasized as one reason for the present unsatisfactory conditions of broadcasting in Canada. Many have expressed the feeling, with which we fully concur, that Canada's insistence upon a more equitable division of the broadcast band with the United States should not be relinquished.

Announcers. — It has been stressed to us and we strongly recommend the importance of having competent and cultured announcers (French and English) and the desirability of having special training and tests of capability for such persons.

Interference

Complaints of interference with radio reception, from electrical distribution lines, machinery, and apparatus, have been brought to our attention in different parts of the country. It has been gratifying at public sessions to hear spontaneous tribute paid by disinterested persons to the efficient work of the Marine Department radio inspectors in removing much of the trouble caused in this way. Their work appears to be made more difficult, however, in that there is no law in effect compelling the users of interfering apparatus to correct faults which interfere with radio reception once such are pointed out by the inspector. The desirability of having legislation to meet such cases has been suggested to us. We recommend the earnest consideration of this suggestion.

Control

The Minister of Marine and Fisheries under the Radiotelegraph Act is the licensing authority for all classes of Radio Stations, which includes Radio Broadcasting Stations and receiving sets. Direct control over such technical questions as wavelengths, power of stations and the collection of licence fees should, we consider, remain with this authority. In order to promote good reception conditions, it is most desirable that the radio activities of other departments of the Government should conform to the regulations and be subject to the authority of the Radiotelegraph Act. We are also of the opinion that the Radio Branch of the Marine Department should continue to carry on the service to broadcast listeners, which includes the suppression of inductive interference.

Summary of Recommendations

The following is a summary of our principal recommendations, viz:—

(a) That broadcasting should be placed on a basis of public service and that the stations providing a service of this kind should be owned and operated by one national company; that provincial authorities should have full control over the programs of the station or stations in their respective areas;

(b) That the company should be known as the Canadian Radio Broadcasting Company; that it should be vested with all the powers of private enterprise and that its status and duties should correspond to those of a public utility;

(c) That a Provincial Radio Broadcasting Director should be appointed for each province to have full control of the programs broadcast by the station or stations located within the boundaries of the province for which he is responsible;

(d) That a Provincial Advisory Council on radio broadcasting should be appointed for each province, to act in an advisory capacity through the provincial authority;

(e) That the Board of the company should be composed of twelve members, three more particularly representing the Dominion and one representing each of the provinces;

(f) That high-power stations should be erected across Canada to give good reception over the entire settled area of the country during daylight; that the nucleus of the system should possibly be seven 50,000 watt stations; that supplementary stations of lower power should be erected in local areas, not effectively covered by the main stations, if found necessary and as experience indicates;

(g) That pending the inauguration and completion of the proposed system, a provisional service should be provided through certain of the existing stations which should be continued in operation by the Canadian Radio Broadcasting company; that the stations chosen for this provisional service should be those which will give the maximum coverage without duplication; that all remaining stations not so needed should be closed down;

(h) That compensation should be allowed owners of existing stations for apparatus in use as may be decided by the Minister of Marine and Fisheries; that such apparatus should become the property of the Canadian Radio Broadcasting Company; that the more modern and efficient of these sets of apparatus should be held available for re-erection in local areas not effectively served by the high-power stations; that the cost of compensation should be met out of an appropriation made by Parliament;

(i) That expenditure necessary for the operation and maintenance of the proposed broadcasting service should be met out of revenue produced by licence fees, rental of time on stations for programs employing indirect advertising, and a subsidy from the Dominion Government;

(j) That all facilities should be made to permit of chain broadcasting by all the stations or in groups; that while the primary purpose should be to produce programs of high standard from Canadian sources, programs of similar order should also be sought from other sources;

(k) That time should be made available for firms or others desiring to put on programs employing indirect advertising; that no direct advertising should be allowed; that specified time should be made available for educational work; that where religions broadcasting is allowed, there should be regulations prohibiting statements of a controversial nature or one religion making an attack upon the leaders or doctrine of another; that the broadcasting of political matters should be carefully restricted under arrangements mutually agreed upon by all political parties concerned; that competent and cultured announcers only should be employed.

(l) That consideration should be given to the question of introducing legislation which would compel users of electrical apparatus causing interference with broadcast reception to suppress or eliminate the same at their own expense;

(m) That the licensing of stations and such other matters prescribed in the Radiotelegraph Act and Regulations issued thereunder for the control of radio stations in general should remain within the jurisdiction of the Minister of Marine and Fisheries; that that authority should continue to be responsible for the collection of licence fees and the suppression of inductive interference causing difficulties with radio reception.

This report would be incomplete without an expression of appreciation of the many courtesies extended to the commission in Canada and abroad. In Great Britain all the authorities concerned, and especially the executive officers of the British Broadcasting Corporation, were unremitting in responding to the requests of the commission for information and enlightenment. The national radio authorities in France, Germany, Belgium, Holland, the Irish Free State, and the National Broadcasting Company of the United States similarly received the commission most cordially and helpfully. At Geneva, the commission met the officers of the Union Internationale de Radiophonie.

It has been greatly to the advantage of the commission that the Department of Marine has extended all available facilities for the gathering of information regarding the present radio situation in Canada.

The department most considerately acceded to the request of the commission to be allowed to have the service of the Chief Inspector of Radio, Mr Donald Manson, as Secretary; his intimate knowledge of radio activities in Canada and abroad, combined with unremitting industry and foresight, has contributed much toward the satisfactory organization of the commission's tour.

JOHN AIRD (*Chairman*).

CHARLES A. BOWMAN.

AUGUSTIN FRIGON.

DONALD MANSON (Secretary).
September 11, 1929.

From *Report of the Royal Commission on National Development in Arts, Letters, and Sciences, May 1951* (Massey Commission)

Part 2, Chapter 18: Television

1. We were given the grave responsibility of making recommendations on the principles upon which the policy of Canada should be based in the field of television, this new and unpredictable force in our society. Our recommendations, however, as well as the evidence we bring forward in support of them, can be short and simple. They follow from the fact that the considerations leading us to recommend the continuation of a national system of radio broadcasting seem to us to dictate much more strongly and urgently a similar system in television. Television, like radio, is akin to a monopoly, but its much more limited channels give added importance to a system of co-ordination and control. Like radio, it is a valuable instrument of national unity, of education, and of entertainment; how much more valuable it is difficult to say at present, but it promises to be a more popular as well as a more persuasive medium.

2. The position of private stations in Canadian television broadcasting requires special consideration. In radio broadcasting Canada has achieved maximum coverage for national programs at minimum cost by using some commercial programs, and by co-ordinating private stations within the national system under the control of the Canadian Broadcasting Corporation. We think the same principles of national control should be applied to television broadcasting but with certain special precautions. It seems apparent that the most difficult problem of television in Canada will be to provide programs in our remote and thinly populated areas; and television advertising will raise difficult questions. Even in radio broadcasting the programs of all private stations are likely to suffer from excessive control by the advertising sponsor. Only to a limited degree can the private station operator determine the character of his own programs. Because of greater capital investment and greater operating costs the unfortunate tendencies of radio broadcasting will be intensified in television. The pressure on uncontrolled private television operators to become mere channels for American commercial material will be almost irresistible. In radio broadcasting, Canada experimented with a purely commercial system before changing to a national system. Such an experiment with the more costly and powerful television would be dangerous. Once television were established in commercial north–south channels it would be almost impossible to make the expensive changes necessary to link the country by national programs on east–west lines of communication. Canadians will welcome good American programs in television as they now do in radio, but as we have been informed, they do not want them at the cost of a Canadian national system, provided that the CBC can make attractive programs available in the not too distant future. It seems desirable to use appropriate American television programs, and to make suitable agreements with Canadian pri-

Report of the Royal Commission on National Development in Arts, Letters, and Sciences, May 1951, from *Documents of Canadian Broadcasting*, ed. Roger Bird (Ottawa: Carleton University Press, 1989), 234–9. Reprinted by permission of McGill–Queen's University Press.

vate stations. These arrangements, however, should follow and should depend on the organization of a national system of television production and control.

3. It has been stated in Part I that many Canadians believe that in view of the high costs of television, and since it is in a stage of rapid transition as a technique and of experiment as an art, Canada would do well for the next few years to move very slowly if at all. As has happened so often, however, our neighbour has set the pace. Some 25,000 Canadians now own television receiving sets and the number will no doubt increase very rapidly here just as it has in the United States. It seems necessary, therefore, in our interests, to provide Canadian television programs with national coverage as soon as possible.

Principles of Control

4. The interim policy of the Canadian government now leaves the Board of Governors of the CBC in control of television broadcasting, authorizes it to open a production centre in Toronto and another in Montreal, to advise the licensing of one private station in any city or area of Canada, and to extend coverage by all practicable means as soon as possible.

5. The principles which underlie this general policy are well calculated to serve the needs and interests of the Canadian people. We do not propose to make detailed recommendations on the policy of development which it is the duty of the Board of Governors with its special knowledge and experience to determine. We understand that the Board is proceeding with the plans laid down in the interim policy announced in March 1949, and that coverage will be extended as rapidly as possible both through the CBC's own transmitting stations and by kinescope recordings provided to private stations which may come into being and serve as national outlets. We are, however, much concerned with three matters. One is that television development should not be precipitate, but should be carefully planned to avoid costly experiments which our country can scarcely afford. The second matter is related to the first. In the national interest, the Board of Governors should not yield to pressure to advise the licensing of any commercial station before it is ready with national programs which all stations may carry. Finally, we also urge, that since this continent is predominantly English-speaking, such programs in the French language be produced as will meet the needs and interests of French-speaking Canadians.

We therefore recommend:

   a. *That direction and control of television broadcasting in Canada continue to be vested in the Canadian Broadcasting Corporation.*

   b. *That the Canadian Broadcasting Corporation proceed with plans for the production of television programs in French and English and for national coverage by kinescope recordings or by any other practicable means.*

   c. *That no private television broadcasting stations be licensed until the Canadian Broadcasting*

Corporation has available national television programs and that all private stations be required to serve as outlets for national programs.

d. *That recommendations previously made in connection with radio broadcasting, and numbered a., c., d., e., f., g., h., and p., apply to television broadcasting.*

Finances

6. We have said something in Part I of the cost of television coverage. As with radio, costs in Canada for coverage will certainly be unusually high, because of the size of the country and our limited population. Program costs will also be very high, again for the same reasons. Television, like radio broadcasting, must be in two languages and must appeal to various interests.

7. In the United States the profits of commercial radio have helped to pay the large initial losses of television. Canada's national radio, as we have seen, shows no profits, and is indeed operating at a loss. If licence fees are charged, they may reasonably be higher for television than for radio. The Board of Governors of the CBC suggests ten dollars a year. But licence fees cannot be charged until Canadian programs are being received; this will involve heavy capital expenditure for equipment as well as the initial program costs. Under the interim policy, the Government provided a loan of $4,000,000 for the first year. The Board of Governors of the CBC had asked for a loan of $5,500,000. We attach the utmost importance to the establishment of a minimum national service as soon as possible. We do not think that the national system should be imperilled by any proposal that television be supported by commercial revenues alone. Nor do we think that radio programs should be impoverished for the sake of the new development.

We therefore recommend:

e. *That the finances of the radio and television broadcasting systems of the Canadian Broadcasting Corporation be kept separate.*

f. *That the capital costs of the national television broadcasting system be provided from public money by parliamentary grants.*

g. *That the costs of the national television broadcasting system for programs and current needs be provided by licence fees on television receiving sets at rates recommended by the Board of Governors of the Canadian Broadcasting Corporation and approved by Parliament, by commercial revenues, and by such statutory grants as may be necessary.*

Programs

8. We do not propose to make recommendations on television programs except in a general way. It has been suggested that television may eventually supersede radio; if this

should happen, most of what we have said of radio programs will apply to television. Again, television may develop and come to concentrate on its more immediately popular capacities such as variety shows, and sports and news actualities, leaving more serious programs to radio and films. For such television programs it will be essential to ensure the maintenance of good taste and a suitable and adequate use of Canadian material and Canadian talent. Finally, as many serious observers have suggested, there may and indeed should emerge from television's combined limitations and advantages an entirely new art essentially distinct from both radio and films. We do not think it useful to speculate on these various possibilities; but if a new art is to develop, it seems to us apparent that television producers must have the greatest freedom for experiment in their work and the most favourable working conditions possible.

9. We do, however, consider it essential that the Board of Governors exercise the greatest care to control excessive commercialism and other possible abuses both in its own programs and in the programs of private stations. The element of control necessary and now exercised by governments and by producers in radio and the cinema will be far more important and far more difficult to achieve in the persuasive and subtle medium of television. We think it important also that, as with radio, the Board of Governors of the CBC endeavour at once to import the best programs from abroad, while developing so far as possible Canadian talent in Canadian programs.

We therefore recommend:

h. *That the Canadian Broadcasting Corporation exercise a strict control over all television stations in Canada in order to avoid excessive commercialism and to encourage Canadian content and the use of Canadian talent.*

i. *That the whole subject of television broadcasting in Canada be reconsidered by an independent investigating body not later than three years after the commencement of regular Canadian television broadcasting.*

10. There is one additional point which should be noticed but upon which we do not propose to make recommendations. Since television programs are costly and since national television networks in Canada cannot be expected for some time, it seems probable that extensive use will be made of films in television programs. We understand that in the United States films occupy about 25 per cent of all television broadcasting time, and that this percentage will no doubt increase. It therefore seems apparent to us that in the interests of economy, and in accordance with the implications of accepted broadcasting and film policies in Canada, there must be close co-operation between the National Film Board and the CBC in the production of films and in their diffusion by television. The National Film Board could not possibly produce all the films or even all the sorts of films which the CBC will probably require, even if it were desirable for the Film Board to do so; and it would be regrettable if the Film Board were to become merely or principally a supplier of films for television purposes. But the Film Board can and should act as principal adviser to the CBC on film matters, including their production by private commercial producers and their procurement from abroad, and the CBC in turn, through the use of a proper proportion of National Film Board films, will no doubt be able to extend very greatly the effectiveness of the Film Board's work and Canadian appreciation of it. We can also readily believe that in the broadcasting and filming of events of national importance, whether in politics, the arts or in Canadian life generally, there will be many opportunities for close collaboration between these two important governmental agencies.

The Marriage of Computers and Communications

The outstanding technological achievement of the past decade, the conquest of space, overshadows the development of digital computer applications that made it possible. Computers are already indispensable tools of scientific research, government, business, and industry, but as yet they have had little direct impact on the man in the street except when they make mistakes. But many observers predict that the computer age is only in its infancy. The development of time-sharing techniques has led to a rapidly growing demand for remote access to computer services, a demand that is already beginning to strain existing telecommunications facilities. Some computer experts forecast that the marriage of computers and communications systems, if it can be successfully consummated, may generate, within the next few decades, social changes more profound than those of the past 200 years.

Telecommunications systems designed primarily for the transmission of information in any form, making the contents of databanks and the processing power of computers commonly and readily available, may open the way to new dimensions of knowledge, not only in business and industry but equally in the home and at school. Moreover, the interactive two-way capabilities of such systems suggest the possibility of much wider participation by individuals in politics, community affairs, broadcasting, and the arts. Eventually, for those who can afford it, the standard telephone may incorporate videoscreen, keyboard, and print-out equipment, giving instant access to all available information and, by simulating face-to-face communication, reduce the need for personal movement and transportation.

It may be useful, especially for those who dismiss these forecasts as visionary, to give a brief account of what is technically feasible today. First, computers have already been developed to a point where human capability for logical thought has been vastly accelerated and extended, while time-sharing techniques have made direct dialogue between man and machine economically practical in some applications. Second, the interaction between a computer and many remote users can be effectively instantaneous, given the proper connections. Third, any information, public or private, can be electronically stored and processed in almost any conceivable way, and can be made available simultaneously to everybody who has access to suitable terminal and transmission equipment, with reasonable protection against unauthorized access. In short, it is now technically feasible to provide the full power of a large-scale computer complex to anyone in the world who is served by efficient telecommunications facilities.

The social and economic benefits to be expected from a computer utility network are predicated on an assumption of virtually universal access, one aspect of which has given rise to the concept of 'The Wired City'.[1] The title is perhaps misleading, for the idea is not

From *Instant World: A Report on Telecommunications in Canada* (Ottawa: Industry Canada, 1971), 161–9. Reprinted by permission of the Minister of Public Works and Government Services, 2003.

restricted in its application to cities alone, and the connections are likely to take other forms than wires. The name may in itself give rise to as many misunderstandings as that of the Holy Roman Empire, which Voltaire described as:

> Ce corps . . . qui s'appelle encore le saint empire romain n'était en aucune manière ni saint, ni romain, ni empire.[2]

The hope, indeed the expectation, is that the benefits of the so-called 'Wired City' may gradually be extended to all Canadians, wherever they work and live. High-capacity co-axial cable and microwave systems have created a revolution in transmission, and another revolution is to be expected from the development, to the point of economic practicability, of local and long-distance transmission systems employing millimetre waves, waveguides, and lasers. The communications satellite modifies the traditional relationship between cost and distance of transmission, for a two-station system costs much the same whether it serves points two miles or two thousand miles apart, and an eventual convergence of local and long-distance costs is conceivable.

Universal access to telecommunications requires, in contemporary terms, much more than telephones and CATV connections, for the services that a computer utility can provide through sophisticated terminal equipment extend far beyond those to which people have become accustomed. The technical problems are on the way to being solved, but multi-service systems will be extremely costly, and the demand, particularly for household and personal services, is at present unpredictable. Also, the heavy capital investment in existing systems cannot be instantly written off. Thus the vision of universal access is unlikely to be realized until the late 1980s, if even then, but it will never be realized at all unless it is recognized as a desirable ultimate objective for plans that are being made now.

Many lists have been made of the new services that may become available through the agency of an information-oriented computer/communications network. In some of these lists, the imagination of the authors challenges credulity, for some of the services they suggest appear, at first glance, to be either inherently unattractive or prohibitively expensive, or both. But such flights of imagination should not be allowed to deflect attention from more practical forecasts. For government, business, industry, and the professions, obvious benefits can be foreseen in the improved effectiveness and economy of operation that result from access to a broader base of information, which can be better organized and processed in any desired way by computer/communications systems. But improved effectiveness and economy of operation can also be provided in the home, through readier access to business and general information and the simplification and compressed storage of personal records and accounts. Remote-access computers are already in experimental use by some school systems, and the spread of computer-assisted instruction in schools, although still some years away, could radically affect the whole process of education. There are knowledgeable skeptics, however, who observe that computer/communications applications have not so far fulfilled the promise of the early 1960s, and who doubt the economic feasibility of implementing the distant prospects sketched in by the enthusiasts.

In fact, a fairly wide variety of data-processing services is already being offered on a remote-access basis to business, industry, and the professions; examples, in addition to information storage and retrieval, are payroll preparation, inventory and process control, on-line banking, accounting and cost control, and billing and payment services. Other current applications include airline, railway, and hotel reservation services; order tallying; stock market quotations; police records; credit reports; and repositories of medical, legal, and scientific information.

For the future, it is significant that few predictions of the availability of new services are related to any precise time-frame; one reason, of course, is that it is a matter of uncertainty as to when a comprehensive information-oriented network might become available. Another is that the installation of sophisticated and sufficiently versatile terminal equipment is still very expensive, and the reduction of costs to a level at which such terminals can be brought into common use will take time; how much time is still a matter for speculation. A third requirement is the ability to forecast the demand for or likelihood of acceptance of new services, a procedure for which effective methods have yet to be devised.

The most immediate developments forecast by technical experts are extensions or refinements of business services already in use or being tried under experimental conditions, and their application to other similar requirements that can be served by the same facilities. A trend is foreseen towards a so-called 'cashless society', when a personal 'money key' might replace most normal cash and cheque transactions if appropriate safeguards can be devised; however, large numbers of Canadians, like Stephen Leacock before them, have not yet become accustomed to using a bank account as a substitute for cash—a fact that is amply demonstrated in any supermarket on payday. Among more personal services, the earliest emphasis is likely to be on information-retrieval television (IRTV) in schools[3] and on-demand pay-as-you-go entertainment in the home, to be followed perhaps by a growing demand for access to educational programming and computer-aided instruction for both children and adults.

Ultimately, as has been said, the existence of a comprehensive all-purpose universal-access telecommunications system may entail profound changes in the day-to-day nature and quality of living experience. Some work now done in offices or schools may come to be done at home, with the side effect of ameliorating urban congestion; it is even possible that, given sufficient transmission capacity, there may be a reversal of the present population trend of movement away from rural to urban areas. There is a real danger, however, in the use of such words as 'ultimately', 'eventually', and 'in the future'. There is little room for complacency, for the shape of things to come will be determined, to a large extent, by actions that are being taken and plans that are being made today. And, so far as Canada is concerned, most of the action and planning for multi-service computer/communications systems has been going on in the United States.

Although Canada has an efficient and sophisticated east–west telecommunications system, the United States lead in the development of large computer utilities could result in a north–south flow of business that would hinder, or even prevent, the establishment of an indigenous computer-utility industry—an industry that may, some experts believe, eventually become one of the largest and most vital in Canada. Already, there are examples of Canadian industrial and commercial information being stored exclusively in databanks in the United States, including vital information about resources; quite apart from the possibly negligible risk of access to this information being denied for political purposes in a time of crisis, there is the real danger of its being used for the exclusive benefit of foreign commercial interests.

The establishment of an exclusively north–south structure for Canadian computer/communications systems might have a number of other serious aspects. First, a concentration in foreign databanks of information about Canadian individuals, transactions, and institutions might render ineffective Canadian laws dealing with such matters as personal privacy and corporate operations. Second, partial storage of Canadian information in the United States, although possibly cheaper in the short run, may jeopardize the economic viability of future computer/communications systems in Canada and result in a permanent fragmentation of sources of Canadian information. Third, and perhaps most serious, is the possible effect on the benefits to be expected in Canada from computer-aided methods of education.

A telecommunications network that leads generally to computers and databanks in the United States is likely also to lead to much information and instruction that is not particularly related to Canadian needs; this might perhaps become a matter for much greater concern about the native characteristics of Canadian education than is already aroused by the prevalence of foreign textbooks and teachers. These considerations cannot be dismissed as chauvinism or naive nationalism. The value of Canadian independence lies in the belief that life in Canada has advantages not available elsewhere and, as has been said, it is precisely in the quality of life that computer/communications systems are expected to have the most far-reaching effects—for good or for ill.

The demand for remote access to computer facilities, which heralds the developments under discussion, can be fully met only by the provision of suitable telecommunications systems. Many applications can now be foreseen that will require greater bandwidths than can be provided on normal voice circuits. In addition, overall systems efficiency could be substantially increased by telecommunication facilities capable of transmitting digital signals without changing their format. Traditional rate-structures, based on experience of the normal time taken to connect and communicate by voice, are ill suited to the transmission of data in digital form, for many remote-access computer applications are distinguished by very long holding times, hours rather than minutes, but a low factor of line utilization. Traffic tends to flow in short rapid bursts, lasting seconds rather than minutes on which existing rates are based, at relatively long intervals; and connections could be made, given suitable carrier equipment, in milliseconds rather than the seconds charged for at present. Users of computer/communications facilities accordingly argue that productivity could be greatly increased if 'time-and-distance' tariffs could be replaced by flat rates for units of information transmitted. The telecommunications carriers are thus faced with problems that go much farther than those of interconnection discussed in the preceding chapter, namely the unpredictability both of data-transmission loading and of new developments in computer technology.

Governments, however, are faced with even more complex problems in the formulation of policy for the development of Canadian computer/communications networks. A tendency has appeared in the United States for data-processing firms to attempt to diversify into communications functions hitherto reserved for the telecommunications carriers; if this were to be permitted in Canada, serious damage might be done to the economic base on which public service is provided. The telecommunications carriers would be open to competition of a kind not easily susceptible to regulation, and the preponderance of foreign ownership in the data-processing industry might have serious implications for Canadian ownership of telecommunications systems. A converse circumstance is that some Canadian carriers, notably CN/CPT and Québec-Téléphone, are now directly or indirectly offering data-processing services. This latter development raises grave questions that were discussed in a paper[4] tabled in Parliament by the Minister of Communications in June 1970, and have been further examined in a Telecommission[5] study, but no conclusions have yet been reached by the federal Government.

The problems raised by the entry of telecommunications carriers into public data processing are, in essence, those of protecting the public against the exercise of monopolistic privilege to take unfair advantage of competitors. But the issues in this instance, and in Canada particularly, are even more complex, for some analysts are of the opinion that the data-processing and computer-utility industry is unlikely to remain highly competitive, and that economies of scale and other factors will tend to concentrate the market in favour of the largest suppliers. The largest suppliers in Canada are multi-national corporations controlled from the United States, which have already acquired some 80 per cent of the Canadian market. Therefore, it is argued, one way to ensure the development of a Canadian data-processing industry would be to permit the telecommunications carriers to offer computer facilities, which they already have and could extend if sufficient capital could be secured, to purveyors of data-processing services operating on a competitive basis.

There is, however, another school of thought which contends that computer power and its applications cannot be so clearly distinguished that a hard and fast line could be drawn. Therefore, the argument runs, if the carriers are to be in the business at all, they should not be artificially excluded from one part of what might be regarded as an integral operation. If this view were accepted without restriction, competitive purveyors of data-processing services might then be placed at a grave disadvantage, in more ways than one, because of their absolute dependence on the carriers, their competitors, for essential transmission facilities and services. They, in turn, would have to be protected by some measures imposed on the carriers, which might be difficult to make totally effective, requiring absolute separation of financial, technical, and management resources applied to the data-processing and communications segments of the carriers' operations, together with enforceable safeguards against cross-subsidization between services and preferential treatment of customers and suppliers. Effective measures might indeed have to be so restrictive as to destroy the original rationale for allowing the carriers into the business in the first place.

The Telecommission studies of Canadian computer/communications systems have revealed the complexity of the problems involved and the bewildering profusion of policy options they entail. Above all, the studies convey a sense of the need for urgency in the determination of objectives and the formulation of plans in circumstances of rapid change which could easily get out of hand. Accordingly, on 27 November 1970, the Minister of Communications announced the formation of a special task force to continue the investigation of all these problems in depth, and to make recommendations for technical, financial, and institutional policies to ensure the orderly and efficient growth and development of computer/communications systems in Canada. This task force, which is already at work, is expected to produce a definitive report around the end of 1971.

One of the most difficult problems confronting the Computer/Communications Task Force is to balance the advantages and disadvantages of developing separate voice and data-transmission networks. Several countries—Britain, Sweden, and the Federal Republic of Germany, for instance—are constructing dedicated digital networks, and in the United States the Federal Communications Commission has indicated its willingness to consider applications from non-carrier organizations for licences to construct and operate such systems in competition with the existing carriers.

A factor that has to be taken into account is that the rapid development of CATV systems represents an area of technical uncertainty with important implications for the future of computer-utilities. Redesigned CATV systems could not only afford viewers a much wider choice of programs but could also provide a range of new services, many involving two-way communication. Information-retrieval services, for instance, could combine broadband transmission of pictorial material with narrow-band channels, in the same cable, for subscribers' queries and responses to a central computer. So far, however, there is no agreement among experts about the optimum approach to the provision of broadband services, or about the best means of incorporating them into the universal-access computer/communications systems that are envisioned for the future.

Some proponents argue that the full exploitation of broadband distribution systems can be achieved only if they are fully integrated with the switched networks of the telecommunications carriers, who should then be required to meet all demands for service. Others, however, contend that the granting of a broadband service monopoly to the existing carriers would stifle innovation and retard the development of the very services that offer the greatest social and economic advantages in prospect. They propose, instead, that new carrier organizations be formed, perhaps through interconnection and amalgamation of existing CATV systems, which could be licensed to compete with the established carriers in providing a limited range of video services.

There appear to be some persuasive technical and short-term economic arguments in favour of promoting the development of a coast-to-coast network of dedicated digital transmission systems. One proposal made by participants in the Telecommission studies is that all publicly accessible remote-access databank and information-processing organizations in Canada should be linked together by a national dedicated digital network to form what the Science Council of Canada has suggested might be called the Trans-Canada Computer Network. Two sub-networks would be involved—one, a circuit-switch system built up from the existing voice network and, possibly, the CATV systems; the other a completely new store-and-forward message-switched system which might share certain trunks and local loops with the first, but would be otherwise independent.

The implementation of a proposal on these lines would require the establishment of a central organization to coordinate the integrated operation of the many independent systems and functional components that would be embodied in a Trans-Canada Computer Network. Such a body might be responsible for overall planning, the establishment of common standards, the promotion and coordination of related research and development, and possibly for the administration of the subsidies that might be necessary if all Canadians are to be given access to the system so that they can exercise to the full their 'right to communicate'.

The development of comprehensive multi-service computer/communications systems, whatever form they might take, would involve massive capital expenditures. Difficult decisions would be faced in defining the boundaries between monopoly and competitive markets, and in enforcing desirable limits on corporate diversification within the industry. National and international standards would be required for such matters as interconnection of systems and terminal equipment. Should a decision be made to proceed with an undertaking of this kind, it would seem desirable that no Canadian political, social, industrial, or commercial organism capable of contributing resources to the system should be discouraged or prevented from doing so.

It will be noted that, earlier in this chapter, in describing the benefits from computer/communications integration that are being forecast, virtually all the new applications expected to become available during the next few years are likely to be oriented to business and industry, or to the protection of property. Some cynics would suggest that all the fine-sounding social and personal benefits that are being predicted are no more than pie in the sky and, if developments are to be controlled only by market forces, they may well prove to be right. To redress the balance, authorities—federal, provincial, and municipal alike—may find it worthwhile to collaborate in addressing themselves to these problems, so that the greatest possible benefits can be derived from the individual, regional, provincial, and national opportunities that Canadian computer/communications system may be expected to provide, with a significant impact on social, cultural, political, and economic activity.

Notes

1   See Telecommission Studies 6(d) and 8(d).

2   'This body . . . that still calls itself the Holy Roman Empire was in no way holy, nor Roman, nor an Empire.' [Ed.]

3   An interesting experiment in IRTV, now nearing completion, has been undertaken in Ottawa during the past two years under the joint sponsorship of Bell Canada, Northern Electric, the Ontario Institute for Studies in Education, and the Ottawa Board of Education.

4   'Communications Canada: Participation by Telecommunications Carriers in Public Data-Processing'.

5   Telecommission Study 5(a), (c), (d), (e)—'Policy Considerations with Respect to Computer Utilities'.

Contributors

MAURICE CHARLAND conducts research on the philosophy of communication and public culture. He is an associate professor of communication studies at Concordia University.

PETER DESBARATS is a former dean of the School of Journalism at the University of Western Ontario. He has written widely on journalism history and practice in Canada.

GARY EVANS teaches in the Department of Communication at the University of Ottawa, and has published books on the National Film Board of Canada.

GERALD FRIESEN is a professor of history at the University of Manitoba. His research interests include prairie and cultural history.

GEORGE GRANT was a professor of philosophy at Dalhousie and McMaster universities from the 1940s until the 1980s. He died in 1988.

DAVID HOGARTH is an assistant professor in the Communication Studies Program at York University. His research examines the globalization of documentary television.

HAROLD A. INNIS taught in the Department of Political Economy at the University of Toronto until his death in 1952.

RUSSELL JOHNSTON specializes in the history of mass media in Canada and cultural and communications policy. He is an associate professor in the Department of Communications, Popular Culture, and Film at Brock University.

RICHARD KESHEN is a professor of philosophy at University College of Cape Breton. His teaching and research interests include natural science and the concept of self-esteem.

VALERIE J. KORINEK is an associate professor of history at the University of Saskatchewan. Her research explores the history of sexuality, culture, and gender.

KENT MACASKILL recently graduated with an MA in philosophy from McMaster University.

ROBERT W. MCCHESNEY is a professor of communication at the University of Illinois at Urbana-Champaign, where he teaches and writes on the political economy of media.

MARSHALL MCLUHAN was director of the Centre for Culture and Technology and a professor of English at the University of Toronto until his death in 1980.

JEFFREY L. MCNAIRN is Canada Research chair and an assistant professor in the Department of History at Queen's University. His research interests lie in the history of political and economic concepts and the organization of knowledge.

TED MAGDER is an associate professor and the chair of the Department of Culture and Communication at New York University. His publications deal with the political economy of media and contemporary media culture.

MICHÈLE MARTIN is a professor of mass communication at Carleton University. Her scholarship examines historical and gendered aspects of communication technologies.

LAURENCE B. MUSSIO, Ph.D., is a historian and senior communications consultant working in the telecommunications and financial services sectors. He is also a lecturer in the Communication Studies Program at McMaster University.

BRIAN OSBORNE is a professor of geography at Queen's University. In his writings he focuses on the culture of communication and the development of Canadian nationalism.

ROBERT PIKE is a professor emeritus at the Department of Sociology, Queen's University, with publishing interests in the social aspects of the diffusion of communications.

DANIEL J. ROBINSON is an assistant professor of media studies and journalism at the University of Western Ontario. He conducts research on advertising and marketing history in North America.

PAUL RUTHERFORD is a professor of history at the University of Toronto. His publishing interests include historical television advertising and political communication.

MINKO SOTIRON is a historian at John Abbott College in Ste-Anne-de-Bellevue, Quebec, whose research focuses on the history of Canadian print media.

WILL STRAW is an associate professor and the director of Graduate Programs in Communication Studies at McGill University. He has published in the areas of urban culture, film studies, and globalization and Canadian culture.

MARY VIPOND, a professor of history at Concordia University, specializes in twentieth-century English-Canadian intellectual, cultural, and media history.

IRA WAGMAN is a Ph.D. candidate in the graduate program in communication at McGill University and an instructor in the Department of Mass Communication at Carleton University.

JEFF A. WEBB's research explores the history of radio broadcasting in Canada. He is a visiting assistant professor in the Department of History at Memorial University of Newfoundland.

DWAYNE WINSECK writes on the political economy of communication and media history. He is an associate professor in Carleton's Department of Mass Communication.

ROBERT A. WRIGHT is an assistant professor of history at Trent University with publishing interests in the history of youth culture and popular culture.

Index